Popular Culture in Early Modern Europe

'Qui dit le peuple dit plus d'une chose: c'est une vaste expression, et l'on s'étonneroit de voir ce qu'elle embrasse, et jusques où elle s'étend.'
La Bruyère, *Les Caractères*, Paris 1688, 'Des Grands'

PETER BURKE

POPULAR CULTURE IN EARLY MODERN EUROPE

Revised reprint

SCOLAR PRESS

First published by
Maurice Temple Smith Ltd

Revised and reprinted in 1994 by
Scolar Press
Gower House
Croft Road
Aldershot
Hants GU11 3HR
England

Ashgate Publishing Company
Old Post Road
Brookfield
Vermont 05036
USA

Reprinted 1996

British Library Cataloguing in Publication Data
Burke, Peter
    Popular culture in early modern Europe.
    1. European culture, 1500–1800
New ed.
    I. Title
    940.2

ISBN 1 85928 102 8

Printed in Great Britain at the University Press, Cambridge

Contents

Illustrations

(between pages 98 and 99)

Acknowledgements

In the course of writing this book I have incurred even more debts than usual. I should like to thank the British Academy for an exchange grant which made it possible to visit people and museums in Norway and Sweden, and the University of Sussex for two terms' leave and for refunding my typing expenses. Ruth Finnegan of the Open University and my Sussex colleagues Peter Abbs, Peter France, Robin Milner-Gulland, John Rosselli, and Stephen Yeo were kind enough to comment on draft versions of all or part of the book. My raid into their territory was abetted by a number of Scandinavian scholars, notably Maj Nodermann in Stockholm, Marta Hoffmann in Oslo and Peter Anker in Bergen. I am also grateful to the many historians in Britain who have passed me references or replied to queries. Alan Macfarlane gave me an opportunity to try out ideas from Chapter 7 on a lively group of social anthropologists and historians gathered in King's College, Cambridge. An early draft of Chapter 3 was read to a conference at the University of East Anglia in 1973 and has now appeared in C. Bigsby (ed.), *Approaches to Popular Culture*, 1976; I should like to thank Edward Arnold Ltd for permission to reprint.

I should also like to thank Margaret Spufford for comments which arrived just before the proofs.

For Sue

Note

A book of this scope is inevitably stuffed with names and technical terms. The reader is advised that brief biographical details about persons mentioned in the text will be found in the index, which also contains a glossary. Many references given in the notes are abbreviated; they are spelt out in full in the bibliography. Unless stated otherwise, translations are my own.

Prologue

The aim of this book is to describe and interpret the popular culture of early modern Europe. 'Culture' is an imprecise term, with many rival definitions; mine is 'a system of shared meanings, attitudes · and values, and the symbolic forms (performances, artifacts) in which they are expressed or embodied'.[1] Culture in this sense is part of a total way of life but not identical with it. As for popular culture, it is perhaps best defined initially in a negative way as unofficial culture, the culture of the non-elite, the 'subordinate classes' as Gramsci called them.[2] In the case of early modern Europe, the non-elite were a whole host of more or less definite social groups of whom the most prominent were craftsmen and peasants. Hence I use the phrase 'craftsmen and peasants' (or 'ordinary people') as convenient pieces of shorthand for the whole non-elite, including women, children, shepherds, sailors, beggars and the rest (cultural variations within these groups are discussed in Chapter 2).

To discover the attitudes and values of craftsmen and peasants it is necessary to modify the traditional approaches to cultural history developed by men such as Jacob Burckhardt, Aby Warburg, and Johan Huizinga, and to borrow concepts and methods from other disciplines. The natural discipline from which to borrow is that of folklore, since folklorists are centrally concerned with 'the folk', with oral traditions, and with ritual. Much of the material to be discussed in this book has long been studied by specialists in European folklore.[3] Some of it has been studied by literary critics; their emphasis on the conventions of literary genres and their sensitivity to language has given them insights which a cultural historian cannot afford to do without.[4] In spite of the obvious differences between the culture of the Azande or the Bororo and that of the craftsmen of Florence or the peasants of Languedoc, the historian of pre-industrial Europe can learn a good deal from social anthropologists. In the first place, anthropologists are concerned to understand the whole of an alien society in its own terms, while historians have tended till recently to restrict their empathy to the upper classes. In the second place, anthropologists do not stop when they have discovered the actor's view of the meaning of his action, but go on to study the social functions of myths, images and rituals.[5]

The period with which this book is concerned runs from about 1500 to about 1800. In other words, it corresponds to what historians often call the 'early modern' period, even when they deny its modernity. The area under discussion is the whole of Europe, from Norway to Sicily, from Ireland to the Urals. These choices may be thought to need a few words of explanation.

Originally conceived as a regional study, this book has turned into an attempt at synthesis. Given the size of the subject, it will be obvious that no kind of comprehensive coverage is intended; the book is rather a set of nine linked essays on major themes, concerned with the code of popular culture rather than the individual messages, and presenting a simplified description of the main constants and the principal trends. The choice of such a vast subject has serious drawbacks, most obviously the fact that no region can be studied in detail and in depth. It was also necessary to be impressionistic, to renounce certain promising quantitative approaches because the sources were not sufficiently homogeneous over these long stretches of space and time to be exploited in this way.[6] Yet there are compensating advantages. In the history of popular culture there are recurrent problems which need to be discussed at a level more general than that of the region – problems of definition, explanations of change, and, most obviously of all, the importance and the limits of regional variation itself. Where local studies rightly emphasise these variations, my purpose is the complementary one of trying to assemble the fragments and see them as a whole, as a system of related parts. I hope that this small map of a vast territory will help to orient future explorers, but I have also written with the general reader in mind; a study of popular culture is the last kind of book to be esoteric.

The years from 1500 to 1800 have been chosen as a period long enough to reveal the less obtrusive trends, and as the best-documented centuries in the history of pre-industrial Europe. In the long run, print undermined traditional oral culture; in the process, it also recorded much of it, making it appropriate to begin when the first broadsides and chap-books were coming from the press. The book ends in the late eighteenth century because of the enormous cultural changes set in motion by industrialisation, although these changes did not affect the whole of Europe equally in 1800. As a result of industrialisation, we need to make a considerable leap of the imagination before we can enter (in so far as we ever can) into the attitudes and values of the craftsmen and peasants of early modern Europe. Think away television, radio and cinema, which have standardised the vernaculars of Europe within living memory, not to mention changes which are less obvious but may be more profound. Think away the railways, which probably did even more than conscription and government propaganda to erode the culture peculiar to each province and to turn regions into nations. Think away universal education and literacy, class consciousness and nationalism. Think away the modern confidence (however shaken) in progress, science and technology, and the secular modes in which hopes and fears are expressed. All this (and more) is necessary before we can re-enter the cultural 'world we have lost'.

As an attempt at synthesis some people may find this work premature; I hope they will not make up their minds before examining the Bibliography. It is true that popular culture has only moved from the periphery of the historian's interests towards the centre in the course of the last fifteen years or so, thanks to the work of Julio Caro Baroja on Spain, of Robert Mandrou and Natalie Davis on France, of Carlo Ginzburg on Italy, of Edward Thompson and Keith Thomas on England. However, there is a long-standing tradition of interest in this subject. There have been generations of historically-minded German folklorists, like Wolfgang Brückner, Gerhard Heilfurth, or Otto Clemen. In the 1920s one leading Norwegian historian, Halvdan Koht, was interested in popular culture. At the beginning of the century, the Finnish school of folklorists, like Kaarle Krohn and Anti Aarne, were interested in history. In the later nineteenth century, outstanding students of popular culture like Giuseppe Pitrè in Sicily and Theofilo Braga in Portugal were well aware of its changes over time. But the work of Pitrè and Braga is part of a tradition of collecting which goes back to the intellectuals' discovery of the people in the late eighteenth and early nineteenth centuries. To that movement I now turn.

Introduction to the revised reprint[1]

Since this general survey was first published in 1978, many studies of popular culture have appeared, probably more than in the previous thirty or forty years. Not only monographs but some subtantial collections of articles have been devoted to the history of popular culture in France, Britain, Germany and Poland as well as in Europe as a whole.[2] These new studies have illuminated many details. To take an example almost at random, two articles have been devoted to a topic to which I gave a few lines in chapter 6, the role of Admiral Vernon as a popular hero.[3] More important, larger areas of the popular culture of the past have now come into sharper focus. In the domain of religion, for instance, the voluminous literature on popular Catholicism and Protestantism is beginning to be supplemented by studies of popular Judaism.[4] Particularly worth emphasizing are the studies of women's culture. These studies are still relatively sparse (compared with studies of women's work, for instance), but they do something to fill the gap pointed out in the first edition of this book (p.49), especially in the domain of religion and medicine. For instance, judicial records have been studied for references to supernatural powers transmitted from mother to daughter or from aunt to niece.[5]

Meanwhile, historians of other parts of the world have discovered popular culture, or, to be more precise, some of them have decided, after an initially suspicious reaction, that the concept of popular culture may be useful in their research.[6] Historians of Japan, for instance, have been studying popular culture for some time.[7] Historians of China have recently turned towards it.[8] In the case of South Asia, the major event in the field has been the emergence of the 'Subaltern Studies' group (so-called in homage to Gramsci's *classi subalterni*, discussed in chapter 1), who are rewriting the history of India 'from below'.[9] Historical studies of the popular culture of South-East Asia are beginning to make their appearance. Ray Ileto, for instance, has studied religion and protest in the nineteenth-century Philippines in the manner of Eric Hobsbawm's *Primitive Rebels*.[10] There is increasing interest in the history of the popular culture of the Caribbean, following the pioneering study of Kemal Brathwaite, and also in that of Brazil (carnival, witchcraft, religious syncretism and so on).[11] Studies of Spanish American popular culture abound, and one historian has gone so far as to organise a history of Latin America in the nineteenth century around the conflict between the culture of the westernising, cosmopolitan elite and the traditions of the people, rooted more deeply in their regions.[12]

The growing concern with popular culture is of course far from being confined to historians. It is shared – and it has long been shared – by sociologists, by folklorists and by students of literature, joined more recently by art historians and social anthropologists, not to mention teachers of that loosely-defined area known in Britain as 'cultural studies'. Between them, these groups have produced an impressive body of work.[13]

As a result of all this effort, the popular culture of early modern Europe no longer looks quite the same as it did in 1978, to my eyes at least. It is obvious enough that the multiplication of monographs on particular themes or regions will modify any general picture of Europe, but it may be worth stressing the point that studies of China or India or Latin America (and, let us hope, future studies of Africa or the Middle East), also have their relevance to such a synthesis. They define by contrast what is specifically European and they reveal the strengths and weaknesses of fundamental concepts by testing them in situations for which they were not originally designed (such as societies in which tribes or castes cut across divisions into 'elite' and 'people').

It is impossible to sum up in a single formula all the suggestions made in the course of the last fifteen years of debate about popular culture in general and that of early modern Europe in particular. They include a recent challenge of an early modern historian to his colleagues, accusing them of 'elevating' their subject, and of inconsistency in idealising popular culture in the past while condemning it in the present.[14] He may be right about the inconsistency, but the ideal for a historian remains neither to idealise nor to condemn, but simply to try to understand the attitudes and values of our ancestors. However, debate has tended to concentrate on two main issues, or two main questions. The first question is, What is 'popular'? The second, What is 'culture'?

The problem of the 'popular'

The notion of the 'popular' has long been recognised as problematic. All the same, recent discussions have uncovered even more problems, or brought difficulties more sharply into focus.

One point frequently made nowadays is that the term 'popular culture' gives a false impression of homogeneity and that it would be better to use the term in the plural, 'popular cultures', or to replace it with an expression such as 'the culture of the popular classes'.[15] The point about the importance of differences, divergences and conflicts is well worth making, though I believe that it was answered in advance in chapter 2, with its stress on varieties of culture and indeed on the existence of more or less sharply defined 'sub-cultures'.

Another objection to what is sometimes called the 'two-tier model' of elite and popular culture is as follows. The border-line between the different cultures of the people and the cultures of the elites (which were no less various) is a fuzzy one, so the attention of students of the subject ought to be concentrated on the interaction rather than the division between the two.[16] The increasing interest in the work of the great Russian critic Mikhail Bakhtin, much of which has now been translated into western languages, both reveals and encourages this shift of emphasis. His stress on the importance of the 'transgression' of boundaries is of obvious relevance here. His definition of Carnival and the carnivalesque by its opposition not to elites but to 'official' culture marks an important shift in emphasis which comes close to redefining the popular as the rebel in all of us (as Freud once described it), rather than as the property of any social group.[17] There are indeed many possible relations between learned culture and popular culture, as I tried to show in a recent study of four Italian writers – Giovanni Boccaccio, Teofilo Folengo,

Ludovico Ariosto and Pietro Aretino – arguing that Boccaccio drew on a popular tradition in which he participated, that Folengo played with the tensions between the two traditions, that Ariosto reappropriated popular themes which had once been borrowed from high culture, and that Aretino used popular motifs to subvert high culture, or at least those parts of it which he disliked.[18] Early modern elites also used popular culture on occasion for political purposes, for example in the defence of traditional festivals by such English poets as Jonson and Herrick, Milton and Marvell.[19]

Since the notion of the 'popular' leads to such difficulties, historians ought perhaps to attempt to do without it. One way of avoiding (if not evading) these difficulties is to talk about history 'from below'; but this notion is more ambiguous than it looks. A history of politics from below might involve a study of the 'subordinate classes', but it might equally well be concerned with what Americans call the 'grass-roots', in other words the provinces. The history of the Church from below might well deal with the laity, whatever their level of culture. The history of education from below might be concerned with the ordinary teacher (as opposed to the ministers or the school inspectors) but it might more reasonably still present the point of view of the pupils. A history of war from below might present the war experienced by common soldiers rather than the generals, but a place ought to be found for the point of view of the civilians caught up in military operations.

A notion which has been much employed in the last few years, notably by Edward Thompson, in analysing the interactions between 'above' and 'below', is Gramsci's idea of 'cultural hegemony', with its implication that 'above' should be translated into 'dominant' and 'below' into 'dominated' or 'subordinate'.[20] Discussions with Gramscian historians of popular culture in Britain, France, Italy, Poland, Brazil, India and elsewhere have made me realise that my own study was not political enough, and that the process of state-building in early modern Europe had important consequences for popular culture. On the other hand, if a historian is working on any period before (say) 1789, he or she runs the risk of over-estimating the political consciousness of dominated groups, or describing this consciousness in anachronistic terms, or overestimating the power of the state. For example, I still think that Robert Muchembled's *Popular Culture and Elite Culture* (1978) overemphasised the active role of the state in changing popular culture, at the expense of other historical agents, such as the small provincial publishers of the *Bibliothèque Bleue*.[21]

Again, it is my impression that the historians of India associated with *Subaltern Studies* assume rather too easily that the dominated classes with whom they are concerned were conscious of belonging to the dominated classes; that is, that the peasants of certain villages in Bengal, for example, over and above any particular local experience of domination, were aware of what they had in common with peasants from other parts of Bengal and indeed India. It is actually extremely hard to answer the question, in what places and at what times the people (whoever 'they' are) have seen themselves as 'The People'.[22] Again, the celebrated studies of popular culture by Christopher Hill, Eric Hobsbawm and the late Edward Thompson (brilliant, original and influential as they have been), are all vulnerable to the criticism that these historians tend to equate the 'popular' with the 'radical', ignoring evidence for popular conservatism.

I am indeed still a little uneasy about the constant appeal to the politics of culture and more especially to 'cultural hegemony' in recent studies, and even more about the way in which a concept used by Gramsci himself to analyse specific problems (such as the influence of the Church in southern Italy), has been taken out of its original context and used more or less indiscriminately to deal with a much wider range of situations. As a corrective to this inflation or dilution of the concept, I should like to suggest the following three 'directions for use', in the form of questions.[23]

(i) Is cultural hegemony to be assumed to be a constant factor, or has it only operated at certain places and times? If the latter, what are the conditions and the indicators of its existence?

(ii) Is the term descriptive or explanatory? If the latter, does it refer to the conscious strategies of the ruling class (or of groups within it), or to the unconscious or latent rationality of their actions?

(iii) How are we to account for the achievement of this

hegemony? Can it be established without the collusion or connivance of some at least of the dominated? Can it be resisted with success? If so, what are the major 'counter-hegemonic strategies'?[24] Does the ruling class impose its values on the subordinate classes, or is there some kind of compromise, with alternative definitions of the situation? The concept of 'negotiation', as it is currently used by sociologists and social historians, to include the unconscious as well as the conscious adaptation of the attitudes of one group to those of another, might well be of value in this analysis.[25]

The ideas expressed in the last paragraph may help clear up a possible misunderstanding of the process of the 'reform' of popular culture, discussed in chapter 8 below. Objections have sometimes been raised to the description of this process as essentially the work of elites.[26] At one level, the micro-level or level of detail, the objectors have a good case. It is not difficult to find documented examples of godly artisans, whether Protestants, like Nehemiah Wallington in seventeenth-century London, or Catholics, like Pierre-Ignace Chavatte in seventeenth-century Lille. It may well have been the case that the movement of reform would have been unsuccessful without this kind of support.

At the macro-level , on the other hand, and over the long term, it still seems to me that the initiative for reform came originally from an elite, more especially the upper clergy, before it spread more widely through society. It was part of what is variously called, following the rival social theorists Norbert Elias and Michel Foucault, a process of 'civilising' or 'disciplining', which began as an attempt by elites to control the behaviour of ordinary people but was gradually internalised (up to a point, and among certain groups, at least) and so turned into self-control.[27] The apparent importance of elites in this process may of course be an optical illusion, the result of the relative lack of evidence for popular attitudes, but given the evidence we have, to speak of village Luthers or Loyolas before the time of Martin Luther and Ignatius Loyola would be unwarranted speculation.

All the objections to the idea of popular culture discussed so far are relatively mild in the sense that they involve qualifications or shifts of emphasis. Other objections are more radical and involve attempts to replace the concept altogether.

Two of these objections are particularly worth discussion; those of the American anthropologist William Christian and the French historian Roger Chartier.

In his study of vows, relics and shrines in sixteenth-century Spain, Christian argues that the kind of religious practice he is describing 'was as characteristic of the royal family as it was of unlettered peasants', and he therefore refuses to use the term 'popular' at all. In its place he proposes to use the term 'local', on the grounds that 'the vast majority of sacred places and monuments held meaning only for local citizens'.[28] This may well have been the case – though it is surely worth adding that the minority of sacred places remaining (among them Rome, Jerusalem, and Santiago de Compostela in Galicia) held meaning for many European Catholics, as the influx of pilgrims demonstrates.

Christian's discussion of the local features of what is generally called 'popular' religion is important, though new only in its emphasis. What is most original is the suggestion that we scrap one binary model, that of the elite and the people, and replace it by another, that of centre and periphery.

Centre-periphery models of this kind have come increasingly into use by historians in the last few years, in economic history, political history, religious history, and even in the history of art. They certainly have their value, but they are not free from problems and ambiguities. The notion of 'centre', for example, is difficult to define, since spatial centres and power centres do not always coincide (think of London, Paris, Peking...). In the case of Catholicism, discussed by Christian, we may reasonably assume Rome to be the centre with which he is contrasting Spanish 'local religion'. It is clear, however, that unofficial devotions were as current in that holy city as they were elsewhere. In the course of smoothing out one conceptual difficulty, another has been created.

The basic problem is that a 'culture' is a system with rather vague boundaries. The great value of Roger Chartier's recent essays on 'the cultural uses of print' is that he keeps this vagueness constantly in mind.[29] Chartier argues that it is pointless to try to identify popular culture by some supposedly specific distribution of cultural objects, objects such as books or ex votos, because these objects were in practice used or 'appropriated' for their own purposes by different social groups, noblemen and clerics as well as craftsmen and peasants.

Following the French social theorists Michel De Certeau and Pierre Bourdieu, Chartier suggests that everyday consumption is a kind of production or creation, since it involves people imposing meanings on objects. In that sense we all engage in the *bricolage* which Lévi-Strauss considered part of *la pensée sauvage*. Recent German literary theorists, such as Hans-Robert Jauss and Wolfgang Iser, have reached similar conclusions about the reception of texts and the responses of readers from a different starting-point.[30]

The moral Chartier draws from his studies is that historians should study not sets of texts or other objects which they define from the start as 'popular' but rather the specific ways in which these objects have been appropriated in particular places and times and by particular groups. In a similar way, more or less independently, a group of American historians and anthropologists have been studying what they call 'the social history of things', emphasising the different uses and meanings of the same object in different contexts.[31]

This analysis of the creative uses of objects is a development from earlier discussions of 'sinking' and 'rising', abandoning the misleading mechanical imagery and emphasising the transformation of cultural items in the course of their reception (below, pp.58). It strikes me as the most important contribution to the popular culture debate in the last fifteen years. Historians are far from having absorbed all its lessons.

All the same, problems remain. The 'appropriation' model is most useful for the study of material culture and texts. It forces the historian, or anthropologist, to focus on the objects, the 'social life of things' rather than on the life of the social groups who use them. On the other hand, other concepts will be needed if we wish to focus on these social groups themselves, to try to understand their mentalities, the logic of their different appropriations and adaptations of diverse objects. If we wish to study the ways in which different groups created their particular life-styles, often by means of *bricolage*, in other words 'cobbling together' elements from diverse sources (as Dick Hebdige demonstrated in the case of some postwar British subcultures), we may have to return to some version of the 'two-tier model', modified to allow for the circulation of

objects.[32] It may for example be unwise to describe public
festivals, for example, whether religious or civic, as 'popular',
because on such occasions different social groups often walked
in procession, or lined the streets to watch the others. All the
same, it may be useful to describe some festivals, in some places
and times as more popular than others, to speak of processes
of 'popularization' or 'aristocratization'.

It is hard to deny the fact that lower-status groups often
imitated the cultural practices of higher status groups. Ex-
plaining the imitation is rather more difficult. The lower groups
may have done this because they wanted to rise socially, or
to appear to have risen socially, because they accepted the
'cultural hegemony' of the upper classes. On the other hand,
they may have imitated the habits of their so-called 'betters'
as an affirmation of equality.

The implication of this recent historical concern with
consumption, 'uses' and 'practices' is that the notion of
'culture', as well as that of 'the people' is in serious need of
re-examination and redefinition.

The notion of 'culture'

The problems raised by utilising the concept 'culture' are, if
anything, even greater than those raised by the term 'popular'.
One reason for these problems is that the concept has widened
its meaning in the last generation as historians and other
intellectuals have widened their interests. In the age of the so-
called 'discovery' of the people, in the early nineteenth century,
the term 'culture' tended to refer to art, literature and music,
and it would not be unfair to describe the nineteenth-century
folklorists as searching for popular equivalents for classical
music, academic art, and so on.

Today, however, following the example of the anthropologists, historians and others use the term 'culture' much
more widely, to refer to almost everything that can be learned
in a given society – how to eat, drink, walk, talk, be silent
and so on.[33]

In other words, the history of culture now includes the
history of the assumptions underlying everyday life. A concern
with everyday life is a striking feature of the social history
practised in the last few years, especially in Germany, where

Alltagsgeschichte has become a slogan.[34] The aim is not simply to describe the everyday, but rather, following the lead of social theorists such as Henri Lefebvre, Michel de Certeau, or Juri Lotman, to discover its 'poetics', in other words the various rules or principles which underlie everyday life in different places and times.[35] What used to be taken for granted, in other words treated as obvious, normal, or 'common sense' is now viewed as part of a cultural system, something which varies from society to society and changes from one century to another, something which is socially 'constructed' and so requires social and historical explanation or inter-pretation.[36] The concept of time, for example, has been studied in this way.[37] This new cultural history is sometimes called 'socio-cultural' history to distinguish it from the more traditional histories of art, literature and music.

In the first edition of this book, I did try to take account of everyday life. I defined culture in terms of the attitudes and values expressed or embodied in artifacts and performances, intending the key terms 'artifacts' and 'performances' to be understood in a wide sense; extending the notion of 'artifact' to include such cultural constructs as the categories of sickness, or dirt, or gender, or politics, and widening the notion of 'performance' to cover such culturally stereotyped forms of behaviour as feasting and violence.

In practice, I have to admit, the book concentrates on a narrower range of objects (notably images, printed matter, and houses), and activities (especially singing, dancing, acting in plays and engaging in rituals), despite the attempt to set these objects and activities in a wider social, economic and political context. Popular revolt was discussed in some detail, but sex, marriage and family life, for example, were virtually omitted.[38]

Was this decision to opt in practice for the narrower definition of culture a wise one? In the early 1970s, when I began research for this study, very few examples of the new type of socio-cultural history had yet been published, so that the time was hardly ripe for a synthesis. If I were writing the book now, the idea of writing a general socio-cultural history of early modern Europe would certainly be tempting, difficult as the enterprise would be. On the other hand, I remain convinced that there is room for a book like this one which concentrates on artifacts and performances in the narrower sense, because this more limited subject allows a more rigorous comparative study than the wider subject affords.

In any case it is impossible to draw any precise boundary between the wider and the narrower sense of 'culture', and it may be useful to end these comments by discussing a few examples of recent research which falls between the two. Take, for example, the case of insults, which may be regarded, at least in some cultures, as an art-form or a literary genre as well as an expression of genuine hostility. In seventeenth-century Rome, for example, private insults took written and pictorial as well as oral forms, employed verse as well as prose, and alluded to, or parodied, epitaphs and official notices.[39]

Recent studies of material culture also fall between the wide and the narrow senses of culture. The German social historian Hans Medick, for instance, has analysed the ways in which conspicuous consumption on food and clothes 'functioned as a vehicle of plebeian self-consciousness' in the eighteenth century.[40] Again, in the case of North America in the middle of the eighteenth century, archaeologists have argued that changes in burial practices, in the mode of food consumption, and in the organisation of living space all suggest a shift in values. A rise of individualism and privacy is revealed by the increase in the number of chairs (instead of benches), cups (instead of communal bowls) and bedrooms (instead of beds being placed in living-rooms).[41]

Examples like these suggest that although it is useful to distinguish the concept of 'culture' from that of 'society', rather than using it to refer to almost everything, this distinction should not follow traditional lines. Keith Baker has suggested that intellectual history should be understood as 'a mode of historical discourse' rather than 'a distinct field of enquiry with a clearly demarcated subject matter'. In similar fashion, cultural historians might usefully define themselves not in terms of a particular area or 'field' such as art, literature and music, but rather of a distinctive concern for values and symbols, wherever these are to be found, in the everyday life of ordinary people as well as in special performances for elites.[42]

Notes

1 This introduction is a revised version of a paper given at conferences on the 'New History' (Delhi, 1988), 'Mensch und Objekt im Mittelalter' (Krems, 1988), and 'Popular Culture in Question' (Colchester, 1991). I should like to thank the participants at these conferences for their comments and suggestions. I have also learned much from discussions over the years with Roger Chartier, Natalie Davis, Carlo Ginzburg, Gábor Klaniczay and Bob Scribner, as well as with my ex-pupils David Gentilcore, Maria-José Del Río and Tim Harris.
2 On France, Beauroy (1976), Bertrand (1985); on Britain, Yeo and Yeo (1981); Storch (1982); Reay (1985); on Germany, Dülmen (1983, 1992); Dülmen and Schindler (1984); Brückner, Blickle and Schindler (1985); on Poland, Geremek (1978); on Europe, Ginzburg (1979), Kaplan (1984); Dinzelbacher and Mück (1987). All abbreviated references are to the supplementary bibliography.
3 Wilson (1988); Jordan and Rogers (1989).
4 Davis (1982); Cohen (1988); Horowitz (1989, 1991).
5 Below, pp.49–50. On women's culture generally, see S. Ardener, *Perceiving Women* (1975); on the early modern period, see especially Ankarloo and Henningsen (1990); Dekker (1987); Dekker and van de Pol (1981); Delumeau (1992); Henningsen (1990); Klapisch (1984); Medick (1984); Roodenburg (1983); Roper (1989); Ruggiero (1993); Wiesner (1988); Zarri (1990). See also the contributions of Amussen and Seleski in Harris (forthcoming).
6 For examples of suspicion, see R. Gombrich, *Precept and Practice* (Oxford, 1971) and Vrijhof and Waardenburg (1979). Gombrich's distrust of the notion 'popular Buddhism' is not shared by W.J. Klausner, 'Popular Buddhism in North-East Thailand', in F.S.C. Northrop and H.H. Livingston (eds), *Cross-Cultural Understanding* (New York, 1964) or Southwold (1982).
7 Gluck (1979); cf Walthall (1986), Shively (1991).
8 Rawski (1979); Johnson, Nathan and Rawski (1985).
9 Guha (1982–88). Other recent studies include Aris (1987), Kumar (1988) and O'Hanlon and Washbrook (1991).
10 Ileto (1979) Cf Lê Thành Khôi (1986).
11 E.K. Brathwaite, *Folk Culture of the Slaves in Jamaica* (1971: revised ed., London and Port of Spain, 1981). On Brazil, Matta (1978); Pereira de Queiroz (1992); Mello e Souza (1987).
12 Burns (1980). For a survey of recent work, see Rowe and Schelling (1992).
13 Paulson (1979); Stallybrass and White (London, 1985); Frykman and Löfgren (1986).
14 Strauss (1991).

15   Ginzburg, cit., (1979); *Culturas populares* (1986).
16   Gurevich (1981); Kaplan (1984).
17   Below, pp.185. For a survey of some recent work inspired by Bakhtin, Burke (1988b).
18   Burke (1992b).
19   Marcus (1986).
20   Thompson (1991), 76ff; cf. Guha (1983), cit., Hall (1981), and Bailey (1987), 9ff.
21   Muchembled (1978).
22   Burke (1992a).
23   Cf. Lears (1985), which raises questions additional (but complementary) to mine.
24   Sider (1980); Scott (1987).
25   Burke (1982, 1987 ch.5).
26   E.g. Mullett (1987), 110, 164.
27   N. Elias, *The Civilizing Process* (1939: English trans, 2 vols, Oxford 1981–2); M. Foucault, *Discipline and Punish* (1975, English trans London, 1977).
28   Christian (1981b), especially pp.8, 177.
29   Chartier (1987).
30   H.R. Jauss, *Towards an Aesthetic of Reception* (1974, English translation Minneapolis 1982): W. Iser, *The Act of Reading* (1976, English translation Baltimore 1978).
31   Appadurai (1985), especially the contributions by Appadurai and Kopytoff. This group has learned from the social theorists Jean Baudrillard and Pierre Bourdieu.
32   Hebdige (1979).
33   An influential (and controversial) explicit discussion in R. Wagner, *The Invention of Culture* (Englewood Cliffs, 1975).
34   E.g. Kuczynski (1980–1); Dinges (1987); Bergsma (1990); Scribner (1990); Mohrmann (1993).
35   H. Lefebvre, *Critique de la vie quotidienne* (3 vols, Paris 1946–81); M. de Certeau, *The Practice of Everyday Life* (1980: English trans, Berkeley 1984); Lotman (1984).
36   C. Geertz, 'Common Sense as a Cultural System', in his *Local Knowledge* (New York, 1983), ch.4.
37   See, for example, T.C. Smith, 'Peasant Time and Factory Time in Japan', *Past and Present* 111 (1986), 165–97 (modelled on E.P. Thompson's article in the same journal in 1967).
38   As remarked by M. Ingram in Reay (1985), p.129. For an anthropological study of family structure as part of culture, see D.M. Schneider, *American Kinship* (Englewood Cliffs, 1968); cf Frykman and Löfgren (1979).
39   Burke (1987), chapter 8.

40 Medick (1983), 94. Cf. Sandgruber (1982).
41 Deetz (1979).
42 K. Baker 'On the Problem of the Ideological Origins of the French Revolution', in *Modern European Intellectual History*, ed. D. LaCapra and S.L. Kaplan (Ithaca and London, 1982), 197.

PART 1

In Search of Popular Culture

CHAPTER ONE

The Discovery of the People

It was in the late eighteenth and early nineteenth centuries, when traditional popular culture was just beginning to disappear, that the 'people' or the 'folk' became a subject of interest to European intellectuals. Craftsmen and peasants were no doubt surprised to find their homes invaded by men and women with middle-class clothes and accents who insisted they sing traditional songs or tell traditional stories. New terms are as good a guide as any to the rise of new ideas, and this was a time when a whole cluster of new terms came into use, especially in Germany. *Volkslied*, for instance: 'folksong'. J. G. Herder gave the name *Volkslieder* to the collections of songs he made in 1774 and 1778. There is *Volksmärchen* and *Volkssage*, late eighteenth-century terms for different kinds of 'folktale'. There is *Volksbuch*, a word which became popular in the early nineteenth century after the journalist Joseph Görres had published an essay on the subject. Its nearest English equivalent is the traditional term 'chap-book'. There is *Volkskunde* (sometimes *Volkstumskunde*), another early nineteenth-century term which might be translated as 'folklore' (a word coined in English in 1846). There is *Volkspiel* (or *Volkschauspiel*), a term which came into use about 1850. Equivalent words and phrases came into use in other countries, usually a little later than in Germany. Thus *Volkslieder* were *folkviser* for the Swedes, *canti popolari* for the Italians, *narodnye pesni* for the Russians, *népdalok* for the Hungarians.[1]

What was happening? Since so many of the terms began life in Germany, it may be useful to look for an answer there. The ideas behind the term 'folksong' are expressed with force in Herder's prize essay of 1778, on the influence of poetry on the morals of peoples in ancient and modern times. His main point was that poetry had once possessed an effectiveness (*lebendigen Wirkung*) which is now lost. Poetry had been effective in this way among the Hebrews, the Greeks and the northern peoples in early times. Poetry was regarded as divine. It was a 'treasury of life' (*Schatz des Lebens*); that is, it had practical functions. Herder went on to suggest that true poetry belongs to a particular way of life, which would later be described as the 'Organic Community', and wrote with nostalgia of peoples 'whom we call savages (*Wilde*), who are often more moral than we are'. The implication of his essay seems to be that in the post-Renaissance world, only folksong retains the moral effectiveness of early poetry because it circulates orally, is recited to music, and performs practical functions, whereas the poetry of the educated is poetry for the eye, cut off from music, frivolous rather than functional. As his friend Goethe put it, 'Herder taught us to think of poetry as the common property of all mankind, not as the private possession of a few refined, cultured individuals'.[2]

The association of poetry with the people received even more emphasis in the work of the Grimm brothers. In an essay on the *Nibelungenlied*, Jakob Grimm pointed out that the author of the poem is unknown, 'as is usual with all national poems and must be the case, because they belong to the whole people'. Their authorship was communal: 'the people creates' (*Das Volk dichtet*). In a famous epigram, he wrote that 'every epic must write itself' (*jedes Epos muss sich selbst dichten*). These poems were not made; like trees, they just grew. Hence Grimm described popular poetry as 'poetry of nature' (*Naturpoesie*).[3]

The ideas of Herder and the Grimms were extremely influential. Collection after collection of national folksongs appeared.* To mention only some of the most famous, there was a collection of Russian *byliny* or ballads, published in 1804 under the name of a certain Kirsha Danilov; the Arnim–Brentano collection of German songs, *Des Knaben Wunderhorn*, which drew on oral tradition and printed broadsheets and was published in parts between 1806 and 1808; the Afzelius–Geijer collection of Swedish ballads, collected from oral tradition in Västergötland and published in 1814; the Serbian ballads edited by Vuk Stefanović Karadžić, first published in 1814 and enlarged later; and Elias Lönnrot's Finnish songs, which he collected from oral tradition and arranged to form an epic, the *Kalevala*, published in 1835.

The Mediterranean countries were backward in this movement, and one famous English editor was less of a pioneer

*Appendix 1 lists the principal publications on popular culture from 1760 to 1846.

than he may look. Thomas Percy, a Northamptonshire clergyman, published his *Reliques of English Poetry* in 1765. These 'reliques', as he called them with deliberately archaic spelling, included a number of famous ballads, such as *Chevy Chase*, *Barbara Allen*, *The Earl of Murray* and *Sir Patrick Spence*. Percy (who was something of a snob and changed his name from 'Pearcy' in order to claim noble descent) did not think ballads had anything to do with the people, but rather that they were composed by minstrels enjoying a high status at medieval courts. However, the *Reliques* was interpreted, from Herder onwards, as a collection of folksongs, and received with enthusiasm in Germany and elsewhere.[4]

Although unbelievers could be found, the Herder–Grimm view of the nature of popular poetry quickly became orthodox. The great Swedish poet-historian Erik Gustav Geijer used the term 'poetry of nature', asserted the communal authorship of the Swedish ballads and looked back with nostalgia to the days when 'the whole people sang as one man' (*et helt folk söng som en man*).[5] Similarly, Claude Fauriel, a French scholar who edited and translated the popular poetry of the modern Greeks, compared folksongs to mountains and rivers and used the phrase 'poésie de la nature'.[6] An Englishman of an older generation summed up the trend:

> The popular ballad . . . is rescued from the hands of the vulgar, to obtain a place in the collection of the man of taste. Verses which a few years past were thought worthy the attention of children only, are now admired for that artless simplicity which once obtained the name of coarseness and vulgarity.[7]

It was not only the folksong which became fashionable, but other forms of popular literature as well. Lessing collected and appreciated what he called *Bilder-reimen* ('verses for pictures'), in other words German satirical broadsheets. The poet Ludwig Tieck was an enthusiast for German chap-books, and produced his own versions of two of them, *The Four Sons of Aymon* and *The Beautiful Magelone*. Tieck wrote:

> The common reader should not make fun of the popular stories (*Volksromane*) which are sold in the streets by old women for a groschen or two, for *The horned Siegfried*, *The sons of Aymon*, *Duke Ernst* and *Genoveva* have more true inventiveness and are simpler and better by far than the books currently in fashion.[8]

A similar admiration for chap-books was expressed by Joseph Görres in his essay on the subject. Then there was the folktale, transmitted by oral tradition. Several volumes of folktales were published in Germany before the famous collection of the Grimm brothers came out in 1812.[9] The Grimms did not use the term 'folktale', calling their volume 'childrens' and domestic tales'(*Kinder-und Hausmärchen*), but they did believe that these stories expressed the nature of the 'folk', and followed them up by two volumes of German historical tales or *Sagen*. The example of the Grimms was soon followed all over Europe. Georg von Gaal published the first collection of Hungarian folktales, in German, in 1822. He made his collection not in the countryside but in Vienna, from the hussars of a Hungarian regiment whose colonel, a friend of his, issued an order to his men to write down any stories they knew.[10] Two particularly famous collections of tales were published in Norway and Russia: P. C. Asbjørnsen and J. Moe's *Norske Folk-Eventyr* (1841) which included the story of Peer Gynt, and A. N. Afanasiev's *Narodnye russkii skazki* (1855 on). Finally there was the 'folk-play', a category which included the puppet-plays about Faust which inspired both Lessing and Goethe; the traditional Swiss play on William Tell which Schiller studied before writing his own; the Spanish *autos sacramentales*, which the German romantics discovered with enthusiasm; the English mystery plays published by William Hone, and the German ones published by F. J. Mone.[11]

This interest in different kinds of traditional literature was itself part of a still wider movement, which might be called the discovery of the people. There was the discovery of popular religion. The Prussian aristocrat Arnim wrote, 'for me, the religion of the people is something extremely worthy of respect', while in his famous book on the 'genius of Christianity' the French aristocrat Chateaubriand includes a discussion of *dévotions populaires*, the unofficial religion of the people, which he saw as an expression of the harmony between religion and nature.[12] Then there was the discovery of popular festivals. Herder, who was living in Riga in the 1760s, was thrilled by the midsummer festival of St John's Eve.[13] Goethe was excited by the Roman Carnival, which he witnessed in 1788 and interpreted as a festival 'which the people give themselves'.[14] This excitement led to historical research, and to books like Joseph Strutt's book on sports and pastimes, Giustina Renier Michiel's study of Venetian festivals, and I. M. Snegirov's book on the holidays and ceremonies of the Russian people.[15] There was the discovery of folk-music. In the late eighteenth century V. F. Trutovsky (a court musician) published some Russian folksongs together with their music. In the 1790s, Haydn made arrangements of Scottish folksongs. In 1819 a government decree ordered the collection of folk-tunes by the local authorities in Lower Austria on behalf of the Society of the Friends of Music. A collection of Galician folksongs published in 1833 gives melodies as well as texts.[16] Attempts were made to write the history of the people rather than the history of the government; in Sweden, Erik Geijer, who had already edited folksongs, published *The History of the Swedish People*. Although it devoted most of its space to the policies of kings, Geijer's history did include separate chapters on 'land and people'. The same can be said for the Czech historian František Palacký (who had gone folksong collecting in Moravia in his youth) and his *History of the Czech People*; for the historical works of Jules Michelet (an admirer of Herder who had once planned an encyclopedia of folksongs), and for Macaulay, whose *History of England*, published in 1848, contains his famous third chapter on English society in the late seventeenth century, based in part on the broadside ballads he loved.[17] The discovery of popular culture made considerable impact on the arts. From Scott to Pushkin, from Victor Hugo to Sándor Petöfi, poets imitated the ballad. Composers drew on folk-music as in Glinka's opera of 1836, *A Life for the Tsar*. The painter Courbet was inspired by popular woodcuts, but a serious interest in folk-art did not develop till after 1850, perhaps because popular artifacts were not threatened by mass-production until that time.[18]

Perhaps the most vivid illustrations of the new attitudes to the people come from travellers, who now went in search not so much of ancient ruins as of manners and customs, the simpler and wilder the better. For this purpose, in the early 1770s, the Italian priest Alberto Fortis visited Dalmatia and his account of his travels devoted a chapter to the way of life of the 'Morlacchi', their religion and 'superstitions', their songs, dances and festivals. As Fortis put it, 'the innocence and the natural liberty of the pastoral centuries still survives in Morlacchia'. At one

point he compared the Morlaks to the Hottentots. Samuel
Johnson and James Boswell toured the Western Islands of
Scotland, 'to speculate', in Johnson's words, 'upon the remains
of pastoral life', to look for 'primitive customs', to enter the huts
of shepherds, listen to the bagpipes, and meet people who spoke
no English and still wore the plaid. At Auchnasheal, Boswell
remarked to Dr Johnson, 'it was much the same as being with a
tribe of Indians', for the villagers 'were as black and wild in their
appearance as any American savages whatever'.[19]

Where Johnson and Boswell observed the Highlanders with
detachment, other members of the upper classes tried to identify
with the people, an identification which seems to have gone
furthest in Spain. Goya's *Duchess of Alba as a Maja* reminds us
that Spanish noblemen and noblewomen sometimes dressed like
the working classes of Madrid. They were on friendly terms
with popular actors. That they also participated in popular
festivals is suggested by a contemporary remark that on such
occasions, 'a gentleman who, either out of curiosity or depraved
taste, attends the amusements of the vulgar, is generally
respected, provided he is a mere spectator, and appears
indifferent to the females'.[20]

It is because of the breadth of the movement that it seems
reasonable to speak of the discovery of popular culture as taking
place in this period; Herder did in fact use the phrase 'popular
culture' (*Kultur des Volkes*), contrasting it with 'learned culture'
(*Kultur der Gelehrten*). Antiquaries had described popular
customs before, or had collected broadside ballads. What is new
in Herder and the Grimms and their followers is, first, the
emphasis on the people, and second, their belief that 'manners,
customs, observances, superstitions, ballads, proverbs etc.'
were all part of a whole, expressing the spirit of a particular
nation. In this sense the subject of this book was discovered – or
is it invented? – by a group of German intellectuals at the end
of the eighteenth century.[21]

Why did the discovery of popular culture come when it did?
What exactly did the people mean to the intellectuals?
Naturally, there is no simple answer to this question. A few of
the discoverers were themselves the sons of craftsmen and
peasants: Tieck was the son of a ropemaker, Lönnrøt the son of
a village tailor, William Hone was himself a bookseller, Vuk
Stefanović Karadžić and Moe were the sons of peasants. Most of

them, however, came from the upper classes, to whom the people were a mysterious Them, described in terms of everything their discoverers were not (or thought they were not): the people were natural, simple, illiterate, instinctive, irrational, rooted in tradition and in the soil of the region, lacking any sense of individuality (the individual was lost in the community). For some intellectuals, especially in the late eighteenth century, the people were interesting in an exotic sort of way; in the early nineteenth century, by contrast, there was a cult of the people in the sense that intellectuals identified with them and tried to imitate them. As the Polish writer Adam Czarnocki put it in 1818, 'We must go to the peasants, visit them in their thatched huts, take part in their feasts, work and amusements. In the smoke rising above their heads the ancient rites are still echoing, the old songs are still heard.'[22]

There were a number of reasons for this interest in the people at this particular point in European history; aesthetic reasons, intellectual reasons, and political reasons.

The main aesthetic reason was what might be called the revolt against 'art'. 'Artificial' (like 'polished') became a pejorative term, and 'artless' (like 'wild') a term of praise. The trend can be seen clearly enough in Percy's *Reliques*. Percy liked the old poems he published because they possessed what he called 'a pleasing simplicity and many artless graces', qualities which his generation found lacking in the poetry of their own age. His other literary enthusiasms reveal more about his tastes. Percy's first publication was the translation of a Chinese novel and some fragments of Chinese poetry, written at a time (he suggested) when the Chinese lived in a state of 'wild nature'.[23] His next publication was of *Five pieces of runic poetry translated from the Icelandic*, with a preface noting the fondness for poetry of that 'hardy and unpolished race', the North Europeans. In short, like other men of his time, Percy was an enthusiast for the exotic, whether it was Chinese, Icelandic, or, like *Chevy Chase*, Northumbrian. The appeal of the exotic was that it was wild, natural, free from the rules of classicism.[24] This last point was perhaps of particular importance in the German-speaking world, since J. G. Gottsched, professor of poetry at Leipzig, was at that moment laying down the law for literature and insisting that playwrights should observe Aristotle's supposed unities of time, place and action. The Swiss critic J. J. Bodmer, who published a collection of traditional English and Suabian ballads in 1780, was in revolt against Gottsched. Goethe too was a rebel against the rules of classical drama, and wrote that 'The unity of place seemed as oppressive as a prison, the unities of action and time burdensome fetters on our imagination'.[25] Puppet-plays and mystery plays were objects of interest precisely because they ignored these unities. So was Shakespeare; Herder wrote an essay on Shakespeare, Tieck and Geijer translated him.

The aesthetic appeal of the wild, unclassical and (to use another favourite word of the time) the 'primitive' can be seen most vividly, perhaps, in the vogue for 'Ossian'.[26] Ossian, or Oiséan MacFinn, was a Gaelic bard (reputedly third-century) whose works were 'translated' by the Scottish poet James Macpherson in the 1760s. In fact, the translation was not a translation, as we shall see. The Ossianic poems were enormously popular all over Europe in the late eighteenth and early nineteenth centuries. They were translated into ten European languages, from Spanish to Russian. Names like 'Oscar' and 'Selma' owe their vogue to them; Mendelssohn's overture 'Fingal's Cave' (written in 1830 after a visit to the Hebrides) was inspired by them; Herder and Goethe, Napoleon and Chateaubriand were among the enthusiasts. What the readers of the time saw in Ossian may be gathered from the 'critical dissertation' on him written by Macpherson's friend Hugh Blair. Blair described Ossian as a Celtic Homer. 'Both are distinguished by simplicity, sublimity and fire.' He admired the poems in particular as examples of the 'poetry of the heart', and suggested that 'many circumstances of those times which we call barbarous are favourable to the poetical spirit', because men in those days were more imaginative. It was in this frame of mind that Herder collected folksongs in Riga, Goethe in Alsace, or Fortis in Dalmatia.[27]

In short, the discovery of popular culture was part of a movement of cultural primitivism in which the ancient, the distant and the popular were all equated. It is no surprise to find that Rousseau had a taste for folksongs, which he found touching because they were simple, naïve and archaic; for he was the great spokesman for cultural primitivism in his generation. The cult of the people grew out of the pastoral tradition. Boswell and Johnson went to the Hebrides to see a pastoral society, and around 1780, porcelain figures of Norwegian peasants joined Dresden shepherdesses in the decoration of fashionable drawing-rooms.[28] This movement was also a reaction against the Enlightenment, as typified by Voltaire; against its elitism, against its rejection of tradition, against its stress on reason. The Grimms, for instance, prized tradition above reason, what grew naturally over what was consciously planned, the instincts of the people over the arguments of intellectuals. The revolt against reason can be illustrated by the new respect for popular religion and the attraction of folktales concerned with the supernatural.

The Enlightenment was disliked in some quarters, in Germany and Spain, for example, because it was foreign, another example of the dominance of the French. The fashion for popular culture in late eighteenth-century Spain was a way of expressing opposition to France. The discovery of popular culture was closely associated with the rise of nationalism. Not in the case of Herder, who was a good European, indeed a good citizen of the world; his collection of folksongs included translations from English and French, Danish and Spanish, Latvian and Eskimo. The Grimms, too, published Danish and Spanish ballads and took considerable interest in the popular culture of the Slavs.[29] However, later collections of folksongs were often nationalist in inspiration and sentiment. The publication of *Wunderhorn* coincided with the invasion of Germany by Napoleon. One of its two editors, Achim von Arnim, intended it to be a song-book for the German people, to encourage national consciousness, and the Prussian statesman Stein recommended it as an aid to the liberation of Germany from the French.[30] In Sweden, the Afzelius–Geijer collection of folksongs was inspired by the 'Gothic Society' founded in 1811. Its members took 'Gothic' names and worked for the revival of the old Swedish or 'Gothic' virtues. They read old Swedish ballads aloud together. The impulse to the formation of this society, which was at once literary, antiquarian, moral and political, was the shock to the Swedes caused by their loss of Finland to Russia in 1809.[31]

The Finns were happy enough to escape from the Swedes, but they feared Russia too; they did not want to lose their identity in the Russian Empire. They had already begun to study their traditional literature in the later eighteenth century; an

important early study of folklore is H. G. Porthan's Latin
dissertation on Finnish poetry, published in 1766. This study of
the national past took on more of a political meaning after 1809.
As one Finnish intellectual put it at the time,

> No fatherland can exist without folk poetry. Poetry is nothing more
> than the crystal in which a nationality can mirror itself; it is the
> spring which brings to the surface the truly original in the folk
> soul.[32]

It was in this political-cultural atmosphere that Lönnrot found
himself when he went up to Turku university. He was
encouraged by his professor to collect folksongs, and out of this
collection grew the *Kalevala*.[33]

Elsewhere, too, enthusiasm for folksongs was part of a
movement of self-definition and national liberation. Fauriel's
collection of Greek folksongs was inspired by the Greek revolt
against the Turks of 1821. The Pole Hugo Kołłątaj drafted a
programme for research into popular culture in the prison
where he was confined after taking part in the Kościuszko rising
against Russian occupation; and the first collection,
Gołębiowski's *Lud Polski* (The Polish People) coincided with
the revolt of 1830. Niccolò Tommaseo, the first important
Italian folksong collector, was a political exile because of his
opposition to Austrian rule in Italy. The Belgian Jan-Frans
Willems, the editor of Flemish and Dutch folksongs, is regarded
as the father of the Flemish nationalist movement, the *Vlaamse
Beweging*. Even in the case of Scotland, where it was too late –
or too early – to speak of national liberation, Walter Scott
declared that he compiled his *Minstrelsy of the Scottish Border* in
order to illustrate 'the peculiar features' of Scottish manners and
character.[34] To a considerable extent the discovery of popular
culture was a series of 'nativistic' movements in the sense of
organised attempts by societies which were under foreign
domination to revive their traditional culture. Folksongs could
evoke a sense of solidarity in a dispersed population which
lacked traditional national institutions. As Arnim put it, they
'united a divided people' (*er sammelte sein zerstreutes Volk*).[35]
Ironically enough, the idea of a 'nation' came from the
intellectuals and was imposed on the 'people' with whom they
desired to identify. In 1800 craftsmen and peasants usually had a
regional rather than a national consciousness.

Of course, the political significance of the discovery of popular culture was not the same in each part of Europe, and to illustrate its complexities it may be useful to discuss one example in a little more detail: the Serbian. The folksongs of Serbia were edited by Vuk Stefanović Karadžić, the outstanding figure in the culture of what is now Yugoslavia. Karadžić came from a family of peasants, in the part of Serbia which was under Turkish rule. He took part in the Serbian rising of 1804 against the Turks, and when it was crushed in 1813 he crossed the border into the Habsburg Empire and went to Vienna. There he met Jernej Kopitar, a Slovene who was imperial censor for Slavonic languages. Kopitar wanted Vienna to become the centre of Slav culture, so that the Serbs and Czechs and others would prefer Austria to Russia. He knew the Herder folksong collection and showed it to Karadžić, who came of a family of singers, and Karadžić decided to follow Herder's example. He did not collect the songs for his song-book, he remembered them (he did go song-collecting later). He published the first part of his anthology in 1814, with a preface in pastoral style describing the songs as 'such as are sung by simple innocent hearts naturally and without artifice', and saying that he had learned them when, 'in the happiest condition known to mortals, I kept sheep and goats'. The preface was probably written tongue-in-cheek for the benefit of the educated reader; Karadžić was indignant whenever he was referred to as an uneducated goat-herd and had set his heart on an honorary degree from a German university. He was not reacting against the rococo, or classicism, or against literacy; in fact he believed that 'whatever man may have invented in this world, nothing can be compared with writing', and he went on to write a grammar of Serbian, a spelling-book, and a dictionary. Where he *was* serious in his preface was in his hope that his collection of songs would please 'every Serb who loves the national spirit of his race'. To publish Serbian songs, including songs about outlaws, in 1814–15 at the time of the suppression of the Serbian rising, was a political act. It is not surprising to find that Metternich would not allow Karadžić to publish his enlarged collection of songs in Vienna, for fear that the Turkish Government might find it subversive; the second edition was in fact published in Leipzig in 1823–4.[36]

It should be clear from the majority of examples quoted so far that the discovery of popular culture took place in the main in

what might be called the cultural periphery of Europe as a whole
and of different countries within it. Italy, France and England
had long had national literatures and a literary language. Their
intellectuals were becoming cut off from folksongs and folktales
in a way that Russians, say, or Swedes were not. Italy, France
and England had invested more in the Renaissance, in
classicism, and in the Enlightenment than other countries had
and so they were slower to abandon the values of these
movements. Since a standard literary language already existed,
the discovery of dialect was divisive. It is not surprising to find
that in Britain it was the Scots rather than the English who
rediscovered popular culture, or that the folksong movement
came late to France and was pioneered by a Breton,
Villemarqué, whose collection, *Barzaz Braiz*, was published in
1839.[37] Again, Villemarqué's equivalent in Italy, Tommaseo,
came from Dalmatia, and when Italian folklore was first studied
seriously, in the later nineteenth century, the most important
contributions were made in Sicily. As for Spain, the discovery of
folklore in the 1820s started not in the centre, in Castile, but on
the periphery, in Andalusia. In Germany too the initiative came
from the periphery; Herder and Arnim were born east of the
Elbe.

There were thus good literary and political reasons for
European intellectuals to discover popular culture when they
did. However, the discovery might have remained purely
literary had it not been for an older tradition of interest in
manners and customs, an antiquarian tradition which goes back
to the Renaissance but was taking on a more sociological
colouring in the eighteenth century. The variety of beliefs and
practices in different parts of the world was coming to seem
more and more fascinating, a challenge to reveal the order
underlying the apparent chaos. From the study of manners and
customs in Tahiti or among the Iroquois it was only a step for
French intellectuals to look at their own peasants, scarcely less
distant from them (they thought) in beliefs and style of life.
Interest did not necessarily imply sympathy, as the frequent use
of terms like 'prejudice' or 'superstition' makes abundantly
clear. So in 1790, the abbé Grégoire sent out a questionnaire
about French regional customs and dialects. In 1794, J. de
Cambry visited Finistère to observe the manners and customs of
the region. His attitude to the people was ambivalent. As a good

republican he found the Bretons backward and superstitious, but he could not help admiring them for their simplicity, their hospitality, their imagination.[38] In Scotland in 1797 a committee of the Highland Society circulated a six-point questionnaire about traditional Gaelic poetry. In 1808 J. A. Dulaure and M. A. Mangourit, members (like Cambry) of the newly-founded Celtic Academy (concerned with early French history), drew up a 51-point questionnaire about French popular customs: festivals, 'superstitious practices', popular medicine, songs, games, fairy stories, places of pilgrimage, religious fraternities, sorcerers and the argot of beggars. 'Do people engage in any particular superstitious practices during Carnival?' they asked, or 'Are there any so-called sorcerers, diviners or old women who make their living in this way? What is the people's opinion of them?'[39] When Italy was under Napoleonic rule, a five-point questionnaire of the same type was sent out to teachers and public officials, asking for information about festivals, customs, 'prejudices and supersti- tions' and 'so-called national songs' (the term *canti popolari* had not yet come into use). A few years later, in 1818, a local official, Michele Placucci, published a book on the 'customs and prejudices' of the peasants of the Romagna, a regional study inspired by the Italian questionnaire and drawing on the answers to it. Placucci included folksongs and proverbs in his book, which was described on the title-page as 'a serious-facetious work', suggesting that he felt some embarrassment at publishing on a subject which was not yet quite respectable.[40] Similar embarrassment may lurk behind the pseudonyms adopted by a number of writers on popular culture in this period and even later: 'Otmar', 'Chodokowski', 'Merton', 'Kazak Lugansky' and, more recently, 'Saintyves' and 'Davenson'.[41]

The popular culture of the years around 1800 was found just in time, or so the discoverers thought. The theme of a vanishing culture which must be recorded before it is too late recurs in their writings, making them reminiscent of the concern with disappearing tribal societies today. Thus Herder in Riga was concerned at the retreat of Latvian popular culture before the advance of German culture. 'Otmar' collected folktales in the Harz Mountains at a time when (he wrote) 'they were falling fast into oblivion'.

In fifty or a hundred years, most of the old folk tales which still
survive here and there will have disappeared . . . or have been
driven into the lonely mountains by the industry of the plains and
towns, whose inhabitants play a more and more lively part in the
political events of our age of change.[42]

Sir Walter Scott declared that he collected border ballads in
order to 'contribute somewhat to the history of my native
country; the peculiar features of whose manners and character
are daily melting and dissolving into those of her sister and ally'.
He believed that his contemporaries really were hearing the lay
of the last minstrel. He described one singer as 'perhaps the last
of our professed ballad reciters' and another as 'probably the
very last instance of the proper minstrel craft'. Arnim believed
that folksong was doomed all over Europe; in France, he wrote,
folksongs had disappeared almost entirely before the French
Revolution. 'In England too, folksongs are sung but rarely; in
Italy they have declined into opera, thanks to an empty desire
for innovation; even in Spain many songs have been lost.'[43] In
Norway a few years later, one collector compared the country
to a 'burning house' from which there was just time to snatch the
ballads before it was too late.[44] No doubt Arnim was
exaggerating wildly, but the other witnesses, who were
speaking of regions they knew well, deserve to be taken
seriously. Even before the industrial revolution, the growth of
towns, the improvement of roads and the spread of literacy were
undermining traditional popular culture. The centre was
invading the periphery. The process of social change made the
discoverers all the more aware of the importance of tradition.

If the discovery had not taken place when it did, it would have
been virtually impossible to write this book or any other study
of the popular culture of early modern Europe. We are deeply in
the debt of the men who snatched all they could from the
burning house, collecting, editing and describing. We are their
heirs. However, we need to take a critical look at this
inheritance, which includes corruptions and misconceptions as
well as good texts and fruitful ideas. It is all too easy to continue
to see popular culture through the romantic, nationalist
spectacles of the intellectuals of the early nineteenth century.

To begin with the heritage of texts. It was one of the glories of
this age of discovery that the antiquaries were poets and the
poets were antiquarians. The Belgian Jan-Frans Willems and the

Italian Niccolò Tommaseo were both poets as well as editors of folksong. In Portugal, Almeida Garrett was at once the reviver of Portuguese poetry and the rediscoverer of popular ballads. Scott was as much antiquary as poet and combined his interests when he wrote *The Lay of the Last Minstrel* (1805) on the theme of a vanishing culture. Geijer, who was, at least in his young days, as much poet as historian, wrote the Swedish equivalent of Scott's poem, *Den sista skalden*, 'the last skald' (1811).

This combination of poets and antiquaries has one serious disadvantage – from the point of view of the historian. Poets are too creative to make reliable editors. By modern standards, which came to be accepted in this field in the later nineteenth century, the work of the pioneer editors of popular poetry was little short of scandalous. The most notorious case is that of James Macpherson, the discoverer of the Celtic Homer, the Gaelic bard 'Ossian'. Not all contemporaries shared Hugh Blair's belief in the antiquity of the Ossianic poems; some, like Dr Johnson, thought Macpherson an 'imposter' who had written the poems himself. After a generation of controversy, the Highland Society of Scotland set up a committee in 1797 to investigate the authenticity of the poems, asking old men in remote parts of Scotland whether they had ever heard the epics. No one had, but many had heard songs about the same heroes, such as Fion or 'Fingal' and Cù Chulainn, songs which sometimes resembled passages of Macpherson quite closely, allowing for the problem of translating medieval Gaelic into eighteenth-century English. In other words, parts of Macpherson were authentically traditional (whether they went back to the third century is another matter) but the whole was not. The committee reported its belief that Macpherson 'was in use to supply chasms, and to give connection, by inserting passages which he did not find, and to add what he conceived to be dignity and delicacy to the original composition, by striking out passages, by softening incidents, by refining the language . . .' The judgement of modern scholars is more or less the same. Macpherson collected songs from oral tradition, he studied the manuscripts of recent collections, and he may well have thought he was reassembling the fragments of an early epic rather than constructing something new.[45]

There is a difference in degree rather than a difference in kind between Macpherson, who is commonly considered a 'forger', and Percy, Scott, the Grimms, Karadrić, Lönnrot and others usually considered as 'editors'. The most obvious parallel is with Lönnrot, who constructed the Finnish national epic out of the songs he collected, and added passages of his own. He justified himself like this:

> Finally, when no rune-singer could any longer compare with me in his knowledge of songs, I assumed that I had the same right which, in my opinion, most of the other singers freely reserved to themselves, namely the right to arrange the songs according as they seemed to fit best.[46]

According to the classical scholar F. A. Wolf, who wrote at the end of the eighteenth century, this is just what Homer had done with the traditional material of the *Iliad* and the *Odyssey*. Similarly, in 1845 Jacob Grimm asked Karadžić whether the songs about Prince Marko Kraljević could be joined together to make an epic.[47]

On a small scale, many editors followed the method of Macpherson and Lönnrot. Percy 'improved' his ballads, as he confessed:

> By a few slight corrections or additions, a most beautiful or interesting sense has started forth, and this so naturally and easily, that the editor could seldom prevail on himself to indulge the vanity of making a formal claim to the improvement; but must plead guilty to the charge of concealing his own share in the amendments under some such general title as a Modern Copy.

These amendments were not always 'slight'. In the case of *Edom o'Gordon* (Child 178), a letter of Percy's survives criticising the ending of the ballad (in which the wronged husband commits suicide) and suggesting the omission of that stanza and the addition of a line suggesting that the husband went mad.[48] Something about the ballads seems to have encouraged invention. John Pinkerton tried to pass off *Hardyknute*, a composition of his own, as a traditional ballad collected from oral tradition in Lanarkshire, and Sir Walter Scott rewrote (if he did not compose) *Kinmont Willie*. Arnim and Brentano did not go as far as that, but they did 'improve' and bowdlerise the songs in their famous collection.[49] Editors of folktales followed the same principles as editors of ballads. For their famous book of *Märchen*, the Grimms collected stories from oral tradition in Hesse, asking their helpers to send the stories 'without additions and so-called improvement' (*ohne Zusatz und sogennante Verschönerung*). However, the brothers did not publish exactly what they found. For one thing, the stories were current in dialect, but the Grimms translated them into German. They created a masterpiece of German literature as a result. What I want to stress here, however, is what was lost and the fact that in Germany at this time the middle classes quite literally spoke a different language from the craftsmen and peasants, and that the original versions of the stories would not have been intelligible to the readers for whom the book was intended. Translation was necessary, but it necessarily involved distortions. Some stories were bowdlerised, because they would otherwise have shocked their new readers. Individual idiosyncrasies in the telling were smoothed out so that the collection had a uniform style. Where the different versions of the same tale completed one another, the Grimms amalgamated them (reasonably enough, given their theory that it is not individuals but 'the people' who create). Finally, a study of the differences between the first edition of the *Märchen* and later ones shows that the Grimms emended the tales in an effort to make them sound more oral. For example, they inserted traditional formulaic phrases into *Snow White*, from 'once upon a time' (*Es war einmal*) to 'they lived happy ever after' (*sie lebten glücklich bis an ihr Ende*). 'Improvement' went out through the door, but came back again through the window.[50]

In the case of folk-music, the changes made by the discoverers and collectors in transmitting what they found to a new public are particularly obvious. The music had to be written down, since there was no other way of preserving it, and written down according to a system of conventions which were not made for music of this kind. The music was published in order to appeal to a middle-class public with a piano and ears attuned to the songs of Haydn, and later Schubert and Schumann: so it had to be, as the title-pages confess, 'harmonised'. V. E. Trutovsky published a collection of Russian folksongs in the late eighteenth century; as a modern writer explains, 'Not only did he deliberately change the melodic outline . . . in some cases, but he also introduced sharps and flats into otherwise modal tunes, and gave them harmonic accompaniments.'[51] William Chappell published a collection of 'national English airs' (popular songs) in the early nineteenth century; in these printed versions, 'academic harmonic patterns were imposed on popular melodies, ancient modalities suppressed, irregular tunes squared off'. He also omitted the words whenever they were 'too coarse for publication'.[52]

Thus to read the text of a ballad, a folktale or even a tune in a collection of this period is much like looking at a Gothic church which was 'restored' at much the same time. One cannot be sure whether one is looking at what was originally there, at what the restorer thought was originally there, at what he thought ought to have been there, or at what he thought should be there now. Not only texts and buildings were subject to 'restoration', but even festivals. Some surviving traditional festivals have had a continuous existence from medieval or early modern times or even longer, but others have not. The Carnival of Cologne was revived in 1823, the Carnival of Nuremberg in 1843, the Carnival of Nice in the mid-nineteenth century.[53] The tradition of the Eisteddfod has not survived from the time of the Druids; it was revived by a stonemason from Glamorgan, Edward Williams (Iolo Morgannwg), who set up the Gorsedd Circle at Carmarthen in 1819; and the costumes were designed by Sir Hubert Herkomer, RA, later in the century.[54]

We have inherited from the intellectuals of the early nineteenth century not only texts and festivals, but also ideas, some of them fruitful and others misleading. The main criticism to be made of the ideas of the discoverers is that they were not discriminating enough. They did not distinguish (or they did not distinguish sharply enough) between the primitive and the medieval, the urban and the rural, the peasant and the whole nation.[55] Percy described ancient Chinese poems, Icelandic poems and border ballads in much the same terms. He lumped them together because they were not classical without worrying about the differences between them. Herder called Moses, Homer and the authors of the German *Minnesang* 'singers of the people'. Claude Fauriel lectured on such 'popular poetry' as Homer, Dante, the troubadours, and the ballads of Greece and Serbia. The intellectuals of this period liked to compare the peasant societies they visited with the tribal societies they read about, a parallel which was frequently illuminating but sometimes misleading. When Boswell and Johnson were at Glenmorison in the Hebrides, they offended their host: 'his pride seemed to be much piqued that we were surprised at his having books'. They were a little too eager to see the Highlanders as 'American savages'.[56]

Herder, the Grimms and their followers made three points in particular about popular culture which were highly influential but also highly questionable. It may be useful to label these points, calling them 'primitivism', 'communalism' and 'purism'.

The first point was about the age of the songs and stories and festivals and beliefs which they had discovered. They tended to locate them in an undefined 'primitive period' (*Vorzeit*) and to believe that pre-Christian traditions had been handed on unchanged for thousands of years. There is no doubt that some of these traditions are very old; the Italian Carnival, for example, may well have developed from the Roman Saturnalia, and the *commedia dell'arte* from classical farces. However, for lack of precise evidence these suggestions cannot be proved. What can be proved is that in relatively recent times, between 1500 and 1800, popular traditions have been subject to change, in all sorts of ways. The design of farmhouses might alter, or one popular hero might be replaced in the 'same' story by another; or the meaning of a ritual might change, while the form remained more or less the same. In short, popular culture does have a history.[57]

The second point was the Grimm brothers' famous theory about communal creation; *Das Volk dichtet*. The value of this theory was that it drew attention to an important difference between the two cultures; in European popular culture in 1800, the role of the individual was smaller and the role of tradition, the past of the community, was greater than in the learned or minority culture of the time. As metaphor, the Grimms' phrase is illuminating. Taken literally, however, it is false; studies of popular singers and storytellers have shown that passing on an oral tradition does not inhibit the development of an individual style.[58]

The third point might be called 'purism'. Whose culture is popular culture? Who are the people? On occasion they were defined as everyone in a particular country, as in Geijer's image of the whole Swedish people singing as one man. More often, the term was restricted. The people were the uneducated, as in Herder's distinction between *Kultur der Gelehrten* and *Kultur des Volkes*. Sometimes the term was narrowed still further:

Herder once wrote that 'The people are not the mob of the streets, who never sing or compose but shriek and mutilate' ('Volk heisst nicht der Pöbel auf den Gassen, der singt und dichtet niemals, sondern schreit und verstümmelt').[59] For the discoverers, the people *par excellence* were the peasants; they lived close to nature, they were less tainted by foreign ways and had preserved primitive customs longer than anyone else. But to say this was to ignore important cultural and social changes, to underestimate the interaction between town and country, learned and popular. There was no pure, unchanging popular tradition in early modern Europe, and perhaps there never had been. Hence there is no good reason for excluding town-dwellers, whether respectable craftsmen or Herder's 'mob', from a study of popular culture.

The difficulty of defining the 'people' suggests that popular culture was not monolithic or homogeneous. In fact it was extremely various. To discuss some of these variations and the unity which underlay them will be the task of the next chapter.

CHAPTER TWO

Unity and Variety in Popular Culture

The upper classes and the 'little tradition'

If everyone in a given society shared the same culture, there
would be no need to use the term 'popular culture' at all. This is,
or was, the situation in many tribal societies, as they have been
described by social anthropologists. Their descriptions might be
summarised, in simplified form, as follows. A tribal society is
small, isolated and self-sufficient. Carvers, singers, storytellers
and their public form a face-to-face group sharing basic values
and the myths and symbols in which these values are expressed.
The craftsman or singer hunts, fishes or tills the soil like other
members of the community, and they carve or sing like him,
even if they do this less frequently and less well. Audience
participation in performance is important. They answer riddles
and they sing choruses. Even carving may be a semi-communal
acitivity; among the Tiv of Nigeria, if a man carving a stick is
called away, a bystander may pick up the knife and carry on
with the work.[1]

This simplified description, or 'model', has its relevance to
early modern Europe, at least in the poorer and more remote
regions, where noblemen and clergymen were thin on the
ground. Students of the ballad in Scotland or Serbia, Castile or
Denmark have sometimes described the 'ballad community', as
they call it, in similar terms to the anthropologist on tribal
society.[2]

However, it is clear that this model does not apply to most
parts of Europe in our period. In most places there was cultural
as well as social stratification. There was a minority who could
read and write as well as a majority who could not, and some of
the literate minority knew Latin, the language of the learned.
This cultural stratification makes a more complex model more
appropriate. Such a model was put forward in the 1930s by the
social anthropologist Robert Redfield. Within some societies,
he suggested, there were two cultural traditions, the 'great

tradition' of the educated few, and the 'little tradition' of the rest.

> The great tradition is cultivated in schools or temples; the little tradition works itself out and keeps itself going in the lives of the unlettered in their village communities . . . The two traditions are interdependent. Great tradition and little tradition have long affected each other and continue to do so . . . Great epics have arisen out of elements of traditional tale-telling by many people, and epics have returned again to the peasantry for modification and incorporation in local cultures.

The point about the two-way traffic between the two traditions is an important one, and we shall return to it later. What should be emphasised now is that Redfield, like Herder, offers what might be called a 'residual' definition of popular culture, as the culture or tradition of the non-learned, the un-lettered, the non-elite.[3]

Applying this model to early modern Europe, we can identify the great tradition easily enough. It includes the classical tradition, as it was handed down in schools and universities; the tradition of medieval scholastic philosophy and theology, far from dead in the sixteenth and seventeenth centuries; and some intellectual movements which are likely to have affected only the educated minority – the Renaissance, the Scientific Revolution of the seventeenth century, the Enlightenment. Subtract all this from the culture of early modern Europe, and what residue is left? There are folksongs and folktales; devotional images and decorated marriage-chests; mystery plays and farces; broadsides and chap-books; and, above all, festivals, like the feasts of the saints and the great seasonal festivals such as Christmas, New Year, Carnival, May, and Midsummer. This is the material with which this book will be primarily concerned; with craftsmen as well as peasants, with printed books as well as oral traditions.

Redfield's model is a useful point of departure, but it is open to criticism. His definition of the little tradition as the tradition of the non-elite can be criticised, paradoxically enough, on the grounds that it is too narrow and also on the grounds that it is too wide.

The definition is too narrow because it omits upper-class participation in popular culture, which was an important fact of

European life, most obvious at festivals. Carnival, for example, was for everyone. In Ferrara in the late fifteenth century, the Duke joined in the fun, going masked in the streets and entering private houses to dance with the ladies. In Florence Lorenzo de' Medici and Niccolò Machiavelli took part in carnival. In Paris in 1583, Henri III and his suite 'went about the streets masked, going from house to house and committing a thousand insolences'. In the carnivals of Nuremberg in the early sixteenth century, the patrician families played a prominent part.[4] Festive societies like the Abbey of Conards at Rouen or the Compagnie de la Mère Folle at Dijon were dominated by the nobles, but still performed in the street for everyone. Henry VIII went to the woods on May Day, just like other young men. The Emperor Charles V took part in bull-fights during festivals, and his great-grandson Philip IV loved to watch them.[5]

It was not only at such times of ritualised collective rejoicing that the upper classes or the educated took part in popular culture. In towns at least, rich and poor, nobles and commoners attended the same sermons. Humanist poets like Poliziano and Pontano have recorded the fact that they stood in the piazza like everyone else to hear the singer of tales, the *cantastorie*, and that they enjoyed the performance. Leading seventeenth-century poets like Malherbe and P. C. Hooft enjoyed folksongs. Among the lovers of ballads were kings and queens like Isabella of Spain, Ivan the Terrible of Russia, and Sophia of Denmark.[6] The same was true of the nobility. In Denmark and Sweden, sixteenth- and seventeenth-century versions of ballads have survived because noblemen and noblewomen wrote them out in their manuscript song-books or *visböcker*. One of these books was compiled by no less a man than Per Brahe the younger, a member of one of the greatest noble families of Sweden, who became lord chancellor and member of the regency council. In a similar way a number of Gaelic songs have survived because they were collected, about the year 1500, by Sir James MacGregor, Dean of Lismore in Argyll. Nobles offered their patronage to distinguished traditional performers. The poet Tinódi lived at the courts of András Báthory and Tamás Nádasdy, the harper John Parry was supported by Sir Watkin Williams Wynne.[7]

Clowns were popular at courts as well as taverns, and often the same clowns. Zan Polo, the famous Venetian buffoon, performed before the doge in 1523. Richard Tarleton's clowning was much appreciated by Queen Elizabeth, who 'bade them take away the knave for making her laugh so excessively', and Latin elegies were written on his death. The French buffoon Tabarin played before Queen Marie of France in 1619, and the dedication to a collection of his jokes makes the point that it is intended for courtiers, nobles, merchants, in fact for everyone. Ivan the Terrible was, as an English visitor noticed, extremely fond of 'jesters and dwarfs, men and women that tumble before him and sing many songs after the Russe manner'. He was also addicted to bear-baiting, and he used to listen to blind men telling folktales before he went to sleep. Even at the end of the eighteenth century, in Russia, blind men advertised in the newspapers for the position of storyteller to gentry families.[8] Nobles and peasants seem to have shared the taste for romances of chivalry. In the sixteenth century, a Norman squire, the Sieur de Gouberville, read *Amadis de Gaule* aloud to his peasants when it rained. Broadsides and chap-books seem to have been read by rich and poor, educated and uneducated. It has been suggested that the seventeenth-century German broadsheet (which combined a simple visual presentation with Latin tags) aimed to please everyone. Copies of French almanacs have survived in leather bindings decorated with the arms of French nobles. Folk-healers were patronised by the upper classes. In Sweden in 1663 there were only twenty physicians in the whole country, so the nobles had nowhere else to go for treatment. The nobles made use of objects which are usually described today as the products of folk art, like Finnish *kåsor,* carved wooden buckets used for ceremonial drinking. Some surviving examples from the sixteenth and seventeenth centuries have the arms of Swedish noblemen painted on them.[9]

It was not only the nobility who participated in popular culture; the clergy did so too, particularly in the sixteenth century. During Carnival, as one Florentine remarked,

> men of the church are permitted to enjoy themselves. Friars play ball with each other, perform comedies, and, dressed in costume, sing, dance, and play instruments. Even nuns are permitted to celebrate by dressing as men . . .

It was not at all uncommon for the priests to be seen singing, dancing, or wearing masks in church on festive occasions, and it was the junior clergy who organised the Feast of Fools, a major festival in some parts of Europe. An eccentric case will make the point more vivid. When Richard Corbet was a Doctor of Divinity (so Aubrey tells us),

> he sang ballads at the cross at Abingdon on a market-day . . . The ballad singer complained he had no custom, he could not put off his ballads. The jolly doctor puts off his gown, and puts on the ballad-singer's leathern jacket, and being a handsome man, and had a rare full voice, he presently vended a great many and had a great audience.

In eighteenth-century Sweden the parson had the first dance with the bride at rural weddings, carved the joint at the feast, and often lent the bridegroom his clerical clothes to be married in, facts which strongly suggest that he participated in peasant culture.[10]

At this point, someone may object that I have painted too rosy a picture of the relations between the classes. Did not the ruling class, and the educated, despise the 'many-headed monster', the people? Indeed they did. 'To speak of the people is really to speak of a mad beast', wrote Guicciardini. Sebastian Franck wrote of 'the unstable fickle rabble called the common man'. Such quotations can be multiplied.[11] However, the point which needs to be made here is that educated people did not yet associate ballads and chap-books and festivals with the common people, precisely because they participated in these forms of culture.

Another possible objection to this participation thesis might be to argue that the nobility and clergy did not listen to folksongs or read chap-books in the same way or for the same reasons as craftsmen and peasants. 'Participation' is an imprecise term: it is easier to see how nobles could take part in a festival than in a belief system. When members of the élite read chap-books, they might have been taking an interest in folklore, just like some intellectuals today. This is certainly possible, and the later one gets into the eighteenth century the more likely this interpretation becomes. For the earlier part of the period, however, one needs to remember that many of the nobles and the clergy could not read and write, or could do so only with difficulty, just like the peasants; in the Cracow area about 1565, more than 80 per cent of the poor nobles were illiterate.

The style of life of some rural nobles and parish priests was not so different from that of the peasants around them. They were also more or less cut off from the great tradition. Most noblewomen were equally cut off, because it was rare for them to have much formal education. Perhaps one should see noblewomen as mediators between the group to which they belonged socially, the elite, and the group to which they belonged culturally, the non-elite; it is interesting to find that several of the *visböcker* were compiled by women. Educated noblemen maintained contact with popular culture through their mothers, sisters, wives and daughters, and they would in many cases have been brought up by peasant nurses who sang them ballads and told them folktales.[12]

Redfield's model needs to be modified, and it might be restated like this. There were two cultural traditions in early modern Europe, but they did not correspond symmetrically to the two main social groups, the elite and the common people. The elite participated in the little tradition, but the common people did not participate in the great tradition. This asymmetry came about because the two traditions were transmitted in different ways. The great tradition was transmitted formally at grammar schools and at universities. It was a closed tradition in the sense that people who had not attended these institutions, which were not open to all, were excluded. In a quite literal sense, they did not speak the language. The little tradition, on the other hand, was transmitted informally. It was open to all, like the church, the tavern and the market-place, where so many of the performances occurred.

Thus the crucial cultural difference in early modern Europe (I want to argue) was that between the majority, for whom popular culture was the only culture, and the minority, who had access to the great tradition but participated in the little tradition as a second culture. They were amphibious, bi-cultural, and also bilingual. Where the majority of people spoke their regional dialect and nothing else, the elite spoke or wrote Latin or a literary form of the vernacular, while remaining able to speak in dialect as a second or third language. For the elite, but for them only, the two traditions had different psychological functions; the great tradition was serious, the little tradition was play. A contemporary analogy to their situation is that of the English-speaking elite of Nigeria, whose western-style education does not prevent them from participating in their traditional tribal culture.[13]

This situation did not remain static throughout the period. The upper classes gradually withdrew from participation in the little tradition in the course of the seventeenth and eighteenth centuries, a movement which will be discussed in Chapter 9 below. All that is being offered here is a simplified description, a model. A more serious objection to the model is that it fails to distinguish different groups within the 'people', whose culture was not the same. Since popular culture is a residual concept, it is important to see how that residue may be structured.

Varieties of popular culture: the countryside

Redfield's definition of the little tradition may be regarded as too narrow, because it excludes those people for whom popular culture was a second culture. It may also be regarded as too wide; speaking of the 'little tradition' in the singular suggests that it was relatively homogeneous, whereas this was far from being the case in early modern Europe. As Antonio Gramsci once put it, 'The people is not a culturally homogeneous unit, but it is culturally stratified in a complex way'.[14] There were many popular cultures or many varieties of popular culture – it is difficult to choose between these phrases because a culture is a loosely bounded system, so that (as Toynbee found when he tried to enumerate world civilisations), it is impossible to say where one ends and another begins. What we cheerfully call 'popular culture' was often the culture of the most visible of the people, the YAMS (young adult males), who represented the whole people no better than the WASPS (white Anglo-Saxon Protestants) represent the USA.

For the discoverers of popular culture, the 'people' were the peasants. The peasants formed between 80 per cent and 90 per cent of the population of Europe. It was their songs which Herder and his friends called 'folksongs', their dances which were called 'folkdances', their stories which were called 'folktales'. Was their culture uniform? Looking back on the Hungarian peasants as he had known them about the year 1900, Zoltan Kodály was sure that it was not:

Folk   tradition   should   not   be   thought   of   as   one   uniform, homogeneous whole. It varies fundamentally according to age, social and material conditions, religion, education, district and sex.

It would of course be dangerous to apply this statement without more ado to the period before 1800 and to the whole of Europe. Kodály was writing of a peasant society so conscious of social distinctions that married men and bachelors, for example, sat not only in different parts of the church but also at separate tables in the inn.[15] However, there are reasons for thinking that Kodály's point was generally valid for early modern Europe.

Culture grows out of a total way of life, and the peasants of early modern Europe did not have a uniform way of life. Some lived in villages, as in England; some in towns, as in southern Italy; some in isolated homesteads, as in Norway. They were not socially homogeneous. Some were freemen, others were serfs – in the whole vast area east of the river Elbe, the peasants were generally made into serfs in the course of the sixteenth and early seventeenth centuries. There were rich peasants and there were poor ones. In a relatively limited region, like the Beauvaisis in the seventeenth century, rural society could be extremely stratified, with considerable differences in style of life between the rich *laboureur* (yeoman, not labourer) and the poor *journalier*.[16] In many parts of Europe this distinction between the rich peasant, who owned his land and employed others to help him work it, and the farm labourer 'with no land to live on but his hands' was a prominent one. This aspect of the traditional 'organic community' must not be forgotten.

It is less easy to say whether there was cultural as well as social stratification within the peasantry. Here as elsewhere in this chapter, we are approaching systems of shared meanings through a small number of outward signs or indicators, and it is easy to read these signs amiss. The richer peasants were more likely to be literate, because they could afford the time to learn to read and write, and they were more likely to own chap-books. They were also more likely to possess painted plates and jugs, embroidered pillows and hangings, and elaborately carved ox-yokes or marriage chests, obvious symbols of wealth and status in the village as well as embodiments of popular culture. It has been suggested, plausibly enough, that what we call 'folk art' or 'peasant art' is really the art created for a peasant aristocracy.[17] Now to say that the poorer peasants were culturally deprived is not to say that they had an alternative culture; they may have aspired to that of the peasant aristocrats. Yet Kodály found that 'the well-to-do like to distinguish themselves from the poorer even in their songs', and many traditional folksongs are appropriate only for one social group, like the Scandinavian *drängvisor*, or farm hands' song, and the *pigvisor*, the 'complaints' of ill-treated maidservants.[18]

If culture grows out of a total way of life, one might expect peasant culture to vary according to ecological differences as well as social ones; differences in physical environment involve differences in material culture, and encourage differences in attitudes as well. The most obvious illustration of this point is surely the contrast between the culture of the mountains and the culture of the plains. Dr Johnson observed that 'As mountains are long before they are conquered, they are likewise long before they are civilised', retaining traditional habits longer than the plains. When the 'cultivated parts' (in both senses) change their language, the mountaineers may 'become a distinct nation, cut off by dissimilitude of speech from conversation with their neighbours', as in the case of the Scottish Highlanders, the Basques and the 'Dalecarlians'. Mountaineers, he continued, are 'warlike' and also 'thievish', 'because they are poor and having neither manufactures nor commerce, can grow richer only by robbery'; and in any case the arm of the law can hardly reach them.[19]

Dr Johnson's ideas have been elaborated and reinforced by a variety of scholars. In Britain archaeologists have stressed the difference between the lowland zones and the poorer and more conservative highland zones; a difference of language, of house-types, and many other features of culture. In Andalusia the mountaineers of the Alpujarras were the last to go over to Islam, and also the last to abandon it.[20] Otmar was right (above, p.15) to look for traditional folktales in the Harz Mountains. Highland zones are the obvious refuge for bandits and other fugitives who 'take to the hills', and these zones remained the home of traditional 'heroic poetry', extolling their exploits. Leaping dances seem to be associated with mountainous regions, in the Basque country, in Norway, in the highlands of Bavaria, Poland and Scotland, probably because this was an old form of dance which did not survive in the plains.[21] The witch-hunts of the sixteenth and seventeenth centuries seem to have been particularly intense in mountainous areas such as the Alps and the Pyrenees, whether, as scholars used to think, because mountain air encourages fantasies, or, rather more plausibly, because of the hostility of lowlanders to highlanders and the differences between the two cultures.[22] More surprising, at first glance, is the fact that at the end of the period some mountainous regions were areas of high literacy. Norway and Sweden are obvious examples, while in France the present department of the Hautes-Alpes had a literacy rate of 45 per cent in the late seventeenth century, more than twice the national average. Perhaps this was, as an observer remarked in 1802, because 'the cold climate does not allow them any other activity in winter-time'. We find some of the surplus population of the French Alps becoming schoolmasters, while many pedlars of chap-books came from the Haut Comminges in the French Pyrenees.[23]

Overlapping with the contrast between lowlanders and highlanders was another important division, between farmers and herdsmen – swineherds, goatherds, cowherds (in Spain the *vaqueros*, the original 'cowboys'), and above all, shepherds*. Shepherd culture in particular was so distinctive, so different from peasant culture that it deserves to be described in some detail.[24] The distinctiveness was symbolised by special clothes, like the smock. Shepherds might come from a farming village, but they could not live in it for much of the year because they had to migrate with their flocks. In Spain, for example, the flocks spent the summer in the highlands around Soria, Segovia, Cuenca and León, but wintered in the southern plains. Shepherds were poor and isolated. A Jesuit missionary who sought them out in their huts near Eboli in South Italy regarded them as so ignorant that they were scarcely human. 'Asked how many gods there were, one said "a hundred", another "a thousand"'.[25] Shepherds were also free; in Poland, where the peasants were enserfed, a serf shepherd was a rare exception. Shepherds were far away from interference by clergy, nobles and officials. No wonder their way of life was idealised in pastoral poetry. They had time on their hands which they could spend carving crooks and walking-sticks and powder-horns.[26]

---

* Highland zones were usually pastoral zones, but not all lowland zones were arable – the obvious exception at this time was the Great Hungarian Plain.

They could make music, playing the bagpipe, made out of the skin of a sheep or goat and popular wherever herdsmen were numerous, from the Scottish Highlands to the Great Hungarian Plain, or they would play the flute, slowly and sadly when the sheep were lost, and gaily when they were found again. As the Catalan proverb has it (perhaps expressing the envy of the peasants), 'Vida de pastor vida regalada/Cantant i sonant guanya la soldada' (The shepherd's life is a pleasant one, he is paid for playing and singing). Shepherds were often credited with magical powers, with knowledge of the stars, which they were well placed to observe (hence the title of the *Calendrier des Bergers*), or with the ability to heal animals and men.[27] Neither their knowledge nor their ignorance corresponded with that of the farmers.

In compensation for their lonely working life, shepherds developed an elaborate set of festivities, at least in central Europe. They had their own guilds and fraternities. They had their own saints like St Wendelin (of whom the story went that he was a king's son turned shepherd) or St Wolfgang, or St Bartholomew, whose festival on 24 August marked the transition from summer to winter quarters. On this day the local shepherds converged on certain towns in South Germany, like Markgröningen, Rothenburg and Urach, to elect their king and queen, to feast, and to dance their special dances. At Christmas, too, they played a lively part; in Spain and elsewhere they acted out the adoration of the shepherds in *autos del nacimiento* or nativity plays.[28]

It is not surprising to find that shepherds often intermarried, as in Hanover in the seventeenth and eighteenth centuries. They had their own pride and they were rejected by the rest of society, as men without fixed abode often are. Farmers often accused them of being lazy and dishonest. Many German guilds regarded the sons of shepherds as *unehrlich*, 'without honour', and so ineligible for membership. When, in the late seventeenth century, some shepherds of Brie were accused of *maleficia*, of doing harm by supernatural means, this looks like a miniature version of the witch-hunts of the Alps and Pyrenees, the persecution of the outsiders.[29]

Some important groups of country people were neither farmers nor herdsmen; how far they had distinctive attitudes and values it is very hard to say. There were the village craftsmen, such as blacksmiths, carpenters or weavers (full-time or part-time), whom it is natural to imagine as culturally midway between other villagers who were not craftsmen and other craftsmen who were not villagers. Blacksmiths in particular seem to have enjoyed a certain prestige, and Novak Kovač, 'Novak the smith', was a hero of Serbian epic. Then there are the woodlanders, in particular woodcutters and charcoal-burners, who might live in the woods for weeks at a time. They are an obscure group, cut off from village culture like the shepherds but apparently (unlike modern lumberjacks) without an alternative culture of their own, living on the margins of society. Sometimes (as in the case of the *cagots* of south-west France) they were treated as outcasts, pursued as sorcerers, associated with leprosy. In Russia, however (like the Balkans), woodlanders' culture was dominant, and English visitors noticed with surprise that 'their churches are built of timber' or 'No pewter to be had, cups cut out of birch are very good'. Axes were sacred as well as utilitarian objects for the Russians as for the Serbs, symbols of protection. Trees had an important function in Russian rituals – firs at Christmas, birches in Trinity week.[30]

The Cossacks, and other groups like them, such as the *hajduks* of Central Europe, were not exactly peasants, or soldiers, or even robbers, but something of all three. They were proud of their status and often despised their peasant neighbours. Their values were distinctively democratic and egalitarian – the Cossacks, for example, elected their leaders or *atamans*. They were well-dressed in their own way. As Vuk Stefanović Karadžić remembered,

> The *hajduks* of our time in Serbia usually wore bright blue cloth trousers . . . a silken embroidered cap from which silken tassels would hang down on one side over their chest – these were worn by few except *hajduks*. They particularly liked to wear silver discs on their breast.

They had their own weapon-dances and their own songs, 'mainly songs about *hajduks*'.[31] If Cossack and other bandit heroes have so often found their way into the popular culture of Central and Eastern Europe, this need not mean that the bandits were always popular among the peasants in their own day.

Another proud, self-conscious group, about whom there is

rather more information, is that of the miners. No doubt the danger of their work, the precious metals they discovered, the difference between their work and 'normal' work and the concentration of miners in a few regions all helped create their self-awareness. In Central Europe the mines were prospering at the beginning of our period: Kutná Hora, a mining town in Bohemia, was the second city of the kingdom, and new towns were springing up near the mines, such as Jachymov in Bohemia, known in German as Joachimstal, or the three Annabergs in Saxony, Silesia and Styria. The miners had their own patron saints, such as St Anne (because of the hidden treasure she carried within her), St Barbara (because she fled to the mountains), and the prophet Daniel (because of his association with the ages of gold and silver). Their clothes were distinctive, in particular their hoods. They had their own chapels, their own plays, and their own songs, the *Bergreihen* or *Bergmannslieder*, and collections of these songs were published in the sixteenth century. They had their own dances, like the dance of the miners of Durrenberg which mimed their work; it is documented for the seventeenth century. The miners had their own legends, dealing in particular with the spirits of the mines (the *Berggeist*, the *Bergmönch*, and the *Bergmännlein* or dwarf), who guarded the treasure and needed to be appeased by offerings. Legends of this kind, dealing with the discovery of treasure by supernatural help, were current not only in Germany but in mining areas all over Europe, from Cornwall to the Urals. Given the existence of this rich miners' culture, it is not surprising to find that the Lutheran clergyman Johann Mathesius, pastor of Joachimstal, wrote hymns and sermons specially for them.[32] Miners, like shepherds, may have developed their own culture because they were rejected by the world around them. The seventeenth-century Scottish colliers were enserfed and despised, and in Fife they were not allowed to be buried in the same churchyards as free labourers. This Spanish verse has a rather patronising tone:

Pobresitos los mineros,	*Unhappy the miners,*
Qué desgrasiáitos son,	*How unfortunate they are,*
Pasan su bida en las minas,	*They spend their life in the mines,*
Y mueren sin confesión.	*And die without making their confession.*

One fifteenth-century painting suggests that the outside world did not distinguish carefully between the dwarfs or gnomes who lived in the mines and the miners themselves, small and hooded as they were.[33]

Varieties of popular culture: the towns

Rural popular culture, then, was far from monolothic. It may be contrasted all the same with the popular culture of the towns. In towns, festivals could take place on a much grander scale; still more important, every day was a festival, in the sense that professional entertainment was permanently available. In large towns, at least, ballad-singers and clowns were performing all the time, whereas villagers would see them only once in a while. Towns housed ethnic minorities who often lived together and shared a culture from which outsiders were excluded. The Jews in their ghettoes are the most obvious example, but there were also the Moors in the towns of southern Spain, the Greeks and Slavs in Venice, and many smaller groups.

The guild system helped give craftsmen and shopkeepers a common culture, different from that of the peasants. Guilds had their own patron saints, their own traditions and their own rituals, and they organised the leisure as well as the working lives of their members. The religious plays performed in many towns for the feast of Corpus Christi were often organised on a guild basis, and so were some secular pageants, like the London Lord Mayor's Show. In some German carnivals the butchers' guild played a prominent part, sometimes performing a weapon-dance with their carving-knives, or making their apprentices jump into the river. Religious fraternities were often recruited from specific guilds. Craftsmen had their own myths, like the London myth of Dick Whittington, or the many stories about the founders of particular crafts. They were particular about whom they admitted to the craft, and not only the sons of shepherds but the sons of beggars, hangmen, gravediggers or minstrels might be excluded because they were not 'honourable people'.[34]

Perhaps one should be more precise and speak of craftsmen cultures in the plural, distinguishing the weavers, the shoemakers, and so on. Every craft has its own culture in the sense of its own skills, handed down from generation to generation, but some crafts, at least, seem to have had a culture of their own in a wider and a fuller sense. The documentation for these cultures is a mixture of what members of the craft said about themselves and what others said about them; if not altogether reliable, this evidence is at least suggestive. One might begin from the fact of occupational costume. Carpenters tended to wear leather aprons and carry a ruler. A tailor would be fashionably dressed, with a needle and thread stuck in his coat.[35] There is also the occupational song (*Ambachtslied, Yrkevisa*).

Weavers were more likely to have a separate culture than most craftsmen. They included some relatively proud and prosperous workers in expensive materials, like silk; they were numerous, and indeed dominated certain towns, like Norwich, Lyons and Segovia; their work enabled them to read if they wanted to, propping the book on the loom. In eighteenth-century Lyons, nearly three-quarters of the silk-workers were literate. Their literacy helps explain the prominence of weavers in heresy trials in England, France or Italy in the early sixteenth century. Lollardy appealed to clothworkers in Colchester, Newbury, Tenterden and elsewhere. The English example is an obvious one to take here, since England had an important place in the European textile industries. Thomas Deloney, the silk-weaver turned professional writer, never lost his pride in his former craft. His famous story *Jack of Newbury* presented a weaver-hero, and the book was dedicated to clothworkers because it showed 'the great worship and credit which men of this trade have in former time come unto'. In the seventeenth and eighteenth centuries, Deloney was often reprinted, sometimes in abbreviated chap-book form. He was not the only writer to consider the weaving public. The presbyterian divine John Collinges, for example, might be described as a spiritual Deloney. He was a minister at Norwich, and his *The Weavers' Pocket-Book* was addressed in particular to the numerous worsted-weavers of that city. His aim was to 'spiritualise' the art of weaving by instructing his readers 'how to raise heavenly meditations from the several parts of their work'. Special almanacs were printed for the use of weavers, and a poem, *The Triumphant Weaver*, published in chap-book form in the late seventeenth century, dealt in its three cantos with the antiquity, the utility and the excellence of the craft. The praises of the linen-weavers were sung in a similar German poem, printed in 1737:

> *Dass Gott sei ein Erheber*
> *Des Handwerks der Leinweber,*
> *Macht mir die Bibel kund.*

(The Bible tells me that God extols the craft of linen-weaver)

Even more telling evidence for the existence of a weaver culture comes from their work songs, sung to the rhythm of the loom. Many of them were recorded in the nineteenth century, from Lancashire to Silesia, at a time when handloom-weaving was in decline. They are likely to date from the eighteenth century, if not before, and they suggest that weaver culture had an international stamp.[36]

A good case might also be made out for the existence of a shoemaker-culture, since shoemakers were another self-conscious and literate group. Sixty-eight per cent of the shoemakers in eighteenth-century Lyons could sign their names, a figure which puts them not far behind the weavers. Deloney appealed to this group with his panegyric, *The Gentle Craft*, which reads like an attempt to give literary form to oral traditions, and themes from Deloney were taken up and turned into plays by Dekker and Rowley. In these stories, shoemakers become saints, while the sons of kings do not disdain to practise the 'gentle', that is noble, craft. Shoemakers appear as heroes on the Continent too; in the famous French folksong *Le petit cordonnier*, it is the shoemaker who wins the much sought-after girl. German songs and stories in praise of shoemaking have survived; so have Scandinavian *skomakarvisa*, shoemakers' work songs, and a shoemaker's dance, the *szewc*, is recorded from Polish Pomerania.[37] Members of the gentle craft were also credited with specific attitudes. The shoemaker-philosopher stereotype goes back at least as far as Lucian, in the second century A.D., but it is easy to find true examples from early modern Europe of shoemakers who did not stick to their last but cobbled up heresies instead. Jakob Boehme of Görlitz in Lusatia is no doubt the most famous heterodox shoemaker of the period, followed by the Portuguese sixteenth-century Gonçalo Anes Bandarra, whose prophecies were taken seriously for centuries, despite his arrest by the Inquisition and his abjuration of his errors. Bandarra was not the only shoemaker in sixteenth-century Portugal to become famous for his religious opinions. Luis Dias of Setúbal was tried for having proclaimed himself a messiah in 1542, and the 'holy shoemaker' Simāo Gomes prophesied in the later sixteenth century. The heterodoxy of these three men may be explained in terms of their background as 'new Christians', the descendants of Jews; that of other shoemakers cannot. When Calvinism spread in the Cévennes in the sixteenth century, it was carried by shoemakers. England too can contribute its share of examples: John White, of Rayleigh, Essex, who claimed to be St John the Baptist in 1586; Samuel How, the shoemaker-preacher, who published *The sufficiency of the spirit's teaching* (1639); Jacob Bauthumley of Leicestershire, a Ranter; Nicholas Smith, of Petworth in Sussex, who published his *Wonderful Prophecies* in 1652; and of course George Fox the Quaker. In Vienna in the 1790s, three shoemakers were members of a group which denied the divinity of Christ.[38] Shoemakers can also be found in the vanguard of political movements, like 'Captain Cobbler' (Nicholas Melton), a leader of the Lincolnshire rising in 1536, and the 41 *cordonniers* among the 514 militant *sansculottes* of L'An II (1793) studied by Albert Soboul.[39] What have shoes to do with heresy and revolution? Perhaps it is just that this sedentary occupation offered the leisure for reflecting on life – it was the urban equivalent of herding sheep.

One could go on through the roster of guilds in this way, and that would not exhaust the complexities of craftsman culture. The guilds were dominated by the masters of the crafts, but the journeymen and apprentices also had their organisations and traditions. French journeymen, for instance, had their *compagnonnages* or *devoirs*, whose active members were mainly unmarried men between eighteen and twenty-six. The economic historian has long been interested in these groups, like the 'Bold Defiance' of the London weavers in 1768, as prototype trade unions which sometimes organised strikes. From the cultural historian's point of view, it is more relevant to say that they were secret societies with initiation rites and myths about their founders, forming a 'closed culture' parallel to popular culture, as a French historian has recently put it. Thus the printers' journeymen in sixteenth-century Lyons belonged to the company of the Griffarins, which had a secret initiation rite, a handshake, a password, and oaths. Similar rituals were practised by a number of *compagnonnages* in Paris, condemned by ten doctors of the faculty of theology in 1655. Important for French journeymen was the *tour de France*, the convention that they should in fact 'journey' or work their way round the country along more or less fixed routes, knowing that they would find a welcome among colleagues of their craft wherever they found them. This institution must surely have encouraged a national journeyman culture.[40]

The *compagnonnages* were not unique to France. In England, Thomas Gent, a printer's journeyman, has recorded his initiation at an inn in Blackfriars about 1713, which involved 'striking me kneeling, with a broadsword; and pouring ale upon my head' and giving him the title of 'earl of Fingall'. In Germany the migrations of the journeymen, which were compulsory and lasted three to four years, are particularly well-attested; Hans Sachs, for example, tells us that between 1511 and 1516 he went south to Innsbrück, west to Aachen, north as far as Lübeck, and then back to Nuremberg again. The wanderings of seventeenth-century Polish journeymen regularly took them to Bohemia, Germany and Hungary. A number of German journeymen's songs from this period have survived, including a special genre, which the Swedes call *Veckodagsvisa*, about the work they have not done each day of the week. A Hungarian example of the genre – which I have not been able to date – goes like this:

Vasárnap bort iszom,	*Sunday I drink wine,*
Hétfón nem dolgozom.	*Monday I do no work.*
Jó kedden lefekudni,	*Tuesday it is good to lie down,*
Szeredán felkelni.	*Wednesday, to get up again.*
Czütörtök gyógyulni,	*Thursday to recover,*
Pénteken számolni,	*Friday to reckon up,*
Hej! Szombaton kérdezni,	*Hey! Saturday to ask,*
Mit fogunk dolgozni?	*What work do we have to do?*[41]

With the journeymen we should perhaps include the masons, even the masters of their craft. Because the masons moved from job to job, their unit of organisation was not the town guild but the 'lodge', the workshop on the building site. Like a guild, the masons had their patron saints, notably the 'Quatuor Coronati' (four Roman stoneworkers who were early Christian martyrs);

but in other respects the masons' organisation was more like that
of journeymen than masters – they initiated new members with
terrifying rituals, swore them to secrecy and taught them secret
signs to know one another, ritual which was passed on by the
professional masons to the 'speculative' free-masons who began
to found their own lodges in the eighteenth century. There were
also rituals for laying the foundations of a new building. A
well-known East European ballad (*Kelémen* or *Manole the
mason*), records the belief that this ritual sometimes included
human sacrifice. Masons also had a jargon of their own,
recorded in the nineteenth century, and probably existing long
before.[42]

Finally we reach the apprentices. There is evidence that they
sometimes operated as a self-conscious group, if not as a
formally-organised one. In London they were said to be more
prone to playgoing and to rioting – at the shout of 'clubs' – than
mature craftsmen were. Some of the English chap-books seem
to have been aimed at the apprentice market; at least, they
gratified the natural fantasies of that group. Thus a ballad called
The honour of a London prentice, current in the eighteenth
century, and probably long before, tells of an apprentice of
Queen Elizabeth's time who fights in a tournament and marries
a king's daughter. Given the literacy of French craftsmen and
the popularity of chap-book romances of chivalry on the other
side of the Channel, it is rather curious that equivalent stories
are lacking in France. In England, at any rate, it seems useful to
speak not only of 'craftsman culture' but also of 'apprentice
culture', which is an early form of youth culture.[43]

It is easy to exaggerate, to be carried away by the impulse to
subdivide. We must not forget that apprentices turned into
journeymen and even, sometimes, into masters; that masters,
journeymen and apprentices worked together in the shop,
talking and singing as they worked; that the different guilds of
the town cooperated during major festivals. Another factor
holding craftsman culture and urban culture together, and
separating it from peasant culture, was literacy. Townsmen had
a much better chance of learning to read and write than peasants
had, because they had more access to schoolmasters. They were
exposed to writing more than peasants were, whether to books,
to placards or to graffiti. Town pageants, whether in London,
say, or Granada, often included figures carrying explanatory

placards, which made the more unusual images intelligible. In Rome, from the early sixteenth century onwards, the statue of 'Pasquino' was regularly plastered with satirical verses for passers-by to read and repeat.[44]

The wanderers

At this point it may be worth pausing to take stock. It has been argued that the popular culture of this period was far from homogeneous; that craftsman culture and peasant culture differed in many ways; that the culture of shepherds and of miners was distinct from that of farmers. *How* distinct is at once the most crucial and the most difficult question to answer. The more picturesque diversities should not be exaggerated. Miners had 'their' saints, their songs, their plays, dances and legends, but these were a selection from the common stock of popular culture. A special devotion to St Anne, for example, is only meaningful within the context of a more general devotion to the saints; and in any case, the miners did not monopolise St Anne. The idea of Christ as 'the Lamb of God' or 'the good shepherd' or the phrase 'he shall set the sheep on his right hand but the goats on the left' (Matthew 25.33) may have had a special meaning for shepherds, but this special meaning was dependent on the ordinary meaning of these ideas in the culture at large. To describe the differences between the songs, rituals or beliefs of our four major groups, 'sub-culture' may be a more useful term than 'culture', because it suggests that these songs, rituals and beliefs were partly autonomous rather than wholly autonomous, distinct yet not completely severed from the rest of popular culture. The sub-culture is a system of shared meanings, but the people who participate in it also share the meanings of the culture at large.[45]

Neither urban nor rural, a number of itinerant occupational groups also formed sub-cultures, even more obviously international in character than any mentioned so far: soldiers, sailors, beggars and thieves.[46]

In the first half of the period, the soldiers of early modern Europe were an international group of mercenaries who took to the roads in winter, when the campaigning season was at an end, and also between wars. Disbanded soldiers (genuine or fake) were recognised as a separate category of beggar, described by the French as *Drilles* and by the Italians as *Formigotti*. They might be effective robbers, like the bands of *Rougets* and *Grisons* who preyed on Parisians in the early 1620s. After 1650, mercenary armies were gradually replaced by national armies, including conscripts as well as volunteers, and the soldiers were confined to barracks when they were not on campaign. Distinctive in dress, hated, feared – and admired – by civilians, it is easy to see how soldiers formed a sub-culture. They were on the margins of ordinary society; their job was a dangerous one; the men were uprooted from their traditional local culture; a regiment was a 'total institution', making unlimited demands on its members. Soldiers had their own slang and their own songs to sing on the march or in camp; songs of battle, songs of farewell, recruiting songs, (like the eighteenth-century *verbunkos* in the Habsburg Empire), songs of demobilisation, songs expressing pride in the soldiers' occupation and songs expressing disillusionment with it. One thinks of the song of the sixteenth-century *Landsknecht*, without booty and without pay ('Es ging ein Landsknecht über Feld . . . Er hat kein Beutel noch kein Geld'); or that of the Prussian hussars of the seventeenth century, with the same worries, and the same rhymes:

> *Wir preussischen Hussaren, wann kriegen wir das Geld?*
> *Wir müssen ja marschieren ins weite, weite Feld . . .*
> *Und wer sich in preussische Dienst will begebn,*
> *Der soll sich sein Lebtag kein Weibel nicht nehmn . . .*
>
> *(We prussian Hussars, when will we be paid? We have to march far, far, into the field . . . and whoever enters Prussian service cannot take a wife all his life long . . .)*

Like the culture of miners and sailors, soldiers' culture was a cultre of men without women (more or less). It was incidentally a soldier's farewell, a song written for the soldiers of the Württemberg regiment, ordered to South Africa in 1787, which inspired Arnim to compile the *Wunderhorn*.[47]

The sailor sub-culture was even more distinctive than the soldier sub-culture, no doubt because crews were even more isolated from ordinary popular culture than regiments were. Everyone knows the sea shanties or sailors' work songs. In the 1480s friar Felix Fabri described sailor songs as a dialogue 'between one who sings and orders and the labourers who sing in response'. The anonymous author of the *Complaynt of Scotland* (1549) records seeing a galleass and hearing the master order the sailors to haul out the bowline:

> than ane of the marynalis began to hail and to cry, and al the marynalis ansvert of that samyn sound, hou hou. pulpela pulpela. boulena boulena. darta darta. hard out steif, hard out steif. afoir the vynd, afoir the vynd. god send, god send. fayr vedthir, fayr vedthir . . .

Whether this dialogue was shouted or sung is not clear. Again, when the sixteenth-century Portuguese poet Camões describes the raising of the anchor (*Lusiads* 2. 18) it is 'with the sailors' usual shout' (*com a nautica grita costumada*). In any case, in the 'classic' form of the shanty, the leader does not sing out orders but sings a song, and the chorus does not repeat the words of the leader but sings a refrain, as in this traditional Portuguese shanty for raising the anchor:

Leader:	
A grande nau Catharineta	The great ship Catharineta
Tem os seus mastros de pinho:	Has its masts of pine:
Chorus:	
Ai lé, lé, lé,	Ai le, le, le,
Marujinho bate o pé,	The sailor stamps his foot.
Leader:	
O ladrão do dispenseiro	The thief of a steward
Furtou a ração do vinho:	Has stolen the wine ration:
Chorus:	
Ai lé, lé, lé	Ai le, le, le
Marinheiro vira à ré.	The sailor turns astern.

It should be added that the leader of the shanty was traditionally licensed to improvise as he wished and insult the officers with impunity. This form of dialogue between leader and chorus may have been taken over from traditional African work songs, and if so would illustrate the exotic influences helping to make the sailor sub-culture a distinctive one.[48]

Sailors stood out from landsmen in a variety of ways. In the first place by their dress; the sixteenth-century Gascon sailor could be recognised by his red cap, the eighteenth-century English sailor by his pigtail, his check shirt, and, oddest of all at this time, his trousers. Sailors were also recognisable by their speech, in which technical terms, slang and oaths had thickened to produce a private language. Terms like 'marlin-spike', 'yard-arm', or 'the main-top-gallant sail' formed a system of shared meanings from which landsmen were excluded, creating solidarity within the sub-culture. This private language tends to be presented by outsiders with a hint of mockery, as when Ned Ward describes the old sea-dogs or 'tarpaulins' in London taverns as talking naval 'dialect' and complaining of a tankard that 'there's no stowage in her hold'.[49]

Sailors also had their own rituals, like the christening of boats or the casting of libations into the sea at dangerous points in the voyage (Greek and Turkish sailors threw bread into the sea as they sailed past Lectum, near Troy), or the mock-baptism or mock-shaving of anyone who was crossing the equator for the first time, or passing Cape Kullen (in Danish waters) or Cape Raz (in Brittany). Sailors had their own folklore, with particular emphasis on mermaids (seen as sinister figures) or phantom ships, like the 'Flying Dutchman', a maritime version of the traditional 'Wild Hunt', in which ghosts are seen riding through the air. They had their own magic, such as whistling to make the wind blow; their own art, such as painted sea-chests or carved mangle-boards (ships in bottles go back only to the mass-production of bottles in the mid-nineteenth century), and their own dances, especially the hornpipe, which is easy to dance alone and in a small space. They had their own rhythm of work and leisure, with long periods of boredom and mounting frustration on board (like shepherds and prisoners, they had the leisure for elaborate carving), alternating with short violent periods of relaxation on shore. If their readiness to brawl was not altogether distinctive, their rolling gait certainly was. Sailors were often literate, at least in eighteenth-century Marseilles (50 per cent, compared to 20 per cent of the male peasants), and they had their own almanacs, with information about full tides and the soundings in different harbours. They had their own inns in ports and their own fraternities, often dedicated to St Nicholas, as in Lübeck and Riga. It is scarcely surprising to find clergymen making special efforts to penetrate the sailor sub-culture, as they did in the case of the miners. John Ryther of Wapping, called 'the seamens' preacher', took Jonah as his text and published his sermons as *A plat for mariners* (1675). John Flavel, a minister at Dartmouth, also concentrated on the sailor public with his *Navigation spiritualised* (1682), in which he compared the body to a ship, the soul to its merchandise, the world to the sea and heaven to the port to which the sailor needs direction.⁵⁰

Once again, we must beware of drawing the boundaries of the sub-culture too sharply. It was not only sailors who sang sea songs, and it was not only sea songs that sailors sang. Fishermen lived in villages and saw their wives more often than sailors did, but they still shared a good deal of maritime culture with them. They too christened new boats (in Brittany the boat was given a godfather and a godmother). Fishermen and sailors had a common concern for storm and shipwreck, and made vows to the same shrines if they were in danger, like Our Lady of Bonaria in Sardinia or Notre Dame de Bon Port near Antibes. Their proverbs drew on the same experience. 'Make hay while the sun shines' has a salty flavour in Dutch — 'One must sail while the wind is favourable' (*men moet zeilen, terwijl de wind dient*). Again it is difficult to know whether to include or exclude the boatmen of major rivers like the Danube, the Volga and the Vistula. They too lived a different life from landsmen, and developed a private language. The slang of the Vistula boatmen was recorded by a Polish poet in the seventeenth century; it has a rather Germanic flavour. 'Fritz' was the name for an apprentice pilot, and *ląd* (land) the term for the bank of the river.⁵¹

Most distinctive of all popular sub-cultures was that of the beggars and thieves, which was recognised and evoked in the literature of the picaresque, notably in Alemán's *Guzman de Alfarache* and in the 'exemplary novel' of Cervantes, *Rinconete and Cortadillo*. The values of thieves and professional (especially counterfeit) beggars were necessarily different from those of the normal world they exploited. The separation was clearly marked out by language. Beggars and thieves had their own argot or jargon, terms which referred to the private language of this social group before they came to signify any kind of slang; appropriately enough, because the jargon of a criminal sub-culture is necessarily more self-conscious, more carefully designed to exclude outsiders, than that of other occupational groups. In the thieves' slang of fifteenth-century Italy, recorded by the poet Luigi Pulci, a girl was *pesce*, 'a fish'; the road was *polverosa*, 'the dusty one'; florins were *rughi*, 'wrinkles'; and so on. In Elizabethan London, a 'cony' was a vìctim, a 'cony-catcher' was a confidence trickster, a 'prigger of prancers' was a horse-thief, a 'nip' cut purses, and had nothing to do with a 'foist' who picked pockets.[52] In Spain, specialisation seems to have gone even further, and one contemporary, García, distinguishes thirteen kinds of thief, such as the *devotos,* who only raid churches, and the *mayordomos,* who only cheat innkeepers. Such division of labour suggests a high degree of organisation, and García goes on to describe the 'republic' of robbers and thieves, their captain, their hierarchy and their laws. The idea of guilds of thieves, complete with apprentices and masters, was widespread in the period. Cervantes built *Rinconete and Cortadillo* round this idea, while two folktales in the Grimm collection, numbers 129 and 192, refer to master thieves and their professional pride. There is a story from seventeenth-century Paris about the way in which a boy 'passes master' among the cut-purses by carrying out a difficult operation set him by his seniors. It is hard to decide whether these guilds really existed; if they did not, it would have been necessary to invent them, to satirise the straight world and to illustrate the commonplace of 'the world turned upside down'. However, thieves really did have their own initiation rite, known in Elizabethan London as 'stalling to the rogue'; like other initiations of craftsmen, it involved pouring a quart of beer over the head of the candidate for admission. They had their own training institutions; Recorder Fleetwood of London wrote to William Cecil in 1585 of the discovery of a 'schoolhouse set up to learn young boys to cut purses', near Billingsgate. This exotic criminal world was a boon to the professional writers of early modern Europe, to whom we are beholden for most of what we know about it. It is not always easy to decide whether a given detail is the fruit of the fertile imagination of the criminal, or of the man who wrote about him; but if specific details can be doubted, the existence of the criminal sub-culture can not.[53]

Religious and regional variations

Beggars and thieves might be described as a 'counter-culture' rather than a sub-culture, in the sense that they not only differed from the world around them, but rejected it. The same point might be made of some Christian sects, notably the Anabaptists in Germany and the Netherlands; the Huguenots in France; the Quakers in England, a 'peculiar people' whose counter-culture was particularly obvious, since it affected their speech and dress; and the Old Believers in Russia. Looking at Europe as a whole, from 1500 to 1800, the differences in religion are among the most striking of cultural differences. Christian Europe was already, in 1500, divided into Catholic and Orthodox; it was soon to be divided still further, with the rise of Protestantism. Some of the differences between Catholic and Protestant culture will be discussed below (p.215f).

In any case some Europeans of the period were not Christians. There were Jews, notably in the towns of southern Spain and eastern Europe, and there were Muslims, in more or less the same areas; each group with its own values and its own rituals. The Jews of Spain and of eastern Europe had their own minstrels, their own folksongs, their own plays, such as the Esther plays recorded in the sixteenth century. The Jews of Spain took ballads from the culture surrounding them, but adapted them for their own use by purging them of christian references. The Muslims of Bosnia spoke a similar language to the Orthodox Serbs, and they sang similar heroic epics about the wars between Christians and Muslims, but, as Karadžić noticed when he collected these songs, 'in their versions their own people usually win'.[54] The Muslims of Spain were forcibly converted after the capture of Granada by the Christians in 1492, but this did not wipe out their separate culture, which remained strong throughout the sixteenth century and even longer. The Moriscos secretly practised their own religion, keeping Friday as a day of rest, fasting during Ramadan, and afterwards running through the streets throwing scented water and oranges like the Christians during Carnival. They had their own holy men or *fakirs* and their own amulets, with verses from the Koran. They were forbidden to speak, read or write Arabic, but this did not stop them; and when they spoke Spanish, it was Spanish of a distinctive kind. They took many more baths than Christians, for religious reasons, and their women continued to wear the veil. In spite of the denunciations of the clergy, they went on dancing the *zambra*. They shared the taste for ballads and romances of chivalry with their Christian neighbours, but in their versions, as in Bosnia, it was the heroic Muslims who won.[55]

Jews and Moriscos were of course ethnic as well as religious minorities, and their distinctive cultures cannot be analysed in religious terms alone. Equally distinctive was the culture of another ethnic minority, the gypsies. The gypsies, often described in this period as 'Egyptians', 'Saracens' or 'Bohemians', appeared in Europe early in the fifteenth century. Respectable people frequently associated them with beggars and thieves, but the gypsies appear to have remained a group distinct from the rest in customs as in language. In the sixteenth and seventeenth centuries, they already practised the occupations for which they are known today. The men were tinkers, horse-traders, bear-leaders and musicians, while the women danced and told fortunes by reading palms. They were suspected of magic, of pacts with the devil, and of ignorance or rejection of true religion. 'They do not know what the Church is, and do not enter it except to commit sacrilege. They do not know any prayers . . . they eat meat all the time, without respecting Friday or Lent.' However, the gypsies' interest in the performing arts made for some interaction between them and more sedentary people. Gypsy musicians were popular in Hungary and elsewhere in Central Europe in the eighteenth century, and they have left indelible traces on the popular music of that region.[56]

The most obvious variations in popular culture have been left almost till last – sexual and regional variations.

There is too little to say about women, for lack of evidence. There is a 'problem of women' for historians of popular culture as there is for social anthropologists. The difficulty of reconstructing and interpreting the culture of the inarticulate is here at its most acute; women's culture is to popular culture what popular culture is to culture as a whole, so that it is easier to say what it is not than what it is. The culture of women was not the same as that of their husbands, fathers, sons or brothers, for although much was shared, there was also much from which women were excluded. They were excluded from guilds, and often from fraternities as well. The world of the tavern was not for them either. The occupational variations in culture between farmers and shepherds, miners and sailors, can have meant relatively little to their women. In eastern Europe, at least, women had their own songs. A collection of folksongs from Galicia distinguishes between 'women's songs' (*pieśni żeńskie*), mainly love-lyrics, and 'men's songs' (*pięśni męskie*), mainly ballads. Karadžić made the same distinction for Serbia, although he pointed out that young men did sometimes sing what he called the 'women's songs'. The women of French villages met for *veillées,* where they would spin, sing and tell stories (with or without male visitors). Women had their own work-songs, such as spinning songs, waulking songs (for shrinking cloth) and songs for grinding the grain. If anything is clear in this obscure area, it is that women's culture was more conservative than that of their men, and came to differ from it ever more sharply as time went by. Women were much less literate than men. In Amsterdam in 1630, 32 per cent of the brides could sign their names, compared to 57 per cent of the grooms, and in France as a whole, in the late seventeenth century, about 14 per cent of the brides could sign, compared to 29 per cent of their grooms. Thus the written word was added to the list of cultural items which women did not share, and women began to take over from men as guardians of the older oral tradition. Where they did read, women read distinctive kinds of book, or, to keep closer to the evidence, writers and printers in England and the Netherlands aimed some books at an audience of women. Religion, particularly ecstatic religion, afforded women a means of self-expression. Women preachers could be found among the English Civil War sects and among the Huguenots of the Cévennes.[57]

If all too little can be said about sex variations in popular culture, the opposite is true of regional variations. The evidence is everywhere, whether one looks at material culture or at the immaterial, at artifacts or performances. Popular culture was perceived as local culture. *A cada terra el seu ús*, as the Catalan proverb has it, 'to each land its own custom'. It was the region, or town, or even village which commanded loyalty; these units formed closed communities with hostile stereotypes of outsiders, reluctant to admit new people or new ways. The German peasants' war of 1525 failed essentially because the bands of peasants from different regions did not cooperate enough with one another. At the end of the seventeenth century, a parish priest from the Sologne described his parishioners as follows: 'They love only their own region (*leur pays*) . . . they are not interested in the news or the fashions of other parts, but are quite detached from everything that happens in the rest of the world.'[58] He might have been speaking of many parts of Europe.

Regional variation in culture was in fact very great, and went back a long way. Celtic mythology had not died out in Scotland or Ireland, Wales or Brittany in this period, the cult of springs remained, and a Celtic language was still spoken in Cornwall. The Bretons were proud of their local saints, like Nonna and Corentin, many of whom were not known elsewhere and may have been pre-Christian divinities, baptised. The Celtic pattern of dispersed settlement distinguished sixteenth-century Wales from neighbouring England. Similarly, Norse mythology had survived in parts of Scandinavia. In the Scandinavian Alps and in Lapland the Norse god Thor was still venerated in the eighteenth century, and Thursday observed as a holy day. Norse myths survived in Scandinavia as traditional ballads. In Lithuania (which became officially Christian only in the fourteenth century) and in Russia, pre-Christian cults were most obvious. In 1547 it was said that Lithuanians still worshipped their traditional gods Perkūnas, Laukosargas and Zemepatis; in 1549, the imperial ambassador Herberstein remarked that in the Perm region of Russia 'Idolaters are still to be found in the forests' and that the old god of thunder, Perun, was still reverenced.[59] (Forests, like mountains, are effective barriers to the spread of new customs and beliefs.)

Long-standing ethnic traditions like these contributed to regional variation, but they were not the only reason for it. The region was a cultural unit for ecological reasons, because the differing physical environment encouraged, if it did not impose, different ways of life. Italians built in stone, Dutchmen in brick, and Russians in wood for sufficiently obvious reasons. The English and Scottish border ballads reflect the way of life of a frontier community, with its stress on cattle and kin, raiding and feuding. When folktales migrated from one region to another they might be modified to make them more relevant by introducing references to local occupations. In a Greek folktale about St Nicholas, he came to the aid of sailors in distress; in the version current in Russia, he helped a peasant whose cart was stuck.[60]

The importance of the region for the study of popular culture was given its most precise and magisterial formulation by one of the great folklorists of our century, Carl von Sydow, who took over from the botanists the term 'ecotype', which refers to a hereditary plant-variety adapted to a certain milieu by natural selection, and used it in his studies of folktales. He argued that a given tradition will 'undergo a process of unification within its own area through the mutual control and reciprocal influence of its bearers', so that a folktale ecotype is formed. He emphasised the importance of the barriers to diffusion. There are linguistic barriers, which hinder the spread of verse in particular; and there are political barriers, frontiers which hinder the movement of the bearers of traditions. Villagers, von Sydow remarked, do not learn from their neighbours, to whom they are often hostile; this is a third barrier to diffusion. Two beliefs may have the same function, and so exclude one another; where one is present in popular tradition, it forms a fourth barrier, for the other is then superfluous, and if it is introduced it will not catch on.[61]

These points are important, and historians will probably find them plausible enough. All the same, they are not the whole story. It is one of the central arguments of this book – and its only justification – that the regional level is not the only level at which popular culture should be studied.

The concept 'region' is in fact less precise than it looks. Is it possible to enumerate the regions into which Europe is divided? If not, doubt is cast on the efficiency of the barriers. The most obvious units to take are the provinces, like the old French provinces before the *départements* were introduced at the end of our period. Is Brittany a region? Or is it two regions, Haute-Bretagne and Basse-Bretagne? The division between the two was not just administrative, it was cultural: Haute-Bretagne was French-speaking in the seventeenth century, while Basse-Bretagne was Breton-speaking. However, ecotypes can be found at a lower level than that. In Basse-Bretagne, it was possible to distinguish the dialect of Breton spoken in Cornouaille from that current in Morbihan or Finistère. Is Cornouaille a 'region'? Or can it be dissolved into its constituent villages? Is there ever any reason to stop dividing till one reaches families or even individuals? It would be the same story if we took other criteria, other regions. The popular art of eighteenth-century Norway and Sweden stands out distinctively from that of the rest of Europe. If we look at Sweden more closely, we find it possible to distinguish the painting of central Sweden (especially Dalarna and Hälsingland) from that of the

south (especially Småland and Halland). To look more carefully
at Dalarna is to find it dividing into two regions, Rättvik and
Leksand . . . The costume of the peasants in nineteenth-
century Moravia differed from that of neighbouring Slovakia.
But Moravian Slovakia formed a unit of its own, subdivided into
no less than twenty-eight 'costume districts'.[62] We seem to have
returned to Toynbee's problem, the impossibility of
enumerating cultures or sub-cultures because they are loosely
bounded systems.

Just as provinces can be broken down into smaller cultural
units, so they can usefully be joined to make larger units,
nations and even groups of nations. Language forms a barrier, it
is true, but it is a barrier which can be broken. Ballads could
follow the trade-routes from Scandinavia to Scotland, helped by
the fact that the languages are not so very different in structure,
so that some ballad commonplaces could be taken over with
very little change. Thus the Danish half-line 'Op staar' or 'Op
stod' could be rendered 'Up then started' or 'Up and spake';
'Ind saa kom' could turn into 'In then came'; 'den liden
Smaadreng' could be translated 'his little foot-page'. The same
goes for some Norwegian ballad formulas: *fager og fin*
corresponds to the Scots 'fair and fine', *baka og bryggje* to 'bake
and brew'.

That the real barriers are those separating language groups
rather than languages is suggested by the spread of the
subversive couplet which we associate with John Ball and the
peasants' revolt of 1381:

> When Adam delved and Eve span,
> Who was then the gentleman?

This couplet was virtually confined to the Germanic languages,
which could all take over the rhyme without alteration; it is
recorded in German, Dutch and Swedish, all in the late fifteenth
century:

> Da Adam reütet und Eva span
> Wer was die Zeit ein Edelman?

> Wie was doe de edelman
> Doe Adam graeff ende Eva span?

> Ho war tha een ädela man
> Tha Adam graff ok Eva span?

It was less well known in the Slav languages, into which it did
not go so easily; in Polish, for example, it became:

> *Gdy Adam z Ewą kopał*
> *Kto komu na ów czas chłopał?*[63]
> *(When Adam and Eve were digging, Who was the peasant then?)*

Stories could travel still more easily. Apparent regional
variation sometimes masks an underlying unity. The people of
Cava in the kingdom of Naples were represented as fools in a
number of local stories, which one suspects to have been
propagated by their rivals in nearby Salerno. What could be
more local? However, a survey of Europe brings to light stories
about the fools of Beira in Portugal; of Fünsing in Bavaria; of
Mundinga in Suabia; of Mols in Denmark; of 'Malleghem' in
Flanders; or, to come still nearer home, of Gotham in
Nottinghamshire. Some of the same stories are current in these
different regions, for example 'four men carry the horse in order
not to tramp up the field', or 'a rider takes the meal-sack on his
shoulder to relieve the ass of his burden'.[64] The local colour has
been applied to a standardised outline. This example is not an
isolated one; many ballad plots and folktales have been recorded
at opposite ends of Europe. A famous example is the ballad the
Dutch call *Heer Halewijn*. It concerns a girl who goes with a
man to the forest only to find that he plans to murder her; but
she manages to trick him and kill him with his own sword. This
ballad is well-known in Germany and Scandinavia, and it turns
up in Britain in the form of 'Lady Isabel and the Elf-Knight'
(Child no. 4). It is also known outside the Germanic
language-area, in Poland and in Hungary, where it is known as
'Molnár Anna'. Again, the story of the 'rescued maiden' who
appeals in vain for help from each member of her family, but is
finally rescued by her lover, is known in regions as far apart and
as different in their cultural traditions as England, Finland and
Sicily. Of course one still needs to ask what proportion of its
tales a given region shares with others, but in this field, research
is still to be done.[65]

Christianity had long been making European culture into
more of a whole. The same festivals were celebrated all over
Europe; the same major saints were venerated everywhere;
similar kinds of religious drama were played. Even Muslims
were affected by popular Christianity. In eighteenth-century

Dalmatia, Muslims went to Christian priests to ask for a *zapis*, a piece of paper with holy names written on it, worn as a talisman in the hat or placed on the horns of cattle to protect them from harm. Tunes travelled from one end of Europe to the other – and beyond – even if they became detached from their original words on the way. House-types recur when the need for them recurs. The Apulian stone house or *trullo* was long thought to be unique, but there are parallels to it in Spain and Ireland. Even formal patterns like the geometrical decorations on marriage-chests can be found from one end of Europe to the other.[66]

Indeed, it would be a mistake to stop at the edge of Europe. A distinguished folklorist has emphasised that 'the lands from Ireland to India form an important tradition area where the same stories are found'. Arab folktales like those in *The book of Sinaibad* and Indian folktales (like those in the *Panchatantra*) were circulating in Europe long before 1500. The traditional Turkish popular theatre included one kind of play, *orta oiunu*, built round comic dialogues between a master and his clownish servant, for all the world like Pantalone and Pulcinella. The Holi festival in India, in which roles are reversed, and the village leaders are drenched with water – or worse – and made to ride backwards on an ass, is, to put it mildly, 'carnivalesque'. One is tempted to follow the example of the early nineteenth-century linguists and of Jacob Grimm, and to think in terms of 'Indo-European' culture.[67] Or is this going too far?

There have been all too few serious studies to help us decide. What the Indo-European area has in common culturally cannot be discovered without systematic comparison with other parts of the world, for example with Japan. The most serious of these attempts so far has been Murdock's 'world ethnographic sample' (concerned with societies as well as with culture in our sense) which divided the world into six regions; he grouped Europe, the Near East, and North Africa together as the 'Circum-Mediterranean' region, but he did not include India.[68] To be convincing, studies of Indo-European unity and variety will have to be as rigorous as the work of von Sydow. They will have to be quantitative, trying to establish what proportion of its culture a given region shares with its neighbours.

Meanwhile, it seems permissible to confine ourselves to Europe; to suggest that the regional level is not the only level at which traditional popular culture should be studied, and that it may be useful to speak of regional sub-cultures in the same way as we have spoken of occupational sub-cultures. The separation of the sub-culture from the rest of popular culture should not be exaggerated in either case. Catalan culture, say, is, like miners' culture, a selection from the common stock rather than something entirely different. It is not the motifs, but the specific combination of motifs, which enables the specialist to say that a given painting comes from Rättvik and not from Leksand. The purpose of this book is to say something about the common stock, the elements from which the local patterns were made.

To put the point another way: there was great regional variation in the popular culture of early modern Europe, but this variation was structured, and coexisted with other kinds of variation. Folklorists have compiled atlases of popular culture at a national or regional level, a student of the ballad has identified seven 'ballad provinces', and anthropologists have divided Africa into 'culture areas', but no one, so far as I know, has tried to describe the cultural geography of Europe as a whole.[69] This is a task for a book, not a paragraph; but the way in which such a book might be structured is extremely relevant to the argument of this chapter.

A cultural geography of Europe would have to be historical, concerned with change over the long term. It would also have to take into account a large number of cultural differences or oppositions which often overlap but rarely coincide with one another. There is the contrast between hamlets and villages, for example; hamlets dominant along the Atlantic coast and among the South Slavs, villages elsewhere. Village living – and above all involvement with the market – seems to have encouraged political consciousness, from the German Peasants' War to the French Revolution. The compact irregular village type contrasts with the planned linear village, associated with the colonisation of the waste. Then there is a geography of vernacular architecture, shaped in part by the availability of building materials; areas where stone was dominant, around the Mediterranean, areas where wood was dominant, as in Norway or Russia, and areas of brick, which was replacing wood in the Netherlands and elsewhere in the seventeenth century. There is a geography of literacy. In France in the seventeenth and eighteenth centuries the split between the literate north-east and the relatively illiterate south-west followed a diagonal line from

Mont-St-Michel to the lake of Geneva. In Europe as a whole in the eighteenth century, there was an area of high literacy in the north-west (Sweden, Prussia, Britain), and an area of low literacy in the south and east. Literate Protestants contrasted with less literate Catholics and still less literate Orthodox Christians; overlapping with the contrast between the colder, darker north, where cultural activities were mainly indoors, and the brighter, warmer south, where popular culture was associated with the open air, with the *piazza* or *plaza*.[70] In the south, the spring festival of Carnival was more important; in the north, the summer festival of St John's Eve. Then there was the linguistic division into Romance, Germanic and Slavonic, complicated by smaller language-groups like the Celtic and the Finno-Ugrian. There was the social division between the peasants east of the Elbe, who were enserfed in the sixteenth and seventeenth centuries, and the peasants to the west, who were relatively free.

Then there are the contrasts which can be found in different parts of Europe, between highland and lowland zones, forests and clearings, coastal and inland regions, and between central areas and frontiers. Students of the English and Scottish ballad know well how it grew out of the conditions of life on the border; but the border between England and Scotland was only one among several where a frontier region encouraged a heroic world-view and heroic ballads. The frontier between the Turks and the Habsburgs in Croatia and Hungary was a heroic world on a grander scale than that of the West, Middle and East Marches between England and Scotland, but its values, its songs, were similar in many ways.[71] Cossacks, too, were a kind of frontiersman.

The pattern made by the interaction of all these contrasts might be summed up, very crudely, as a distinction between three Europes: north-western, southern, and eastern. Thus southern Europe, Mediterranean Europe, was Romance-speaking, Catholic (with pockets of Huguenots, Muslims, etc.), with an outdoor culture, 'the 500-ton stone house' (as Chaunu calls it), low literacy (with pockets of high literacy in sixteenth-century Italy), and a value-system laying great stress on honour and shame.[72] However, to understand the culture of a particular community one would need not only to place it within one of these Europes but also to place it in relation to the

axes of contrast which have just been described. The culture of a
Breton fishing-village, say, needs to be seen as part of not one
whole but several: part of French culture, maritime culture,
Celtic culture, Catholic culture, and so on. Relatively sharp
cultural differentiation could be seen whenever a number of
contrasts coincided. Huguenot weavers in Spitalfields in the
eighteenth century were at once an ethnic, a religious and an
occupational sub-culture, like Jewish shoemakers in Central
Europe. Indeed, the Reformation may have appealed to some
ethnic or occupational groups because it reinforced their sense
of a collective identity; it can hardly be an accident that in
Transylvania, where three language-groups lived together, the
Germans generally went over to the doctrines of their
fellow-countryman Luther, the Hungarians turned Calvinist,
and the Rumanians remained Orthodox.

Interaction

Given the existence of both great and little traditions, however
various, in early modern Europe, it was natural that there would
be interaction between them. The nature of this interaction has
been much debated. Swift described 'Opinions like Fashions' as
'always descending from those of Quality to the middle Sort,
and thence to the Vulgar, where at length they are dropt and
vanish'.[73] The discoverers of popular culture, such as Herder
and the Grimms, reversed this view, believing that creativity
came from below, from the people. The folklorists in Germany
early in the twentieth century, who discussed this question most
fully and explicitly, returned to the earlier view. They held that
the culture of the lower classes (*Unterschicht*) was an
out-of-date imitation of the culture of the upper classes
(*Oberschicht*). Images and themes, songs and stories gradually
'sank', as they put it, to the bottom of the social scale.[74]

Which theory is right? The debate has been complicated by
differences in definition, but if we continue to use the terms
'learned culture' and 'popular culture' as they were defined
earlier in the chapter, it can be stated with confidence that there
was two-way traffic between them. As Redfield put it, 'Great
tradition and little tradition have long affected each other and
continue to do so'. A few examples will make the point clear.[75]

Popular art offers a number of obvious examples of 'sinking'.

The English yeomen of the late sixteenth and early seventeenth centuries built houses in the style of the local gentry. In Central Europe in the eighteenth century, there was a peasant baroque, about a century behind the original baroque style. The peasant art of Norway and Sweden in the same period borrowed motifs from the renaissance, baroque and rococo styles. Church furnishings and engravings were their main sources of inspiration.[76]

Literature also descended the social scale. When Addison visited Italy, he remarked 'a custom at Venice, that they tell me is particular to the common people of this country, of singing stanzas out of Tasso. They are set to a pretty solemn tune, and when one begins in any part of the poet, 'tis odds but he will be answered by somebody else that overhears him.' The custom is well-attested by Italians as well as foreigners. In Florence between the fourteenth and the sixteenth centuries, Dante seems to have formed part of popular culture. Grazzini wrote a madrigal on the death of an owl, beginning:

Nel mezzo del cammin della sua vita
Il mio bel gufo pien d'amore e fede
Renduto hal l'alma . . .;

which would lose most of its point if the parody of Dante were not recognised.[77] In England, the mummers borrowed verses from more sophisticated drama; the Ampleforth Play contains fragments of Congreve's *Love for Love*, and the Mylor Play includes scraps from Addison's own *Fair Rosamond*, just as nineteenth-century Russian folk-plays contain verses from Lermontov and Pushkin. In eighteenth-century Flanders, village plays show a love of acrostics, as if the literary baroque had reached the countryside just when it had been abandoned by the town.[78]

Another example in favour of the sinking theory is the gradual diffusion of the romances of chivalry. It seems reasonable to assume that the romances of chivalry were originally created for the nobility; they deal with the adventures of the nobility, they present events and people from the standpoint of the nobility, and they express aristocratic values. However, by 1500 the stories of Charlemagne and his paladins were sung in the Italian market-places for everyone to hear them, and by 1800 the romances of chivalry had been abandoned to the peasants, most notably in Sicily. Why the Sicilian peasants should have found the deeds of Orlando and Rinaldo so attractive it is not easy to say; but it was not only in Italy that the romances of chivalry had this wide appeal. In France, in the seventeenth and eighteenth centuries, some 10 per cent of the chap-book 'Bibliothèque Bleue' was made up of such books, with *Pierre of Provence, Ogier the Dane* and *The Four Sons of Aymon* among the most popular titles. *Pierre of Provence* was also popular in Portugal, *Ogier the Dane* (it is hardly surprising to learn) in Denmark, and *The Four Sons of Aymon* in the Netherlands. In England, the adventures of Guy of Warwick and Bevis of Hampton were part of the minstrel repertoire in the sixteenth century, and still more widely available as broadside ballads and chap-book romances.[79] Religious ideas also descended the social scale; the ideas of Luther, Calvin, Zwingli, and those of their Catholic opponents as well.

Yet the sinking theory is too crude, too mechanical, suggesting as it does that images, stories or ideas are passively accepted by popular painters, singers, and their spectators and audiences. In fact they are modified or transformed, in a process which looks from above like misunderstanding or distortion, from below like adaptation to specific needs. The minds of ordinary people are not like blank paper, but stocked with ideas and images; new ideas will be rejected if they are incompatible with the old. Traditional ways of perceiving and thinking form a kind of sieve which will allow some novelties through, but not others. This is most obvious in the case of painting. Swedish peasant painters took over baroque details but the structure of their works remained medieval. In the case of religion Edward Thompson makes the same point when he describes ordinary Christians as 'accepting from the church only so much doctrine as can be assimilated to the life-experience of the poor'. Official texts and rituals may be imitated but the imitation often slides into parody (below p.122f)[80]

The other major defect of the sinking theory is to ignore traffic in the opposite direction, up the social scale. One obvious example is that of the dance. The nobility regularly took over lively dance-forms from the peasantry, gradually made them more sedate, and so had to borrow once more. An example from the end of our period is the social rise of the waltz. Another example of 'rising' is that of the Renaissance court festival. Court festivals often took place at the same time as popular festivals, such as Carnival and the twelve days of Christmas. In some cases early in the period there seems to be little distinction between them except in the status of the participants. In the course of the sixteenth century, court festivals became more private, more elaborate, and more formal. They made use of more properties, they developed a greater unity of plot, and they came to require professional organisers, like the English Master of the Revels. Informal 'masking' turned into the formal 'masque'. Court festivals continued to bear the marks of their popular origins. The mock king or 'Lord of Misrule' still played a prominent part, masks were still worn, and mock battles were still fought. Here too we see both borrowing and the creative transformation of what was borrowed.[81]

Court festivals are far from being the only example. The great Hungarian epic of the seventeenth century, Miklós Zrínyi's *The Sziget Disaster,* was a poem in two traditions: that of the literary epic in the manner of Tasso, whom Zrínyi much admired, and that of the popular oral epic of the Croats – Zrínyi had estates in Croatia and spoke Croat as well as Hungarian and Italian. Goethe's *Faust* borrowed something from the traditional puppet-plays of Faust. When Handel was in Rome for Christmas 1709 he heard the shepherds of the Abruzzi playing the bagpipes; he wrote the music down and used it in his *Messiah.* John Playford's *Dancing Master* was a collection of dances for 'ingenious gentlemen' and their ladies, but the titles of many pieces suggest a popular origin: 'Gathering Peascods', 'Jack a Lent', 'Milkmaid's Bob' or 'Row ye well, mariners'.[82]

This kind of borrowing may take place for different reasons, and the borrowers may have very different attitudes to popular culture. When Pulci writes to Lorenzo de' Medici in thieves' jargon, he is just having fun and showing off his ingenuity. When Villon uses the jargon, it may express his identification with the thieves, as in the case of his sixteenth-century Spanish equivalent, Alonso Alvarez de Soria, the son of a rich merchant who turned *pícaro,* and wrote poems about the picaresque world until his execution in 1603. Or the borrower may have a more ironic attitude to his material, as John Gay surely did in his *Beggar's Opera,* which adapts some of the street songs of the day. Gay's attitude to the beggars and thieves from whom he took his material seems one of affectionate mockery – which is not to say that he was not mocking his own world as well. When an educated Venetian of the seventeenth century makes use of Venetian dialect to write an anonymous political satire, he is suggesting that ordinary people are not happy with the policy of the government, and leaving it to the reader to decide whether he means anything more. When Perrault draws on French folklore for his *contes*, what is he doing? Equating the common people with children? Striking a blow for the moderns in their battle with the ancients?[83]

In other cases, we can be reasonably sure that a particular theme moved backwards and forwards between the two traditions over the centuries. We know that Rabelais drew on popular culture; the early part of his *Pantagruel*, in particular, drew on the chap-book *Grandes et Inestimables Chroniques de l'Enorme Geant Gargantua*. On the other hand, the seventeenth-century clowns Bruscambille and Tabarin drew on Rabelais. In the nineteenth century, Breton oral traditions included many legends about Gargantua, and it is impossible to tell whether these traditions go back before Rabelais or reflect the impact of his book.[84] Ariosto is another example of two-way traffic. He derived his story from the traditional oral epics of the Italian singers of tales, and elaborated it (like Zrínyi later) in accordance with the ideas of the sophisticated. Cantos of his *Orlando Furioso* returned to popular culture in simplified form as chap-books. French songs moved from the streets to the court and back. Pastoral poetry drew on shepherds' culture but we also find genuine shepherds singing songs influenced by the conventions of learned pastoral.[85]

One of the most striking instances of interaction between the learned and the popular traditions is that of the witch. Jacob Grimm thought that witch-beliefs came from the people; Joseph Hansen, later in the nineteenth century, argued that they were elaborated by theologians out of material taken from the Christian and classical traditions. More recent research suggests that both men were right – in part; that the image of the witch current in the sixteenth and seventeenth centuries involved both popular elements, like the belief that some people had the power to fly through the air or do their neighbours harm by supernatural means, and learned elements, notably the idea of a pact with the devil.[86]

These interactions between learned and popular culture were made all the easier because, to add a final qualification to Redfield's model, there was a group of people who stood in between the great and the little traditions and acted as mediators. A case could certainly be made for describing the culture of early modern Europe as three cultures rather than two, since the literacy barrier did not coincide with the Latin barrier. Between learned culture and traditional oral culture came what might be called 'chap-book culture', the culture of the semi-literate, who had gone to school but not for long. (English unfortunately lacks the distinction Italians draw between *literatura popolare* and *literatura popolareggiante*.) This chap-book culture might be regarded as an early form of what Dwight Macdonald calls 'midcult', situated between the great and little traditions and drawing on both.[87] That broadsides disseminated traditional ballads is well known. What needs more emphasis here is the fact that broadsides and chap-books also drew on the great tradition. I have just mentioned the fact that Italian chap-books of the sixteenth century presented cantos of Ariosto in simplified form. Similarly, Spanish chap-books offered short and simple versions of the plays of Lope de Vega and Calderón; French chap-books included plays by Corneille, adaptations of Ariosto, and popularisations of Rousseau; English chap-books included versions of *Moll Flanders* and *Robinson Crusoe*, reduced to twenty-four pages each. The existence of these booklets suggests that a public existed which was interested in the authors but could not afford, or could not understand, the full texts. Authors who do not fit easily into the learned or the popular traditions might be placed in this category instead: Italians like Giulio Cesare Croce, Spaniards like Juan Timoneda, Germans like Hans Sachs, Englishmen like Thomas Deloney.[88] One might hazard the hypothesis that the backbone of this chap-book culture was provided by the journeymen printers, who participated in craftsman culture yet were familiar with the world of books. Like noblewomen, they were in a good position to mediate between the great and the little traditions.

In this chapter I have attempted to define popular culture, and a long and complicated job this definition of the indefinite has turned out to be. It should now be possible to review the sources for our knowledge of popular culture between 1500 and 1800. In fact they are generally contaminated. We are faced with the problem of the 'mediator' in another sense, not the mediator between the great and little traditions, but the mediator between us and them. The problems posed by this kind of mediation will be discussed in the next chapter.

CHAPTER THREE

An Elusive Quarry

The popular culture of early modern Europe is elusive. It eludes the historian because he is a literate, self-conscious modern man who may find it difficult to comprehend people unlike himself, and also because the evidence for their attitudes and values, hopes and fears is so fragmentary. Much of the popular culture of this period was oral culture, and 'words fly away'. Much of it took the form of festivals, which were equally impermanent. We want to know about performances, but what have survived are texts; we want to see these performances through the eyes of the craftsmen and peasants themselves, but we are forced to see them through the eyes of literate outsiders.[1] It is hardly surprising that some historians think it impossible to discover what popular culture was like in this period. It is important to be aware of the difficulties, and so, in the section which follows, I shall play devil's advocate and put the case of the sceptic. At the same time, I do believe that we can find out a good deal about the popular culture of this period by more or less indirect means, and in the second section I shall try to suggest what these indirect approaches may be.

The mediators

Historians are used to dealing with texts, with 'the documents', whether manuscript or printed. However, it is one thing to study a society such as Britain in the early twentieth century, in which most people were literate, through texts; quite another to study the craftsmen and peasants of early modern Europe, most of whom could not read or write. Their attitudes and values were expressed in activities and performances, but these activities and performances were only documented when the literate upper classes took an interest in them. The only surviving seventeenth-century texts of Russian popular songs and stories were recorded by two British visitors, Richard James and Samuel Collins; it took a foreigner to think that these oral traditions were worth writing down. Much of what we know about the great carnivals in Rome and Venice between 1500 and 1800 comes from the descriptions left by foreign visitors like Montaigne, Evelyn and Goethe. Foreign visitors are likely to miss all sorts of local or topical allusions and may misunderstand what the festivities mean to the participants.

Other popular activities are documented simply because the authorities in church or state were trying to suppress them. Most of what we know about the rebellions, the heresies and the witchcraft of the period was recorded because the rebels, heretics and witches were brought to trial and interrogated. If historians know something about the culture of the Moriscos of Granada in the sixteenth century, this is mainly because of the descriptions recorded in the proceedings of the synod of Guadix in 1554, a synod which was trying to stamp that culture out. We know about the 'Summer Lord Game' in the village of South Kyme in Lincolnshire in 1601 only because the game satirised the Earl of Lincoln, who brought a bill of complaint before the Star Chamber. In all these cases the situation in which the activity was documented may distort the record because the questioners were not concerned to establish what rebellions or heresies or satires meant to the accused.[2]

Another class of documents, which looks less likely to be distorted, is that of the 'works' of popular actors, poets or preachers, which might be published during their lifetimes or soon after their deaths. One thinks of Richard Tarleton's *Jests*; of *The Braveries of Captain Terror of Hell Valley*, a collection of 'boastful soldier' speeches published by Francesco Andreini, who specialised in that role; of the songs of Cristofano dell'Altissimo and Sebastyén Tinódi; of the sermons of Olivier Maillard and of Gabriele Barletta.[3]

These texts are indispensable sources for the historian of popular culture, but they are not exactly what he wants. A text cannot record a performance adequately, whether it is a clown's or a preacher's. The tone of voice is missing, so are the facial expressions, the gestures, the acrobatics. Thomas Fuller made the crucial point in his life of Tarleton: 'Much of his merriment lay in his very looks and actions . . . indeed the self-same words, spoken by another, would hardly move a merry man to smile; which uttered by him, would force a sad soul to laughter'. The historian has the frustrating task of writing about

Tarleton without being able to see him.[4]

There is another problem as well. We cannot afford to assume that these printed texts are faithful records of performances, even to the limited extent that texts can be. The text may have been aimed at a different audience from that of the performances; indeed it should have been aimed at a better-educated, better-off audience simply in order to sell. We know very little about the process by which these printed texts came into being. Were the clowns, preachers or poets consulted? Andreini put his own name to *Captain Terror*, but Altissimo's poems were edited for publication, and we cannot be sure what 'editing' meant. One of his poems, the *Rout of Ravenna*, survives in manuscript form, but the manuscript breaks off with the note: 'Here some stanzas are missing, the last ones, because the poet was so inspired at the conclusion that the pen or the memory of the man who was taking this down could not keep up with him.'[5] In other cases we do not know what happened. Was the text taken down faithfully during the performance? Was it censored? Was anything added? Were additions or subtractions made with the consent of the performer or without?

In the case of sermons, there is an additional complication. Maillard preached in French and Barletta preached in Italian, but their sermons were published in Latin, making it clear that the audience envisaged was very different from the original listeners. The point of the publication was not to record the performance; it was to make the themes and the *exempla* available to other preachers all over Europe. Hence a famous sermon collection was known as *Dormi secure* because it ensured that preachers slept well on Saturday night. The Latin of these sermon collections is not very literary – it may be 'macaronic', or mixed with the vernacular – but it forms an additional obstacle to the recovery of the performance, not just the specific performance, but, what matters still more from our point of view, the typical performance. Printed sermons may be full of learned references. Barletta's text refers to Livy, to Eusebius and to Bede – would he have done so in the sermon itself?[6]

Behind this problem of the relation between text and performance lies another, still more serious. The texts are rarely produced directly by the craftsmen and peasants whose attitudes and values we are trying to reconstruct; we are not approaching them directly, but through mediators. The historian of popular culture in early modern Europe has the same sort of problems as the historian of traditional black Africa. The documents of African history were written by outsiders, travellers or missionaries or officials, men who were often ignorant of the local language, who did not know the local culture well and were sometimes trying to suppress it. To study the history of the attitudes of the illiterate is necessarily to see that history through two pairs of alien eyes, our own and those of the authors of the documents, who mediate between us and the people we are trying to reach. It may be useful to distinguish six kinds of mediator.

(i) The problem can be seen at its most obvious in the case of the great writers who have been studied as sources for popular culture, such as Villon and Rabelais. Villon and Rabelais were of course familiar with the little tradition of their day, the culture of the tavern and the market-place; but they were also familiar with the great tradition, and they drew freely on it. They were not unsophisticated examples of popular culture but sophisticated mediators between the two traditions.

The mistake is particularly easy to make in the case of Villon, who led the life of a vagabond and a criminal. He was gaoled in 1461 and again in 1462 and he was condemned to death after a brawl, although it is not known whether the sentence was carried out. He wrote some poems in *argot*, probably in the jargon of the Coquillards, a group of criminals who were investigated at Dijon in 1455. In one *ballade* he refers to the police of medieval Paris, the *sergents*, as 'angels', a euphemism which may have been suggested by paintings of the Archangel Michael weighing souls. He made use of the forms of popular culture like the mock testament and the proverb – in fact he constructed a *ballade* out of proverbs:

> *Tant grate chièvre que mal gist,*
> *Tant va le pot à l'eaue qu'il brise . . .*
> *Tant crie l'on Noël qu'il vient.*

> (*The goat scratches so much it spoils its bed, The pitcher goes to the well so often that it breaks, People cry 'Christmas' so long that it comes.*)

However, one needs to remember that Villon was a university

man, with a master's degree from Paris. His poems refer not only to criminals and taverns but also to classical writers like Aristotle and Vegetius and to scholastic philosophers like Jean Buridan. His *ballades* are part of a literary tradition, and if the proverbial elements of one of them are popular, the whole poem is not.[7]

The case of Rabelais is analogous. Rabelais did not invent Gargantua, a giant who already existed in French chap-books and oral traditions. The style of Rabelais also owes a good deal to popular culture, as the gifted Russian critic Mikhail Bakhtin has pointed out, drawing attention to 'the language of the market-place in Rabelais' and to his use of 'popular-festive forms', notably the carnivalesque. Bakhtin was absolutely right, but one must not forget that Rabelais was also a learned man, professionally trained in theology and medicine, well-read in the classics and well-informed about the law. His use of popular culture was self-conscious rather than spontaneous; Rabelais was (as a French critic has recently suggested) well aware of 'the subversive possibilities' of the chap-book, which he imitated in order to undermine the traditional hierarchy of literary genres. Twentieth-century readers, who stand outside both the learned and the popular traditions of sixteenth-century France, may easily fail to see when Rabelais is working within one tradition and when he is mixing the two.[8]

The mistake is as easy to make in the case of minor writers in the great tradition who draw on popular culture for their own purposes. Carlos García wrote a book which purports to record a discussion in prison between the author and a celebrated thief, who describes the specialisms within his profession and the statutes and laws which govern it. It does not give us direct access to the world of the *pícaro*, any more than the more obviously literary works of Cervantes, Alemán, or Quevedo. The *Pentamarone*, a collection of stories in Neapolitan dialect published in the seventeenth century, has been studied from the time of the Grimms as a source for Italian folklore. Yet it was written by Gianbattista Basile, a nobleman and a baroque poet in the style of Marino. He was attracted to the stories because they were fantastic and bizarre. He may not have altered the plots, but the way in which he tells the stories is characteristic of the learned culture of his day – the long sentences, the profusion of synonyms, the extraordinary 'conceits'.[9]

(ii) The sermons of the friars, the Franciscans in particular, are among the most important sources for the popular culture of Catholic Europe. The friars were not infrequently the sons of craftsmen and peasants; Abraham a Sancta Clara, the great German preacher of the late seventeenth century, was the son of a serf-innkeeper. The simple way of life of the friars kept them close to the people. Their sympathies were often with Pauper against Dives, with the powerless against the powerful. They were often in trouble for denouncing prominent clerics and laymen, and even for inciting rebellion, like the Dominican John Pickering during the Pilgrimage of Grace.

The friars were popular preachers in the sense that they deliberately appealed to the uneducated and often drew large audiences. Savonarola preached to tens of thousands at a time in Florence. Friars often preached in the open air, and men climbed trees or sat on rooftops to hear them. It took sixty-four days to repair the roofs after a visit of Olivier Maillard to Orleans.[10] The friars drew on the oral culture of their time. They preached in a colloquial style, making much use of puns, rhymes and alliteration, shouting and gesturing, drawing on folktales to illustrate their message, and composing songs for their congregations to sing. It is not surprising that folklorists have drawn on sermons in order to study the folktale in this period.[11]

They are right to do so, but caution is necessary. The friars were amphibious or bi-cultural, men of the university as well as men of the market-place. They had often been trained in scholastic philosophy and theology and they were interested in passing on at least something from the great tradition in their sermons. Savonarola, for example, was the son of a physician and had studied theology at the university of Ferrara. In one sermon he explained the universe (according to the Ptolemaic system) to his listeners by comparing it with an onion with the earth as centre and each skin of the onion corresponding to one of the crystalline spheres in which the planets moved. The image is a homely one, but we should not assume that this world-picture was part of the culture of most of his audience; Savonarola may have been popularising science. Thomas Murner, the Franciscan who wrote lively and colloquial pamphlets against Luther, was an academic. He was a doctor of 'both laws' (canon law and civil law) and the author of an introduction to scholastic logic, who wrote in Latin as well as

German. Even in his German works Murner sometimes uses technical terms from the schools like 'Text und Gloss', where the 'gloss' is the commentary written between the lines of the text. Abraham a Sancta Clara, whose pamphlets were even more lively and colloquial than Murner's, was a doctor of theology who had been trained in rhetoric and who preached at court.

The friars usually preached in the colloquial style, but this does not mean that they were just talking naturally. The choice of the colloquial style was a conscious literary choice from three possible styles, the others being the plain style and the ornate style.[12] Each style had its own rules. The audience may not have known this, but the preachers did. The friars drew on popular themes but often transmuted them. They told traditional tales but gave them a moral which was not necessarily traditional. They used popular tunes but wrote new words for them. Some of the elements of their performances may be popular culture, but, as in the case of Villon's proverbs, the whole is not.

(iii) If the sermons of the friars do not give us direct access to popular culture, perhaps broadsides and chap-books will do so. Yet here too there are problems. The songs and stories printed in thic cheap format *may* have expressed the values of craftsmen and peasants (especially craftsmen), but this is not the only possibility. Take the so-called *genre poissard*, for instance, current in seventeenth-century France. These booklets purport to reproduce the speech of peasants or the fishwives from Les Halles, but they are literary imitations, probably written by members of the upper classes for members of the upper classes, with no more to do with real fishwives than Renaissance pastoral had to do with real shepherds.[13]

Eulenspiegel is a chap-book which went into many editions in Germany and elsewhere, and was much better known than any examples of the *genre poissard*. It is a collection of stories with the same hero, a trickster, and the stories read like folktales. Its anonymous author claims not to know Latin. In spite of this, some of the chapters appear to be derived from stories in a Latin collection which had not been translated when *Eulenspiegel* first appeared. Perhaps the two books simply drew on common oral traditions, but it is also possible that the book was written by a mediator, a man who was just pretending to be ignorant of Latin. It has sometimes been ascribed to Thomas Murner, yet another friar.[14]

The possibility of propaganda has always to be borne in mind when one is studying broadsides and chap-books. These were the 'mass media' of the period, and it was obvious to political and religious leaders that these media must be used in order to influence as many people as possible. During the German peasants' war of 1525, a number of broadside ballads were printed which dealt with current events. They are in general hostile to the peasants, and frequently point out that the rebels have broken their word in taking up arms. Perhaps they simply express the hostility of townsmen to countrymen, but some towns did in fact collaborate with the peasants in 1525, so it is possible that these ballads were commissioned by the ruling classes as propaganda. In any case, what the ballads do not express are the attitudes of the rebels. It is worth bearing in mind the comment of Andrew Fletcher of Saltoun, made at the end of the seventeenth century: 'I knew a very wise man, that believed that if a man were permitted to make all the ballads, he need not care who should make the laws of a nation'. In similar fashion a writer in *The London Magazine* for 1769 wondered why

> no administration in this country for their own good, or no worthy magistrates for the public good, have been at pains to have ballads of a proper tendency circulated among the people. I am sure money could not be better employed, and I am certain that no placemen, or pensioners, can be of so much service as a set of well chosen ballad singers might be.

In other words, some contemporaries were aware of the value of the mass media as a means of social control.[15]

This German example should make us a little wary of accepting the claims which French scholars have recently made for the Bibliothèque Bleue as a mirror of the attitudes of the French peasants of the old regime. This 'library' was a collection of chap-books, published at Troyes and elsewhere from the early seventeenth century onwards, and distributed throughout the country by *colporteurs* or pedlars. So many copies were sold that they must have reached at least some of the peasants, and if only 29 per cent of adult males could read in late seventeenth-century France, others could have listened when the books were read aloud. The chap-books were also bought and read by craftsmen.

However, it would be unwise to conclude without more ado

that the conformist attitudes to the king, the nobles and the clergy expressed in these texts were the attitudes of the craftsmen and peasants of early modern France. In the first place, we should not assume that the Bibliothèque Bleue represented the whole culture of French craftsmen and peasants. It coexisted with oral traditions, and in some regions it was much less important than oral traditions. Chap-books may have been an important part of the culture of late eighteenth-century Champagne, where they were printed and three-quarters of adult males were literate, but they could hardly have been taken very seriously in Morbihan in the late seventeenth century, where the literacy rate for adult males was below 10 per cent and the language spoken was not French but Breton.

In the second place, we must not forget the mediator. The books which the chapmen carried round had often been composed by priests, nobles, doctors and lawyers, sometimes centuries earlier. *Melusine*, for example, had been written in the late fourteenth century by Jean D'Arras at the command of the Duc de Berry. Someone revised, abridged or translated the book, and someone else chose to print it. A pedlar selected it for his pack, and thus the book arrived at a given village. There is thus a whole chain of mediators between a particular text and the peasants whose attitudes it is supposed to express, and we cannot assume that the peasants passively accepted the ideas expressed in the texts any more than contemporary viewers believe all they see on television.[16]

(iv) If printed sources are misleading, we can surely rely on oral tradition. The discovery of popular culture in the late eighteenth century led to the collection of many songs and stories from individual craftsmen or peasants or their wives. Yet between these individuals and the modern reader there is, once more, a whole chain of mediators. The editor may, as we have seen, have taken liberties with the texts he collected (above, p.18f). Even if he did not, his informants may have done so. Percy printed ballads which acquaintances sent him, and the Grimms were helped by their friends. In any case the presence of the collector, an outsider with a notebook, in the singing or storytelling situation is going to affect what he wants to record. Singers may refuse to perform altogether. Karadžić has recorded the problems he had in persuading Serbian women to sing, and as most collectors have been men, much of traditional women's culture has been lost.

Even the individual singer or storyteller may be a mediator in a sense, because in early modern Europe oral and written, town and country, great tradition and little tradition all coexisted and interacted. Twentieth-century examples show this interaction most vividly. One American collector went to great trouble and expense to visit a remote region in the south-west to record folksongs, 'only to discover . . . that much of what he had gathered had been learned from recent eastern radio broadcasts'. In Yugoslavia, songs recorded from oral tradition in the 1930s had sometimes been learned from printed sources, including the Karadžić collection itself. Thus one folklorist helps create the folklore others will collect. [17]

This kind of situation can occasionally be documented for the period before 1800. The classic British example is that of Mrs Brown of Falkland, a singer who provided versions of thirty-three Child ballads, including five not otherwise known. She was, however, no peasant but a professor's daughter, who knew her Ossian and her Percy. It is likely that this knowledge affected her ballad versions, and in any case her interest in the supernatural, her sentimentality and her avoidance of the erotic reflect middle-class attitudes of the late eighteenth century. She was a mediator. What can be documented for Mrs Brown may be suspected in other cases. Twenty-one tales from the Grimm collection go back to one informant, a woman called 'Die Frau Viehmännin'. She was born in 1755 and was of Huguenot descent, from refugees after the Revocation of the Edict of Nantes. Did she know the Perrault collection? Are some of the similarities between the Perrault and Grimm collections the result of this accident of dependence on a particular informant? Izaak Walton once recorded having heard a milkmaid singing 'Come live with me and be my love'. What was the source of this oral tradition? Quite possibly a printed broadside. [18]

(v) If early folklorists cannot be trusted to record oral traditions, perhaps inquisitors can. The trials and confessions of heretics and witches are obviously an important source for popular attitudes. In the trial records the historian can discover the favourite turns of phrase of the accused, and almost hear their voices. Yet here too there are mediators, for the confessions were not often spontaneous. The confessions of witches, for example, are the product of a situation in which an interrogator, usually a friar, an educated man, is face to face with the accused, while a clerk takes down what is being said. The historian has access to the clerk's record, often in Latin, of a dialogue in which the interrogator, who may have been new to the region, probably spoke a standard form of the vernacular while the accused replied in dialect. The possibilities for misunderstanding were considerable. The interrogator had been through the whole business many times before and knew, all too well, what he was trying to find. The accused did not know what was happening and may well have been searching frantically for cues and clues to what was wanted. The situation was like a parody of the interviews between modern anthropologists and their informants in the field – anthropologists are much concerned about the possibility that the answers they receive may be little more than what they have suggested, unconsciously, to the informant. Interrogations of supposed witches were all the more unreliable a guide to their true opinions because the interrogator had power over the accused and the accused knew this, and also because torture might be used to extract confessions. As the famous Italian physician Girolamo Cardano pointed out in the mid-sixteenth century, confessions of the standard type were not to be trusted, because 'these things are said under torture, when they know that a confession of this type will bring the torture to an end'. In other words, the accused may have told the interrogators what they expected to hear, and what they expected to hear was what they had read about in the treatises on witchcraft. The treatises described what was confessed in the trials, but the trials also followed what was described in the treatises. It is very hard for the historian to escape from this vicious circle and to discover what, if anything, the accused thought he or she had been doing.[19]

(vi) If the trials for heresy and witchcraft are tainted evidence, perhaps riots and rebellions give us more direct access to popular culture. Instead of listening to isolated and defeated individuals we can look at large groups. Actions speak louder than words, and riots and rebellions may be seen not only as expressions of 'blind fury', but also as dramatic expressions of popular attitudes and values. This approach has recently proved a fruitful one, but to employ it safely the historian has to remember the mediator.

One source for this history of rebellions is the interrogation of captured participants, a source which has the same kind of built-in distortions as the interrogations of heretics and witches. Another kind of source is the narrative or description written down at the time, usually in reports by officials who were trying to suppress the rebellions. Thus we know about the many revolts which took place in France between 1620 and 1648 almost exclusively through the reports of provincial officials to the chancellor, Séguier, whose papers happen to have survived. The values of these officials, so different from those of the rebels, may have affected not only the judgements they passed, which can easily be discounted, but also the descriptions they gave. It would be natural for the officials to interpret as a 'blind fury' a movement which the participants saw as a planned defence of specific traditional rights. The officials are mediators between us and the rebels, and unreliable mediators at that.[20]

The historian is not always forced to see revolts exclusively through official eyes. The demands of the rebels often survived in manuscript or even in print, and they are obviously an extremely valuable kind of source, if only they are authentic. When the Breton peasants rose in 1675, they drew up their demands in a *Code Paysan*. Such a document, in a seventeenth- or eighteenth-century hand, survives, and if genuine tells us much about the mentality of the rebels. It contains the following clause: 'It is forbidden, on pain of running the gauntlet, to give refuge to the gabelle and to her children . . . but on the contrary everyone is enjoined to fire on her as they would on a mad dog.' In other words, the Bretons thought that the dreaded salt-tax, the *gabelle,* against which they had revolted, was a person. Or did they? The text may have been tampered with, and these 'folkloristic' details added to make the movement seem absurd. The existence of a mediator is more obvious in the case of the surviving text of the demands of the peasants in the diocese of Speyer in 1502, for he could not resist the comment: 'Oh, the sinfulness of the peasant mind! What a bane it has always been to the clergy!'[21]

The demands of the rebels during the German peasants' war of 1525 survive in a more reliable form because they were printed at the time to gain publicity for the cause. Yet a problem remains, because we do not know how the articles were drawn up. The famous Twelve Articles of Memmingen (a small town in

Suabia where one of the peasant armies had assembled) begin
with the demand that each parish should be allowed to choose
its own priest. The articles were drafted with the help of
Memmingen men, including the town clerk, Sebastian Lotzer,
and a preacher, Christoph Schappeler. Was this demand what
mattered most to the peasants, or to the men who drew up the
demands in their name? In fact, this right of *Pfarrerwahl* is
mentioned in only 13 per cent of the local lists of grievances of
the Swabian peasants, and in only 4 per cent of those drawn up
before the Twelve Articles.[22]

The leaders of peasant risings were often noblemen or priests,
not peasants, whether they were chosen in order to legitimate
the movement or because the peasants lacked experience of
leadership. On occasion it is possible that these noblemen or
clergymen were not even voluntary leaders, but forced to take
command; at least they often said this afterwards, perhaps
because they were trying to escape responsibility. Whether
voluntary leaders or not, these men were also mediators, and it
is difficult for the historian to discover what the rank and file of
the movement — like the witches — really thought they were
doing.

The local grievance lists of 1525 are something like an early
public opinion poll, but a distorted one, and the same objection
can be made to the famous French *cahiers* of 1789. There are
40,000 such documents, which were discussed in village
assemblies. The assembly might include all men aged
twenty-five or over paying taxes, but we rarely know how they
drew up their grievances. In one case a local *commerçant*
brought a list out of his pocket, and this was accepted with little
modification.[23]

Oblique approaches to popular culture

We have seen that there is some force in the objections made by
traditional historians to the history of popular culture on the
grounds that the undertaking is impossible because the
documents are lacking or untrustworthy, contaminated by
misunderstandings or their desire to make propaganda for some
cause. However, historians never can trust their documents
completely. The point about the different classes of document
discussed so far is not that they are worthless, but that they are

distorted, and distortion can to some degree be allowed for –
indeed, it is the historian's traditional business to do so. Some of
the documents may be less unreliable than others, and some
parts of them less unreliable than other parts, as a
re-examination of the witch-trials should suggest.

Some historians working on witchcraft have recently reached
new conclusions not by discovering new kinds of source but by
using old sources in a new way. One student of Italian
witch-trials has paid particular attention to the cases in which
the interrogator seems to have been disconcerted by the answers
of the accused, because it is clear that in these cases the answers
did not conform to the inquisitorial stereotype. In Friuli, in
north-east Italy, in the 1570s, the accused declared that they
were not witches but opponents of witches, whom they fought
at night with sticks of fennel, while the witches were armed with
sticks of maize, 'and if we win, that year is an abundant one, and
if we lose, there is famine that year'. Two students of English
witchcraft have used trial records to answer questions which did
not interest the investigators at the time and are therefore
unlikely to be distorted: questions about the social status of the
accused and the accuser, the relations between them and the
situations out of which accusations developed. If this does not
bring us much nearer to understanding the mentality of the
witch herself, it does cast a clear light upon her neighbours.[24]

The essential point is surely to accept the fact that we cannot
often reach the craftsmen and peasants of early modern Europe
directly, but that we can reach them via preachers, printers,
travellers, officials. These men were brokers between learned
culture and popular culture, and in a situation where great and
little traditions coexisted, they were a fundamental fact of
cultural life, welcome or unwelcome missionaries to the little
community from the outside world. Given that a direct
approach is impossible, an oblique approach to popular culture
via these mediators is the least likely to put us on the wrong
track. In fact there are several oblique approaches.

One oblique approach is to study texts when what one wants
to recover is the performance. The dangers of this approach
have already been discussed, but there is also a more positive
point to be made, which is that some texts are much closer to
performances than others are. Among the documents which
have survived are manuscripts in which minstrels recorded their

repertoire. One famous English example is MS. Ashmole no. 48, associated with the sixteenth-century minstrel Richard Sheale. If we know some popular preachers only through posthumous Latin editions of their works, we know others through records made on the spot. Some of the sermons of St Bernardino of Siena have been printed from a manuscript of the fifteenth century, copied out by a man who went to the sermons with wax tablets in order to take down every word in shorthand. Calvin's sermons were also taken down in shorthand as he delivered them so that they could be printed immediately and accurately.[25]

A second approach to popular culture might be described as socially oblique. It consists of studying the attitudes of craftsmen and peasants through the witness of the clergy, the nobility and the bourgeoisie. The dangers of this procedure have already been underlined; but they are not insuperable. For one thing, the upper classes genuinely participated in popular culture, especially in the first half of the period, so that they were not total outsiders. They would have understood ballads and carnivals from the inside, if not riots and rebellions. Particularly valuable is the testimony of men who were born craftsmen or peasants and rose socially afterwards. Some of them wrote their autobiographies, men such as Benvenuto Cellini or Giulio Cesare Croce, John Bunyan or Samuel Bamford, and texts like these bring the historian as close to this vanished world as he will ever get.[26]

Three more oblique approaches need to be discussed in rather more detail – the iconographical method, the regressive method and the comparative method.

Iconography was defined by one of its greatest practitioners, the late Erwin Panofsky, as 'that branch of the history of art which concerns itself with the subject matter or meaning of works of art as opposed to their form'.[27] It includes relatively pedestrian tasks like the identification of saints by their attributes, and at a deeper level of analysis, which Panofsky came to call 'iconology', it involves the diagnosis of the attitudes and values of which works of art are the symptoms. Roughly speaking, one might say that iconography is concerned with what contemporaries knew about works of art, iconology with what they did not know about themselves – or at any rate, did not know they knew. There is no reason why we should not study popular imagery in this way as well as the works of art produced for princes and noblemen, whether we look at Staffordshire pottery figures, the hand-coloured woodcuts produced at Epinal, or the peasant paintings of Dalarna.

Since the craftsmen and peasants with whom we are concerned were often illiterate and better at using their hands than at using words, the iconographical approach to their attitudes and values ought to be a fruitful one. The artifacts which they produced are our most immediate contact with the dead whose world we are trying to reconstruct and interpret, so much so that it may seem odd to call this approach 'oblique' at all. The reason for doing so is simply that history is written, so that when a cultural historian interprets an artifact he translates from paint or wood or stone into words.

This kind of translation is always somewhat presumptuous. It is particularly difficult in the case of popular art for the same reason that it is so necessary, because of the lack of reliable literary evidence for the world-view of the illiterate. It is hardly surprising to find that little work has been done in this field. The artifacts have been collected into museums of folk art, their distribution has been carefully plotted on maps, and many iconographical problems, in the narrow sense of the term, have been solved, so that it is possible to recognise the charity of St Martin, or the mill of youth, or the world turned upside down. But what did the world turned upside down mean to ordinary people? Were its associations frightening or exhilarating? Does the frequency with which soldiers turn up in eighteenth-century popular art mean that ordinary people approved of wars? Attempts to answer questions like these have hardly begun; the iconological approach to popular culture remains just out of reach.

The iconology of rebellion might lead us more directly to the aims of the rank-and-file than the confessions of the leaders do. The German peasants of the early sixteenth century often marched to revolt behind a banner bearing the image of a shoe, the *Bundschuh*; what exactly did this image mean to them? In the English Pilgrimage of Grace, the banner of the Five Wounds was prominent; in the Norman revolt of 1639, the banner displayed by the rebels represented St John the Baptist. The participants were used to marching behind banners of this kind, in religious processions. The religious images perhaps

An Elusive Quarry   81

legitimated revolt in their eyes by transforming it into a
pilgrimage or a crusade. The image of St John the Baptist, who
went barefoot, was perhaps one with which it was easy for the
poor to identify . . .

The whole vast area of material culture is a potential subject
for iconological analysis. Clothes, for example, form a
symbolic system. In a given community, within which
meanings are shared, there are certain rules governing what can
be worn, by whom, on what occasions, so that the clothes worn
by an individual transmit various messages to members of the
community. At the iconographical level this is obvious enough;
a glance at a peasant girl would tell the initiated what village she
came from, how prosperous her family was, and whether she
was married or not. Could a historian also study the iconology
of clothes? Strong regional variations in clothes tell the observer
that the wearers identify strongly with their region; a sharp
distinction between ordinary working days and festivals may be
expressed by a sharp distinction between working clothes and
'Sunday best'. An iconological approach to houses may also be a
possibility, for a house is not just a machine for living in but also
a centre of ritual. The hearth and the threshold were places of
symbolic importance – hence witch-bottles were buried under
them in East Anglian houses of the sixteenth and seventeenth
centuries. Houses are bound to reflect, and to shape, family life
and habits of work or leisure; they too may be seen as systems of
signs. The organisation of space and the placing of major items
of furniture transmit messages at one level about the men and
women who live in it and at another level about the culture in
which they live.[28] We need to remember, of course, that we
cannot enter an eighteenth-century house, that the interiors we
see in museums of folk art are reconstructions – that is,
interpretations.

If it is ever possible to study the material culture of the early
modern period as a system of signs, it will involve another
oblique approach, chronologically oblique this time, the
so-called 'regressive method'. This term was coined by the great
French historian Marc Bloch when he was studying rural
history. He tried to read the history of the French peasantry
from the fields they tilled, and found that the evidence was
relatively good for the eighteenth century (when field maps, for
example, were common), but fragmentary before this. Hence

Bloch proposed to read history backwards.

> Is it not inevitable that in general, the facts of the most distant past are also the most obscure? How can one escape from the necessity of working from the better- to the less well-known?[29]

The historian of traditional popular culture is in a similar position. Popular prints, broadsides and chap-books of the eighteenth century are very much more common than earlier ones, whether because more were printed or because a greater proportion have survived. A high percentage of the artifacts preserved in museums of popular art are eighteenth-century or later.[30] It was only in the late eighteenth century that ballads and stories were systematically collected from oral tradition, as we have seen, and that popular customs and festivals were systematically described. There is therefore a strong case for writing the history of popular culture backwards and for using the late eighteenth century as a base from which to consider the more fragmentary evidence from the seventeenth and sixteenth centuries.

In certain areas, where the evidence is particularly thin, the historian may even be forced to take a later period as a base and work back from there. That he needs to be very cautious in doing this goes without saying. Suppose, for example, that we want to reconstruct the culture of the serfs in central and eastern Europe in the seventeenth and eighteenth centuries. It would surely be a mistake to neglect the folktales collected in Mecklenburg, for example, in the early twentieth century: stories collected from old men and women whose grandparents were probably alive in the late eighteenth century, oral traditions which reveal something of the attitudes of the serfs towards their masters.[31]

Again, if we want to study the folksongs of early modern Europe the regressive method is indispensable and the years around 1900 need to be taken as a point of departure. It was as late as this that the serious study of folk-music began, that an attempt was made to record it as it was sung, and not to harmonise it. It was in 1903 that Cecil Sharp recorded his first folksong, 'The seeds of love', in a vicarage garden in Somerset, and it was a year later that, at the other end of Europe, in Transylvania, Béla Bartók began collecting. It was just at this time that sound-recording devices were becoming available.

Sharp did not like the cylinder phonograph because he thought that it made the singers self-conscious, but Bartók recorded a good deal of peasant music on wax cylinders, which made it possible to compare individual performances.[32]

No one interested in the techniques of oral poets or singers of tales can afford to ignore records made in the field in the nineteenth and twentieth centuries. Russian *byliny* were written down before 1800, but it was only in the mid-nineteenth century that the man who was recording them paid any attention to variations between performances. Even more useful, from this point of view, are the tape-recordings of Yugoslavian singers of tales made in the 1930s by the American scholar, Milman Parry, which make it possible to compare two singers' versions of the same song, and the same singer singing the same song on different occasions. Parry's aim, incidentally, was to test hypotheses about the poetic techniques of Homer, an ambition which makes our attempt to get back no further than the sixteenth century appear quite faint-hearted! More recently, another American scholar, also armed with a tape-recorder, has studied the verbal art of black preachers in parts of the USA. Again, the information we possess on the techniques of divining and folk-medicine in France or Norway or Yugoslavia is incomparably more detailed for the twentieth century than for earlier periods. Historians whose sources consist of fragmentary texts have a lot to learn from folklorists whose sources are living people, who can be observed at work and even questioned.[33]

To avoid misunderstanding, let me say at once what the regressive method is not. It does not consist of taking descriptions of relatively recent situations and cheerfully assuming that they apply equally well to earlier periods. What I am advocating is a rather more indirect use of the modern material, to criticise or interpret the documentary sources. It is particularly useful for suggesting connections between elements which can themselves be documented for the period being studied, or for making sense of descriptions which are so allusive or elliptical that they do not make sense by themselves.[34]

The regressive method as advocated here is a great deal less ambitious than the approach of Wilhelm Mannhardt, Sir James Frazer, and other nineteenth-century scholars who took the customs of the peasants of their own day, like the ritual of the last sheaf or the mock battles of the mummers, as the basis for the reconstruction of what they liked to consider 'the primitive religion of the Aryans'. They were preoccupied with the study of origins at the expense of the study of what these rituals meant for later generations, and they were prepared to jump over thousands of years, neglecting the social and cultural changes of the period between Tacitus and themselves. They accepted too easily the myth of an unchanging popular culture, a myth created by the educated townsman who sees the peasants as part of nature rather than part of culture, in other words, as animals rather than men. Marc Bloch did not make this mistake. His aim was not to jump millennia but to work his way back, step by step, a century or two. His point was not that change was absent from the French countryside but that it was slow.

In village communities where a majority of families remained from one generation to the next, living in the same houses as their fathers and grandfathers and tilling the same soil, it is reasonable to assume a good deal of cultural continuity. In this kind of community oral traditions were probably stable and so a more reliable guide to the past than modern historians have been willing to admit. There are men living in the West Highlands even today who occupy the same land as their ancestors did in the seventeenth century and possess family traditions which go back as far. Elsewhere in contemporary Britain, as the Opies have shown, children are faithful guardians of oral tradition.

> In their self-contained community their basic lore and language seems scarcely to alter from generation to generation. Boys . . . ask riddles which were posed when Henry VIII was a boy. Young girls . . . rebuke one of their number who seeks back a gift with a couplet used in Shakespeare's day.[35]

Of course, oral traditions do change as they are handed down. Incidents which took place centuries apart may be conflated, or modern concerns projected on to the past. However, the historian who is aware that he is employing an oblique approach will remember to make allowances for this. He will rely on the regressive method more for structures than for details, more to interpret attitudes than to establish what attitudes were. His basic problem remains that of knowing how much to allow for change in any given case, the problem of making ends meet.

The history of the English mummers' plays may serve to illustrate this difficulty. More than 600 texts survive, but almost all of them come (like the texts of the Tuscan *maggi* or the Swedish 'star-plays') from the nineteenth century or later. A number of these texts have St George as the hero. In Norfolk in 1473, Sir John Paston referred to a man he had kept 'this three year to play St George'. The problem is to make ends meet and to reconstruct the fifteenth-century play from versions recorded some four hundred years later. We may begin by subtraction, by the elimination of such figures as Oliver Cromwell, King William (whether William III or William IV), and Admiral Vernon, who all occur in nineteenth-century versions. Textual criticism has enabled scholars to recover some names and phrases which had become corrupted in the process of oral transmission, to read 'Turkey Snipe' as 'Turkish Knight'. We must allow something for the fact that some nineteenth-century versions were recorded in bowdlerised form by local vicars, the ubiquitous mediators. Like a picture-restorer stripping off layer after layer of overpainting, the historian finds himself left with the fundamental structure of the action: the sequence of combats, the slaying of the hero, and his revival.[36]

In this last example, the regressive method may be supplemented by a last oblique approach: comparison. The earlier forms and the possible meaning of some of the English mummers' plays have been illuminated by a comparison with the St George plays performed in Thrace at the beginning of this century. The Greek plays make it easier to imagine what the English plays were like before bowdlerisation. If we are trying to decide how far back the comic doctor figure goes, then it is useful to know that a similar figure occurs in German carnival plays of the fifteenth and sixteenth centuries.[37]

It may be useful to follow Marc Bloch still further and to distinguish two varieties of the comparative method.

The first is the neighbourly comparison. Child Ballad 4, *Lady Isabel and the Elf-Knight*, is brief and cryptic. The versions collected across the North Sea, in the Netherlands, where the ballad is called *Heer Halewijn*, are fuller and more numerous, and so they serve to interpret the English variant. The historian of rituals has an even greater need of the comparative method than the historian of ballads. It would be difficult either to reconstruct or to interpret Roman sixteenth-century carnivals without making some comparison with Florence or Venice. The more fragmentary the surviving evidence from one region, the more useful the comparative approach. It has to be practised with care – one cannot afford to ignore regional variation any more than change over time – but, employed as a consciously oblique approach, it has its uses.[38]

More controversial is the second variety of this approach, comparisons between two societies relatively remote in space or time. Has the historian of early modern Europe something to learn from social anthropologists who have studied the Trobriand Islanders, or the Nuer, or contemporary Sicily or Greece? That he cannot simply take over their conclusions goes without saying. However, anthropologists have experienced at first hand what historians try so hard to imagine, the quality of life in pre-industrial societies, and they have come back to tell us about it in our own language. Anthropologists are often more at ease with concepts and more articulate about their methods than their historical colleagues, and this makes their example particularly worth following in a field like the history of popular culture, which has not been cultivated by historians long enough for any consensus on methods to have been reached.

An obvious example of what a historian of popular beliefs can learn from social anthropologists working in another continent comes from recent research on witchcraft. Students of African witchcraft have consulted witch-doctors and even become their apprentices, so they have come to understand witchcraft from the inside. Historians cannot imitate these methods, but the example of the anthropologists has helped liberate them from the pressure exerted by the documents to look at witches through the eyes of their judges.[39]

For historians concerned with the attitudes and values of peasants who have rarely left written records, the study of public rituals is obviously important, and in this field too the anthropologists have long been at home. A student of European carnivals has something to learn, as a later chapter will suggest, from recent work on 'rites of reversal' in India and Africa. Again, I would not have dared to suggest that historians may one day analyse the houses of European peasants as systems of signs, if the anthropologist Pierre Bourdieu had not made an analysis of this kind for the Berber house of modern Algeria, describing the contrast between male space and female space, between 'the light-filled, noble, upper part of the house', the place of fire, and 'the dark and nocturnal, lower part of the house, place of objects that are moist, green or raw'.[40]

Anthropologists turned ethno-historians have also provided two outstanding examples of the careful and self-conscious use of the regressive method. To assess the influence of Spain on the culture of Latin America, George Foster has attempted to reconstruct the culture of the sixteenth-century Spanish peasantry, and to do this he has worked back from the twentieth century, doing his own fieldwork in Spain and drawing on the research of folklorists. Georges Balandier has written a history of the kingdom of the Congo in the sixteenth and seventeenth centuries. The documentary sources for this period are the work of white officials and missionaries, and naturally enough express their point of view. To supplement these sources Balandier has had recourse to oral traditions collected in the nineteenth and twentieth centuries. Oral traditions may not provide reliable narrative of events, but they are invaluable as evidence of reactions to these events, for seeing them with 'the vision of the vanquished'. The analogy between Balandier's problems and those of a historian of European popular culture will be obvious enough.[41]

The comparative method, like the regressive method, involves speculation. If it seems too speculative, the reader should remember that the method is not to be employed by itself but in conjunction with all the other methods, and in particular to make sense of surviving fragments of evidence, not as a substitute for them. Herder once called folksongs 'the archive of the people' (*Das Archiv des Volkes*). To read in that archive is impossible without techniques of this kind. Since the popular culture of early modern Europe is so elusive, it has to be approached in a roundabout manner, recovered by indirect means, and interpreted by a series of analogies. The difficulties should receive vivid illustration in the next chapter, concerned with the singers and storytellers, actors, carvers and painters who transmitted popular culture in our period. Some of them were celebrated in their own day, but all of them are shadowy figures now.

PART 2

Structures of Popular Culture

CHAPTER FOUR

The Transmission of Popular Culture

Every craftsman and peasant was involved in the transmission of popular culture, and so were their mothers, wives and daughters. They passed it on every time they told a traditional story to someone else, while bringing up children necessarily involved transmitting the values of their culture or sub-culture. Life in a pre-industrial society was organised on a hand-made, do-it-yourself basis to a degree that we can scarcely imagine now. Shepherds made their own bagpipes as well as playing them. The men of the household made the furniture, and the women made the clothes; these were obvious winter occupations in the countryside. Anyone who fell ill or had an accident would be treated at home. Most entertainment was also organised on a do-it-yourself basis.

Most, but not all. Neither the household nor the village was culturally autonomous. Within the village, some men and women told stories or sang better than others, like 'Die Frau Viehmännin', a tailor's widow from the Kassel area whose ability is on record because the brothers Grimm wrote down twenty-one of her stories.[1] If he or his cattle were sick and home-made remedies were of no avail, a peasant would have recourse to a 'cunning man' or a 'wise woman', in other words a semi-professional healer. If he wanted a metal tool he would go to the local blacksmith, a professional craftsman, or wait for a travelling pedlar to come to the village. Wandering minstrels or actors provided sporadic professional entertainment. In short, it is useful to distinguish what the Swedish folklorist Carl von Sydow called the 'active bearers' of popular traditions from the rest, who were relatively passive. It is with this minority of active tradition-bearers or 'carriers' that this chapter is mainly concerned, describing the manner of people they were and the social settings in which they operated, and attempting to determine whether they were innovators or simply 'keepers' or 'guardians' of tradition.[2]

The professionals

It is impossible to avoid the problem of definition. What is a 'popular' artist? The most useful definition would seem to be an artist who works mainly for a public of craftsmen and peasants. This will exclude Dürer, say, or Hogarth; although some of their graphic works probably circulated widely. A marginal case is that of the seventeenth-century Dutch engraver Romeyn de Hooghe. De Hooghe (the nephew of the painter Pieter de Hooghe) was a doctor of law. His prints appealed to the upper classes, and he was ennobled by the King of Poland. I would count him as a popular artist because his most important works were political prints with a wide circulation. Similarly, I would include the eighteenth-century English cartoonist James Gillray. There is all too little to say about most of their colleagues. We know the names, but little more than the names, of some families of French engravers in the rue St-Jacques in Paris who produced popular prints: the Mariette family (active *c*.1600–1774), the Jolain family (active *c*.1650–1738), or the Basset family (active *c*.1700–1854), best known because one of them produced prints in favour of the French Revolution. It is difficult to say whether we should regard these families as entrepreneurs, engravers, or artists – probably all three. The same is probably true of the Abadal family, who were active in different towns in Catalonia from the seventeenth century to the early twentieth, or the Didier family of Epinal in Lorraine, which was already in the eighteenth century an important centre of *imagerie populaire*. We can get some idea of the scale of their operations from the fact that Jean-Charles Didier died in 1772 leaving a stock of over 56,000 images.[3]

In Norway and Sweden, something is known about hundreds of craftsmen who worked in country districts in the eighteenth century, because they not infrequently signed and dated their works and because the local records tell us not only their dates of baptism, marriage and burial but also something about their literacy, their knowledge of the catechism and even the amount of furniture in their homes. Oral traditions about some of them have also survived. Some of these craftsmen emerge as well-defined artistic personalities and as men enjoying a considerable local reputation: men such as Clemet Håkansson from Småland and Corporal Gustaf Reuter, from Hälsingland, two leading Swedish exponents of *bonadmåleri,* paintings on hangings; Kittil Rygg, of Hallingdal, and Ola Hansson, of Telemark, leading 'rose-painters' from east Norway; or Jakob Klukstad, of Gudbrandsdal, perhaps the greatest of the Norwegian wood-carvers of the eighteenth century.

Some painters, carvers and weavers of the eighteenth century were definitely professionals, although they might, like Corporal Reuter, have exercised another occupation before turning artist, and they might own a farm and derive an income from that. They were often itinerant, working in the houses of their clients. Their training was informal. Painters might enlarge their repertoire by copying or adapting Dutch or German woodcuts or engravings, and they might try to pass their skills on to their children. Clemet Håkansson's son and grandson were painters like him, while the Swedish painter Per Nilsson had not only sons but no less than five daughters following in his footsteps, which suggests that the family worked as a team and produced their paintings at home. Specific innovations can sometimes be traced back to individual artists; for example, Erik Eliasson of Rättvik in Dalarna, who painted floral designs on cupboards, is credited with the invention of the *kurbits* or stylised gourd. What artists and their clients thought about innovation we do not know; and in the present state of research it is still difficult to generalise with any confidence even about the recruitment, training and status of these country craftsmen.[4]

About makers of popular artifacts elsewhere it is only possible to speak in still more vague and general terms. In large towns there was a living to be made by specialist painters, like sign-painters in London, who clustered in Harp Alley, or *madonneri,* painters of votive pictures to the Madonna, in Venice or Naples. Other painters tramped the countryside in search of work, whether painting portraits or painting signs. In some regions, where the clay was right, as in the Italian Marches, whole villages of semi-professional potters might be found. Elsewhere the nearest thing to a professional artist might be the village blacksmith, for blacksmiths did not confine themselves to shoeing horses or repairing tools but made weather-vanes and other decorative pieces of wrought iron as well. In Alsace, south Germany and Austria the blacksmith made votive figures out of iron, and in Sweden, which was rich in the ore, he made grave monuments of the same material.[5]

There is rather more to say about performers. These successors of the medieval minstrels were a motley and versatile group.[6] To use only terms which were current in England between 1500 and 1800, they included ballad-singers, bear-wards, buffoons, charlatans, clowns, comedians, fencers, fools, hocus-pocus men, jugglers, merry-andrews, minstrels, mountebanks, players, puppet-masters, quacks, rope-dancers, showmen, tooth-drawers and tumblers (for even tooth-drawers, operating in the open, surrounded by spectators, were a kind of performer). Many of the names overlapped because the functions overlapped; these professional entertainers certainly put on a variety show. A 'comedian' was not confined to comic parts. A 'player' (compare the German *Spielmann*, Slavic *igrec*) might play instruments, play a part, play the fool, or all of these. He would need to be a master of mimicry and quick-change acts. English troupes could make a success of continental tours because their effects did not depend on language. In the words of a Danish document, the English players were *instrumentister och springere*, 'musicians and acrobats'. A buffoon or clown might sing or improvise verses, fence or dance on a rope, tumble or juggle with balls in the air. So might a minstrel. One of the few English minstrels of the sixteenth century whose name has come down to us, Richard Sheale (whose version of the ballad *Chevy Chase* was printed in Percy's *Reliques*), described himself as a 'merry knave', in other words a clown. The old Spanish terms for minstrel, *juglar* – somewhat out of date by the sixteenth century – reminds us that the same man might tell stories or juggle with balls; and the Latin word from which it is derived, *joculator,* 'joker', suggests that a minstrel was a general entertainer. So impressive were the feats of these men that 'juggler' came to mean 'magician', while the term 'conjurer', which had originally meant someone who conjured up spirits, came by the eighteenth century to refer to someone who practised legerdemain, eating fire or pulling long coloured ribbons out of his mouth. Actors and actresses too were sometimes believed to be in league with the Devil, who was the great master of illusions.

We are left with the 'showmen', whether they showed puppets or relics or waxworks or performing bears or monkeys or a 'peep-show', with views of battles or exotic cities like Constantinople or Peking; and also with a cluster of terms

which have become pejorative, such as 'charlatan', 'mountebank' and 'quacksalver' or just 'quack'. These terms were not
always pejorative in the sixteenth and seventeenth centuries, and
their meanings were more precise then than later.* The
charlatan, or *opérateur*, as he sometimes called himself in
France, was an itinerant seller of pills or other medicines, who
clowned or developed an amusing patter to attract the attention
of potential customers. Antoine Girard, known as 'Tabarin',
was a famous example of the charlatan, and perhaps one should
add his seventeeth-century contemporary Guillot-Gorju, who
alternated the roles of stage-doctor and real physician, and even
the great Austrian actor Josef Anton Stranitzky, who doubled
as a drawer of teeth. This combination of healer and entertainer
is in fact an extremely old one. Healing was, and in some parts of
the world still is, a social drama, a public performance involving
elaborate rituals.[7] In Italy, the word *ciarlatano* (or *ciurmatore*)
might mean a hawker of medicines or a street actor. The
ciarlatani who performed on the piazza were distinguished
from the higher-status *comedianti* who acted in private houses.
The 'mountebank' was the charlatan mounted on a bench or
stage, surrounded by somewhat more elaborate properties.
There were also *saltimbanchi*, acrobats on benches, and
cantimbanchi, singers on benches (the German *Bänkelsänger*).
These singers were often furnished with a set of illustrations to
their ballads and a pointer to direct the attention of the audience,
not to mention copies of the ballad itself, which they sold
afterwards, for they were as much hawkers, 'ballad-mongers',
as they were performers (Plate 1). Charlatans sold ballads too.
In German these singers were also known as *Gassensänger* or
Marktsänger because they sang in the streets or market-places,
or as *Avisensänger* (news-singer), when they specialised in
songs about current events. Women sometimes did this job; in
Vienna there were fifty *Liederweiber* or 'song-wives' active in
1797.[8]

   These associations of names, ideas and occupations were not
merely west European. The Russian term *skomorokh* might be
translated variously as 'player', 'buffoon' or 'acrobat'. The
skomorokhi of the sixteenth and seventeenth centuries recited
byliny, played the fool, wrestled, juggled, put performing bears

---

* The term 'charlatan' seems to have first been applied to fake scholars by J. B.
Menckenius in 1715.

through their repertoire of tricks, and gave puppet-shows in the street.[9] (Plate 4)

Rarely described at any length, these performers were often mentioned in passing, and from these many fragments some kind of a general picture does emerge. The performing profession had its hierarchy of success. At the top were a few entertainers who worked in large cities, were summoned to court, and had their works published, like Tabarin in Paris, Tarleton in London, or Gil Vicente in Lisbon, who was a poet, actor and musician, in other words a *jogral*, a minstrel. (Shakespeare is excluded on the grounds that he did not work *mainly* for craftsmen or peasants.) Also highly placed were a few entrepreneurs, like Martin Powell, who showed his puppets at Bath and moved to Covent Garden in 1710, or his French contemporary François Brioché, who had a puppet-stall at the Foire St-Germain. On a visit to Switzerland, Brioché was once arrested as a suspected magician, but he went on to be mentioned by Boileau and appointed *opérateur de la maison du roi*, which might be translated as 'charlatan by appointment'. The men who worked such pitches as Piazza S. Marco in Venice, Piazza Navona in Rome, or the Pont-Neuf in Paris must have been among the aristrocrats of their profession. Given the size of these cities, they will have had little need to move. Some of them founded dynasties, like the Brioché family or the Bienfait family, who were also puppet-masters at the Foire St-Germain, or the Hilverding family, puppet-masters in Central Europe. The Venetian clowns Zan Polo and Zane Cimador were a successful father-and-son team. With these men we might include a new type of entertainer for the post-Gutenberg age, the professional ballad-writer, like the ex-attorney William Elderton or the ex-weaver Thomas Deloney, and also men on the edge between learned and popular culture, like Elkanah Settle, an Oxford man who thought himself a worthy rival to Dryden and had Shaftesbury for his patron, yet worked for Mrs Mynn, a show-woman at Bartholomew Fair, and in one play was said to have been reduced to playing the dragon. In more remote parts of Europe, traditional bards still enjoyed noble patronage and high status, like Sebestyén Tinódi in sixteenth-century Hungary, who was ennobled, and, perhaps, John Parry in eighteenth-century Wales.[10]

Below this small and respectable group came the mass of the profession, who spent their lives on the move. Since the population density of early modern Europe was low relative to that of the twentieth century, many more services had to be provided on an itinerant basis. Entertainers, like tinkers and pedlars, travelled from place to place. It was easier to change their audience than their repertoire, and to change their audience they had to travel from town to town or from fair to fair, stopping at such villages as might be on the way. In Central Europe, in particular, they were no respecters of political frontiers, and it is to men like these – as much as to archaic Indo-European traditions – that European popular culture owed its unity.* The puppet-showman, J. B. Hilverding, was in Prague in 1698, in Danzig in 1699, in Stockholm in 1700, in Nuremberg in 1701, and in Basel in 1702.

Itinerant entertainers might travel alone or in troupes. According to a sixteenth-century Russian church council, the *skomorokhi* wandered about 'in bands of up to sixty, seventy or even one hundred men'. In eighteenth-century England, troupes of strolling players could be seen on the road, some too poor to travel by coach but still smartly dressed to attract attention. Two actors would be sent ahead of the rest to get permission to play in the towns and villages on their route. Their properties and costumes would be secondhand, even dilapidated, and they would perform in inns or barns; hence the nineteenth-century term of contempt for their 'barnstorming'.[11]

The French *bateleurs* lived a similar life and so did the Spanish *farsantes*. One of them, Agustín de Rojas, has left a lively description of the hard life of the players. He distinguished eight kinds of company according to the size of the group, its repertoire, its wealth, and the number of days it spent in a given place before taking to the road again. The bottom four types described by Rojas might be described as 'popular'. Of these the largest was the *cambaleo*. 'The *cambaleo* is a woman who sings and five men who weep'; they could stay from four to six days in the same place because they could perform a comedy, two *autos* (religious plays), and three or four comic interludes. Rather less

---

*It is to be hoped that a historian will one day follow these wanderers across Europe (via the permissions to perform still preserved in municipal archives), and so discover how far they usually travelled before turning back.

grand was the *gangarilla*, composed of three or four men, 'one who can play the fool and a boy who plays the women's roles . . . they eat roast meat, sleep on the ground, drink their draught of wine, travel constantly, perform in every farmyard'. Next came the *ñaque*. 'The *ñaque* is two men . . . they sleep in their clothes, go barefoot and don't satisfy their hunger'; their only props are a false beard and a tambourine. At the very bottom of the scale came the *bululú*, 'an actor by himself, who travels on foot. He enters a village, goes to the priest and tells him that he knows a play and a *loa* or two'. (A *loa* was a verse prologue to an *auto*.)[12]

The *bululú* was only one of many nomadic individual entertainers. A vivid impression of one of them has been left by Georges de la Tour, in a painting now in the Musée des Beaux-Arts at Nates; (Plate 3) a blind old man is singing and accompanying himself on the *vielle*, a sort of rustic lute known in England as a 'hurdy-gurdy'. Such wandering musicians often figure in the records of almsgiving by the Church in sixteenth-century Languedoc. Some were priests, which tells us something about the wealth and status of the lower clergy at this time. Some played the *vielle*, others the serpent. By the eighteenth century the hurdy-gurdy had been replaced by the fiddle, but *chanteurs-chansonniers* or ballad-mongers still wandered about like journeymen on their *tour de France*. In Italy the *cantastorie*, or 'singers of tales', wandered from place to place, singing in the piazza and accompanying themselves on some instrument, usually the *viola*. Their epics were sometimes so long that the recital might have to be spread over several successive days. In Serbia, such singers of tales were called *guslari*, because they accompanied themselves on the *gusle*, a kind of one-stringed fiddle. In Russia they were known as *kobzari* because they played the *kobza*, another variety of lute; their rivals were the *kaleki*, who specialised in songs about the saints. In Wales and Ireland, it was the harp which was the favourite instrument of the nomadic entertainer; in Spain, by the end of the period, it was the guitar. Other individual wanderers were the puppet-showmen, like Master Pedro in *Don Quixote*.[13]

Professional entertainers were in many ways a distinctive group. They wore unusual clothes, gay and parti-coloured; the *skomorokhi* wore short tunics in the western style; Tabarin was

1 Street Singers. German, 17th century. Nuremburg: Germanisches Nationalmuseum

2   Newsvendor. German, 16th century. Paris: Bibliothèque Nationale

3 Georges La Tour, "The hurdy-gurdy man". French, 17th century.
Nantes, Musée des Beaux-Arts

4 Skomorokhi at Ladoga in 1634. Engraving from A. Olearius, *Reisen,* 1647.
London, British Library

5 Charlatans on Piazza S. Marco. From G. Franco, *Habiti d'Huomini e Donne,*
Venice 1609. London: British Library

6　Charlatans in Paris, early 17th century. Paris, Bibliothèque Nationale

7　King Karvel and Ogier the Dane. Painted chest from Gudbrandsdal, Norway (perhaps by Jakob Klukstad). Oslo, Norsk Folkemuseum

8　Björn Frøysak, a Norwegian peasant and family. Painting 1699 Oslo, Norsk Folkemuseum

Credit est mort
(il faut prier Dieu)

CREDIT   EST   MORT

Courons petits et grands à cet enterrement
Nostre credit est mort, sa gloire est en fumée,
Il ne nous reste plus qu'un peu de renommée,
Que nous allons poser dessus son monument.

Si preste non tât, si tât non tout, si tout non tel, si tel non gré.
15 Car a prester cousin germain, au rendre fils de putain

Rotisseurs, Hosteliers, Charcuitiers, boulengers,   Les grands et les petis souffrent fort maintenant
Depuis que le Credit fut mis dessous la tombe,   Qu'ils n'ont plus de credit l'assistance propice;
Ne prestent a pas vn soient voisins ou estrangers,   Chacun pleure et larmoye, hautement se plaigna
Par les mauuais payeurs, sur tout ce malheur tombe. Comme vn enfant qu'on seure de sa nourice.

9   "Credit is dead". Engraving from J. Lagniet, *Recueil des Plus Illustres Proverbes*, Paris 1657. London, British Library

10 The mice bury the cat. Russian broadside, c1725 (perhaps by Vasily Koren)

The text within the image (in old Swedish script):

Carolus för man minns
jor med har wari fäll.
Pror knapt den förrek finnes
uppå de gansse wätt
fienden han twinga ått som
en dröra man ded här ån
ne bekräftes oth om
wär säies han
1746
F.R.

11 & 12 Medal of Admiral Vernon, 1739. London, British Museum:
Department of Coins and Medals

13 Charles XII. Painted hanging by Gustaf Reuter, 1746. Stockholm,
Nordiska Museet

Mascharç da Ebrei

14   The Four Sons of Aymon. Detail from 17th-century Dutch painting by
Pieter Saenredam. London, National Gallery

15   Chap-book version of the *Four Sons of Aymon,* Amsterdam 1602.
London, British Library

16   Musicians masked as Jews, from F. Bertelli, *Il Carnevale Italiano
Mascherato,* Venice 1642. London: British Library

LA FOLIE DES HOMMES.

La Femme porte Le Fuzi Le mari porte Lenfan sur ses Genou

Le chasseur chase sur la mer et le poison vollé en la ir

17 The World Upside Down. 18th century French broadside

18 Political plate, c1790. Nevers, Musée Municipal

19 & 20 Political prints, 1789, by Andre Basset. Paris: Musée Carnavalet. Photo: Girardon

famous for the unusual shape of his hat. They had unusual nicknames like 'Sourmilk', a lute-player who turned up in Ochsenfurt in 1511, or 'Brûle-Maison', a noted singer from eighteenth-century Lille. Many were gypsies, much in demand in central Europe as musicians and sometimes becoming famous like the Czinka family in eighteenth-century Hungary. Many were from Savoy, where the land was not fertile enough to support the whole population and many young men had to leave, especially for the winter months. Where the Swiss became mercenaries, the Savoyards turned pedlars, fiddlers, flute-players, organ-grinders, fortune-tellers or showmen, with a peepshow strapped to their backs or a marmot on a leash. Others were from southern Italy, from Basilicata for example, where the peasants 'learn from their infancy to wield the mattock with one hand and the flageolet or bagpipe with the other' and could be found travelling Italy, France and even Spain.[14]

Like other nomads, these travelling folk did not always enjoy a good reputation with more sedentary people. The sons of the German players were considered *unehrlich*, 'lacking in honour', and so ineligible for membership in guilds, like the sons of hangmen and grave-diggers. The German players were not infrequently accused of witchcraft, and the *skomorokhi*, too, had the reputation of sorcerers, no doubt because of their conjuring tricks.[15]

The travelling entertainers were often regarded as beggars, and it must sometimes have been difficult to distinguish the professional singer who had fallen on evil days from the beggar who sang or played because he could not ask for charity without losing his self-respect. In any case, the distinction can scarcely have meant much to the magistrates, sedentary members of the upper classes concerned with the virtues of order and hard work. Their attitudes are reflected in the notorious English Act for the 'restraining of vagabonds' passed in 1572, which lumped together 'all fencers bear-wards common players in interludes and minstrels . . . all jugglers pedlars tinkers and petty chapmen', and forebade them all to 'wander abroad' without a licence from two justices of the peace.[16]

Many of these vagabond-entertainers seem to have been blind. In Spain the common name for a street singer used to be *ciego*, 'blind man'. Such terms often reflect stereotypes rather than realities, but in this case there is a good deal of supporting evidence. In eighteenth-century Palermo and Madrid, for instance, the blind ballad-singers had their own fraternity and their own privileges. The Russian *kobzari* and *kaleki* – whose name means 'cripple' – were often described as blind. Vuk Stefanović Karadžić wrote that the heroic epics of Serbia owed their circulation in his day to blind singers: 'The blind men go begging from house to house right round the country. In front of every house they sing a song, and then ask for something to be given them; when something is offered they will sing more.' Filip Višnjić told Karadžić 'he became blind as a young man as the result of smallpox and then went round the whole pashalik of Bosnia and right down to Skadar, begging and singing to the *gusle*'. Višnjić, one of the greatest of the *guslari*, eventually prospered, acquired his own horse and cart and, according to Karadžić, became 'a proper gentleman'.[17] He was only one of a number of distinguished blind performers in the eighteenth century, which included the Welsh harper John Parry and the Irish harpers Arthur O'Neill and Carolan.[18] In the seventeenth century there was the ballad singer Philippot. In the sixteenth century, famous blind singers included the Portuguese Balthasar Dias, the Hungarian Sebestyén Tinódi, the Italian Niccolò d'Arezzo, the German Jörg Graff, a former *Landsknecht*. The reader may well be wondering what percentage of the population of Europe was blind in those days – presumably it was considerably higher than now – or why blind men should have predominated in Homer's profession – perhaps because a gifted man with all his faculties was unlikely to choose this dishonourable occupation. (cf.p.255 below)

Among this crowd of travelling performers, there were a few whose chief aim was not to entertain. Schoolmasters and preachers took to the roads on occasions in this period. Itinerant schoolmasters were known in eighteenth-century Wales, where they were sometimes said to be converted harpers or fiddlers, and in eighteenth-century France, where they hired themselves out at fairs, wearing one, two or three feathers in their caps according to whether they taught reading, reading and writing, or arithmetic as well. Then there are the wandering holy men – orthodox or unorthodox – like the prophet calling himself 'Missus a Deo', who arrived in Bologna in 1517 and preached against the religious orders until the authorities expelled him from the city.[19]

Prominent among the Catholic preachers are the friars. St Francis had described his own order as 'god's minstrels' (*joculatores Domini*), and the parallel was in fact a close one in many respects. Like the minstrels, the friars wandered from town to town and often performed in the market-place – for the churches were not big enough to hold everyone who came to listen to them. Contemporaries estimated some of the crowds at 15–20,000, and some people came the night before to be sure of a place. The friars seem to have learned a trick or two from the minstrels in whose steps they followed, for disapproving references can be found to preachers who, 'in the manner of buffoons, tell silly stories and make the people roar with laughter'. Bernardino da Feltre took his sandal off and threw it at a man who was sleeping during his sermon. Some Franciscans certainly acted in the pulpit; even St Bernardino had been known to imitate the sound of a trumpet or the buzzing of a fly. Roberto Caracciolo, preaching a crusade, was said to have thrown off his gown in mid-sermon to reveal a suit of armour underneath. Barletta's sermon-notes frequently say 'shout' (*clama*). Olivier Maillard wrote himself the following stage-directions in the margin of a sermon: 'sit down – stand up – mop yourself – ahem! ahem! – now shriek like a devil'.[20]

The parallel – and the competition – between preachers and professional entertainers was often remarked in our period, notably by Diderot, describing Venice as a city where 'in a single square you can see on one side a stage with mountebanks performing merry but monstrously indecent farces, and on the other, another stage with priests performing farces of a different complexion and shouting out: "Take no notice of those wretches, gentlemen; the Pulcinello you are flocking to is a feeble fool; here (displaying the crucifix) is the genuine Pulcinello!" '.[21] The story that the French Jesuit preacher Emond Auger had been a bear-ward in secular life was certainly *ben trovato* and may even have been true.

Some Protestant preachers followed the example of the friars. Anabaptist lay preachers wandered sixteenth-century Germany, and Calvinist preachers wandered the Cévennes. In North Wales in the mid-seventeenth century a notable figure was Vavasor Powell, 'the metropolitan of the itinerants', as his opponents called him; he preached in Welsh at markets and fairs. In England at the same time there were many 'enthusiastic' sectarian lay preachers about, making their way from one market or barn to another, performing cures as well as preaching sermons, learning from the cunning folk as well as from the clergy. The greatest of these preachers, John Bunyan, was already familiar with the wandering life from his tinker's trade. As for histrionics, the seventeenth-century dissenting preacher was described as one who 'acts much with his hands, striking them together or beating his breast, or flinging them about in a rapturous manner'.[22]

The amateurs

The professional tradition-bearers described so far are only the tip of the iceberg, but the others are barely visible. There were the amateurs and there were the semi-professionals, part-time specialists who had another occupation but might derive a supplementary income from their singing, playing or healing. We know about them only when they were organised into societies, or attracted the attention of the upper classes or the authorities for some reason, because they were outstanding performers, or suspect of sedition, heresy or witchcraft.

In south-western Europe, where cities were more important than elsewhere, plays and other festivities were often mounted by town craftsmen, grouped into guilds, fraternities, or clubs with fancy titles like the 'Abbeys' of Folly and Misrule. The English mystery plays were performed by the guilds, like the butchers or the carpenters of York, the shearmen or the tailors of Coventry, sometimes with the help of professional actors who took the leading parts. The Spanish guilds likewise mounted pageants for the feast of Corpus Christi. In Paris, the Confrérie de la Passion, which put on many mystery plays in the fifteenth and sixteenth centuries, was a fraternity of craftsmen, described contemptuously in 1542 as 'gens ignares, artisans mecaniques, ne sachant ni A ni B'. In Florence, the guilds, or guild-based clubs like the so-called 'powers' (*Potenze*), played an important part in mystery plays and pageants, especially for the feast of St John the Baptist, the patron of the city. In sixteenth-century Siena, plays were written by members of a club called the 'Rustics' (*Rozzi*), from which people of high status were formally excluded. Among the leading members of the *Rozzi* were a paper-seller called Silvestro, who took the nickname 'Smoky' (*Fumoso*), and a tailor called Gianbattista, whose nickname was 'Fantastic' (*Falatico*). In German towns, too, groups of craftsmen mounted plays and pageants, especially for Carnival. In Nuremberg in particular, craftsmen achieved fame for writing plays, notably the tinsmith Hans Rosenplüt and the barber Hans Folz (both in the fifteenth century), and, above all, the shoemaker Hans Sachs, who wrote 200-odd plays and some 2,000 shorter pieces. One wonders how he found the time to make any shoes.[23]

Alternatively, the various wards of the city might organise festivities, as they did in Siena, where the *contrade* mounted the famous race, *il palio*, in this period as they do today. Towns might compete with one another to compose and perform the best play. These competitions were particularly important in the Netherlands; nineteen dramatic societies or 'chambers of rhetoric' (*rederijkkamers*) took part in the competition in 1539. Fourteen of these societies represented towns, and the remaining five came from the countryside. Rural amateur dramatics seem to have been exceptionally important – or exceptionally well-documented – in Flanders, perhaps because the region was more highly urbanised than elsewhere, making it easier for villagers to imitate the ways of townsmen. It was said that in eighteenth-century Flanders, every village had its club, often run by the local schoolmaster or by a professional *liedzanger*, performing at fairs or on Sunday evenings. The English mummers do not seem to have matched this enthusiasm. They too performed plays in the eighteenth century, but only once or twice a year. References in the Essex records suggest that they were already doing this kind of thing in the sixteenth century.[24]

Poems as well as plays were composed and recited by craftsmen in the chambers of rhetoric in the Netherlands and in the French *puys*. There were regular poetry competitions and prizes, like the *jocs florals* in Toulouse. Sixteenth-century German *Meistergesang* was largely an art-form of craftsmen, notably tailors, weavers and shoemakers; the complicated metres must have made the craft as difficult to master as the elaborate goldsmith's work cultivated at the time in the same German cities. These organisations were at once expressions of civic patriotism, the cultural equivalent of the citizen-militia, with its feasts and shooting-competitions, and an indication of how seriously the performing arts were taken in those days.[25]

Of course, craftsmen and peasants did not have the monopoly of festive organisations. Noblemen belonged to some of the societies which organised street entertainments, like the Abbey of the Conards in sixteenth-century Rouen or the *Infanterie de la Mère Folle* in seventeenth-century Dijon. In Paris, some of the farces played during Carnival were the work of the Basoche, a club of lawyers' clerks. At Montpellier and elsewhere, students were prominent in this kind of performance and even now, some four hundred years after the event, some of their pieces have not lost the atmosphere of a rag or a student revue.[26]

In these cases (which all come, significantly, from the first half of our period), we see the educated, the upper classes, participating collectively in popular culture. It is hardly surprising, then, to find some well-known individuals helping to create it. The authors of French mystery plays include one princess, Marguerite de Navarre, and the authors of Florentine mystery plays include a professor of canon law at Pisa, Pierozzo Castellani, and the ruler of Florence, the 'magnificent' Lorenzo de' Medici. Lorenzo also composed songs for Carnival, and so did his younger contemporary Niccolò Machiavelli. The sixteenth-century nobleman, Gian Giorgio Alione, wrote farces in the dialect of Asti. Among the known composers of ballads which circulated on broadsheets we find Fray Ambrosio Montesino, who was confessor to Queen Isabella of Spain; and in England, among others of less note, we find Andrew Marvell, MP; Thomas Warton, MP, the author of *Lilliburlero*; and Jonathan Swift. In Scotland there was Mrs Brown of Falkland, a professor's wife. As this juxtaposition suggests, what was unusual about Mrs Brown was not that she composed ballads but that she composed them in the traditional manner, by extemporisation.[27]

After the upper-class amateurs we know most about the lower-class semi-professionals. Of the *chanteurs-chansonniers* of eighteenth-century France, Alexandre was a mason, Hayez a *mulquinier*, while Bazolle 'La Joie' was, or had been, a soldier. John Graeme of Sowport in Cumberland was described by Walter Scott as 'by profession an itinerant cleaner of clocks and watches'. It is likely that off the main routes it was the semi-professionals who were dominant in this period, and that they were mainly recruited from itinerant occupations, which included that of tailor. Adam Ferguson once recorded a heroic poem from a travelling tailor working in his father's house; Adam Puschman, a sixteenth-century German *Meistersinger*, was another tailor; and in nineteenth-century Russia, an important source of *byliny* for Rybnikov was the tailor Leonty Bogdanovich.[28] A few of this group who achieved fame or turned professional have left valuable details about their earlier lives. Some emerge into visibility at just the moment when they were ceasing to be popular poets. Giovan Domenico Pèri began as a shepherd who improvised songs while he looked after his sheep, learning his craft from Ariosto and Tasso. (It was the same with Divizia, the illiterate peasant woman Montaigne met near Lucca: she learned to compose verses by listening to her uncle reading Ariosto). Pèri attracted the attention of Archduke Cosimo II of Tuscany and was enabled to publish his poems – and to abandon the popular style. The same might be said for Stephen Duck, who learned the poet's craft by studying Milton while he was a Wiltshire thresher, was taken up by Queen Caroline, and became a clergyman. Pietro Fullone, a miner from seventeenth-century Palermo, became a legend in his lifetime for the facility with which he improvised verses, but there is a curious gap between this legend and the published poetry attributed to him, which is not popular at all. Other poets seem to have remained within the popular tradition after they were well-known, like John Taylor, the Thames waterman, or Giulio Cesare Croce, who worked as a blacksmith in Bologna before turning professional. From his autobiography we learn that he was inspired to write verses after a neighbour had given him a broken-down copy of Ovid's *Metamorphoses*.[29]

More obscure are the part-time storytellers, musicians, preachers and healers, who were not taken up by the great as the poets were. How many storytellers of the calibre of Die Frau Viehmännin existed before 1800? Were traditions of storytelling of equal importance all over Europe? In Ireland the *seanchaidhthe*, or shanachies, seem to have played a particularly important role between the mid-seventeenth century, when the English destroyed the old Irish nobility on whom the traditional bards depended, and the mid-nineteenth century, the time of the Great Famine. The shanachie was an ordinary countryman with extraordinary skills as a raconteur. He told his stories in Irish and learned his repertoire either in the family or from travelling entertainers. His Welsh equivalent, the *cyfarwydd*, was also active in the eighteenth century. Foreign tourists allow us a few precious glimpses of Italian story tellers at the end of the eighteenth century. An English clergyman recalled – with some distaste – having seen 'on the quay at Naples, . . . a thin emaciated object reading with infinite gesticulation and emphasis the *Orlando Furioso* and translating it into the Neapolitan dialect'. On the quay at Venice, Goethe saw a man telling stories in dialect to a mainly lower-class audience, and admired the variety and the force of his gestures. Was Straparola a storyteller like these?[30]

About the musicians we know something only when the authorities tried to regulate them, as they did, for example, in Sweden and Switzerland. In Sweden in the seventeenth and eighteenth centuries, musicians were attached to a particular hundred or parish and had to be furnished with a *garningsbrev* or permit to work in this way. In French Switzerland, too, the *ménétriers* or players were subject to regulation by Calvinist consistories and from the record it emerges that they were rarely full-time professionals, but servants, shoemakers, tailors, masons or carpenters. It may well be significant that these were all itinerant occupations. Other part-timers, in all probability, were the 'old women that are hired in Calabria to howl at burials', as an English visitor so unkindly put it, the keeners, familiar figures in Ireland, the Scottish Highlands and in Russia; but we know all too little about these performers.[31]

A greater worry to the authorities – and vice versa – were the lay preachers, prophets, healers and diviners. A few achieved fame before their mouths were stopped, like Hans Böhm, 'the drummer of Niklashausen', a shepherd from the Würzbürg area (and a drummer on holidays), who was inspired to preach the egalitarian millennium in 1476; or Pietro Bernardo, a Florentine goldsmith who began to preach and prophesy in Savonarolan style about the year 1496, and was executed six years later; or Gonzalo Anes Bandarra, a Portuguese shoemaker turned poet and prophet, who fell into the hands of the Inquisition.[32]

Less spectacular were the majority of the popular healers and diviners, who can be found in many parts of Europe with different names but similar techniques. In England they were known as 'cunning men' and 'wise women'; in Sweden, similarly, as *kloka gubbarna* and *visa käringarna*; in Poland as *mądry,* 'wise ones'; in Spain, as *saludadores,* 'healers'; in Sicily, as *giravoli,* 'wanderers'; and so on. They treated their patients with herbs, or, as in Spain, with bread moistened in the healer's mouth, with their spittle, and, not least, with a variety of charms, prayers, and rituals in which candles and (in Catholic countries) even consecrated wafers had their part. Some specialised in particular ailments, as the *giravoli* did in snakebite, others were more general practitioners, treating both animals and men. Some of them practised 'soothsaying' or divination as well, finding lost money, discovering the faces of thieves in a bowl of water (for the crystal ball is a more recent piece of equipment), or revealing their names by means of the oracle of the sieve balanced on the points of a pair of shears, and turning when the guilty person is named.

The wise woman was often a midwife, who might assist the woman in labour with spells as well as the official prayers; the cunning man might exercise all sorts of occupations. In northern Italy in the sixteenth century, there are references to healers who were peasants, priests, shepherds, masons and weavers. In Sweden the *kloka* included Lapps, whom the Swedes regarded as not quite human, and also clergymen, smiths, and musicians, three occupations traditionally associated with magical powers.* Some healers boasted that they had been born under a favourable constellation or with their heads covered with the 'caul' (a fragment of the amniotic membrane). How they learned their craft we rarely know; presumably much of it was handed down in the family, perhaps supplemented by memories of an urban charlatan, a cunning man on a grander scale.[33]

An occupational hazard of the cunning folk was to be accused of sorcery, on the grounds that 'whoever knows how to heal knows how to harm' (*qui scit sanare scit destruere*), as a witness said at a trial in Modena in 1499. In France, the cunning man was sometimes known as a *conjureur* or *maige* (magician), while wise women were commonly described as witches. This fearsome reputation is hardly surprising. Their clients had recourse to them only for complaints which they could not deal

---

* A ballad collected in eighteenth-century Scotland (Child 44) also presents the 'coal-black smith' as an expert in magical transformation.

with by themselves, which suggested a supernatural origin, and how could the cunning folk acquire their familiarity with the supernatural, if not with the devil's aid? Photographs of cunning folk taken in Finland and in Sweden early this century, when the tradition still flourished, show them with wide, staring yet vacant eyes, frightening enough when encountered merely between the pages of a book. It is hardly surprising that they should sometimes have been accused of witchcraft and the evil eye.[34]

Thanks to such accusations, historians have been able to discover something about individual practitioners. Román Ramírez, a Morisco *curandero* and storyteller, arrested by the Inquisition in 1595, was barely literate – the inquisitors tested him – but owned a few books, among them Dioscorides on medicine and the famous romance of chivalry *Amadis de Gaule*. An exceptionally well-documented case is that of Catharina Fagerberg, 'the wise maid', a tailor's daughter from Småland in Sweden, who was tried for sorcery in 1732 – and acquitted. Catharina cured people from *trollskotter*, 'magic shots', as ailments of unknown origin were called, and she cast out evil spirits, and also sent out her own spirit to discover what was happening in other places. She asked her patients if they had enemies, and told them to seek reconciliation. These details suggest that Catharina might be described in traditional terms as a shamaness and in modern terms as a cross between a medium and a psychiatrist. The impression is confirmed if we look at studies of folk-healers today, in Mexico for instance, for they, like her, encourage the patients to 'confess' their problems, and work by first inducing and then relieving anxiety and guilt.[35]

Amateur popular painters are also recorded. Among the church painters of seventeenth-century Norway there were several village clergymen.[36]

Settings

To understand any item of culture we need to place it in context, which includes its physical context or social setting, public or private, indoor or outdoor, for this physical space helps to structure the events which take place in it. In so far as popular culture was transmitted at home, within doors, it virtually escapes the historian of this period. Only by projecting backwards the descriptions of 'tale occasions' given by modern folklorists and juxtaposing them to some fictional accounts of the sixteenth and seventeenth centuries can we imagine the setting for traditional narratives: the storyteller in his chair – if there was one – by the fire on a winter evening, or the group of women congregating in one house to spin and to tell stories while they worked. With the private house we can include the barn, the setting for performances by wandering actors and preachers.[37]

There is much more to say about public settings: the church, the tavern and the market-place. The church was often used for secular purposes in this period as it had been in the Middle Ages, in spite of the objections of both Catholic and Protestant clergy. Mystery plays were performed in the church. The churchyard was used for dancing and feasting by the Lord of Misrule and his merry men. The church itself was the setting for the parish 'wake' (French *veille*, Italian *veglia*). On the eve of the feast of their patron saint, the parishioners might spend the night in church, eating and drinking, singing and dancing. The persistence of this custom tells us something about the lack of social facilities in the villages of the period and something about popular attitudes to the sacred: more intimate, more familiar than they were later to become. The church was especially important as a cultural centre in regions where people lived in scattered homesteads, as in Norway, and might not otherwise meet.[38]

Still more important a centre for popular culture in town and country was the inn, tavern, ale-house or beer-cellar. For England between 1500 and 1800, the evidence is overwhelming. Inns were places for watching cock-fights or for playing cards or backgammon, throwing dice or bowling at nine-pins. Minstrels and harpers performed in taverns and there was dancing, sometimes with hobbyhorses. Ale-houses were a setting for popular art. 'In these houses', we are told, 'you shall see the history of Judith, Susanna, Daniel in the lion's den, or Dives and Lazarus painted upon the wall'. Broadside ballads were sometimes pasted on the walls of inns so that more people could join in the singing. The host and the customers passed on rumours and gossip, criticised the authorities and, during the Reformation, disputed about the sacraments or the innovations in religion. *Robin Goodfellow his mad pranks and merry jests* is set in an ale-house in Kent, and the hostess is presented telling the story to her customers. Even the godly might meet at inns to talk about religion, taking a private room to avoid interruption.

In London in particular, certain inns – and their yards – were important cultural centres, with the innkeeper acting as impresario or *animateur*. If you wanted to see bear-baiting, clowns, cock-fights, fencers, a performing horse, not to mention plays, the places to go, in the late sixteenth century, were the Bell, the Cross Keys, and the Bel Sauvage, all in Gracechurch Street. Leading figures from the entertainment world kept taverns, like Richard Tarleton the clown or, in the eighteenth century, Daniel Mendoza the pugilist (who had fought in inn-yards), and Thomas Topham the strong-man. Certain inns near Covent Garden, like the Harlequin in Drury Lane, were the haunts of eighteenth-century actors, employed or unemployed. Plays were still performed in the yard of the Queen's Arms at Southwark in the eighteenth century.[39]

English inns and taverns have been studied more carefully than their continental equivalents – the French *cabaret* (*oustal* in the south), the Spanish *venta*, the Polish *gospoda*, or *karczma*, the German *Wirtshaus*, and so on – so it is difficult to say whether the English pub was of unique cultural importance or not. Probably not, for the French *cabaretier* has recently been described as 'a key figure in popular culture, a centre of information . . . an organiser of collective rejoicing'. He might organise riots as well as festivals, like François Siméon, called 'the little Moor', in south-west France in 1635. Similarly, innkeepers played a prominent part in the German peasants' war of 1525.[40] Dutch painting reminds us of the importance of the tavern as a place to dance – inside or outside – and so does the Hungarian term *csárdas*, derived from *csárda*, a country inn. Inns were associated with actors on the Continent as in England. References to innkeepers in German Carnival plays suggest that the plays were performed in this setting: one has to imagine the troupe bursting in unexpectedly, asking for silence, and beginning to perform. In eighteenth-century France, singers performed in *cabarets*, and one of them in Paris, the Tambour Royal, was a well-known haunt of actors. In Spain, wandering puppet-showmen like Master Pedro in *Don Quixote* used to perform in inns. In exile on his country estate, Machiavelli relaxed in the local *hosteria* and played *cricca* and *trich-trach* with the miller and the baker.[41]

However, it is likely that the tavern was less important as a centre of entertainment in the south of Europe than in the north. In the Mediterranean countries, the real focus of popular culture was the *piazza*. There were puppet-shows in the market-place in seventeenth-century Seville, while in Madrid you could watch plays, bull-fights, races and tournaments in the Plaza Mayor, or listen to ballads, if the singers were not drowned by the cries of the knife-grinders and the chestnut women. In Rome, people went to Piazza Navona to watch the charlatans and fire-eaters, or to Piazza Pasquino for the latest pasquinades. In Florence, Piazza Signoria was the place for official spectacles, Piazza S. Croce the place to watch buffalo-races, bull-fights or football, and Piazza S. Martino (near Or San Michele) the place to listen to the singers of tales. In Venice, it was Piazza S. Marco where the leading charlatans set up their benches, made their jests and sold their medicines.

Piazza culture extended to Paris, for Place de Grève was the centre for public spectacles like executions – Cartouche was broken on the wheel there in 1721 – or the bonfires on St John's Eve. It extended as far north as Lille, where singers performed on the Petite Place. Bridges were cultural centres as well as squares, and in Paris after 1600 it was the Pont-Neuf which was the great haunt of players and puppet-masters, charlatans and tooth-drawers, ballad-singers and hawkers of pamphlets, not to mention recruiting-sergeants, orange-sellers and cutpurses. One man, nicknamed 'le Rhingrave', sold songs and onions as well. So important were the singers there that the term *pont-neuf* came to mean no more than 'song'.[42]

What happened every day on the Pont-Neuf happened in many parts of Europe on market-days or during fairs. The economic importance of fairs in pre-industrial Europe is well known; they were itinerant shopping-centres, the counterpart to the pedlar, but on a gigantic scale. In a given region the fair was timed to coincide with a major festival: the feast of the Ascension at Venice (a fifteen-day fair), the feast of St Anthony at Padua (another fifteen-day fair), and so on. At fairs the peasants would have a chance to buy chap-books or pottery figures which they might never otherwise see.

What needs more emphasis here are the non-economic aspects of the institution. Fairs were not only places for sheep and horses to be traded and servants hired, but, as in the less developed countries today, they were places for young people to meet away from family supervision, and places for everyone to watch travelling entertainers or dance or hear the latest news.[43] Sixteenth-century Sweden was a small enough country for the king to go to the *marknadsmöten* or 'market-meetings' to explain his policies to the people and discover what they were thinking. Around the year 1600, troupes of English and French actors used to go to Frankfurt twice a year, at Easter and in the autumn, to entertain the crowds at the fairs.[44] Outside Paris, a distinctive form of theatre grew up in the later seventeenth century at the Foire St-Germain, which ran from 3 February till Easter, and the Foire St-Laurent, which lasted from the end of June till about 1 October. Here, among the coffee-shops and toyshops, the acrobats and the exotic animals, Italian actors presented plays, or (when these were forbidden as infringements of the theatrical monopoly of the Comédie Française) put on silent shows, comic operas and pantomimes.[45]

In England, Bartholomew Fair and Stourbridge Fair were leading centres of entertainment. Batholomew Fair was held at Smithfield on 25 August, the feast of St Bartholomew. There, in the seventeenth century, you could see plays, puppet-shows, clowns, rope-dancers and waxworks, introduced by showmen dressed as fools or as wild men of the woods, while your ears were assaulted by drums and penny trumpets, your nose by what Ned Ward described as 'the odoriferous effluvia that arose from the singeing of pigs', for roast pork was a part of the occasion.

The fair held at Stourbridge, near Cambridge, lasted three weeks from 8 September. When James I issued orders against the 'unprofitable games' at Stourbridge, he mentioned 'bull-baiting, bear-baiting, common plays, public shows, interludes, comedies and tragedies in the English tongue, games at loggets, nine-holes', and other seventeenth-century evidence enables us to add horse-races and performances by tumblers, conjurers, preachers, puppets and rope-dancers, perhaps the same puppets and rope-dancers who were to be seen at Bartholomew Fair a few days before. Such was the convenience of meeting at the fair that it even attracted the godly. The Presbyterians held a synod at Stourbridge Fair about 1588, and in 1678 the Muggletonians met there.[46]

Tradition and creativity

The most important question to ask about these craftsmen and performers, professional and amateur, is also the most difficult to answer. How great was their individual contribution? The traditional performer has sometimes been presented, from the Grimm brothers onwards, as no more than the mouthpiece of the community, a spokesman for popular tradition. Yet other scholars and critics, from the time of A. W. Schlegel and Walter Scott, have emphasised the importance of the individual tradition-bearer, who has his own way of singing his song or telling his tale.[47] Who is right? There is something odd in trying to generalise about individuality at all: obviously some singers or storytellers or clowns or painters were more creative than others. In any case there is too little evidence about even the most famous tradition-bearers of the period 1500–1800 to support any clear-cut conclusion. All that can be done at this point is to present some arguments against both extremes and to invite the reader to take his choice from the middle bands of the spectrum.

The extreme position that *das Volk dichtet,* that the people create collectively, is not difficult to refute. We have seen that many individual performers and some craftsmen were known by name in this period and that some of them enjoyed a great reputation. Richard Tarleton, for example, has been described as 'the first actor to achieve stardom'. That some performers were well aware of their gifts and liked to outdo their colleagues we know from the competitions which not infrequently took place. John Parry had a famous playing-contest with a fellow-harper, Hugh Shon Prys, and Carolan had a 'scalding match' with MacCabe. In the seventeenth century, the *sfida* or challenge from one popular poet to another to improvise the best verses seems to have been an institution in Sicily as in Japan.[48]

Modern studies of tradition-bearers suggest that some are 'faithful unto incomprehension', preserving phrases they do not understand, but that others are not dominated by the tradition they guard, and feel free to reinterpret it according to their personal preferences. In most cases they do not learn a song or story by heart but recreate it at every performance, a procedure which gives plenty of scope for innovation. Hence, as the

American folklorist Phillips Barry put it, 'there are texts, but no *text*; tunes, but no *tune*'.[49]

That this was also how performers worked in early modern Europe is suggested by the fact that the ballads recorded in this period, like those recorded later, come in a number of variants. One collector of the late eighteenth century, 'Otmar', pointed out that the singers he knew told their stories differently every time according to their audience or even according to the weather. In the case of a few singers at the end of the period, such as Filip Višnjić, whose performances were recorded in detail by Karadžić, it has even proved possible to study their idiosyncrasies and innovations in some detail. In other cases we have to be content with vaguer contemporary or sub-contemporary comment. The Italian actor Silvio Fiorillo was given the credit for inventing the character of Pulcinella, while Josef Anton Stranitzky's transformation of the traditional clown's role of Hanswurst, which he played in Salzburg peasant costume, has led him to be described as the creator of the Viennese popular drama – although his own performances were principally for the court. It is not uncommon to find words and music of popular songs attributed to individuals, at least in the second half of our period; Scottish examples include *The auld man's mare's dead,* attributed to Patrick Birnie, a seventeenth-century fiddler, and *Macpherson's Rant,* which another fiddler, James Macpherson, is said to have composed and played on the scaffold immediately before his execution, for reiving, in 1700. In the visual arts, significant innovations have been attributed to peasant painters and carvers such as Malar Erik Eliasson of Dalarna in Sweden, and Jakob Klukstad of Gudbrandsdal in Norway, both active in the later eighteenth century.[50]

This evidence is obviously damaging to the Grimm thesis but it should not lead us to conclude that the individual 'authorship' of a variant of a traditional song or story was exactly like the authorship of a literary work of the period. Some urban popular poets signed off at the end of their words, as if to make sure they got the credit for their inventiveness:

Dass aus dem Schwank kein Unrat wachs,
bitt und begehrt mit Fleiss Hans Sachs.

(*Hans Sachs begs and fervently hopes that his joke will not give rise to anything untoward.*)

However, Sachs was, as has been suggested already, on the margin of traditional popular culture. The more traditional attitude was the one that Karadžić noticed on his travels through Serbia. There, no performer would admit to having composed a new song. 'Everyone denies responsibility, even the true composer, and says that he heard it from someone else'.[51] The performer is aware of his debt to tradition, hence, perhaps, the impersonality of traditional songs and stories, the lack of reference to 'me', the narrator himself. The audience is also aware that the performer is following tradition, so they do not pass on his name with his songs or stories – hence the anonymity of folksong and folktale. The individual may invent, but in an oral culture, as Cecil Sharp emphasised, 'the community selects'. If an individual produces innovations or variations which the community likes, they will be imitated and so pass into the common stock of tradition. If his innovations do not meet with approval, they will perish with him, or even before. Thus successive audiences exercise a 'preventive censorship' and decide whether a given song or story will survive, and in what form it will survive. It is in this sense (apart from their encouragement during the performance) that the people participate in the creation and transformation of popular culture, just as they participate in the creation and transformation of their native language.[52]

In short, the traditional performer was no mere mouthpiece for tradition, but he was not free to invent whatever he liked. He was neither 'performer' nor 'composer' in the modern sense of those terms. He produced his own variations, but within a traditional framework. To describe that framework will be the task of the next chapter.

CHAPTER FIVE

Traditional Forms

Genres

The approach adopted in this chapter will be morphological. Its purpose is to describe the principal varieties of artifact and performance in European popular culture, and the formal conventions of each. It is concerned with the code rather than the messages (a cultural code which has to be mastered before the meaning of individual messages can be deciphered). It attempts to provide a brief inventory of the stock or repertoire of the forms and conventions of popular culture, but not a history of them before 1500, although many of these forms and conventions go back a long way.

In any one region this stock or repertoire was fairly limited. Its riches and variety are apparent only when the inventory is extended to the whole of Europe; when this is done, the variety is so bewildering as almost to hide the recurrence of a few basic types of artifact and performance. They are never quite the same in any two regions, but they are not all that different either: unique combinations of recurrent elements, local variations on European themes.

This point is particularly obvious in the case of the dance.[1] The folk-dances current in early modern Europe have so many names that to list them would take a chapter in itself and make the reader dizzy. Many are called after the region in which they are supposed to have originated: the Italian *forlana* (Friuli), the French *gavotte* (Gap in Dauphiné), the Norwegian *halling* (Hallingdal), the Polish *krakowiak* (Cracow), the Scots *strathspey*. However, these local forms are variations on a few basic types of dance: slow dances or quick ones, with or without twists and leaps, dances of love and dances of war, dances for one person, for couples and for groups.

Dances for groups seem to have been dominant in this period, especially the round-dance and the weapon-dance. The Dalmatian *kolo* or 'wheel' was vividly described by an Italian visitor to the region in the late eighteenth century:

All the dancers, men and women, join hands, form a circle and begin to turn slowly . . . the circle keeps changing its shape and becomes now an ellipse, now a square, as the dance goes faster; finally it turns into great leaps into the air.[2]

The *kolo* (Bulgarian *horo*, Rumanian *hora*) had many varieties and was well known in the Balkans. Round dances, whether or not they were danced so wildly, were common in western Europe too; the Catalans had their *sardana*, the French their *branle*, or, in the 1790s, their *carmagnole*, danced round the tree of liberty or the guillotine. The *farandoulo* of Provence, in which the participants hold hands and dance in a line, may be seen as an adaptation of the round to the long, narrow streets of a traditional urban culture.

The round-dance was for men and women, but a second recurrent type of choral dance was a dance for men only. This was the weapon-dance, its central feature a mimed combat. There was the English morris, danced with sticks or swords, and related in the name and form to the Spanish *morisca*, which mimed the battles of the Christians with the 'Moors', and the Polish *zbójnicki* or 'brigands' dance', in which the participants carried long hatchets which they clashed and threw in the air and caught while they were dancing. Sword-dances seem to have been particularly common in towns in the German-speaking world in the sixteenth and seventeenth centuries, often associated with particular guilds or occupations. In Cologne it was the smiths who danced the sword-dance; in Lübeck the bakers and the soldiers; in Zwickau in Bohemia, the butchers; in Leipzig, the shoemakers; in Breslau (now Wroctaw, in Poland), the skinners; in Danzig (now Gdańsk), it was the sailors.[3]

Solo dances, like the hornpipe and the Norwegian *halling*, were often opportunities for acrobatics. The Norwegian dancers somersaulted and kicked the rafters. Dances for couples were usually more sedate, at least in the opening figures. They often mimed courtship: the man approached the women, who encouraged him but then withdrew; he pursued her; finally she yielded. The *furlana* was a wild dance of this type, and so was the Bavarian *Schuhplattler*, in which the man stamped, slapped his thighs, somersaulted, circled the girl and even jumped over her to get her attention. The *sarabande* was another dance of this kind, described by a modern writer as 'a sexual pantomime of unparalleled suggestiveness'; it was introduced into Spain, possibly from the Arab world, in the late sixteenth century, and quickly condemned by moralists. It was succeeded by the *fandango*, which came to Spain from America about 1700 and provoked a witness to comment that 'it seemed to me impossible that after such a dance the girl could refuse anything to her partner'. The witness should have known what he was talking about, for his name was Casanova.[4] In the *fandango* the couples never touched; in the Provençal *volto*, equally condemned by the moralists, the couples embraced, whirled round, and, still entwined, leapt into the air. Other twisting dances, which were also condemned, included the German *Dreher* and above all the *Walzer*, or waltz, which was a peasant dance taken up by the nobility and bourgeoisie at the end of the eighteenth century.

Like dances, folksongs came in a luxuriant variety of local forms with their own metres and rhyme-schemes and their own names. Italian lyrical songs were and are known as *strambotti* in Lombardy, *vilote* in the Veneto, *rispetti* or *stornelli* in Tuscany, *sunette* in Apulia, *canzuni* or *ciuri* in Sicily. Yet folksongs, like dances, can be divided into a comparatively few types.

One of the most important of these is the narrative song, which it is convenient to call the 'ballad' or 'epic' (according to length), although the singers themselves were more likely to use simpler terms like 'songs' (Danish *viser*, Serbian *pjesme*), 'stories' (the Spanish *romances*), or 'old things' (Russian *stariny*). A recurrent north-west European form of ballad, to be found wherever Germanic languages are spoken, in Britain, the Netherlands, Germany and Scandinavia, is the so-called 'common measure', the alternation of lines with four stresses which do not rhyme and lines with three stresses which do:

> *Young Bekie was as brave a knight*
> *As ever sailed the sea;*
> *An he's doen him to the court of France,*
> *To serve for meat and fee. (Child 53)*

> *Es reit der Herr von Falkenstein*
> *Wohl über ein breite Heide.*
> *Was sieht er an dem Wege stehn?*
> *Ein Mädel mit weissem Kleide.*

> *(The Lord of Falkenstein is riding over a wide heath. What does he see standing in his path? A girl dressed in white.)*[5]

In eastern Europe, wherever Slavic languages were spoken,

heroic epic usually took a looser form in which there was no regular rhyme or assonance at all. A more-or-less ten-syllable line was the norm, with a caesura after four syllables:

Vino pije /Kraljevicu Marko,
Sa staricam /Jevrosimom majkam.

(Marko Kraljević was drinking wine /with old mother Euphrosina.) [6]

In the Romance-speaking parts of Europe, there was not even the relative uniformity of the Germanic and Slavic areas. In Spain the dominant form was a line of eight syllables with assonances between the even lines:

Los vientos eran contrarios,
la luna estaba crecida,
los peces daban gemidos
por el mal tempo que hacía.

(The winds were contrary /the moon was full /the fish were groaning /because of the bad weather). [7]

In Italy, the standard form was *ottava rima*, the tightest of all these forms, a twelve-syllable line in an eight-line stanza rhyming *a b a b a b c c*:

O bona gente che avete ascoltato
el bel contrasto del vivo e del morto
Iddio vi guardi di male e peccato
E diavi pace e ogni bon conforto
Christo del cielo re glorificato
alla fin vi conduca nel buon porto
nel paradiso in quella summa gloria
al vostro onore e finita questa historia.

(O good people who have listened to the fine debate between the living and the dead, God keep you from evil and sin and give you peace and every good comfort; may Christ the glorious king of Heaven lead you in the end to the good harbour, to the height of glory in Heaven; in your honour this story is finished.) [8]

The narrative song was of no fixed length – the distinction between the long 'epic' and the short 'ballad' is a modern one. It is likely that some songs were so long that they had to be sung in instalments. This is the practice of singers of tales in Yugoslavia today; that it was also the practice in some parts of early modern Europe is suggested by the survival in print of popular narrative poems divided into cantos or 'fits' like the English *Gest of Robin Hood* (1,824 lines, 8 fits), the Hungarian *Siege of Eger* (1,800 lines, 4 cantos), or the Italian *Reali di Francia* (nearly 28,000 lines, 94 cantos).[9] The various 'fits' of the English poem seem to correspond to separate performances, for several of them begin 'lythe and listin, gentlemen'. The first canto of the *Reali di Francia* ends like this:

> *Per oggi son le mie imprese finite:*
> *Ritornate domane e hor partite.*
>
> *(I have finished for today: go away now and come back tomorrow),*

and the second canto begins, 'Io vi lasciasi nel fin de l'altro canto' (I left you at the end of the other canto). The canto tends to end at a moment of suspense – the singers of tales would have had little to learn from modern writers of serials.

The narrative song has been discussed in relative detail because of its importance in the popular culture of many parts of Europe; other kinds of song will be dealt with more briefly. A few recurrent types may be described as separate genres in the sense of combinations of function, mood, and imagery. There is the praise-song, for example, whether the praises are directed to the singer's beloved, to his profession, to his king, or to God and the saints, as in the case of the Italian *laude* or the Castilian *alabanzas*. Satirical songs were an equally widespread and an equally stereotyped genre, whether directed against political leaders or the singer's neighbours:

Braccio valente	Brave Braccio
vince omni gente.	conquers everyone.
Papa Martino	Pope Martin
Non vale un quattrino.	is not worth a farthing.[10]

Woe be unto Kendal that ever he was born,
He keeps his wife so lustily she makes him wear a horn,
But what is he the better or what is he the worse?
She keeps him like a cuckold with money in his purse.[11]

Still more stereotyped in form is the lament, the French *complainte*, the German *Klagen*, and so on, whether it expresses the sorrows of the lover, the ill-married wife, or the widow, the belated repentance of the criminal or the harsh lot of the weaver or the sailor:

Ah qu'il est lamentable, le sort des matelots,
Il mangent des gourganes, ils boivent que l'eau,
Ils font triste figure quand ils ont pas d'argent,
Ils couchent sur la dure, comme les pauvres gens.

(How unhappy is the fate of sailors /they eat dried beans and drink only water /they are a sorry sight when they have no money /they sleep rough like poor people.)

Just as stereotyped a genre is the farewell, whether it is the lover's farewell to his mistress or the travelling journeyman's farewell to the town of his birth:

Innsbruck, ich muss dich lassen	*Innsbruck, I must leave thee*
Ich fahr dahin mein Strassen	*I am going my way*
In fremde Land dahin.	*To a strange place.* [12]

Popular prose performances need no elaborate classification. The most important solo performance was, of course, the story; the famous distinction drawn by Jakob Grimm between historical stories (*Sagen*) and poetical stories (*Märchen*) was not made explicitly in our period. Another kind of solo performance often contained stories but was organised on different lines – the sermon. Both stories and sermons need to be understood as semi-dramatic forms; the surviving texts often break into dialogue, and descriptions of performances (above, p.106) emphasise the importance of gesture and facial expression in transmitting the message or simply holding the attention of the audience. Thus stories and sermons shade into popular dramas, which tended to be known as 'games' (French *jeu*, Spanish *juego*, German *Spiel*, etc.) whether they were comic or serious. [13]

Two-person performances often took the form of a dialogue between a clown and his stooge – a genre known in France as a *rencontre* – or that of a quarrel or debate, for example between Carnival and Lent, water and wine, summer and winter, and so on, as in the French *débat*, the Italian *contrasto*, or the German *Kampfgespräch*. [14]

Three or more actors were involved in more elaborate comic forms (often known as 'farces') which revolved round a few stock types of husbands, wives, parents, servants, priests, doctors and lawyers. The Italian *commedia dell'arte* was simply the most famous and the most elaborate of the numerous varieties of European farce. Serious popular plays were religious. The threefold distinction between 'mystery' plays with subjects taken from the Bible, 'miracle' plays dealing with the lives of the saints, and the allegorical 'morality' plays was not a distinction drawn at the time, but one which might be argued to be implicit in the plays themselves, provided one adds that allegorical plays might deal with theology as well as morality, as in the case of the Spanish *autos sacramentales*, plays about the Holy Sacrament or other religious themes.[15]

Any list of the genres of popular culture would be seriously incomplete if it omitted parody, notably the parody of religious forms. Mock sermons were a traditional part of the clown's repertoire and a few have survived, like the *Sermon joyeux de M. Saint Hareng*, that 'glorious martyr' who was fished out of the sea and brought to Dieppe, or the *Sermon in praise of thieves*, which a certain parson Haberdyne is said to have 'made at the commandment of certain thieves after they had robbed him besides Hartley Row in Hampshire'.[16] There were parodies of the Catechism, the Commandments, the Creed, the Litany, the Psalms, and, above all, the Our Father, from the medieval *Paternostre du vin* to the political parodies of the Reformation and the wars of religion. A single example will have to stand for many. The following was addressed by the Netherlanders in 1633 to the Marquis of Santa Cruz, the Commander of the Spanish forces:

> *Onsen Vader die te Brussel sijt,*
> *Uwen Name is hier vermalendijt,*
> *Uwen Wille is nerghens van waerden,*
> *Noch in den Hemel noch op der Aerden.*

> *Our Father who art in Brussels,*
> *Thy name is accursed here,*
> *Thy will is not done at all,*
> *Neither in heaven nor on earth.*[17]

Parodies of legal forms were almost as common as ecclesiastical parodies. There were mock proclamations, mock trials, such as the trial of Carnival (or, in England), *The whole trial and indictment of Sir John Barleycorn*: most common of all, there were mock testaments – the cock's, the Pope's, the Devil's, Philip II's, Frederick the Great's, and many more.[18] There were also mock battles, mock weddings and mock funerals, which might be enacted, described, or portrayed in popular prints, like the Dutch *Burial of Transsubstantiation* (1613), the English *Funeral Procession of Madam Geneva* (1736, a comment on the Gin Act), or the Russian print of the mice burying the cat, which is a reference to the relief of his subjects on the death of Peter the Great.[19]

Perhaps the adjective 'mock' is misleading. It does not occur in most contemporary descriptions, which refer only to 'trials', 'testaments', and so on. If we decide to use the term, we should at least be aware of its ambiguity. A mock battle may be no more or no less than a battle with blunt weapons, a mock funeral may simply be the acting out of a funeral without a real corpse. The mock baptism of French journeymen at their initiation ceremonies was taken by the clergy to be deliberate blasphemy, but they probably misunderstood the intention of the participants. In the case of the parodies of the Our Father, the Litany, the Commandments, or the standard procedure for trials and testaments, what seems to have been intended was not a mockery of religious or legal forms but the taking over of these forms for a new purpose. Claude Lévi-Strauss once described mythical thought as 'a sort of intellectual *bricolage*', a new construction out of pre-existing elements.[20] His term seems even more justified in the context of the mock trial or the parody of Our Father. It looks as if the creators of popular culture took over ready-made forms from the official culture of the church and the law because for certain purposes they had no equally appropriate forms of their own, a procedure which illustrates the dependence of popular culture on the culture of the dominant minority and thus offers important evidence in favour of the 'sinking' theory (above, p.58f). Ecclesiastical and legal forms also had the great advantage of familiarity. The audience knew the structure of a trial or a litany, they knew what was coming next, and so they could concentrate on the message. A new form would have distracted attention from the message and so made less of an impact.

However, taking over the forms of official culture did not necessarily involve taking over the meanings usually associated with them. The subversive possibilities of imitation did not go unappreciated; in some cases the forms themselves *were* mocked, the official world turned upside down. Thus the *causes grasses*, the mock trials staged at Carnival by French lawyers' clerks, were surely intended to make fun of the procedures of their elders, procedures which were not infrequently criticised in the early modern period for their unintelligibility. In some literary and pictorial versions of the battle between Carnival and Lent, the combatants wear saucepans for helmets and fight with spoons and forks; it is difficult not to see that knights were being ridiculed. The mock liturgy of the Feast of Fools is harder to interpret. It was seen by some contemporaries as blasphemous (p.210, below), and one wonders whether the congregation experienced it not only as a festive reversal of the everyday but also a criticism of the unintelligibility of the liturgy to the layman. We do not know.

The last few pages have attempted to make an inventory of popular genres, but the term 'genre' must not be understood in too precise a sense. The conventions of different forms of popular culture were less strict than those of French classical tragedy, say, or Renaissance literary epic. Yet there were conventions, and to ignore them is to risk missing the meaning of many images, texts, and performances.[21]

Themes and variations

Popular culture may be described as a stock of genres, but also, in close-up, as a stock of forms (schemata, motifs, themes, formulae), whether these forms are peculiar to one genre or shared by two or more of them. It is the thesis of this section that folksongs and folktales, popular plays and popular prints all need to be seen as combinations of elementary forms, permutations of elements which are more or less ready-made. This point may be illustrated most easily in the case of music, the medium which most nearly approaches to 'pure' form.

The music of the dominant minority in early modern Europe was written down and printed. Popular music, on the other hand, was transmitted orally. The formal consequences of this fact may be summed up in two paradoxes.

(a) In oral tradition, the same tune is different. As Kodály put it, 'In folk music . . . a variation is produced by the lips of the singer on every occasion'.[22] In societies or sub-cultures where music is not written down, the singer or fiddler or piper does not keep tunes note by note in his head: he improvises. On the other hand, he does not improvise quite freely: he plays variations on a theme. He adds ornaments or grace-notes to the basic tune, ornamenting it with slides, turns, trills, and so on, or making slight changes in the rhythm or pitch. Hence folktunes come in a multitude of versions or 'variants'. There is no 'correct' version, for the idea of a correct version is meaningless before tunes are written down. In oral tradition the tune exists only in its variants.

(b) The second paradox is that in oral tradition, different tunes are the same. More exactly, different tunes may contain the same phrase or motif, lasting for perhaps two or three bars. Motifs may be said to 'wander' or 'float' from one tune to another. Indeed, folk-tunes are fundamentally combinations of 'prefabricated' motifs. These tune-foundations or tune-skeletons are the framework for improvisation and ornamentation – but the ornaments too are stereotyped.[23] To put tunes together out of prefabricated elements may seem a somewhat mechanical procedure, but the habit of constant variation counteracts it. When two tunes contain several of the same motifs, it becomes impossible to say whether they are the same tune or not. In a given region the tunes in circulation will be transformations of one another, and it will be impossible to say exactly how many tunes there are.

These points are much easier to demonstrate for the folk-music of the age of Cecil Sharp and Zoltan Kodály than they are for that of early modern Europe, but the fragmentary evidence which survives points in this direction. For example, an Englishman who listened to some itinerant musicians at Otranto in the late eighteenth century commented that they were 'wont to embellish the common tune with variations out of their own fancy'.[24] Two manuscript collections of violin melodies from Slovakia in the 1730s record the tunes in schematic and abbreviated form, as if they were no more than a framework for improvisation. The 750-odd melodies in these collections (which contain over a hundred folk-tunes) may be divided into groups of variants, and there is no difficulty in identifying recurrent motifs.[25]

In oral tradition, texts behave like tunes; the same text is different, and different texts are the same, as the committee of the Highland Society discovered when they were investigating the authenticity of Macpherson's *Ossian* and found a multitude of 'compositions which had never been fixed by publication, but floated . . . in the oral recitation of senachies or bards'.[26] To demonstrate this in detail for all the different regions and genres is of course impossible in a book of this size, so I will offer a case-study of the traditional British ballad, and refer to other regions and other literary genres much more briefly. The reasons for this choice are obvious. The corpus of 300-odd ballads is accessible in an exemplary edition, the work of a nineteenth-century Harvard professor, Francis Child; the many studies of these ballads include some from a formal point of view; and the subject lends itself to discussion in English. Many of these ballads are known not only from the oral tradition of recent times but also from printed broadsides of the seventeenth and eighteenth centuries, a combination of sources which brings us closer than usual to the lost oral culture of early modern Europe.

That the same ballad is often different is clear to anyone who leafs through the Child collection, where the variants are conveniently laid out. The words like the tunes have their grace-notes, their ornaments, their amplifications, according to the performer's skill. One eighteenth-century version of *Barbara Allen* begins like this:

> *It was in and about the Martinmas time,*
> *When the green leaves were a falling,*
> *That Sir John Graeme, in the West Country,*
> *Fell in love with Barbara Allen.*

The opening quatrain of another eighteenth-century version of the ballad has only the girl's name in common with the first:

> *In Scarlet town, where I was bound,*
> *There was a fair maid dwelling,*
> *Whom I had chosen to be my own,*
> *And her name it was Barbara Allen. (Child 84)*

Yet these variants must not be interpreted without more ado as examples of the creative originality of the ballad-singers. Both openings are stereotyped. If one version of *Barbara Allen* begins, 'It was in and about the Martinmas time', other ballads in the Child collection begin 'It fell about the Martinmas time' or 'It fell about the Martinmas'; we have to do with an opening formula which wanders from one ballad to another.

This point was not lost on the early editors. Scott once remarked of traditional minstrels that 'the collections of rhymes, accumulated by the earliest of the craft, appear to have been considered as forming a joint stock for the common use of the profession'. Pinkerton drew attention to 'the frequent returns of the same sentences and descriptions expressed in the very same words', for example 'the delivery of messages, the description of battles'. More recently one scholar has identified 150 different formulae or commonplaces in the 300-odd ballads of the Child collection.[27]

For example, epithets abound; adjectives regularly associated with particular nouns, whether in one ballad or more generally. One thinks of 'doughty Douglas' in Child 161 and 162, or of Robin Hood's 'merry men', or the 'proud sheriff' of Nottingham, or of the many heroes and heroines with 'yellow hair' or a 'milk-white steed'. It is the same in other countries. Swedish ballads are full of phrases like *gular lockar*, 'golden hair'; *fingrar små*, 'small fingers'; *gangare grå*, 'grey steed'; in Russian ballads, hands are 'white', horses 'good', rivers 'swift', and so on. Other formulae include verbs. A favourite Serbian formula for the first half of a line is *vino pije*, 'is drinking wine', leaving the second half of the line to be filled in with the proper name required; *Vino pije/Kraljeviku Marko*, as it might be, or *Vino pije/Aga Asanaga*. Favourite Danish formulae for the first half of the line are *Ind kom*, 'in came'; *Op stod*, 'up stood'; and *Det var*, 'it was'. On a grander scale there are formulae for opening a ballad, such as 'It fell about the Martinmas' (or Lammas, or Midsummer) which locates the story in time, and others which locate it in place; the Serbian *vino pije* formula is developed to tell us who is drinking wine, where, with whom, and why the drinking is interrupted. On occasion British ballads do the same thing:

> *The king sits in Dumferling toune,*
> *Drinking the blude-reid wine;*
> *O whar will I get guid sailor,*
> *To sail this schip of mine? (Child 58)*

> *Young Johnstone and the young Colnel*
> *Sat drinking at the wine:*
> *O gin ye wad marry my sister,*
> *It's I wad marry thine. (Child 88)*

Similarly, there are recurrent closing formulae like the description of the plants or branches growing from two graves, which concludes a number of ballads about ill-fated lovers:

> *Lord Thomas was buried without kirk-wa,*
> *Fair Annet within the quiere,*
> *And o the tane thair grew a birk,*
> *The other a bonny briar. (Child 73)*

Other British lovers and also the Hungarians Kádár Kata and Gyula Márton end in this way:

> *Egyiköt temették ótár eleibe*
> *Másikot temették ótár háta mögi*
> *A kettöböl kinöt két kápóna-virág*
> *Az ótár tetejin esszekapcsolódtak.*

> (The one was buried in front of the altar/The other was buried behind the altar/From the two of them sprang two chapel-flowers/On top of the altar they intertwined.)[28]

This stanza in its different variations surely represents a theme or 'motif' in the musical sense, an elementary form which has been incorporated into a number of stories because it offers a ready-made conclusion which is emotionally and aesthetically satisfying. Whole scenes or episodes may wander or float no less than phrases and lines.

Many other recurrent motifs can be found in the ballads, British and continental. There is the motif of the heroine sitting in her bower sewing, the female equivalent of the drinking scene already described; there is the prophetic dream; the fight; the feast, a favourite of the Russian ballad-singers; Pinkerton's example, the sending or receiving of a letter or other message which serves to introduce a new development in the story; the motif of looking out from a high tower, which recurs in Spanish and Norwegian ballads and serves a similar function; and the motif of the return of the hero, sometimes in disguise and often unrecognisable, which has been popular from Homer's time to our own.

Two points about formulae and motifs deserve emphasis. The first is their frequency. An analysis of 237 traditional Spanish ballads showed that on average 35 per cent of their lines were formulaic, the proportion varying between 2 per cent and 68 per cent in different ballads.[29]

Larger-scale motifs are harder to define and so to count, but it is difficult to find a ballad in the Child collection without thematic analogies both within the collection and elsewhere.

If the reader is getting the impression that ballad-singers were not creative or that they had little to do, the second point about formulae and motifs may serve to cancel that impression out by stressing flexibility and transformations. One should not think so much in terms of phrases, lines, stanzas or episodes migrating unchanged from one ballad to another – though this can happen – as of substitutions within a formal framework. In some traditional Danish ballads, for example, we find a high proportion of formulaic half-lines:

> *Det var* unge herr Marsk Stig
> *Det var* Konning herr Erick
> *Det var* Orm unger Svend, etc.

We also find
> Op stod *unge herr Marsk Stig*
> Høre i det *unge herr Marsk Stig,* etc.

We might therefore say that the completely formulaic lines

> *Det var Konning herr Erick*
> *Op stod unge herr Marsk Stig*

are really the 'same' line, but only in the sense that I have owned the same knife for ten years, in odd years replacing the handle and in even years replacing the blade. The point which needs emphasis is the possibility of dropping almost infinitely various phrases into the same formulaic slot. To take a slightly more complex example, we might compare the following couplets from Child 39 and Child 243:

> *She had na pu'd a double rose,*
> *A rose but only twa . . .*

> *They had not saild a league, a league*
> *A league but barely three . . .*

There is scarcely a word in common between the couplets, and yet the existence of a formula which structures the material will be obvious.

The case of floating episodes or scenes is more complex still. If we look at the motif of the return of the hero, we find that he may be in disguise and may not; that he may find his beloved waiting for him, or about to marry another, or married already, with several children (as in the French ballad *Pauvre soldat revient de guerre*), or gone, perhaps kidnapped by pirates. If we were listing examples of this motif among the British ballads, it would be odd to include Child 17, *Hind Horn*, where the hero turns up at his love's wedding, and not Child 53, *Young Beichan*, which reverses the situation and makes the hero's first true love return as young Beichan is marrying someone else. And what about the return of ghosts? In Child 74, *Fair Margaret and Sweet William*, the first true love returns from the dead to visit the hero after his wedding. If this is to be included, why not Child 47, which is also built round a return from the dead? Yet proud Margaret's visitor is a brother, not a lover. . . . In four large volumes Claude Lévi-Strauss has studied a corpus of Amerindian myths as transformations of one another.[30] It might be possible to make a similar study of the Child ballads or even of the traditional ballads of Europe. At any rate it is difficult in the study of ballads, as of folk-tunes, to say where one ends and another begins, what is theme and what is variation.

Similar points, if not exactly the same ones, can be made about the formal structures of genres other than the ballad. In the case of the epic, for example, the length of the performance makes it even more necessary to distinguish two kinds of wandering unit, the small-scale 'formula' and the larger-scale 'theme' or 'motif', a scene or episode which may, if properly ornamented or amplified, last for hundreds of lines.[31] Child 117, *A Gest of Robin Hood*, is 1,824 lines long, enough to be described as an epic. The motif of the feast or dinner, so sketchy in the ballads, can therefore be developed much more fully. No less than six dinners are described in the *Gest*, of which four take place in the greenwood with Robin as host and are described in much the same way. Two of these episodes, in the first and the fourth 'fits' of the poem, are particularly close in structure. In each case Little John suggests that the band go to dinner, Robin sends them to Watling Street to look for a guest, the guest arrives, dines, and is asked how much money he has, while Little John spreads his mantle on the ground to count it.

In the case of the lyric, one of the two basic paradoxes has to be dropped. We cannot say that 'the same lyric is different' simply because people do not speak of the 'same' lyric in two variants, but rather of two lyrics. On the other hand, formulae are common, so that 'different lyrics are the same'. A study of the German popular lyric of the fifteenth and sixteenth centuries lists scores of verse phrases which can be found in one song after another, whether the lover is describing his beloved (*hübsch und fein*), the time of their meeting (*an einem abend spät*), the place (*so fern in grönem walde*), or his reaction to rejection (*mein hertz wil mir zubrechen*). As in the case of ballads, formulae of this kind occur with great frequency in the lyric, so that verses of four or six lines can be found which are virtually nothing but formulae. But these formulae are flexible, just like ballad-formulae. One does not find the mechanical repetition of *so fern im grönem walde* so much as a set of similar phrases substituting for one another, such as

So fern auf grüner awen
So fern auf jener heide
So fern in gröner heide, etc. [32]

In the case of the folktale, we return to the multiplicity of variants of the 'same' tale. *Cinderella* is an obvious example, 'Aschenputtel' as she is called in German tradition. An Italian, a Swedish and two French versions are known to have existed before the Grimms published theirs in 1812, and since then hundred of variants have been found, in the Romance, Germanic, Slavic and Celtic language-groups, thirty-eight in French alone. [33]

As for the second paradox, 'different tales are the same', it seems that the formula is much less important in the prose tale than it is in popular verse; it is more or less confined to the beginning and end, to set phrases like 'Once upon a time' and its equivalents (*Es war amol, Cc'era 'na vota,* etc.) or 'they lived happily ever after'. In prose there is not the same need for formulae of this kind to help the performer along; it is also possible that the folktales from the early modern period which have come down to us in collections like those of Straparola or Timoneda lost their formulae in the course of preparation for the printer. [34]

Motifs, on the other hand, are particularly obvious here. It has long been noticed that folktales are unstable combinations of elements which lead a semi-independent existence, wandering of floating from one tale to another, and in order to track them down a massive motif-index to the folktale has been compiled by the American folklorist Stith Thompson, while his Russian colleague Vladimir Propp has argued that the Russian fairy-tale draws on a stock of thirty-one motifs (or 'functions', as he calls them), no more and no less, from 'a member of the family leaves the house' to 'the hero marries and ascends the throne'.[35] If we take the tales which Straparola published in 1550 and look them up in Thompson's motif-index, it soon becomes clear that they contain many well-known themes. For example, there is the theme of the animal or bird or fish which helps the hero and often has the power of speech; or the theme of the testing of the suitor, who may have to bridle wild horses, kill a dragon or go on a quest for the water of life.[36] Or suppose we focus on one folktale, like Cinderella; we find that it can be broken down into five basic motifs, A, B, C, D, E, as follows: A, the heroine is mishandled by her relatives; B, she receives supernatural help; C, she meets the hero; D, she passes a recognition-test; E, she marries the hero. Each motif comes in a number of variants, for example D1, only one girl can wear the slipper; D2, only one girl can wear the ring; D3, only one girl can pluck the apple. The Grimms' version of the story might be written in shorthand A1, B1, C1, D1, E. Once the story has been broken down into its elementary motifs in this way, its affinity with other stories in the Grimm collection become obvious; notably with no. 65, *Allerleirauh* (A2, C1, D2, E); with no. 130, *Einaüglein, Zweiaüglein und Dreiaüglein* (A1, B1, B3, B4, D3, E); and with no. 179, *Die Gansehirtin am Brunnen* (A3, B1, C3, E). Once more we find that 'different texts are the same', or rather that they are transformations of one another, different permutations of the same basic elements.[37]

Among the professional storytellers of early modern Europe may be numbered many preachers, who enlivened their sermons with *exempla* or stories with a moral. One handbook for preachers recommends an animal story as an effective means of stirring up a sleeping audience. Indeed, the sermon as a whole deserves study as a popular art-form, 'popular' in the sense that it was often aimed at an audience of craftsmen and peasants, and sometimes composed and delivered by a 'mechanic preacher'. Was the sermon, like the ballad or the folktale, composed of formulae or motifs? There is not, so far as I know, any evidence for the systematic use of stereotyped phrases in the sermons of the period. Of course, they may have existed and been edited out of the texts when they were prepared for publication, as is equally possible in the case of the folktale; but they may have been unnecessary in a prose performance. A recent student of black folk-preachers in the USA, armed with his tape-recorder, noted the use of formulae like 'The Christ of the Bible' (used twenty-four times in one sermon) or 'Am I right about it?' (used fifteen times), but he was studying the chanted sermon, which seems to have been exceptional in early modern Europe, although it could be found in Britain; John Aubrey records that 'our old vicar of Kingston St Michael, Mr Hynd, did sing his sermons rather than read them', and that 'In Herefordshire they have a touch of this singing; our old divines had'. On the other side of the border, the tradition of *hwyl* has survived to our own day. In the late seventeenth century, Dissenters were said to 'think they hear a very powerful preacher, if his voice be sharp and quavering, and near to singing; if he draws out some words with a mournful accent'.[38]

Motifs or themes, on the other hand, were basic to the sermon. That they were employed self-consciously as a means of sermon construction is made clear by the existence of a number of handbooks for preachers which discuss the subject. They even use the word 'theme' in the sense of a text taken from the Bible and used to hold the sermon together. The preacher should begin with the presentation of the text, *thematis propositio*; next should come the greeting of the audience, *salutatio populi*, and the prayer for God's help, the *divini auxilii imploratio* (introductory motifs which were, incidentally, much used by the Italian singers of tales); then came the three main parts of the sermon, first the *introductio thematis*; then the *divisio thematis*, or explanation of the meaning of the text by dividing it into parts and taking them one by one; finally the *conclusio*, or application of the text's message to the audience. This skeleton-structure fitted all sermons, but could easily be made more specific by taking a particular biblical text, or, if the preacher were lazy or unimaginative, by consulting a book of sermon outlines like the famous *Sermones Dormi Secure*, which ensured him a good Saturday night's sleep by providing him with something ready-made for Sunday morning.[39]

Another standard method of holding the sermon together and keeping the attention of the audience was the use of an extended metaphor. John Flavel, who preached to sailors, organised sermons round the image of spiritual navigation (above, p.45), and George Whitefield preached a famous sermon, also to sailors, around the image of spiritual shipwreck. John Bunyan built sermons round the image of Christ the advocate or the image of the waters of life. Hugh Latimer preached two celebrated sermons 'on the card', taking his imagery from the currently popular game of 'triumph', and his equally famous 'sermon of the plough' was organised round a comparison of the preacher to God's ploughman. These two motifs remain the standby of the American folk-preacher, and the card image goes back to the fourteenth century, if no further.[40]

From the preacher gesticulating in his pulpit it was only a short step – too short for some moralists – to the popular play. No doubt the surviving texts are an even more unreliable guide to the nature of performance in the case of plays than in the case of ballads, folktales or sermons, but at least they enable us to see the importance, once again, of variants, formulae and motifs. The same play was different; in Britain the mummers seem to have performed only three basic types of play – the hero-combat, the wooing-ceremony and the sword-dance – but more than 900 variants have been found. In Russia the most popular of the folk-plays, *Tsar Maximilian,* is recorded in more than 200 variants. In Spain and Spanish America a play about the Nativity and the adoration of the shepherds has been preserved in many variants.[41]

Different plays are the same; the drama has its formulae and its motifs, even if these take slightly different forms from those in other media. Verbal formulae abound, from the simple 'Here comes I' of the English mummers to the more elaborately stereotyped phrases of the *commedia dell'arte,* in which each character has its own repertoire of conceits, the rhetoric of his part. Capitano, for example, had his *bravure* or boasts, which appear to have formed a formulaic system, marked by the constant use of hyperbole and by a few recurrent images – Capitano sees the world in military terms, and his favourite soup is iron filings sprinkled with gunpowder.[42]

However, in the popular drama, the basic units were not words but characters and actions. The English mummers built their plays round a few characters – St George, Turkish Knight, Fool, Doctor; the French farces of the sixteenth century had

their stock husbands, wives, mothers-in-law, servant girls and
curés; the Spanish nativity plays had their lazy shepherd and
their quarrelling newly-weds; and the more complex structures
of the *commedia dell'arte* were organised round similar
elements – the sententious Pantalone, the pedantic Gratiano, the
boastful Capitano, and the foolish, sly and agile Zanni. Their
stereotyped personalities, like their stereotyped accents
(Venetian for Pantalone, Bolognese for Gratiano, etc.) served to
identify them like the epithets in the traditional ballad. Actions
too were stereotyped. The *commedia dell'arte* had its *lazzi*,
formulaic pieces of 'business' which are listed in the literary
sources, like the *'lazzo* of the smock', in which Zanni escapes
from a furious Capitano by leaving his smock behind.[43] There
were stereotyped scenes of recognition, misunderstanding,
beating, disguise, and so on. Popular plays from many parts of
Europe also contain such recurrent motifs as combats, wooings,
weddings, trials, wills, executions and funerals, whether singly
or in combination.

From the acrobatics of Harlequin it is only a short step to the
dance. The records of performances before 1800 are not careful
or detailed enough to enable anyone to describe how much, or
in what way, one *krakowiak*, say, differed from another.
However, it does not seem too difficult to interpret folk-dances
as combinations of motifs or elementary forms – of pauses and
movements, quick movements and slow movements, of
different types of step, and so on. Traditional Czech dancers
themselves classified their steps as *obkročák*, 'circular step';
skočná, 'hopping step'; *třasák*, 'trembling step'; *vrták*, 'drill
step', and so on.[44]

From the dance — indeed, from all the media discussed so far
— it is a considerable jump to the visual arts; they are not oral,
they are not performances, and as Lessing pointed out in a
famous attack on analogies between the arts, they are extended
in space rather than in time.[45] And yet there are some
similarities, which should not be forgotten, between popular
painting or carving or weaving and the traditional forms
described in the last few pages. In the visual arts as in the
performing arts we find the variant. The traditional potter or
carpenter or weaver does not produce two jugs, or chests, or
bedspreads which are exactly the same, and they differ
principally in that they are different combinations of

stereotyped elements. There is a visual repertory of geometrical patterns, such as rosettes; and also of stylised plants, animals, birds or people. This repertory corresponds to the stock of formulae and motifs in oral tradition. The saint is identified by his attributes as the epic hero is by his epithet: St Catherine has her wheel, St George his dragon, and St Martin his cloak, sword and beggar. Just as a story wandered from one hero to another, so the same woodcut might be used in different chap-books to illustrate episodes in different stories, thus reducing the cost of production. In one printing-shop in eighteenth-century Catalonia, an image of St James was made to do duty for St George and St Martin as well – after all, they were all soldiers.[46] Here we find instances of the 'stereotype' or 'cliché' in something like the original sense of those well-worn metaphors. Other compositions were more or less free-floating. The image of a king sitting on his throne with a figure approaching him might be used to illustrate many different episodes. The same feast-composition might illustrate Belshazzar's feast, the marriage at Cana, or the Last Supper. A battle-scene might be represented in much the same way, whether the scene was supposed to illustrate the Old Testament or a romance of chivalry.[47] We have already seen that the same funeral procession motif might be used in a variety of different contexts (above, p.123).

The process of composition

Formulae and motifs might be regarded as the vocabulary of the tradition-bearer, whether singer, craftsman or player. Can we also discover his grammar and syntax? In other words, are there rules which govern the combination of wandering motifs? Do they form part of a structure or system? From the time of the Danish folklorist Axel Olrik, whose essay 'Epic laws of folk narrative' was published in 1909, to that of contemporary structuralists, some scholars have argued that this grammar or these laws can be discovered; for example, the Russian critic Viktor Shklovsky suggested that 'folktales constantly disintegrate and are put together on the basis of special, as yet unknown laws of plot formation'. If 'grammar' is too grand a metaphor to describe what they have found, these scholars have at least come up with some interesting conclusions about the use of ready-made combinations of motifs, which we might call 'schemata'.[48]

In the visual arts, a popular schema was to bisect the picture vertically. In one variant, parallel images would be shown to the left and to the right, as if one was the mirror-image of the other, as in the confrontation of Holger Danske and King Karvel, two warriors with their arms raised and drawn back to strike (Plate 7). Alternatively, the images are not in parallel but in contrast; a beautiful woman on one side of a print, say, and a skeleton on the other. In Lutheran propaganda, Christ and the Pope (who was, of course, Antichrist) were often represented in this way, whether in a single print or a series of prints like the *Passional Christi und Anti-christi*. The Hogarth prints of the idle and industrious apprentices are a famous example of this kind of 'antithesis'.[49] A variant on the schema was to show a balance or scale in which one object, of which the spectator was expected to approve, outweighed another; the Bible, for example, might be shown to outweigh the work of St Thomas Aquinas. The time-element may be introduced, so that the pair of images represent before and after or crime and punishment.[50]

This pictorial schema has its literary parallels, as one might have expected; after all, the antithesis is a figure of rhetoric. At the level of the genre, there is the debate or *contrasto* (above, p.121). At the level of the stanza, we find one quatrain balancing or opposing its predecessor, or the second half of the quatrain opposing the first half:

> Some pat on the gay green robes,
> And some pat on the brown;
> But Janet put on the scarlet robes,
> To shine foremost throw the town. (Child 64)

At the level of the story, Axel Olrik drew attention to what he called the 'law of two to a scene' – only two people appear at any one time in traditional popular literature – and to the 'law of contrast', the habit of juxtaposing opposites such as large and small, rich and poor, Goliath and David, Dives and Lazarus, St George and the dragon, Christ and the Devil.[51]

The antithesis is, among other things, a device for handling repetition. Repetition can be found in all works of art, and without it there would be no structure at all, but it is either particularly prevalent or particularly obvious in popular culture. An eighteenth-century Swedish artist will paint the Three Magi as three horsemen galloping in a row, where a Renaissance artist will incorporate them into a more complex, more unified composition.[52] Again, there is much more redundancy within the oral tradition than there is in works intended to be read. At the level of the line, pleonastic constructions are common: 'a loud laugh laughed he', 'lythe and listen', or *llorando de los sus ojos,* 'crying with his eyes'. At the level of the stanza, repetition is no less obvious:

> He was a braw gallant,
> And he rid at the ring;
> And the bonny Earl of Murray
> Oh he might have been a king!

> He was a braw gallant,
> And he played at the ba;
> And the bonny Earl of Murray
> Was the flower amang them a'.

> He was a braw gallant,
> And he played at the glove;
> And the bonny Earl of Murray
> Oh he was the Queen's love! (Child 181)

This trinary pattern is a common one – stanzas often come in linked triads, and the central action of the ballad often develops in three steps. The same pattern occurs in many folktales, as the first three stories from the Straparola collection will serve to illustrate. In the first, a man is told by his dying father to observe three precepts; he breaks them one by one. In the second, an official defies a thief to steal three objects, but the thief succeeds. In the third, a priest is tricked by three rogues, but revenges himself on them in three stages. All these examples illustrate what Olrik called 'the Law of Three', another of his 'laws of folk narrative'. Of course, a trinary structure is not confined to popular literature, but it is interesting to find that when the story of David and Goliath was taken from the Bible to become a Spanish ballad, David was made to shoot at the giant three times before striking him down.[53]

When one finds exceptions to this law in folksongs and folktales, they sometimes signal an unusual twist in the story, a case of 'incremental repetition' which proceeds towards an unexpected climax. In the ballad *Lord Randal* (Child 12), the dying hero is asked what he will leave to his mother, his sister, his brother – and finally, what he will bequeath to his 'true-love', who has, it is now revealed, poisoned him. A similar use of incremental repetition within the mock-testament motif can be found in one of the finest Catalan ballads, *Amalia sta malalta;* the dying Amalia leaves bequests to the poor, to her brother, and to the Virgin Mary:

> *I a vós, la meva mare*
> *us deixo el marit meu*
> *perqué el tingeu en cambra*
> *com fa molt temps que feu.*

> *(And to you, my mother/I leave my husband/so that you can embrace him in your chamber/as you have long been doing.)*[54]

If these remarks on binary and trinary structure suggest what is likely to happen to a motif when it is used in a ballad of folktale, they do not explain how motifs come to be combined, the 'laws of plot formation', as Shklovsky called them. Are motifs combined according to rules, or simply by association of ideas in the mind of the storyteller? A number of scholars, including Lévi-Strauss and the Russian folklorist Vladimir Propp, are convinced that there are rules governing the combination of motifs and that the grammar or the 'algebra' of the Russian or Italian folktale or the myths of the American Indians can be discovered. They are concerned with motifs at a high level of generality: 'A gives X to B' rather than 'the queen gives a ring to Ivan'. They have identified recurrent narrative schemata or sequences of motifs, such as interdiction/violation/consequences/attempted escape, or lack/deception/lack liquidated. Finally, they are concerned with 'transformational grammar' in the sense of the rules for the transformation of tales into other tales, not only by the insertion of different heroes into the roles of A and B, but also by changes in the sequence of motifs itself, which may be amplified, condensed, or inverted. The love/separation/happiness schema may be transformed into love/separation/unhappiness, and so on.[55]

There can be little doubt that narrative schemata of this kind (including some of the very schemata just mentioned) can be found in stories told in early modern Europe. To return to Straparola and his *Piacevoli Notti*: the first tale in the collection takes the common form of interdiction/violation/consequences; the second tale is the inverse of the first – challenge/acceptance/consequences; the third takes the form of deceit/revenge; the fourth returns to the interdiction/violation form of the first; and the fifth returns to the deceit/revenge schema of the third. The Italian religious drama also contains recurrent sequences of motifs: plays which deal with saintly women tend to adopt the schema of innocence persecuted/innocence rewarded. The heroine may be persecuted for her faith and rewarded in heaven, as in the case of Saints Barbara, Margherita, Orsola or Teodora; or, like Saints Guglielma and Uliva, she may be persecuted for more worldly reasons and rewarded on earth. The French comic play is equally stereotyped. The action frequently centres on a married couple, the wife being shown as demanding, obstinate or unfaithful, and a popular schema is the three-motif sequence deceit/discovery/punishment.[56] At a still more abstract level many farces could be described in terms of the schema 'the hero is provoked by adversaries/the hero defeats the adversaries'.

More intricate are the plots of the *commedia dell'arte*, so intricate, indeed, that they are likely to leave the modern reader bewildered. If they did not have this effect on the actors and audiences of the time this was surely because these plays were built round familiar schemata. Indeed, if there is any form of popular art which cries out for structural analysis, it is this one. The first scenario in Scala's famous collection is typical enough to make an appropriate example: 'the two old twins', *Li due vecchi gemelli*. The essence of the plot is a sequence of four motifs which often recur in this genre: A loves B/an obstacle occurs/the obstacle is eliminated/A marries B. In this case, Orazio loves the widow Flaminia; Capitano appears and pursues her; he is driven off, and Orazio marries Flaminia. This sequence is complicated by duplication and by addition. By 'duplication', I mean the insertion of one or more sub-plots which echo the first. In this case, the servant Pedrolino loves the servant-girl Franceschina; Gratiano appears and pursues her; he is driven off, and Pedrolino marries Franceschina. Even this is not enough and the main hero and heroine are doubled up by Orazio's cousin Flavio and a second widow, Isabella, who also fall in love and marry. Finally, the play takes its name from the addition of another motif, the 'return motif', so common in ballads and folktales as well as in plays; the fathers of Orazio and

Flavio are twins who had been captured and sold into slavery, but return in time for the weddings. All that is lacking to make this play stand for the *commedia dell'arte* is an example of the popular disguise motif, for in this genre servants, or necromancers, or madwomen are constantly turning out to be different from what they had appeared to be.[57]

For another example of an intricate pattern of motifs we may return to the British ballad, where one sometimes finds a 'ring' or 'frame', a stanza or person or theme which appears to introduce and again to round off a particular story. In its most elaborate form it involves chiastic structuring, the pattern *a*, *b*, *c*, *c*, *b*, *a*. Thus *The Lass of Roch Royal* (Child 76) has been revealed as a sequence of three motifs which are then repeated in reverse; plaint/journey/rebuff; rebuff discovered/journey/plaint.[58]

It may be too grandiose to speak of universal 'laws' governing the combination of motifs into ballads, plays and folktales, but the examples discussed in the last few pages do suggest that there are patterns of combination rather than a random association of one element with another.

The analyses of the structuralists, illuminating as they are, risk giving a false impression: the impression that 'motifs' combine with one another, whereas they are in fact combined in this way by men and women, by singers, storytellers and actors. Yet thanks to the focus on the not-quite-free-floating motif or formula, it is easier to understand how actors and storytellers and singers create their works of art in an oral culture. They learn by listening to older people and trying to imitate them, and what they learn are not fixed texts but rather a vocabulary of formulae and motifs and the rules for combining them, a kind of 'poetic grammar'.[59] This grammar is best learned when one is young; no wonder that ballad-singing runs in families. Singers also learn how to 'amplify' or 'ornament' the basic structure. By this means they are able to improvise with relative ease, to the amazement of scholars from a literate culture. In Yugoslavia in the 1930s, for example, some singers of tales, like Avdo Mededović, could sing ten to twenty decasyllabic lines to the minute for two hours at a stretch, and continue a story in instalments till it reached 13,000 lines. That he could improvise songs at short notice was shown by the experiment of reading him a text and then asking him to sing the story in his own way, a test which he triumphantly passed.[60]

What of the singers of early modern Europe? There can be little doubt that many of them improvised, in some areas at least. To begin with an example not far from Avdo's own region, Alberto Fortis, on his visit to Dalmatia in the late eighteenth century, listened carefully to 'the heroic song of the Morlaks' and noted that 'there is more than one Morlak who improvises his song – *che canta improvvisando* – from beginning to end'. In another remote, rocky and pastoral society at the other end of Europe–the Western Isles of Scotland–a traveller in the late seventeenth century recorded the fact that 'several of both sexes have a gift of poesy, and are able to form a satire or panegyric extempore, without the assistance of any stronger liquor than water to raise their fancy'. One eighteenth-century Highlander must have had Avdo's stamina, if not his creative powers, for a Scots clergyman told the Committee of the Highland Society of an old man who 'continued, for three successive days, and during several hours in each day, to repeat, without hesitation, with the utmost rapidity . . . many thousand lines of ancient poetry'. The Committee thought that this feat was the result of a good memory, but facility in improvisation seems a more plausible explanation. An extemporised verse-form called the *pennyll* was current in eighteenth-century Wales.

> A person conversant in this art will produce a *pennyll* approximate to the last which was sung . . . like nightingales they support the contest throughout the night . . . parishes often contend against parishes; and every hill is vocal with the chorus.

In Norway in the early nineteenth century, in Telemark and Setesdal, it was common to improvise the *stev*, a four-line stanza composed of two rhymed couplets, and to engage in the *stevleik*, a debate or competition in which alternate stanzas were composed by the two participants. It is likely that this custom went back to the Middle Ages, and almost certain that it was practised in the early modern period.[61]

However, the best evidence of improvised poetry in our period comes from Italy. Montaigne describes meeting an illiterate peasant woman in Tuscany who was able to compose verses 'avec une promptitude extraordinaire'. In Sicily in the seventeenth century, there were improvisation-contests reminiscent of the Norwegian *stevleik,* or the *haiku-*competitions of seventeenth-century Japan.[62] *Provisanti,* 'improvisers', was a common term for popular poets. One of the best-known of these *provisanti* in Tuscany, about the year 1500, was Cristoforo, called 'Altissimo' (possibly because of his predilection for this adjective in his poetic formulae). When the first book of his *Reali di Francia* was published (after his death) in 1534, it was described on the titlepage as a poem 'sung by him extempore' *(cantato da lui all'improvviso),* and the first canto begins with an apology in case this method of composition has led to bad verses.

It is also in Italy that we find the best evidence for improvised drama in the *commedia dell'arte,* often known during this period as *commedia all'improvviso.* Despite the help they had from formulae, motifs, and stock characters (not to mention the scenario, hung backstage for quick reference), it is difficult to imagine how ten or twelve actors were able to coordinate their improvisations, although we know that they did in fact manage this feat successfully, as troupes still do in parts of Asia today. It is easier to understand how a solo performance of this kind could be contrived, like those of the mountebanks on Piazza San Marco who, in the words of an English visitor, Thomas Coryat, 'tell their tales with such admirable volubility and plausible grace, even extempore'.[63]

Whether Italians extemporised more readily than other performers or whether their performances have simply been recorded more carefully, it is difficult to say. Clowns like Tarleton or Tabarin may have improvised their turns, but we cannot be sure. For England, the best evidence of extempore performances relates to sermons, perhaps because of the strength of enthusiastic Protestantism. Seventeenth-century English dissenting preachers, who included laymen, spoke when the spirit moved them, and they were criticised for their 'abrupt' and 'incoherent' discourse, which suggests unskilled improvisation. John Bunyan apparently did not write his sermons out before delivery, although it was said to be 'customary with him to commit his sermons to writing after he had preached them'. The eighteenth-century Methodist George Whitefield preached extempore with great success. The eighteenth-century Scottish ballad singer Mrs Brown of Falkland has also been quoted as an example of the improvising performer.[64] As for storytellers, evidence of their methods has rarely survived, but a certain Román Ramírez, who recited romances of chivalry in public, explained to the Inquisition that he did not know the texts by heart but only 'the substance', and that he would amplify or shorten the stories as appropriate during the performance.[65] Was he typical?

If he was, if the singers and storytellers and preachers and actors of early modern Europe regularly made up their performances as they went along, then we should interpret many of the traditional forms described earlier in this chapter as devices to help them on their way. Formulaic phrases can be (as one American folk-preacher recently admitted) 'a rest on the highway', or even, when another preacher used them, 'stalling for time'. Repetition in an extemporised ballad would give the singer a breathing-space, a relief from the strain of continuous creation, a chance to think of what was to come next. In the British ballad the second line of the four-line stanza, known as the 'filler', was the favourite place for such a rest on the highway, and in the *commedia dell'arte* the *lazzi* provided it. Because phrases or motifs were linked, whether by free association or through schemata, the performer was in no doubt as to what should come next: 'the things come into my head as if I was looking at them, and before one word is finished, the next is there in order'.[66]

There were other aids to performance besides. Vuk Stefanović Karadžić remarked of one singer of tales, a certain Milija, that 'he couldn't recite the ballads in proper order, but only sing them. And not only that; without spirits he wouldn't even sing.' Román Ramírez told the Inquisition that he 'read' his stories from a blank sheet of paper, or 'a book which was not the same as what he read, and kept his eyes on it without turning the pages, and this he did not to distract his memory and attend better to what he was reading'. It is also likely that singers, actors and preachers of the period had recourse to what was known as the 'art of memory', the association of words or motifs with the parts of a real or imaginary building.[67]

It would be difficult to improvise without using these devices, but the use of these devices does not prove that a given performance was improvised; they have their uses for the listeners as well as the performer. Redundancy, for example, which looks so odd and clumsy on the printed page, may be a welcome relief from concentration for people who have been listening for an hour or more. Equally welcome must have been the stereotyped scenes of fighting and feasting, because the familiar is more reassuring and demands less attention than the new. Perhaps the 'Law of Three' holds because three is the maximum number of points the oral narrator can expect his audience to keep in mind. Again, without the stock characters and sequences of action in the *commedia dell'arte,* the public would have been in danger of losing their way in some of the labyrinthine plots. They enjoyed the *lazzi,* as the audiences of variety shows still do, precisely because they knew in advance what was going to happen next. The same devices would also have helped performers learn texts by heart, as in some cases (like that of the Irish bards) they certainly did. These forms are necessary in an oral culture, but they do not tell us whether extemporisation was prevalent or not.

This question of prevalence is unlikely ever to receive a satisfactory answer for the early modern period. Indeed, the term 'extemporisation' is more ambiguous than it looks, for the dichotomy between improvised and memorised is a false one. Every lecturer knows that there is a whole spectrum of possible performances between the extremes of something learned by heart in advance and something created on the spot without forethought. Seventeenth-century preachers, like modern lecturers, often spoke from notes; the poet 'Altissimo' was described as writing his ideas down on pieces of paper; and some Italian actors kept commonplace books of material that they could use in 'improvised' performances, which they did so skilfully that 'what had long been premeditated seemed to come out extempore'.[68] Performers who did not use notes may still, by repeated practice, have produced something which was neither completely spontaneous nor learned exactly by heart, the degree of improvisation varying with the individual or the genre. The Serbo-Croat epic, for example, with its line of variable length and lack of rhyme, lent itself to improvisation more than the British ballad. The existence of numerous variants shows that many performers did not learn the ballads word by word from one another, but performances of the same ballad by the same singer may not have varied in more than minor details, as in the case of Ingierd Gunnarsdotter, whose version of 'Essbiörn Prude och Ormen Stark' was recorded several times in the 1670s. On one occasion this Swedish ballad-singer began with the heroes drinking wine in hall, on another they were drinking mead.[69]

It should now be possible to return to the question of individual versus communal creation (above, p.113), and to look at it from a slightly different angle. The individual is creative in the sense that each artifact or performance is a new creation, a little different from its predecessors. Each craftsman or performer develops his own style, his idiolect, by choosing some formulae and themes rather than others from the common stock. In popular culture individual variation, like regional variation, should be seen primarily in terms of selection and combination. Combining formulae and motifs and adapting them to new contexts is not a mechanical process; indeed, 'every good improvisation is a creative act'.[70] Yet variation takes place not only as a result of conscious individual creative acts but unconsciously as well. 'Ballads resemble gossip', as one American folklorist puts it. 'Their variation comes about in much the same way gossip variation occurs.' That is, people remember selectively and only pass on what interests them, so that a rumour or ballad gets progressively shorter as all that is not memorable is lost.[71] The ballad is gradually stripped down to its essentials – hence the laconic style, the abrupt transition from one episode to another, or the simple juxtaposition of two images without comment. This elliptical style is one of the most attractive aesthetic features of traditional songs and stories, and it is the result not so much of individual decisions as of the wear and tear of oral transmission, a negative form of 'communal creation'. For all these reasons, to listen to a traditional song or story is not so much to hear the voice of an individual, however gifted, as to hear the voice of the tradition which speaks through him.

It may be argued that the points made in this chapter are applicable to all works of art and not just to popular culture. All works of art may be analysed in terms of repetition, commonplaces, motifs, schemata, and variations, as Aby Warburg, Ernst Curtius and Sir Ernst Gombrich (to name no more) have shown.[72] The point may be illustrated from European literature in the sixteenth and seventeenth centuries.

The formulaic element in the Petrarchan sonnet is obvious enough. Treatises on rhetoric gave instruction in the use of formulae and schemata. There is no great difficulty in identifying a folktale motif in a story by Cervantes such as *The illustrious kitchen-maid,* or in identifying stock characters, like the Zanni-figure Sganarelle, in plays by Molière. As late as the eighteenth century, singers and players were expected to improvise the ornamentation of compositions which had been written down and printed.

If there is no difference in kind between the forms of learned and popular culture, there may still be differences of degree, arising especially from the fact that so much of popular culture was, and is, oral culture. In the first place, in popular culture the repertoire of elements from which an indivudual can draw is relatively limited. In the second place, these elements are combined in stereotyped ways with relatively little attempt at modification – this is the principle of *bricolage.* (It may not be an accident that several pioneer structuralists were students of folklore, notably Roman Jakobson and Vladimir Propp.) Writing for the eye and for a sophisticated audience, it is possible to forget about the law of two to a scene, to use formulae less frequently, to amplify descriptions much further, and to create more fully individualised characters, and all this happens more and more in European literature from the invention of printing onwards, although what has been called 'oral residue' did survive.[73] Conscious innovation became easier, no longer held back by the techniques of oral composition.

New stories could, of course, be introduced into the repertoire of traditional performers, but the use of formulae and stock motifs would rapidly assimilate them to the old. There is a traditional Spanish ballad about King Juan of Navarre which cannot be earlier than the early sixteenth century, when Juan lost his kingdom to Ferdinand the Catholic. The ballad tells of the king dreaming that Lady Fortune is warning him of the disaster which is about to happen. The prophetic dream is a stock motif which had been applied, in an older ballad, to King Rodrigo, who had lost his realm to the Moors 800 years before.[74] Here we see recent events becoming stylised and the new being perceived in terms of the old. In similar fashion the ballads about Peter the Great assimilate him to Ivan the Terrible or even to the medieval hero Ilya of Murom. In eighteenth-century France, a print of the famous criminal Cartouche (below, p.165) was adapted to serve for his successor Mandrin. For the printer this may have been no more than a way of cutting his costs, but it probably helped the public to see one man in terms of the other.[75] It is for this reason, among others, that the emphasis in the next chapter will fall on types rather than on individual heroes, villains and fools.

CHAPTER SIX

Heroes, Villains and Fools

What were the fundamental attitudes and values of the craftsmen and peasants of early modern Europe? The question is central to this book, yet to answer it is the most presumptuous part of the whole enterprise, involving as it does the attempt to make explicit what was implicit in the different forms of popular culture. The approach adopted in this chapter depends on the assumption that a culture's heroes, villains and fools form a system, that they reveal the standards of that culture by surpassing them, threatening them and falling short of them respectively.[1]

It is of course highly dangerous, as has already been suggested (above, p.29f), to treat the popular culture of this period as if it were monolithic. Yet the same heroes could be found in many different parts of Europe. The cult of the saints was universal in 1500, and some saints survived in Protestant areas long after the Reformation. St George, for example, remained the patron of England and the leading figure in the mummers' plays; in the Lutheran parts of Germany, the cult of St Martin continued; and even in the officially Calvinist Dutch Republic, St Nicholas continued to fill children's shoes with presents. The heroes of the romances of chivalry were almost equally international figures. The knight we know in England as 'Bevis of Hampton' was a hero to the Italians as Buovo d'Antone, and is just about recognizable in Russian dress as Bova Korolevitch. The story of Pierre de Provence was known not only in France but in Portugal, the Netherlands, Germany and Denmark. The Turks were devoted to Roland, whom they declared a Turk, and even to St George, whom they declared a *spahi*, or Turkish knight.[2]

The first part of this chapter is an essay in composite biography which will describe some of the most loved, hated and despised figures in the popular culture of the time; the second part, more speculative, will attempt to interpret the attitudes expressed in or through these figures.

Prototypes and transformations

Since stories so often wander from one popular hero to another, it seems useful to discuss types rather than individuals. The *Golden Legend*, no less than the Child ballads, might be studied as a corpus of stories which are transformations of one another. There are four main hero types: the saint, the warrior, the ruler, and the outlaw. In many cases it is not difficult to see how latecomers to the tradition were modelled on earlier prototypes. St John the Baptist, for example, was the prototypical ascetic, living in the wilderness, eating locusts and wild honey, dressed in 'raiment of camel's hair' (Matthew 3. 1-4), and other ascetics like St Antony Abbot or St Humphrey (who grew his hair and beard especially long) appear to have been modelled on him. Alexander the Great was the prototype of the ruler who was victorious abroad, just as Solomon was the model of the ruler who governed wisely at home.[3]

Prototypes might be modified to suit new needs. The medieval knight was transformed, as we shall see, into a general, a hussar, even a bandit. The Protestants did not believe in saints but they adopted, and adapted, the martyr, starting as early as 1523, when Luther wrote a broadside ballad about two of his followers who had been burned in Brussels. Crespin's book of martyrs celebrated the heroism of the Huguenots, while Foxe's book, which was ordered to be placed in churches, is important in the making of the English Protestant tradition. Finally the figure of the martyr became politicised, and men as diverse, and as remote from the original conception, as King Gustav Adolf of Sweden and Dr Henry Sacheverell were presented in terms of this stereotype.[4]

The ruler

The image of the ruler calls for treatment at some length because it should reveal popular attitudes to authority. One common image is that of the conqueror. The ruler is often described with adjectives like 'victorious', 'triumphant', 'glorious' or 'invincible' and portrayed as an Alexander-figure on horseback, leading an army against the foe, especially the heathen or heretic foe: Saracens (Charlemagne, Richard I), Moors (Sebastian of Portugal, a hero despite his defeat), Turks (Mátyás of

Hungary), Tartars (Ivan the Terrible, conqueror of Kazan and
Astrakhan), or Papists (Gustav Adolf, William III). William III
was pictured on horseback, galloping across prints – or
northern Irish gables – while accompanying verses emphasised
the theme of conquest and victory.

> *Whilst conquering William with laurels is crowned*
> *His fame and his name through the world shall go round.*

> *The conquering sword does King William proclaim*
> *And crown him with trophies of honour and fame.* [5]

Among the conquering heroes of the eighteenth century, two
rulers stand out. One is Charles XII, the 'brave and renowned'
king of Sweden, as an English chap-book calls him. Corporal
Gustav Reuter inscribed a portrait of the king on horseback,
'You must remember Carolus, the best soldier in the world'.
(Plate 13). The other outstanding conqueror is Frederick the
Great, whom the German broadside ballads present in similarly
glorious terms:

> *Friederikus ist ein Held*
> *Allzeit siegreich in dem Feld.*

> *(Frederick is a hero /always victorious in the field.)* [6]

The second common image of the ruler presented him as a
Solomon-figure, the judge seated on his throne, the
father of his people, described with adjectives like 'just',
'wise', and 'merciful'. St Louis (Louis IX of France) was a
popular figure of this kind, traditionally portrayed dispensing
justice under an oak-tree. His successor Louis XII of France
seems to have acquired a similar reputation. It was said that he
cried when he had to tax the people. A manifesto of the peasant
revolt in Normandy in 1639 looked back with nostalgia to the
time 'when Louis XII presided over a golden age' (*alors que
Louis XII menait un siècle d'or*), and one of the *cahiers* of the
third estate in 1789 addressed Louis XVI as 'heir to the sceptre
and the virtues of Louis IX, Louis XII and Henri IV'. In other
cahiers we are told that 'the name of Henry IV is always known
in the countryside and always repeated with emotion', that he
recognised his subordination to God and the law, and that he
saw himself as the father of his people who had nothing to gain
from their oppression. [7] The Emperor Maximilian was

presented, in his own time and afterwards, as a just and clement ruler, who gladly listened to the petitions of his subjects. In Hungary, the justice of King Mátyás was proverbial. The proverb ran: *Meghalt Mátyás király, oda az igazság*, or, in humanist Latin, *Matthias obiit, justitia periit*: 'King Mátyás is dead, justice is lost'. In Norway, throughout our period, St Olav, the eleventh-century king of Norway, remained a popular hero, and innovations which the peasants disliked were resisted in the name of 'King Olav's law'.[8]

A recurrent story about the ruler tells of his wandering about the land incognito. One might call this the 'Harun al-Rashid' topos after the stories about the Caliph of Bagdad told in the *Arabian Nights*. The Motif-Index calls this motif 'King in disguise to learn secrets of subjects' (K. 1812), which gives an unfortunate impression of snooping, whereas the king is usually presented as trying to ensure that justice is being done or to share the lives of ordinary people. A number of English ballads are built round this motif and deal with the meetings of King Edward and the Tanner (Child 273), King Henry and the Miller, King William and the Forester, or King Richard and Robin Hood (Child 151). A seventeenth-century chap-book, *The History of the King and the Cobbler*, tells us that 'it was the custom of King Henry VIII to walk late in the night into the City disguised, to observe how the constables and watch performed their duty'. In Scotland it was said that James V used to disguise himself as a tinker or a beggar or 'the gudeman of Ballengight'. In Russia, tales circulated of how the Tsar (sometimes specified as Ivan the Terrible or Peter the Great) joined the thieves:

> Sometimes he would associate with them in a disguise and once he advised them to rob the Exchequer; for (says he) I know the way to it; but one of the fellows up with his fist, and struck him a hearty good blow on the face, saying Thou Rogue, wilt thou offer to rob His Majesty, who is so good to us; let us go rob such a rich boyar who has cozen'd His Majesty of vast sums. At this Ivan was well pleased.[9]

The best known of all stories about the ruler as popular hero is the one that he is not really dead. He is only sleeping, usually in a cave, and he will return one day to conquer his enemies, to free his people from oppression, to restore justice and to bring about the golden age (Motif-Index A.570, D. 1960.2). The obvious prototype for this story is Christ, and the identification of the ruler with Christ and his Second Coming is surely a significant one. The story was a widespread one in our period, as it was before and would be later. It was attached to the Emperor Frederick in particular. During the Peasants' War, after the battle of Frankenhausen, thousands of peasants gathered at the Kyffhaüser mountain, where the Emperor was traditionally said to be sleeping, to wait for him to rise up and avenge the innocent blood which had lately been shed. The same story was attached to King Arthur, 'the past and future king', *rex quondam rexque futurus*, asleep in the 'hollow hill'. It was attached to Charlemagne, to 'good king Wenceslas' of Bohemia (*svatý Václav*), to Mátyás of Hungary, to Sebastian of Portugal. The Russian variant of the story contrasted the 'boyars' tsar', the actual tsar who was oppressing the people, with the 'true tsar', who was waiting his moment to come out of hiding.[10]

As the last example should make clear, the fact that some rulers were popular heroes did not mean that all rulers were, that craftsmen and peasants were blind to their faults. The hero-king was not infrequently contrasted with the actual king, Louis XII with Louis XIII, against whom the Norman peasants were rebelling in 1639, 'King Olav's law' with the law of the Danish kings who were ruling Norway during the early modern period.

In any case the image of the tyrant was familiar enough, with obvious biblical prototypes. From the Old Testament there was Pharaoh, and from the New there was Herod, who was well-known in mystery plays in England, Poland, Russia and elsewhere. He was traditionally represented in England as a megalomaniac braggart, claiming to be God: 'For I am even he that made heaven and hell/ And of my mighty power holdeth up this world round'. In time of war, foreign or civil, these odious comparisons were often made. Henry II of France was described as 'Pharaoh' in a Huguenot song, Philip II in a Dutch song during the revolt of the Netherlands; a wall-painting of about 1600 in Sucevița in Moldavia shows the crossing of the Red Sea, with Pharaoh's troops dressed like the Polish army, the Moldavians' chief enemy of the time. The preachers of the Catholic League described Henri III of France as a 'new Herod' after he had had the Duke of Guise assassinated. In Russia the traditional Herod play was transformed, probably in the late seventeenth century, into that of 'Tsar Maximilian', a proud, cruel and pagan ruler who persecutes his Christian son until he is struck down by the vengeance of God. Like the image of the mice burying the cat (above p.10), the play surely implies a criticism of Peter the Great, who imprisoned and possibly executed his son Alexis and subordinated the Church to the State; unless it is early enough to be a comment on the mid-seventeenth-century schism or on Ivan the Terrible, who had killed his son with his own hands.[11]

Cases of plain speaking against reigning monarchs stand out by their rarity, although a handful of French and English examples, at least, can be found. At Dijon in 1630, a portrait of Louis XIII was burned in the street, and something similar happened at Aix in 1637. At the end of the seventeenth century, a political 'Our Father' (above, p.122) was addressed to Louis XIV:

> Notre père qui êtes á Marly, votre nom n'est pas glorieux, votre règne est sur sa fin, votre volonté n'est plus fait ni sur la terre ni sur la mer . . .

One man at Thouars in 1707 is recorded to have said that 'Le roi est un bougre et un voleur', while a Buckinghamshire man said of Henry VIII, in the 1530s, that 'the King is a knave and liveth in adultery, and is an heretic and liveth not after the laws of God . . . I set not by the King's crown, and if I had it here I would play at football with it'. George II was burned in effigy at Walsall in 1750, and in 1779–80 George III appeared in prints as 'Sultan', an oriental despot in a turban.[12]

It is more normal for hostility to be displaced and for criticism to be indirect. This may happen in stories set in the past; in the French chap-book romances of chivalry the heroes – Huon of Bordeaux, Ogier the Dane, the four sons of Aymon – are shown to be justified in rebelling against Charlemagne, but the emperor is not shown to be at fault. It was his son Charlot, or his nephew Bertolais, who was to blame. Similarly, Robin Hood is justified in his rebellion, but the fault is not the king's, the true villain is an official, the sheriff of Nottingham. It is as if the king can do no wrong, although he can be ill advised by 'evil counsellors', to use the consecrated phrase. The testimony of popular literature fits in with the evidence from popular rebellions. The Pilgrimage of Grace claimed to be directed not against Henry

VIII but against Thomas Cromwell. Peasant risings in seventeenth-century France used slogans like 'Long live the king, down with the officials' (*Vive le roi, fie aux élus*).[13] The rebels did not want to know that the taxes had been authorised by the king. I should be inclined to conclude that kings inherited considerable reserves of popular good-will, that they were presumed benevolent, even heroic, until they were proved to be otherwise, that criticism was inhibited not only by the fear of punishment but also by a self-censorship which may not even have been conscious; but that these inhibitions could be broken down by events, in which case the stereotypes of Alexander and Solomon could be replaced by those of Herod and Pharaoh.

If a study of the ruler as popular hero helps illuminate popular political attitudes, other heroes, villains and fools should inform us about social attitudes, attitudes of the different groups making up society: the clergy, the nobility, and the 'third estate', including craftsmen and peasants themselves. In prints and on plates one sometimes finds images of the three estates, the priest saying 'I pray for all', the noble, 'I fight for all' and the peasant 'I work for all'.[14]

The clergy

For a heroic image of men of religion, we have only to go to the legends of the saints. There is the ascetic, for example: the austerities of St Jerome and St Antony Abbot, who fasted, prayed and mortified their flesh in the wilderness, seem to have caught the popular imagination. A second type of clerical hero is the good shepherd, a charitable man devoted to the material as well as the spiritual welfare of ordinary people. St Martin, Bishop of Tours, divided his cloak with a beggar ('The Charity of St Martin'). St Benedict helped a peasant who had dropped his axe in the river by making it float to the surface. St Nicholas, Bishop of Myra, one of the most popular saints of all, helped the sailors when the ship in which he was travelling was caught in a storm, and threw money into the house of a poor man at night so that his daughters would have the dowries they needed ('The Charity of St Nicholas'). St Francis combined the qualities of the ascetic and the pastor, fasting and praying in the wilderness but also giving away his clothes, and pacifying the man-eating wolf of Gubbio and the faction-fighting in Arezzo. St Francis was of course modelled on the prototype of Christ, not only receiving the stigmata but (according to some versions of his legend) being born in a manger.[15]

In other kinds of source, however, a rather different image of the clergy can be found. Friar Tuck, the merry friar who enjoys fighting and loves his dinner, is only one of a number of sympathetic but unheroic priests. Two Austrians, 'Pfaffe Amis' and 'Der Pfarrer vom Kalenberg', were medieval trickster-figures who were still popular in the sixteenth century. Their Tuscan equivalent is the 'merry priest' of fifteenth-century Florence, *il piovano arlotto*, 'a poor country cleric', as he describes himself, barely able to read his missal, and loving wine, women, and jests at the expense of both clergy and laity.[16]

The weaknesses of the clergy do not always receive such a sympathetic portrayal in popular tradition; they are often presented as villains or fools, as ignorant, proud, greedy, lazy, and lusting after other men's wives. These points are made with particular force in the popular literature of the German Reformation. Pamphilus Gengenbach's *Totenfresser* (1521) shows a pope, a bishop, a monk and a nun sitting round a table carving up a corpse. This is of course an attack not only on the greed of the clergy, but also on the doctrine of purgatory. It would be better to look at a less revolutionary decade, if we want to see popular anti-clericalism in its normal form, expressed in anecdotes, plays, or even popular art, like the eighteenth-century Staffordshire figure of the tithe pig chasing the parson. The motif of clerical covetousness is a recurrent one; think of the rich and grasping abbot who is punished by Robin Hood (Child 117), or the story of the priest who won't bury the dead unless he is paid in advance (Motif-Index Q.286.2), or the priest who refuses a small bribe because he will only sell his soul to the Devil for a large one (J.1263). Even more popular is the image of the cleric as seducer. There are Russian statuettes in wood and earthenware of a monk carrying on his back a sheaf in which a girl is hidden, and the clerical seducer is often the butt of sixteenth-century French farces. Friars in particular are mocked in this way in Italian stories from Boccaccio to Bandello, stories which are probably literary elaborations of folktales, like that of Frate Auberto disguised as the angel Gabriel (*Decameron*, day 4 No 2).[17]

The nobility

The nobility seem to have had a better image than might have been expected. The knight was a popular hero. Although the medieval romances of chivalry offer a clear-cut example of literature produced by, for, and about the nobility, there can be little doubt of the popular appeal of these romances in our period, abbreviated into chap-books and ballads or presented in the form of plays, including puppet-plays. The French had their Roland (known in Italy as Orlando), the Danes had their Holger (known in France as Ogier), the English, Guy of Warwick, the Spaniards their Cid, the Russians, Ilya of Murom, the Serbs, Marko Kraljević; the romance of the *Four Sons of Aymon* (pictured astride the famous horse Bayard) was popular in France, the Netherlands and Germany, and the eldest brother, Renaud de Montauban, pursued a glorious and independent career in Italy as Rinaldo.

The warrior-hero is presented in much the same way in one romance after the other. It goes without saying that he is both brave and strong; Marko, for example, might be painted 'grasping a grown ox by the tail slung over his shoulders and carrying it on his back while he walked erect'. A great rock split down the middle could be seen near Turin in the sixteenth and seventeenth centuries and 'the idiot peasants' said that Orlando 'split it with his sword'.[18] The warrior is also proud. The epithet which the Spanish ballads of our period apply most frequently to the Cid is *soberbio*, meaning that he is sensitive to real or fancied insults and quick to avenge them. Similarly, a Russian ballad presents Ilya of Murom as quarrelling with Vladimir, Prince of Kiev, because the Prince did not invite him to a feast; in *Les quatre fils Aymon*, Renaud kills Charlemagne's nephew Bertolais because Bertolais struck him in a dispute over a game of chess. With the important exception of Pierre de Provence, the knight is usually portrayed as a rough diamond, his manners unpolished, his main interest not love but war. The Cid and Guy of Warwick neglect their wives for feats of arms; the love-theme does not enter into *Les quatre fils Aymon* at all. In popular tradition, the *chanson de geste* was more influential than the *roman courtois*.

The popularity of the knight was such that a number of saints were represented in this form, not only St Martin, St Florian and

St Maurice (who were supposed to have served in the Roman army before their conversion), but St George, St James and even St Michael the archangel. In *The Seven Champions of Christendom*, St George and St James were joined by the brave knights St Denis, St Anthony of Padua, St Andrew, St Patrick and St David.[19]

From a military point of view, the knight in armour was already an anachronism in 1500, and as war became more highly organised, he was gradually replaced, in popular imagery as well as on the field, by the professional army officer, like 'the Austrian hero', Prince Eugene of Savoy. Yet Prince Eugene was still cast in the mould of Roland or St George, and celebrated in broadsides as 'the valiant hero', 'the noble knight' (*der tapfere Held, der edle Ritter*), fighting 'like a lion' against the Turks. If inn-signs provide a measure of English popular heroes, then in the eighteenth century the Duke of Marlborough and the Marquis of Granby were prominent among them, and so was Admiral Rodney and, above all, Admiral Vernon, 'Brave Vernon, Britain's Hero' as the ballads called him, 'Admiral Vernon the scourge of Spain'. Over a hundred varieties of a medal struck in his honour have survived, with the inscription 'he took Portobello with six ships only' (plates 11 and 12).[20]

Generals and admirals were not the sole heirs to the glory of the knight. Something rubbed off on the common soldier. By the eighteenth century, when he lived in barracks rather than being quartered on ordinary people, and no longer robbed and raped on the scale of the Thirty Years' War, the soldier could be seen in a heroic light, at least by young men – and women. After all, soldiers 'did not have to work in the fields; they were freed from the domination of their parents; they wore a splendid uniform; and they got to see something of the world'. Hussars, dragoons and guardsmen figured in broadsides and popular prints, or were painted on cupboards, or made into pottery figures or candlesticks. Perhaps it was a concession to popular taste when St Martin dividing his cloak with the Beggar was shown, as he was in Bratislava cathedral, in the uniform of an eighteenth-century hussar.[21]

The noble, like the priest, has an unheroic face, but it is one shown relatively rarely. In the romances of chivalry we find the figure of the treacherous knight, such as Ganelon, or Mordred, or Count Amaury in *Huon de Bordeaux*, or the Counts of

Carrión in the ballads of the Cid. The boastful soldier was a favourite fool-figure in the mystery plays of the Resurrection (the knights guarding the sepulchre), the Florentine pageants, where he took the form of a German *Landsknecht,* and the *commedia dell'arte,* where he took that of a Spanish captain. He may have been inspired by memories of the classical *miles gloriosus,* but he is also a topical figure in that age of mercenary warfare. What one misses in popular literature is the nobleman at home, the nobleman as landlord. The noble landlord, like the king, seems to have benefited from the fact that he was remote from the everyday life of the peasant. For his actions it was often the miller or the bailiff who got the blame. An occasional Italian folktale presents a noble who marries a poor girl and deserts her, or an oppressor who is brought to justice with difficulty. In the Catalan ballad *El Compte Arnau* the Count's ghost says he is in hell for having underpaid his workers – *per pagar mal les soldades.* A celebrated French print of *c.* 1789 shows the nobleman on the peasant's back (Plate 19). It may be relevant to note that in eastern Europe, where the nobles enserfed the peasants during this period, literacy was low so that evidence of popular attitudes has rarely survived; that in eastern Germany in 1525, some peasants declared that 'the gentry of Keymen robbed the poor people of their grain' and also that in Mecklenburg a set of stories about the tyranny of the noble landlord have been collected from oral tradition.[22]

The middle class

It may be that the peasants' potential hostility to their landlords, like their hostility to their rulers, was displaced on to another social group, the middle class – lawyers, officials, merchants and doctors. In a famous popular print, current in France and Germany, the lawyer was presented as a fourth estate: 'I eat all' are the words put into his mouth. A German folktale well known in the period described a rapacious lawyer who, when one of his victims said 'the Devil take you', was literally taken away by the Devil. Another folktale concerns the lawyer who tries to practise without lying and fails. The mask of *Dottore,* in the *commedia dell'arte,* sometimes called *Dottor Grazian* (after a medieval canon lawyer who taught at Bologna), presents the doctor of law as an ignorant, pedantic, pretentious fool. A number of Russian proverbs are concerned with the corruption of judges: 'the court is straight, but the judge is crooked', or 'one cannot talk to the judge if one is empty-handed'. There is also a rich vein of English evidence for popular hostility to 'the two-tongued lawyer', particularly during the Civil War. Lilburne called lawyers and judges 'thieves *cum privilegio*'. Winstanley declared that 'The law is the fox, poor men are the geese; he pulls off their feathers and feeds upon them', and a Digger song included the line 'Gainst lawyers and gainst priests, stand up now'. To understand this bitterness, one needs to remember how widespread litigation was in the early modern period; craftsmen and peasants might well have personal experience of lawyers.[23]

Another hate-figure was the official, whether he advised the ruler or carried his actions out. The unpopularity of the official, the tax-collector in particular, is well-documented from seventeenth-century France, where taxes were 'farmed'; in other words, the right of collecting them was sold, at a discount, to private entrepreneurs known as *partisans*, or *traitants*, or *maltotiers*, or *gabeleurs* (named after the notorious salt-tax, the *gabelle*). These *gabeleurs* were described by the rebellious peasants and others as 'tyrants', 'cannibals', and 'blood-suckers', and they were not infrequently attacked in the course of their operations, a custom which seems to have survived in France till the days of Pierre Poujade.[24]

Other kinds of businessmen were considered scarcely less villainous, particularly if they lent money at interest, hoarded grain, or held monopolies.

> *Thou Usurer with thy money bags,*
> *That liveth so at ease:*
> *By gaping after gold thou dost*
> *Thy mighty God displease,*
> *And for thy greedy usury*
> *And thy great extortion:*
> *Except thou dost repent thy sins,*
> *Hell fire will be thy portion.*

Thus a broadside ballad of 1612. In times of scarcity or inflation, like the later sixteenth and later eighteenth centuries, it was the merchants who were blamed (particularly 'the leeches of Genoa' in Spain) for 'engrossing' or 'forestalling', in other words, creating an artificial scarcity for their own profit. In the same class were monopolists, like Sir Giles Mompesson, whose monopoly of licensing alehouses probably made him one of the best-hated men in England. He was attacked in a print of 1621, inscribed:

> For greedy gain he thrust the weak to wall
> And thereby got himself the devil and all.

Dives, whose story was sung in ballads (like Child 56) and painted on alehouse walls, was the prototype of the selfish rich man, invoked, for example, in an English anonymous letter of 1795 about the distress of the poor. Alternatively, the miser might be presented as a comic figure, a fool who is so upset by the loss of his money that he dies, like Reginald Money-Bags and John Eye-of-the-Penny in the popular plays of eighteenth-century Wales.[25]

Compared to the lawyer and the merchant, the physician escaped relatively lightly. In folktales and in popular plays in England, Germany and Italy he is portrayed as ignorant, pedantic, cunning and greedy, but he is more of a fool than a villain, perhaps because most craftsmen and peasants did not have personal experience of doctors and their fees.[26]

After a view of this rogues' gallery the reader may well wonder where the middle-class heroes have gone. They are certainly rare enough; there is one example of the honest lawyer, and he was canonised for it – the Breton Saint Yves, usually portrayed mediating between a rich man and a poor man. As for that nineteenth-century favourite, the entrepreneur as popular hero, he is almost invisible in the early modern period, with one significant exception. The exception is England in the seventeenth and eighteenth centuries, where we find heroes like 'old Hobson the merry Londoner' (a wealthy haberdasher); the Berkshire clothier, Jack of Newbury; Simon Eyre, Lord Mayor of London; and, above all, Dick Whittington. Dick's popularity in England and the lack of continental parallels to his career goes a little way towards suggesting that England was an 'achieving society' before the Industrial Revolution.[27]

Ordinary people

How did craftsmen and peasants see themselves? The self-image of the weavers, the shoemakers and other crafts has been discussed above (p.36f). It is much harder to discover the self-image of the peasant, Jacques Bonhomme, Karsthans, or Juan Labrador. It is obviously necessary to be suspicious of any printed text which purports to present it. All the same, a few texts do seem worth discussing in this place, because they were frequently reprinted and because they present peasants as heroes.

The story of King Solomon and Marcolf is a medieval one and it was written in Latin, but it was current in sixteenth-century Europe translated into a number of vernaculars, so it should not be dismissed from consideration. Marcolf, who is sometimes portrayed carrying a pitchfork, is a peasant, 'of visage greatly misshapen and foul'. He may look a fool but he triumphs over the proverbially wise Solomon with ease, turning out to be 'right talkative eloquent and wise'. Another peasant who is no fool is the Italian Campriano, who triumphs over a group of merchants in a sequence of incidents which progress from the crude to the sadistic.[28]

Much more attractive is the French peasant, Bonhomme Misère. Misère is a poor man but a kind one. As a result of his hospitality to two travellers, Peter and Paul, Misère has a wish granted. His wish is that 'anyone who climbs my pear-tree' [his only property in the world] 'should be unable to come down until I wish it'. He catches a thief in this way, and releases him on oath never to rob the tree again. Later he is cunning enough to catch Death himself, and only lets him go after he has been promised that he might remain on earth 'tant que le monde sera monde'. Misère is presented as poor, but 'content de sa destinée'; simple, but not as simple as he looks; generous, and ultimately indestructible. It is hardly surprising that the story was a popular one.

A similar picture of the wisdom of contenting oneself with modest comforts emerges from a poem current in eighteenth-century Scandinavia, *Bonde Lyckan*, 'Peasant Success'.

En 8te kiørs bonde	*A peasant with eight cows*
som haver en haest	*who owns a horse*
Gudfrygtig og aer-lig,	*God-fearing and honest,*
god naboe dernaest.	*a good neighbour as well.*
Sin Gud og Kong troe	*Faithful to his God and his king*
med hver mands attest.	*as everyone will bear witness.*

Er lidet louv-halted,	*He limps a little, and is*
god ven med sin Praest.	*good friends with his vicar.*
Ved inted af Laensmand	*Sees nothing of the magistrate,*
ej heller noen rest.	*owes nothing to anyone.*
Boer langt op i skougen,	*Lives high up in the woods,*
har skieldum nogen giaest.	*seldom has a guest.*
Er frie for Herregaarden.	*Is free from the landlord,*
krig hunger og paest.	*war hunger and plague.*
Vel bruger sin ager,	*Makes good use of his land,*
eng, spade og laest.	*meadow, spade and last.*
Og slider sit vadmel,	*He wears homespun,*
skind-buxer og vaest.	*leather trousers and waistcoat.*
Forligt med sin Hustrue,	*Agrees with his wife*
den han haver faest.	*and holds her close.*
Samt glad i sit arbeid,	*Happy in his work,*
den lever aller-baest.	*which he loves best of all.* [29]

If the reader finds this picture too idyllic to be true, it may be worth emphasising that its hero avoids landlords like the plague, that he owes his freedom from them to his living so 'high up in the woods', just as he owes his freedom from military service to the fact that he is lame. The unknown author of these lines – like Marcolf, Campriano and Misère – is not so simple as he looks. If they are not a self-portrait, they present an image to which the peasant might nod his assent.

The craftsman's image of the peasant was a good deal less flattering. Hostility between town and country was strong in many parts of Europe in this period, intensified as it was by the fact that many townsmen, craftsmen included, owned small pieces of land. This practice seems to have been particularly common in Italy, and it may be no accident that some of the most vivid images of the peasant as villain are Italian, such as those expressed in *Le malitie di villani* ('The peasants' dirty tricks'), a song which declares that they are 'like animals' and that

In mal far si sono astuti	*They are cunning in ill-doing*
Si li vecchi come i putti	*The old ones as much as the young*
I me par ribaldi tutti	*They all seem rogues to me*
Con lor non e da praticare	*There is no doing business with them*
De villani non te fidare.	*Don't trust the peasant.*

A sixteenth-century play has as its villain a certain Biagio, 'a treacherous peasant' (*un perfido villano*), who overcharges for the produce he sells at market and is punished for this by a group of citizens. The very word *villano* meant both 'villain' and 'peasant' at this time; in English, too, 'villain' and 'villein' are connected. In more cheerful mood, the townsmen and their spokesmen, notably Hans Sachs, saw the peasants as figures of fun. His *Heinz in Nürnberg* mocks the simple countryman who comes to town to obtain a citizen's privileges, a theme taken up by an Italian song of a peasant who wanted to become a citizen of Ferrara. The moral is clear: peasant, know your place![30]

Women also had to know their place, as is clear not only from the popular (masculine) images of the woman as villain, such as the shrew, but even from the images of the heroine. Most popular heroines were objects, admired not so much for what they did as for what they suffered. For women, martyrdom was virtually the only road to sanctity, and there were many legends of virgin martyrs who are not easy to tell apart except in the manner of their deaths and tortures: St Agatha, whose breasts were cut off, St Catherine, who was to be broken on a wheel, St Lucy, whose eyes were put out, and so on. Particularly popular in the Netherlands, France and Germany was the story of Geneviève of Brabant, the wife falsely accused of adultery and driven out by her husband, living in the forest till her innocence was discovered. Equally passive were two heroines who often took the place of saints in Protestant countries: chaste Susanna (falsely accused but vindicated like Geneviève) and patient Griselda, who were celebrated in German plays, in English puppet-plays, in Swedish ballads, in Danish chap-books. Equally passive is Cinderella, and so are other folktale heroines; almost equally passive is the Virgin Mary, a figure of obedience (the Annunciation) or patient suffering (the Crucifixion). Judith slaying the tyrant Holofernes seems to have been an exception among heroines.[31]

The villainous woman, on the other hand, is portrayed as intensely active, whether she is scolding, seducing, causing bad weather, stealing the milk from her neighbour's cattle, or beating her husband. The preponderance of women among the accused at witch-trials is the best evidence of the strength of popular traditions of misogyny; to it one might add the many anecdotes about the malice of women, some collected in chap-books devoted entirely to that subject. What these anecdotes tend to emphasise is the danger of trusting women: Eve, Delilah and Potiphar's wife were emotionally powerful prototypes of the deceitful female.[32]

The outsiders

No image of society can be complete if it does not include the outsiders. One kind of outsider was often seen as a hero: the outlaw. I use the deliberately neutral term 'outlaw' as a general description of a number of ways of life in opposition to the authorities. On the sea there was the English pirate, or the Dutch *zeeroover*. On the land there was the English highwayman, the Scots reiver, the German *Strassenraüber,* the Italian *bandito* (originally 'exile', later 'bandit'), and the Spanish *bandolero.* On the evidence of ballads, the outlaw seems to have been an even more important figure in the popular culture of eastern Europe than he was in the west: the Russian *razboinik,* the Czech *loupežník,* the Croat *uskok,* the Hungarian *bétyár,* and the south-east European *haiduk*. Low population density and relatively weak central governments allowed outlaws to flourish longer in the east than in the west, and an enserfed poor peasantry is more likely to sympathise with outlaws than a freer or more prosperous one.[33]

Outlaws were more like rulers than saints; they tended to be popular only in their own region. Robin Hood's reputation was confined to England, Joan de Serrallonga's to Catalonia, Stenka Razin's to Russia. For some reason new outlaw-heroes seem to have been particularly numerous in the eighteenth century; perhaps the spread of broadside and chap-book immortalised names which might have been forgotten and fixed exploits which would in time have been transferred to others. In eighteenth-century Russia we find the Cossack rebel Emilian Pugachev; in the Carpathians, Oleks Dovbuš; in Slovakia, Juraj Jánošík; in Andalusia, Diego Corrientes, 'the generous bandit'; in Naples, Angiolillo; in Britain, Captain Kidd (who was born in Scotland), Rob Roy, and Dick Turpin, who was highwayman, burglar, deer-stealer and smuggler; in France, Cartouche, who led a gang of thieves in Paris, and Mandrin, who organised smuggling in Dauphiné.[34] That outlaws were mythogenic in this way suggests that they satisfied repressed wishes, enabling ordinary people to take imaginative revenge on the authorities to whom they were usually obedient in real life.

The central theme of the legends of the heroic outlaw is that he rights wrongs and helps ordinary people. Robin Hood robbed the rich and gave to the poor, as the ballads suggest, notably *A Gest of Robyn Hood* (Child 117) and *A True Tale of Robin Hood* (Child 154). This characteristic was to become a commonplace of outlaw biography in the English-speaking world. Rob Roy, like Robin, gave money to a poor man who was in debt to a rich one, taking it back from the rich man soon after. Dick Turpin threw £6 into the house of a poor woman in a gesture reminiscent of the Charity of St Nicholas. In Spain too a traditional ballad refers to

> *Diego Corrientes, el ladrón de Andalucía,*
> *Que a los ricos robaba y a los pobres socorría.*

> *(Diego Corrientes, the robber of Andalucia*
> *Who took from the rich and helped the poor.)*

Elsewhere the theme undergoes local variations, according to need. The ballads of Stenka Razin show him punishing unjust officials and hanging a tyrannical governor on his own gallows. Angiolillo was said to have defended the honour of virgins and to have sold corn cheap to the poor in times of dearth.[35]

What is more, the outlaw is not infrequently described in terms borrowed from the stereotype of the knight. Robin Hood was described as 'courteous': 'Would he never do company harm/That any woman was in'. Stenka Razin was presented in ballads as a *bogatyr*, a traditional warrior hero. Serrallonga was described as *galán*, 'gallant' in every sense. Mandrin was noted for his 'politesse . . . avec le beau sexe', and is described in one biography as *preux*, 'valiant', an adjective associated with Roland and other heroes of romances of chivalry.

However, the outlaw was not always idealised. Serrallonga may have been a popular hero, but the small fry of his profession were seen rather differently, as some sixteenth-century Catalan chap-books suggest. The verses on a certain Ianot Poch, for example, emphasise the 'evils and disasters' that he and his band have caused, suggest that he is 'posessed by the devil (*endiablada*), and accuse him of cruelty to ordinary people:

La pobra gent robaves
Fins los claus de las parets.

(*You robbed poor people of everything, down to the nails in the*
walls.)

In similar fashion the broadside, *Captain Kidd's Farewell to the*
Seas (1701), presents him as proud and cruel, themes elaborated
in a later eighteenth-century American version.[36]

If attitudes to the outlaw are sometimes ambiguous or
ambivalent, the image of other outsiders is plain enough; they
are wicked and fearsome without qualification. The most
obvious examples are those of the Turk, the Jew, and the witch.

The popular image of the Turk or any other Muslim was that
of a blasphemer who denies God, rather than a man with a
religion of his own. In addition Turks were seen as bloodthirsty,
cruel and treacherous. When Christian solders committed
atrocities, they were described as behaving 'like Turks'. Target
practice in Elizabethan England was known as 'shooting at the
Turk' because the image of a Turk was a favourite butt for
arrows. Turks were scarcely considered human; they were
commonly described as wolves or dogs. In Spain and Serbia,
where Muslims were not so much outsiders as neighbours, they
were sometimes portrayed in ballads as honourable foes, but
not always; the Venetian governor of Split complained in 1574
that the local inhabitants 'have various seditious ballads always
in their mouths; especially one comparing the Turk to a
devouring flood, which they sing at night, under our very
palace windows'.[37]

Even more fearsome, if possible, was the outsider who lived
within the community, the traitor within the gates; for example,
the Jew. Jews, like Turks, were not seen as human beings but as
'dogs' or as pigs; woodcuts showed a Jewish woman who had
given birth to piglets or a sow suckling Jewish babies. They
were regarded as sorcerers and blasphemers and often accused
of desecrating the host or holy images. A popular story, *The*
Wandering Jew, told of the shoemaker who would not let
Christ rest on the way to the crucifixion and was condemned to
wander the world thereafter. Jews were regarded as murderers
because they had crucified Christ and they were often accused
of the ritual murder of children, as in the ballad, *Hugh of*
Lincoln (Child 155). The stereotype of the cruel and greedy

usurer was often applied to them. In mystery plays, Judas was often represented as a typical Jewish usurer of this kind; and in seventeenth-century German prints, Jews were shown profiteering from dearth and debased coinage. Chap-book biographies of Judas relate that he killed his father and married his mother, as if repressed wishes were projected on to the greatest of human villains.[38]

Similarly, the witch was seen as a traitor within the gates, blaspheming against Christianity by insulting the cross and the host, doing harm to her neighbours, eating children and engaging in sex orgies with demons. Again it has been suggested that people projected 'their unacknowledged terrifying desires' on to the witch. Prosecutions for witchcraft increased sharply in many parts of Europe in the sixteenth century. How far the hatred and fear of witches was spontaneous, and how far it was necessary for the clergy to convert ordinary people to the witch-craze, is a question which historians are finding it difficult to answer. It is likely, though hard to prove, that the stereotype of the old woman with supernatural powers which she used to harm people was a popular belief going back to the Middle Ages or before, while the stereotype of the witch as heretic or blasphemer, in league with the Devil, was a learned belief to which ordinary people were converted only gradually. One argument for this view comes from comparative history. In Orthodox Europe there was no great witch-hunt in the sixteenth and seventeenth centuries; Russia, for example, was immune from it. Yet in Russian folklore there was a villain-figure with strong resemblances to a witch: Baba Yaga, a hideous old woman with an iron nose who flew through the air in a mortar and ate children. What was lacking was the idea of a pact between the old woman and the devil.

Two more popular villains were created in the course of the Reformation: the Catholic stereotype of the wicked Protestant and the Protestant stereotype of the wicked 'Papist'. The new images had much in common with the stereotypes of the Jew and the witch, from which elements were obviously taken. In sixteenth-century France, Catholics described Protestants as pigs, as sacrilegious and blasphemous – why else should they have attacked relics and images? – as 'bewitched' by the new religion, as treacherous, as people who indulged in child-murder, cannibalism and promiscuous sex, encouraged by their ministers. Conversely, in seventeenth-century England, Protestants saw Catholics as idolaters, supporters of the Devil, and as plotters, traitors who wanted to destroy English liberty and to bring in papal, Spanish or French tyranny, not to mention the Inquisition.

Hatred of outsiders was so common as to make one wonder whether most ordinary people of the period were not what psychologists sometimes call 'authoritarian personalities', combining submissiveness to authority with aggressiveness towards people outside their group.[39]

Popular attitudes and values

Most of the heroes – and villains – described in the last few pages really existed. Why should some kings, or bishops, or outlaws have become heroes and not others? In trying to answer this question it is important to avoid two opposite errors. Historians tend to be short-sighted, and try too hard to explain the legend of, say, Henri IV of France in terms of the characteristics of the king and of attitudes to his policies. The trouble with this approach is that stories wander from one hero-king to another, and also that there is no obvious correlation between a ruler's power and prestige in his own time and his posthumous reputation, his place in popular tradition. The Emperor Charles V had great power, but there is only a little evidence that he was sometimes seen as a hero after his death. No expense was spared to present Louis XIV as a hero in his own lifetime, but in vain; unlike his grandfather Henri, Louis does not seem to figure in French folktales.[40] On the other hand, relatively colourless personalities like Sebastian of Portugal and William III of England did become popular heroes.

Folklorists, on the other hand, tend to be long-sighted. They stress the fact that the same stories are told of many different heroes, that a well-known stereotype 'crystallises' around a particular individual, without asking why that individual was selected. What was it which made him mythogenic? Why did the process of crystallisation occur around him and not someone else?[41]

There may well be different answers to this question in different cases, but a plausible suggestion might be that certain individuals conform, or are seen as conforming in certain respects, to a hero-stereotype like that of the just king or the noble outlaw. This conformity strikes the imagination of singers or storytellers or painters, so that tales and images of this individual begin to circulate. In the course of circulation, their lives and deeds are assimilated to the stereotype in other respects as well as the original ones. This assimilation takes place partly for technical reasons of the kind already discussed (above, p.141). It is easier to adapt verbal or pictorial formulae to a new hero than to create new formulae. In any case the traditional image corresponds to the expectations of the audience.

This theory is too ambitious for precise demonstration, but a few pieces of evidence which fit it may be pointed out. If a king has the same name as a ruler-hero, this will help to launch him in popular tradition. Frederick the Great inherited something from the traditional 'Emperor Frederick', a figure which was itself the product of the assimilation of Frederick II to Frederick I. If Louis XII of France enjoyed a reputation for justice in the seventeenth and eighteenth centuries, this may be in part because he had been assimilated to St Louis, Louis IX. 'Conquering William', William III of England, may have been conflated with William the Conqueror. If Martin Luther was seen as a Protestant saint, notably in the famous woodcut by Hans Baldung, this may be in part because St Martin was already a popular hero – and conversely, the cult of St Martin may have survived in Evangelical Germany by association with Martin Luther.

A ruler's own actions could, of course, help him to be seen in terms of the stereotype. William III and Charles XII did win victories, Henri IV did bring peace, Louis XII and the Emperor Joseph II were concerned with justice and reform, Sebastian did fight the infidel. If the story of the ruler who is not dead but sleeping attached itself to Sebastian, this may be because he was not seen to die and did not die in Portugal. If the 'Harun al-Rashid' topos attached itself to Peter the Great, this may be because Peter did travel incognito, although he did this in England and the Dutch Republic, not in Russia.

Finally, disasters which take place after their deaths help to make some rulers into heroes, encouraging people to look back to the good old days under their rule. The Turkish invasion of Hungary in 1526 probably helped make King Mátyás, who died in 1490, into a hero; the Spanish takeover of Portugal in 1580 probably did the same for Sebastian, who had been killed in 1578. Perhaps the Russian 'Time of Troubles' about 1600 softened the harsh outlines of the career of Ivan the Terrible, who died in 1584.

The process of crystallisation is not confined to rulers, but seems to work for other kinds of popular hero or villain. British outlaws were assimilated to Robin Hood. Gabriel Ratsey, a minor English outlaw, was said to have intended to rob one man but, finding him to be poor, gave him forty shillings instead, saying that he helped the poor, 'for the rich can help themselves'. Robin Hood-like stories were told of Dick Turpin and also of Rob Roy, who certainly had the right name for success in his chosen career. In Russia, the image of Pugachev was assimilated to that of Razin, whom he resembled in obvious respects such as being a Cossack and a rebel, and the career of Razin was in turn remembered in terms of that of Pugachev. Dick Whittington, about whom some reliable information has survived, is a clear case of crystallisation. He was a rich merchant and he was a generous one, founding Whittington College. Hence he had to be described as coming of humble origin (when he was really of gentry stock) and as marrying his master's daughter (which we happen to know he did not do).[42]

One of the most remarkable cases of assimilation to a stereotype is that of Faust. His story, as told in puppet-plays and chap-books in the early modern period, is a combination of several traditional themes: that of the man who makes a pact with the Devil, like Theophilus; that of the magician with a dangerously close relationship to the forces of evil, like Friar Bacon; and that of the trickster, like Till Eulenspiegel. In the Faust-Book of 1587 these themes combined and crystallised on to a relatively minor figure, a certain Georgius Faustus of Heidelberg who lived in the early sixteenth century and studied magic.[43]

More fundamental are the questions, why these stereotypes existed in early modern Europe, why heroes were presented in these particular ways, and what this tells us about popular attitudes. Here the historian is in a dilemma. The subject is too elusive for him to do much more than offer impressions and speculations; on the other hand, it is too important to leave out. In a small space it is best to make only a few points.

The first point concerns the marvellous, which is present almost everywhere. It dominates the lives of the saints from birth to death. St George was born with a red cross marked on his right hand, St Nicholas when a baby refused the breast on Fridays, and St John the Baptist prophesied in the womb. Accounts of martyrdoms are punctuated with supernatural interventions. When St Agatha's breasts were cut off, they grew again; St Lucy became immobile and a thousand men could not shift her. One might have expected saints to work miracles, but knights, kings and outlaws also do so on occasion. Knights perform superhuman feats of arms. Frederick the Great was said to be unvulnerable and to have two books of magic to help him win battles. King Olav was believed to work miraculous cures. In France and England the royal magic was institutionalised and took the form of touching for the 'king's evil' (that is, for scrofula), a practice which reached its height in the seventeenth century. Where Louis XII touched 500-odd people in a year, Louis XIII touched more than 3,000 and Louis XIV, on one occasion, 2,400 in a single day.[44]

Superhuman powers are also a recurrent feature of outlaw biography. Robin Hood's archery was phenomenal: 'always he sliced the wand'. Turpin rode from London to York in a day, such a feat that his arrival served him as an alibi. However, these feats were nothing compared to those of the Russian *razboiniki*. Bullets and cannon-balls could not harm Stenka Razin, and he once escaped from prison by drawing a boat on the wall and sailing away in it.[45] Villains, too, were believed to have supernatural powers, because they were helped by the Devil. Turks and Jews were regularly associated with the Devil in verses and in prints. Witches and magicians (such as Faust) were supposed to have made a pact with the Devil. Protestants said that the Pope had made a Devil's pact, and Catholics said that Luther had done so. Whatever was outside the experience of ordinary people demanded an explanation in terms of the marvellous. To be learned was abnormal, so a learned man must be a magician, he must (like Friar Bacon and others) have a brazen head in his study which answered his questions (Motif-Index D 1311.7.1). To be rich was abnormal, and a rich man must have oppressed the poor, found buried treasure, or, as in *The History of Fortunatus*, been given a purse which could never be emptied.

As in the case of this magic purse, objects as well as people could have supernatural powers: swords, rings, and so on. The image of a saint might be as potent as the saint and it might, like a person, be subject to persuasion, even threats. The people of San Pedro de Usun threatened to throw their image of St Peter into the river if their prayers were not heard, and the people of Villeneuve-St-Georges actually did throw their St George into the Seine in 1735, after he had failed to look after their vines. Ex-votos were often offered to miraculous images, and different images of the same saint were sometimes believed to be rivals, like the two St Christophers at Tarragona.[46] This 'concrete thought', as it is sometimes called, is also revealed in the use of personifications. In eighteenth-century Serbia, the plague was seen as an old woman who could be kept out of the village if the right rituals were performed. Carnival was a fat man: Lent, a thin old woman (below, p.185). In this context, the threats of the Breton peasants to shoot the *gabelle* 'like a mad dog' do not seem all that implausible (above, p.76). In a seventeenth-century French inn, you would not see such a notice as, 'Do not ask for credit as a refusal might offend', but a picture of a dead man labelled *Crédit est Mort* (Plate 9). This is the language of the image at all times, as a glance at a newspaper or hoarding will reveal, but the example of the Bretons suggests that it may have been taken a little more seriously in the seventeenth century than we take it now. If they did not quite believe that the *gabelle* was a person, they may not have quite disbelieved it.[47] People were made the scapegoats for processes. It was not the system but the individual who was attacked, not the crown but the king or his councillors.

It is for this reason, among others, that popular attitudes in this period may be described as generally 'conservative', or better, 'traditional'. The fact that craftsmen and peasants accepted saints, rulers and knights as their heroes suggests that they identified with the values of church, king and nobility, or at least, that they had to structure their world through models provided by the dominant group.[48] The peasants of Telemark in Norway were described in 1786 as holding one basic principle: 'Follow the old ways. Oppose all innovations' (*Følg gammel Skik. Staae imod alle Anordninger*). This formula is echoed in a number of proverbs of the form 'don't abandon old customs for new ones', or as the Catalans say, *No et deixis els costums vells pels novells*; it will serve as a useful shorthand description of the attitudes of ordinary people in this period, provided that it is not misunderstood.[49]

It does not mean that craftsmen and peasants were satisfied with the social order exactly as it was. They did not see society in terms of harmony but in terms of conflict. They complained of poverty, injustice, unemployment, taxation, tithes, rent, and labour services. They often refer to the exploitation, or, as they put it more concretely, the 'skinning' or the 'devouring' of the poor by the rich. Popular prints sometimes show big fish eating up small ones, an image for which the obvious interpretation is that (as the fisherman says in Shakespeare's *Pericles*) fish live in the sea just as men do on land. Craftsmen and peasants were well aware, as the remarks already quoted about judges and lawyers suggest, of the difficulty of obtaining redress for the wrongs they suffered by means of the law.[50]

What did they think should or could be done about these wrongs? Juxtaposing the evidence from texts – songs, tales, proverbs – with the evidence from actions – the many riots and rebellions of the period – it is possible to discover various responses, and it may be useful to distinguish five points on a broad spectrum of attitudes: fatalist, moralist, traditionalist, radical, and millenarian.

The fatalist response, invisible in action, is expressed in the weary wisdom of the proverbs. Things cannot be different. So many proverbs begin, in their various languages, with 'one has to . . .' (*il faut, man müss, bisogna* . . .) 'God is very high and the Tsar is a long way off', say the Russians, or 'To live is either to beat or to be beaten'. 'Poor folks fare poorly', say the Dutch; or 'God gives, God takes away'.[51] All one can do in this life is to suffer, to endure. However, others thought that 'God helps those who help themselves' (a proverb current in the period as it is today). The fatalist response shades into the moralist response, which is to see the world's troubles and injustices as a symptom of what is wrong with human nature, not of what is wrong with the social order. This is not a passive attitude; it allows action against villains wherever this is possible. It is the attitude expressed in the figure of the avenger, the noble outlaw who struck at unjust or wealthy individuals just as he helped poor or wronged individuals, without trying to reform the social system.[52]

The moralist response shades into the traditionalist, which is to resist, in the name of the 'old order' (*das alte Recht, stara pravda, gammel skik,* etc.), changes which have been taking place. The emphasis may be on wicked individuals who break with tradition, but it may be on new customs (as we would say, new 'trends'). It is not a mindless conservatism but a bitter awareness that change is usually at ordinary people's expense, coupled with the need to legitimise riot or rebellion. Hence the German peasants who rose in 1525 declared they were defending their traditional rights; the Norman peasants who rose in 1639 resisted the demands of Louis XIII in the name of the laws of Louis XII; eighteenth-century English food rioters demanded traditional prices and traditional restrictions on profiteers; and the peasants of Telemark in 1786 opposed new taxes in the name of King Olav's Law.[53]

The traditionalist response shades into a more radical one. In 1675 some of the rebellious Breton peasants demanded *ordonnances nouvelles.* Not all the demands of the German peasants in 1525 were traditional ones, and not all were supported by appeals to old customs. Some demanded the abolition of serfdom, because 'God created everyone free' or because Christ has redeemed all mankind. Michael Gaismair, who led the rising in the Tyrol, had a vision of 'complete equality in the land' (*ain ganze Gleichait im Lande*). Stenka Razin proclaimed that all men would be equal. If this is a return to the past, it is not to the recent past but to a primitive golden age.

When Adam delved and Eve span,
who was then the gentleman?[54]

This attitude shades into the millenarian. Hans Böhm, 'the drummer of Niklashausen', who preached in the Würzburg area in the 1470s, declared that a kingdom was at hand where there would be no taxes, rents or services, while everyone would be equal. 'The time will have to come when princes and lords will work for their daily bread.' In 1525, Thomas Müntzer preached a similar utopia to the peasants and miners of Thuringia. At Münster in 1534, the Anabaptists announced a new order in which 'all things were to be in common, there would be no private property and nobody was to do any more work, but simply trust in God'. The millennium was to come about miraculously, by divine intervention, independently of human effort, like the white man's cargo in modern cargo cults or the fortune of Fortunatus or the image, well known in the sixteenth century, of the land of Cockaigne, where roast pigs with knives in their backs were ready for the taking. We have returned to a fatalist response, though this one is optimistic.[55]

In this spectrum of opinion one can find radical views and activist views but rarely the two combined. A labourer in Elizabethan Essex once asked, 'What can rich men do against poor men if the poor men rise and hold together?' They rarely did. Class consciousness or 'horizontal solidarity' was largely lacking. The 'vertical solidarity' of master and man, patron and client, landlord and tenant often worked against these horizontal ties. In towns, loyalty to the craft (masters and journeymen) against other crafts and other towns worked against class consciousness. In the countryside, loyalty to the village worked against it; it was difficult to persuade peasants to cooperate with outsiders, including other peasants.

This attitude of distrust towards everyone outside a small circle of relatives and friends went with a view of the world (not uncommon in traditional societies) as a place of 'limited good' where no one can prosper save at someone else's expense. (In a society which is not enjoying economic growth there is, of course, something in this idea.) The result was that envy, the 'evil eye' and the fear of envy were widespread. So was the belief that witches had the power to make their own cows give more milk by taking milk by supernatural means from the cows of their neighbours. There were spells for protecting farm animals by directing the evil on to the animals of others. It is as if people believed that the system could not change but only the relative places of individuals within it, most spectacularly in the popular image of the world turned upside down (below, p.185). In the Vivarais in 1670, some rebellious peasants declared that it was the turn of the gentry to become *their* servants.[56]

This is a kind of imaginative poverty, an incapacity to conceive of alternative social worlds, which is surely the result of narrow horizons, limited social experience. In 1944 a study of Turkish villagers revealed that they could not imagine a sum of money larger than five thousand dollars. Similarly, when Misère is asked what he wishes for most, he thinks not of land or more trees, but simply of improved security for the one tree he has. In the world of the folktale he was right; he avoided the nemesis which came on the fisherman and his wife (Grimm, No. 19) who asked for too much, irritated their supernatural helper and lost all they had gained. There is a Russian proverb, 'too much luck is dangerous'.[57] Perhaps people were unwilling rather than unable to imagine alternative ways of life. They were afraid.

They had good reason to be afraid, given the mortality rate and the dangers of war, famine and plague. An underlying insecurity often surfaces in proverbs. Outside the family, the house and the village, the world is hostile. 'There are three things you cannot trust: the king, the weather and the sea.' 'Friends and mules fail you when you need them.' 'So long goes the pot to water that it breaks.' Many rituals and symbols of popular culture seem to have been protections against danger. This was the function of many saints, notably 'the fourteen helpers in need' (*Die Vierzehn Nothelfer*), which spread out from Germany in the fifteenth century. St George protected people from war, St Sebastian from the plague, St Margaret from the dangers of childbirth, and so on. Other popular heroes were seen in a similar light; warriors or soldiers painted on cupboards acted as guardians. Insecurity involves following tradition, for 'the certain is worth more than the uncertain', or is at any rate safer.[58]

It was dangerous to abandon the well-trodden paths of tradition, and yet the existing social order with its injustices and privations engendered frustrations on a massive scale. People needed hate-figures like witches, Turks and Jews, they needed to displace on to outsiders the hostilities created by tensions inside the community. They needed regular occasions on which to express those hostilities, to relieve those tensions. These occasions will be the subject of the next chapter.

CHAPTER SEVEN

The World of Carnival

Myths and rituals

In the last chapter an attempt was made to approach popular attitudes and values by way of popular heroes. One danger of this approach was that the heroes had to be taken out of their setting. In traditional European popular culture, the most important kind of setting was that of the festival: family festivals, like weddings; community festivals, like the feast of the patron saint of a town or parish (*Fête Patronale, Kirchenweihtag*, etc.); annual festivals involving most Europeans, like Easter, May Day, Midsummer, the Twelve Days of Christmas, New Year, and the Epiphany; and finally, Carnival. These were special occasions when people stopped work and ate, drank and spent whatever they had. The Italian priest Alberto Fortis recorded with disapproval on his visit to Dalmatia that 'domestic economy is not commonly understood by the Morlaks, a pastoral people of that region; in this respect they resemble the Hottentots, and finish off in a week what should have lasted for many months, simply because an opportunity to make merry has presented itself'.[1] Dalmatia may have been an extreme case, but it illustrates all the more clearly the place of the festival in traditional society. It was opposed to the everyday, a time of waste precisely because the everyday was a time of careful saving. Its special quality was symbolised by the clothes people wore to take part in it, their best. An English visitor to Naples noticed that 'very little suffices to clothe the *lazaro* [the poor man] except on holidays; and then he is indeed tawdrily decked out, with laced jacket and flame-coloured stockings; his buckles are of enormous magnitude'.[2] The special clothes were a sign that the day was no ordinary one.

Certain kinds of performance took place only during festivals, like the English May games and their Tuscan equivalents the *Maggi* or *Bruscelli,* or the Spanish *auto pastoril,* played at Christmas, or the *auto sacramental,* played at Corpus Christi – not to mention the many kinds of Carnival play. Within the house, the most richly decorated jugs, bowls and plates were often for use only on festival occasions, and so they have survived to mislead the historian, if he is not careful, about the quality of everyday life in the past. Indeed, half the house might be reserved for special occasions; in Sweden in the seventeenth and eighteenth centuries, the common house-type was the *parstuga,* the house with two main rooms, one for everyday use and the other for guests and festivals. If the house had only one main room, it might be transformed for special occasions by bringing painted hangings out of store. Popular themes of this *bonadsmåleri* like the Marriage at Cana or the Queen of Sheba's visit to Solomon were particularly appropriate for these special occasions, presenting an idealised mirror image of the host and guests.[3]

A French sociologist has suggested that in traditional societies, a man lives 'in remembrance of one festival and in expectation of the next'. Thomas Gray made the same point when he wrote from Turin in 1739: 'This Carnival lasts only from Christmas to Lent; one half of the remaining part of the year is passed in remembering the last, the other in expecting the future Carnival.'[4] People reckoned time by major festivals like Michaelmas or Martinmas. For major urban festivals the crowds were swelled by the local peasants, who came into town so as not to miss the fun. Some English travellers who were in Prato for the feast of Our Lady took a good look at the crowd in the piazza, 'whereof we judged one half to have hats of straw and one fourth part to be bare legged'. An English clergyman, in Barcelona for Holy Week in 1787, pointed out that 'many upon such occasions resort to Barcelona from the adjacent villages, and some from distant provinces'. Pilgrimages to holy places on the occasion of major festivals were great events in people's lives. In Provence, a man who had visited the shrine of St Claude in the Jura was known for the rest of his life as a *Romieu,* much as pilgrims to Mecca are given the title of *Haji* today.[5] Pictures on the walls of cottages might often be souvenirs of pilgrimage, for woodcuts of holy images were sold near the shrine, as at Mariazell in Austria or Częstochowa in Poland. Even an article of furniture like a cupboard or bed, in everyday use, might be associated with the festival for which it was made, probably the wedding of the first owners. It would often carry their initials and the date of the great event.

To discuss festivals is necessarily to discuss ritual. 'Ritual' is a difficult term to catch in a definition; in the pages which follow it will refer to the use of action to express meaning, as opposed to more utilitarian actions and also to the expression of meaning through words or images. Everyday life in early modern Europe was filled with rituals, religious and secular, and the performances of songs and stories were no exception. Italian storytellers began with the sign of the cross, and in eighteenth-century Scotland a report to the Highland Society told of 'an old fellow in the parish that very gravely takes off his bonnet as often as he sings Duon Dearmot . . . he told me it was out of regard for the memory of that hero'.[6] For more elaborate rituals, however, one had to wait for special occasions. These more elaborate rituals have left too few traces for the historian to reconstruct them with any degree of accuracy. However, the attempt must be made because a picture of traditional popular culture without ritual would be even more misleading than a historian's reconstruction. For example, the meaning of a popular hero may be modified by the ritual with which he is presented in public.

A notorious example of this modification is that of Robin Hood. Robin was not only a hero of ballads but also of May games. He often formed a part of the English spring festival with its King and Queen of the May. Robin's clothes of Lincoln green and his home in the greenwood made him an appropriate spring symbol, but if Robin was to be King of the May, he would need a Queen. Maid Marion is not recorded in association with Robin until the sixteenth century, hundreds of years after his story was first told, but Robin Hood and Maid Marion were the May King and Queen at Reading in 1502, at Kingston-on-Thames in 1506, in London in 1559, at Abingdon in 1566. It would be misleading to describe Robin, in Frazerian terms, as a 'vegetation demon', for this would be to ignore his social significance, yet Robin the outlaw may have stepped into the role and taken over the attributes of a spirit of spring.[7]

The story of St John the Baptist is better-documented and follows curiously similar lines to Robin's. St John's Eve falls at Midsummer. In early modern Europe this festival was the occasion of many rituals which included lighting bonfires and jumping over them, bathing in rivers, and dipping branches. Fire and water are common symbols of purification, so that it is plausible to argue that the meaning of the festival was renewal, regeneration; and also fertility, for there were rituals to divine whether the coming harvest would be a good one or whether a girl would get married in the coming year. What has all this to do with St John? It looks as if the medieval Church took over a pre-Christian festival and made it her own. Just as the Midwinter festival on 25 December came to be celebrated as the birthday of Christ, so the Midsummer festival came to be celebrated as the birthday of the forerunner of Christ. Bathing in the river was reinterpreted as a commemoration of St John's baptism of Christ in the river Jordan. St John, like Robin Hood, seems to have stepped into the role of a vegetation spirit. He was sometimes shown holding a branch, and often as a hermit, scantily clothed and living in wild places (above, p.150). Hence it would not be difficult to see him as a woodwose or wild man of the woods, a popular figure in medieval art who seems to symbolise Nature (as opposed to Culture).[8]

A famous nineteenth-century theory of myth declared that myths are derived from rituals. In the course of time, so the argument goes, rituals ceased to be understood and myths had to be invented to explain them. This theory is too simple, and examples can be found where the myth came before the ritual, as in the case of the Mass; but the examples of Robin Hood and St John the Baptist suggest that ritual does sometimes influence myth. Even more clear-cut are the examples of St Antony Abbot and St Martin. Why should the hermit-saint Antony be represented with a pig? Because his feast-day falls on 17 January, the time of year when households killed their pigs. Among the traditional songs about St Martin was one which began:

Wann der heilige Sankt Martin   *When the holy St Martin*
Will der Bischof sehr entfliehn   *Wants to avoid the bishop*
Sitzt er in dem Gänse Stall . . .   *He sits in the goose-pen . . .*

There is nothing about this incident in the tradional lives of the saint. However, Martinmas, the feast of St Martin, falls on 11 November. Geese were killed at about this time, and it was traditional, in Germany in particular, to eat them on this day. The goose was part of the ritual, and so it crept into the myth.[9]

Carnival

The example *par excellence* of the festival as a context for images and texts is surely Carnival. In southern Europe in particular Carnival was the greatest popular festival of the year, and a privileged time when what oft was thought could for once be expressed with relative impunity. Carnival was a favourite time for the performance of plays, and many of these plays cannot be properly understood without some knowledge of Carnival rituals, to which they often allude.

Before any interpretation can be attempted, it is necessary to reconstruct a typical Carnival from the fragmentary evidence which has survived. This reconstruction is inevitably a hazardous business. Since the Italian evidence is the richest, there will be some danger of seeing Europe through Italian spectacles. Most of the surviving evidence concerns cities and does not tell us what we would like to know about peasant culture, although some peasants lived in towns and others probably came to town for the festival. Much of the evidence comes from outsiders, foreign tourists who may have misunderstood what they saw and heard (above, p.66). No Carnival was exactly like any other Carnival. There were regional variations, and there were other differences due to the weather, the political situation, or the price of meat at a given time. However, these variations cannot be appreciated without some kind of norm to measure them against, some composite picture of an early modern European Carnival.

The Carnival season began in January or even in late December, with excitement mounting as Lent approached. The place of Carnival was the open air in the city centre: in Montpellier, Place Notre Dame; in Nuremberg, the market-place surrounding the Town Hall; in Venice, Piazza S. Marco, and so on. Carnival may be seen as a huge play in which the main streets and squares became stages, the city became a theatre without walls and the inhabitants, the actors and spectators, observing the scene from their balconies. In fact there was no sharp distinction between actors and spectators, since the ladies on their balconies might throw eggs at the crowd below, and the maskers were often licensed to burst into private houses.[10]

The action of this gigantic play was a set of more or less

formally structured events. The less formally structured events went on intermittently for the whole Carnival season and were spread over the whole town. In the first place, there was massive eating of meat, pancakes and (in the Netherlands) waffles, reaching a climax on Shrove Tuesday, which in seventeenth-century England was described as a time of 'such boiling and broiling, such roasting and toasting, such stewing and brewing, such baking, frying, mincing, cutting, carving, devouring, and gorbellied gourmandising, that a man would think people did take in two months' provision at once into their paunches, or that they did ballast their bellies with meat for a voyage to Constantinople, or the West Indies'. Drinking was also heavy. In Russia, according to an English visitor, in the last week of Carnival 'they drink as if they were never to drink more'.[11] People sang and danced in the streets – not that this was unusual in early modern Europe, but the excitement was, and some of the songs and dances and musical instruments were special ones, like the Dutch *Rommelpot,* a pig's bladder stretched over a jug half full of water. 'When a reed stick is stuck through the middle of the bladder and is moved between the thumb and fingers the instrument produces a sound not unlike one emitted by a stuck pig.'[12] People wore masks, some with long noses (Plate 16), or entire fancy-dress. Men dressed as women, women as men; other popular costumes were those of clerics, devils, fools, wild men and wild animals, for example bears. Italians liked to dress as characters from the *commedia dell'arte,* and Goethe records seeing hundreds of Pulcinellas in the Corso in Rome. An Englishman in Paris for the Carnival of 1786 wrote that 'popes, cardinals, monks, devils, courtiers, harlequins and lawyers all mingled in one promiscuous crowd'.[13] This crowd did not just dress up but acted out their parts. 'One plays the Doctor of Law, and goes up and down the streets with his book in his hand disputing with every man he meets.'[14] Fools and wild men rushed about striking at the bystanders with pig's bladders and even with sticks. People threw flour at one another, or sugar-plums, or apples, or oranges, or stones, or eggs, which might be filled with rose-water but might not. In Cadiz the ubiquitous English visitor noticed women on balconies pouring pails of water on the men below.[15] Animals were common victims of the Carnival madness; dogs might be tossed in a blanket, and cocks pelted to death. Aggression was also verbal, and many insults were exchanged and satirical verses sung.[16]

Other happenings were structured rather more formally, were concentrated in the last few days of Carnival and in the central squares, made more of a distinction between actors and spectators, and were often organised by clubs or fraternities led by 'Kings' or 'Abbots' of Misrule and recruited particularly, but not exclusively, from young adult males of the upper classes, as in the cases of the Abbaye des Conards (Rouen), the Compagnie de la Mère Folle (Dijon), the Compagnie della Calza (Venice), or the Schembartläufer (Nuremberg).[17] The performances which they organised were 'improvised' in the sense that there was no script and (probably) no rehearsal, but they were coordinated by a group who knew one another, who had taken part in such occasions before. The performances were not exactly fixed but not exactly free, just as they were not exactly serious but not exactly pure entertainment, something in between. They often included the following three elements.

In the first place, a procession, in which there would probably be floats bearing people dressed as giants, goddesses, devils, and so on. In Nuremberg there was one float or *Hölle*, which was drawn through the streets on a sledge to the main square. It often took the form of a ship, reminiscent of the German ship-wagon processions which are occasionally mentioned in ancient and medieval times. The floats were particularly numerous and famous in Florence. The actors would represent gardeners, wet-nurses, fencers, students, Turks, *Landsknechten* and other social types, and they would sing songs composed for the occasion, which they addressed to the ladies on their balconies looking down on the procession as it passed. In some French Carnivals, husbands who had been beaten by their wives or had recently got married were carried in procession by the officials of the 'great prince Mardi Gras', or led through town mounted backwards on an ass.[18]

A second recurrent element of the Carnival ritual was some kind of competition; running at the ring, horse-races and foot-races were popular. The Roman Carnival included a race for young men, a race for Jews, and a race for old men. Or there might be jousts or tournaments on land or water; at Lille in the eighteenth century, the jousters stood on two boats in the river. Football matches on Shrove Tuesday were common in Britain and northern France. In Ludlow, there was a tug-of-war; in

Bologna, one side threw eggs at the other, which tried to ward them off with sticks.[19]

A third recurrent element in Carnival was the performance of a play of some kind, usually a farce. However, it is difficult to draw the line between a formal play and informal 'games'. There were mock sieges, popular in Italy, in which a castle erected on the main square would be taken by assault; mock lawsuits, or *causes grasses,* popular in France; mock sermons, popular in Spain; mock ploughings, popular in Germany, with unmarried women pulling the ploughs; and mock weddings, in which the bride might be a man, or the groom a bear (cf. p.122 above, on parody). Many games of this kind centred on the figure of 'Carnival' himself. 'Carnival' usually took the form of a fat man, pot-bellied, ruddy, cheerful, often hung about with eatables (sausages, fowl, rabbits), seated on a barrel, or accompanied (as at Venice in 1572) by a cauldron of macaroni. 'Lent', for contrast, took the form of a thin old woman, dressed in black and hung about with fish – the English 'Jack a Lent', a male figure, seems to have been the exception. This Carnival context should enable us to explain the names and guess at the characteristics of several famous clowns of the period; 'Hans Wurst' was surely a Carnival figure with a sausage, while 'Pickleherring' and 'Steven Stockfish' were emaciated Lenten types.[20]

There is some evidence to suggest that battles between Carnival and Lent were not just figments of the imagination of Brueghel, Bosch and other painters, but were enacted in public; in Bologna in 1506, there was a tournament between 'Carnival', on a fat horse, and 'Lent', on a thin one, each with a squadron of followers. The last act of the festival was often a drama in which 'Carnival' suffered a mock trial, made a mock confession and a mock testament, and was given a mock execution, usually by burning, and a mock funeral. Alternatively, a pig might be solemnly beheaded, as happened every year in Venice, or a sardine might be buried with full honours, as was the case in Madrid.[21]

The world upside down

What did Carnival mean to the people who took part in it? In a sense the question is unnecessary. Carnival was a holiday, a game, an end in itself, needing no explanation or justification. It was a time of ecstasy, of liberation. In another sense the question needs to be multiplied. Why did the game take these particular forms? Why did people wear masks with long noses, why did they throw eggs, why did they execute 'Carnival'? Contemporaries did not bother to record what Carnival meant to them – it must have seemed obvious – so we shall have to proceed indirectly, looking for recurrent themes and their most common associations.[22]

There were three major themes in Carnival, real and symbolic: food, sex and violence. Food was the most obvious. It was meat which put the *carne* in Carnival. Heavy consumption of pork, beef and other meat actually took place and was symbolically represented as well. 'Carnival' had chickens and rabbits hanging from his clothes. In Nuremberg, Munich and elsewhere the butchers played an important part in the rituals, dancing or running through the streets or ducking one of the juniors. At Koenigsberg in 1583, ninety butchers carried in procession a sausage weighing 440 lb.

Carne also meant 'the flesh'. Sex was, as usual, more interesting symbolically than food because of the ways in which it was disguised, transparent as these veils may have been. Carnival was a time of particularly intense sexual activity, as historians of eighteenth-century France have been able to show with their tables of the seasonal movement of conceptions; the peak was in May–June, but there was a second peak in February or thereabouts. Weddings often took place during Carnival, and mock weddings were a popular form of game. Songs with double meanings were not only permitted at this time, but were virtually obligatory. Typical is the one sung by a float of Florentine 'key-makers', who told the ladies, as they passed under their balconies, that

E bella e nuova ed util masserizia	Our tools are fine, new and useful;
Sempre con noi portiamo	We always carry them with us;
D'ogni cosa dovizia,	They are good for anything,
E chi volesse il può toccar con mano.	If you want to touch them, you can.

In Naples in 1664, the ladies were shocked to see a wooden

phallus, 'the size of a horse's' being carried through the streets.[23] Given such an incident, it does not seem too far-fetched to interpret long-nosed masks or horned masks as phallic symbols, let alone the sausage carried in procession at Koenigsberg; or to draw attention to the sexual significance of the 'ploughing' in which unmarried girls had to take part, and of the pig's bladder which was used to make music, play football, and strike people. The cock and the pig were contemporary symbols of lust, while the hairy woodwoses and the bears who frequently appeared at Carnival and might kidnap ladies were surely symbols of potency.

Carnival was not only a festival of sex but a festival of aggression, of destruction, desecration. Indeed, one should perhaps think of sex as the middle term connecting food and violence. The violence, like the sex, was more or less sublimated into ritual. Verbal aggression was licensed at this season; maskers were allowed to insult individuals and to criticise the authorities. This was the time to accuse your neighbour of being cuckolded or beaten by his wife. In a Carnival procession at Madrid in 1637, one figure, who seemed to be skinned, carried the inscription:

Sisas, alcavalas y papel sellado
Me tienen desollado.

(*The excise, the sales tax and the tax on stamped paper have fleeced me.*)[24]

Other figures, alluding to the current traffic in honours, carried the costumes of the military orders, with inscriptions 'For Sale'. Aggression was often ritualised in mock battles, or in football matches, or it was displaced on to objects which could not easily defend themselves, such as cocks, dogs, cats, and Jews, who were pelted with mud and stones on their annual race through Rome. More serious violence not infrequently occurred, whether because the insults went too far or because the season was too good an opportunity to miss for paying off old grudges. In Moscow the number of killings in the street increased during the Carnival season, while an English visitor to Venice at the end of the sixteenth century recorded that 'there were on Shrove-Sunday at night seventeen slain, and very many wounded; besides that they reported, there was almost every night one slain, all that Carnival time'. In London, Shrove

Tuesday violence by apprentices was as regular as pancake-eating: 'Youths arm'd with cudgels, stones, hammers, rules, trowels and handsaws put playhouses to the sack and bawdy-houses to the spoil', with their pockets full of stones to pelt the constable and his men when they arrived on the scene. It was said about 1800 that 'The average of dangerous or mortal wounds on every great festival at Seville' was 'about two or three'.[25]

Claude Lévi-Strauss has taught us to look for oppositions when interpreting myths, rituals and other cultural forms. In the case of Carnival, there were two basic oppositions which provide the context for interpreting many elements in the proceedings, oppositions of which contemporaries were well aware.

The first opposition is that between Carnival and Lent, between what the French called *jours gras* and *jours maigres,* and generally personified as a fat man and a thin woman. According to the law of the Church, Lent was a time of fasting and abstinence – of abstinence not only from meat but from eggs, sex, play-going and other recreations. Hence it was natural to represent Lent as emaciated (the very word 'Lent' means 'lean time'), as a kill-joy, associated with the cold-blooded creatures of Lenten diet. Whatever was lacking in Lent was naturally emphasised in Carnival, so that 'Carnival' was represented as young, cheerful, fat, sexy, a mighty eater and drinker, a Gargantuan or Falstaffian figure. (No doubt the connection was the other way round, and Carnival is the context for interpreting Gargantua and Falstaff.)

The second basic opposition demands more explanation. Carnival was opposed not only to Lent but also to the everyday, not only to the forty days which began on Ash Wednesday but to the rest of the year. Carnival was an enactment of 'the world turned upside down', a favourite theme in the popular culture of early modern Europe; *le monde renversé, il mondo alla rovescia, Die verkehrte Welt.* The world upside down lent itself to illustration, and from the mid-sixteenth century it was a favourite theme of popular prints (p.17). There was physical reversal: people standing on their heads, cities in the sky, the sun and moon on earth, fishes flying, or that favourite item of carnival procession, a horse going backwards with its rider facing the tail. There was reversal of the relation between man and beast: the horse turned farrier, shoeing his master; the ox turned butcher, cutting up a man; the fish eating the fisherman; the hares carrying a trussed hunter or turning him on the spit. Also represented was the reversal of the relations between man and man, whether age reversal, sex reversal, or other inversion of status. The son is shown beating his father, the pupil beating his teacher, servants giving orders to their masters, the poor giving alms to the rich, the laity saying Mass or preaching to the clergy, the king going on foot while the peasant rides, the husband holding the baby and spinning while his wife smokes and holds a gun.[26]

What was the meaning of this series of images? There is no simple answer to the question. They were ambiguous, with different meanings for different people, and possibly ambivalent, with different meanings for the same person. It is most easy to document the attitude of the upper classes, for whom these images symbolised chaos, disorder, misrule. Opponents of change in the early modern period frequently characterised it as quite literally 'subversive', an attempt to turn the world upside down. Their assumption was that the existing order was the natural order, that any alternative to it was simply disorder. Luther, for example, was attacked for turning the world upside down and in turn attacked the rebellious peasants of 1525 in the same way. In England in the mid-seventeenth century, the Quakers, among other groups, were called by their adversaries 'turners of the world upside down'.[27]

Whether ordinary people saw the topsy-turvy world as a bad thing is much less clear. When the peasant rebels of 1525 invaded the house of the Teutonic Order at Heilbronn, they forced the knights to exchange roles with them. While the invaders feasted, the knights had to stand by the table, hat in hand. 'Today, little Junker', said one of the peasants, '*we* are the knights (*Heut, Junkerlein, syn wir Teutschmeister*). The commons in Norfolk in 1549, in Ket's rebellion, declared that 'gentlemen have ruled aforetime and they will rule now'. In the Vivarais in 1670, the peasants made the same claim. 'The time of the prophecy had come, they said, when the earthenware pots would break the iron ones.' Two popular prints circulated after the French Revolution, one with the noble astride the peasant, the other with the peasant astride the noble, inscribed 'I knew our turn was coming.[28] (Plates 19/20). A topsy-turvy world was involved in the popular utopia of the Land of Cockaigne, 'Lubberland' or 'The land of Prester John', where houses were thatched with pancakes, brooks ran with milk, there were roast pigs running about with knives conveniently stuck in their backs, and races where the last past the post was the winner. A French popular poet added his variations to this common theme:

Pour dormir une heure
De profond sommeille,
Sans qu'on se réveille,
On gagne six francs,
Et à manger autant;
Et pour bien boire
On gagne une pistole;
Ce pays est drôle,
On gagne par jour
Dix francs à faire l'amour.[29]

Cockaigne is a vision of life as one long Carnival, and Carnival a temporary Cockaigne, with the same emphasis on eating and on reversals. Carnival was a time of comedies, which often enacted situations of reversal in which the judge was put in the stocks or the wife triumphed over her husband.[30] Carnival costume allowed men and women to reverse roles. The relations of master and servant might be inverted; in England, 'Shrove Tuesday's liberty of servants' was traditional. The everyday taboos on the expression of sexual and aggressive impulses were replaced by encouragements. Carnival was, in short, a time of institutionalised disorder, a set of rituals of reversal. No wonder contemporaries called it a time of 'madness' in which Folly was king. The rules of culture were suspended; the exemplars to follow were the wild man, the fool, and 'Carnival', who represent Nature, or in Freudian terms, the Id. As an Italian poet, Mantuanus, wrote in the early sixteenth century,

Per fora per vicos it personata libido
Et censore carens subit omnia tecta voluptas.

(Desire in his mask goes through the squares and streets,
And in the absence of the censor, Pleasure enters under every roof.)

The lines have a Freudian ring. Of course, the terms *libido* and *censor* have associations for us which were lacking in the sixteenth century, but the poet is pointing out that Carnival provided an outlet for sexual desires which were normally suppressed.[31]

The twin oppositions between Carnival and Lent, the world turned upside down and the everyday world, do not of course exhaust the meanings of the festival. Another theme, which emerges from the Nuremberg Carnivals in particular, is that of youth. In 1510, there was a float representing the Fountain of Youth; in 1514, one of old women being devoured by a giant devil. Perhaps the topsy-turvy world is itself a gigantic symbol of rejuvenation, of return to the licence of the years before the age of reason.[32]

When Sir James Frazer discussed Carnival in his *Golden Bough*, he suggested that it was a ritual to make the crops grow, and interpreted not only the woodwoses but also 'Carnival' as vegetation spirits. Whatever the origin of the ritual, it does not seem that this is what it meant to participants in the cities of early modern Europe. Yet it might well be a mistake to dismiss Frazer without more ado. 'Fertility' is a remarkably useful concept for linking disparate elements in Carnival from eggs to weddings and the many phallic symbols. A sausage might symbolise a phallus; but then a phallus might symbolise something else, whether contemporaries were conscious of this or not. We can do no more than speculate.[33] What is clear is that Carnival was polysemous, meaning different things to different people. Christian meanings were superimposed on pagan ones without obliterating them, and the result has to be read as a palimpsest. The rituals convey simultaneous messages about food and sex, religion and politics. A fool's bladder, for example, has several meanings, because it is a bladder, associated with the sexual organs; because it comes from a pig, the Carnival animal *par excellence*; and because it is carried by a fool, whose 'fatuity' is symbolised by its emptiness.

The carnivalesque

Carnival did not have the same importance all over Europe. It was strong in the Mediterranean area, in Italy, Spain and France; fairly strong in Central Europe; and at its weakest in the north, in Britain and Scandinavia, probably because the weather discouraged an elaborate street festival at this time of year. Where Carnival was weak, and even in some places where it was

lively, other festivals performed its functions and shared its
characteristics. As stories wandered from one hero to another,
so elementary 'particles' of ritual wandered from one festival to
another. Most obviously 'carnivalesque' were a number of
feast-days which fell in December, January and February, in
other words inside the Carnival period in its widest sense.

A famous example is that of the Feast of Fools, held on 28
December (the feast of the 'innocents' massacred by Herod) or
thereabouts, and particularly well-documented for France. The
Feast of Fools was organised by the junior clergy, the
ecclesiastical equivalent of the young mens' societies so
prominent during Carnival. Ordinary people participated in the
same way as they participated at Mass, in the congregation.
During the Feast of Fools a bishop or abbot of the fools would
be elected, there would be dancing in church and in the streets,
the usual procession, and a mock mass in which the clergy wore
masks or women's clothes or put their vestments on back to
front, held the missal upside down, played cards, ate sausages,
sang bawdy songs, and cursed the congregation instead of
blessing them. The 'indulgences' proclaimed in the south of
France (in Occitan instead of the usual Latin) might go like this:

Mossehor, qu'es eissi présen,   My lord, who is here present,
Vos dona xx banastas dé mal dé dens,   Gives you 20 baskets of toothache
Et a tôs vôs aoutrés aoûssi,   And to all you others also
Dona una cóa de Roussi.   Gives a red bum.

One could hardly wish for a more literal enactment of the world
turned upside down. Its legitimation was a line from the
Magnificat, *Deposuit potentes de sede et exaltavit humiles*; He
hath put down the mighty from their seat and hath exalted the
humble. Elsewhere, for example in England before the
Reformation, the occasion took the milder form of the feast of
'the boy bishop' or 'Childermass'. According to the
proclamation abolishing these customs in 1541, they included
'children being strangely decked and apparelled to counterfeit
priests, bishops and women, and so to be led with songs and
dances from house to house blessing the people and gathering
money, and boys do sing mass and preach in the pulpit'.[34] On
the anniversary of Herod's massacre, children were allowed to
take over.

The Feast of the Innocents fell within the twelve days of Christmas, and this whole season was treated as carnivalesque, appropriately enough from a Christian point of view, since the birth of the son of God in a manger was a spectacular example of the world turned upside down. Like Carnival, the twelve days of Christmas were a great time for eating and drinking, for the performance of plays, and for 'Misrule' of various kinds. In England, the custom was to perform 'Plough Plays', which might include mock weddings, on the first Monday after Epiphany. There might also be 'a changing of clothes between men and women' at New Year. As at Carnival, the season was personified. The 'riding', or procession, of Yule (the original Father Christmas) and his wife was a great event in sixteenth-century York, 'drawing great concourses of people after them to gaze', as the corporation admitted when it abolished this ritual in 1572. In Italy it was Epiphany who was personified, as an old woman, *La Befana* or *La Vecchia*, an old witch something like 'Lent' who might be burned at the end of the festivities.[35]

In Russia, according to a sixteenth-century English visitor, at Christmas, 'every bishop in his cathedral church setteth forth a show of the three children in the oven, where the angel is made to come flying from the roof of the church with great admiration of the lookers-on, and many terrible flashes of fire are made with resin and gunpowder by the Chaldeans (as they call them) that run about town all the twelve days disguised in their players' coats and make such good sport for the honour of the bishop's pageant'. The carnivalesque side of the proceedings comes out more vividly from a seventeenth-century German account which explains that these 'Chaldeans', so called after the people who persuaded Nebuchadnezzar to throw Shadrach, Mesach and Abed-nego into the 'burning fiery furnace' (Daniel 3.8-30), were

> certain dissolute people who each year received the patriarch's permission, for a period from eight days before Christmas until the day of the three saintly kings, to run about the streets with special fireworks. They often burned the beards of passers-by, especially the peasants . . . whoever wanted to be spared had to pay a kopek. They were dressed as carnival revellers, wearing on their heads painted wooden hats.

Still in the Carnival season, on 5 February there was the feast of St Agatha, Santa Agueda to the Spanish, for whom the day was an occasion for another rite of reversal; the women gave orders and the men obeyed. It is as if St Agatha's torturers, by cutting off her breasts, had turned her into an Amazon.[36]

Outside the Carnival season, there were festivals which emphasised the themes of renewal, or eating, or sex, or violence, or reversal, and so might be described as carnivalesque. In England, Easter Tuesday, or 'Hock Tuesday', was one of these; the women captured the men and made them pay a ransom for their release. So was May Day, for in England a lively May festival seems to have compensated for a relatively quiet Shrove Tuesday. There were elaborate May Games organised by a May King and Queen, which might include plays about St George (who was a neighbour, since his feast fell a week earlier) or Robin Hood (above, p.180). Men, women and children went to the woods where, as a late sixteenth-century description puts it, 'they spend all the night in pleasant pastimes', returning with birch-boughs and a maypole. In other words, the rites of spring involved sexual licence. In eighteenth-century London, chimney-sweeps covered themselves with flour on May Day, a ritual of reversal if ever there was one. In Italy, maypoles were known as *Alberi della Cuccagna*, 'trees of Cockaigne', another link with the world of Carnival. In Spain, May Day was, like Carnival, celebrated with mock battles and mock weddings, for example (as Covarrubias describes it in his dictionary), 'a sort of play performed by lads and lasses who place a little boy and a little girl on a marriage bed which signifies matrimony'.[37]

Summer, too, had its carnivals, notably Corpus Christi and the feast of St John the Baptist. The festival of Corpus Christi, which spread in Europe from the thirteenth century on, was a day of processions and plays. In late medieval England, this was the time when mystery plays were performed in the market-places of Chester, Coventry, York and elsewhere. In Spain too Corpus Christi was a great day for the performance of religious plays, but proceedings were invaded by carnivalesque elements. Elaborate floats would be drawn through the streets carrying saints, giants, and, most important of all, a huge dragon, explained in Christian terms as the Beast of the Apocalypse, while the woman on his back was supposed to represent the Whore of Babylon. The ears of the crowd would be assaulted by fireworks, bagpipes, tambourines, castanets, drums and trumpets. Devils had an important part to play, tumbling, singing, and engaging in mock battles with the angels. The fool had another chance to strike bystanders with his bladder.[38]

It has already been suggested that St John's Eve, Midsummer, was an important festival organised around the theme of renewal (above, p.181). This feast took a carnivalesque form in some communities where St John was the patron saint. This was the case, for example, in Chaumont in the diocese of Langres, where the weeks preceding the festival were given up to misrule, organised, or rather disorganised, by devils. The devils, rather like the Russian 'Chaldeans', threw fireworks at the crowd, ran about town on Sunday evenings, terrorised the countryside and taxed the market. These activities were interpreted as a representation of the Devil's power over the world, which lasted until the feast of St John. Florence was also dedicated to St John the Baptist and his feast was marked not only by religious plays, processions, and floats, but also by bonfires, giants, fireworks, races, football matches, bull-fights, and *spiritelli,* men walking on stilts. In northern and eastern Europe, St John's Eve was a particularly important festival in our period, whether because pagan survivals were stronger or because the public rituals which took place at Carnival in Mediterranean countries and in May in England were better postponed to June in these colder climes. In sixteenth-century Estonia, St John's Eve was marked, according to one Lutheran pastor, by 'flames of joy over the whole country. Around these bonfires people danced, sang and leapt with great pleasure, and did not spare the big bagpipes . . . many loads of beer were brought . . . what disorder, whoring, fighting and killing and dreadful idolatry took place there!' In the countryside around Riga, another Lutheran pastor described the feast of St John's Eve rather more sympathetically in the late eighteenth century. His name: J. G. Herder (above, p.3f).[39]

The Carnival emphasis on eating and drinking seems to have been absent from these spring and summer festivals, but people made up for this in the autumn. Eating and drinking was the main point of the harvest supper given for the reapers, although other entertainment was not forgotten; 'a fiddler must play for them when they have eaten their bellyfuls, going into the barn and dancing on the wooden floor until they drip with sweat, there being a big can with beer at hand for them and a piece of tobacco for each'. That was in Cardiganshire in 1760. In Sicily a few years later, a French visitor remarked that 'after the harvest the peasants celebrate a popular festival, a kind of orgy', dancing to the sound of drums; 'a young woman dressed in white and seated on an ass . . . is surrounded by men on foot who carry wheat-sheaves on their heads and in their arms, and seem to be doing homage to her with them'. In England, there was a carnivalesque egalitarianism about the proceedings. At the harvest supper, we learn from an eighteenth-century observer, 'the servant and his master are alike and everything is done with an equal freedom. They sit at the same table, converse freely together, and spend the remaining part of the night in dancing, singing etc without any difference or distinction'.[40]

Other autumn rituals of eating and drinking were the feasts of St Bartholomew (25 August) and St Martin (11 November). St Bartholomew, who was said to have been flayed alive, was an appropriate if grisly patron for butchers. In Bologna and in London his day was the occasion of some carnivalesque celebrations. At Bologna, it was called 'the feast of the pig', which was carried in triumph before it was killed, roasted and distributed. In London, the same day was the occasion of, Bartholomew Fair, held in Smithfield, the centre of the London meat trade. Ben Jonson's play describes with accuracy the main ingredients in this festival: Bartholomew pig (sold in booths with a pig's head as a sign), gingerbread, puppet-shows, and several days of licensed disorder. In France, Germany and the Netherlands, St Martin's Day was a great occasion when people cheerfully obeyed the injunction of the song, 'Drink Martin's wine and eat goose' (*trinck Martins wein und gens isz*), all the more cheerfully because in some places, like Groningen in the early seventeenth century, it was customary for the innkeepers to lay on the roast goose for nothing.[41]

The repertoire of public rituals was also laid under contribution on special occasions which were not part of the annual cycle of feasts. Public executions, the solemn 'entry' of important people into town, the celebration of victories (or coronations, or the birth of royal children), and, in eighteenth-century England at least, parliamentary elections, were all carnivalesque. Elections, notably at Westminster, were an occasion for eating, drinking, singing and fighting in the streets, and ended with a ritual of triumph, the 'chairing' of the successful candidate. The violence and ecstasy of such occasions have been caught and preserved for us by Hogarth. Victories meant feasting, fireworks and bonfires; royal entries meant the erection of triumphal arches, speeches, mock battles, fountains flowing with wine, and coins thrown to the crowd.

A much more common ritual in early modern Europe was that of execution. It was a dramatic performance carefully managed by the authorities to show the people that crime did not pay. Hence Dr Johnson's objection to the abolition of public hangings:

> Sir, executions are intended to draw spectators. If they do not draw spectators they don't answer their purpose.

It would begin with a procession of the condemned men and their guards, for example the journey to Tyburn, the condemned men in carts with ropes round their necks. Then they would mount the scaffold, the stage on which their last act was to be performed. The clergy would attend them. The condemned men might be allowed to address the crowd, to declare their repentance or (as at Montpellier in 1554) to describe their crimes in verse. If the criminal had escaped, he might be hanged in effigy, a procedure which must have reminded the spectators of Carnival. The condemned who were present would be beheaded, or hanged, or burned, or broken on the wheel, and the ghastly ritual would end with 'drawing and quartering', the display of their heads at the city gates, and, of course, the selling of ballads recounting their last moments. If the criminal was a priest, he would have to be solemnly 'degraded' or 'unfrocked' before execution, as Savonarola and two other friars were in 1498, on a scaffold in the main square of Florence: 'they were robed in all their vestments, which were taken off one by one, with the appropriate words for the degradation . . . then their hands and faces were shaved, as is customary at this ceremony'.

Lesser forms of public punishment were also presented in dramatic form, like whipping at the cart's tail through the centre of the city or, most carnivalesque of all, the penalty for practising medicine without formal qualifications: 'such people are placed backwards on an ass, with the tail in their hands in place of a bridle, and they are led in this way through the streets'.[42] These performances required the participation of the public, just like Carnival; they offered similar opportunities for sadism, for throwing mud and stones at the criminals as they passed, as at the Jews racing through Rome. The point of the stocks and the pillory was part public shaming, part the exposure of the offender to the violence of the crowd. However, audiences do not always react in the way the playwright expects, or wants, and the crowd did not necessarily interpret proceedings in the same way as the authorities. They might sympathise with the criminal, and the performance was structured in such a way that they were able to express this sympathy. To take two famous English examples: when Lilburne was whipped through Fleet Street to Westminster in 1638, he was supported by the crowd, and when Defoe was pilloried at Temple Bar in 1703, he was pelted with flowers instead of the customary stones or refuse. At executions, notably at Tyburn in the eighteenth century, official rituals had to coexist with popular rituals which presented the hangman as the villain and the criminal as a hero. Girls on the steps of St Sepulchre's Church would throw flowers and blow kisses to the condemned as they passed. The 'Carnival' atmosphere at Tyburn has often been the subject of comment.[43]

Carnivalesque also were the rituals of popular justice, of which the most famous was the charivari. A charivari was, to follow a famous seventeenth-century English definition, a 'public defamation', more especially 'an infamous (or infaming) ballad, sung, by an armed troop, under the window of an old dotard married, the day before, unto a young wanton, in mockery of them both'. It was normally accompanied by 'rough music' (German *Katzenmusik*, Dutch *ketelmusik*), such as the beating of pots and pans; in other words, it was a mock serenade. The charivari was known right across Europe from Portugal to Hungary, although details of the ritual might vary, and so might the choice of victim. It was not only the old man married to the young woman (or vice versa) who might be the object of a charivari, but anyone marrying for the second time, or a girl marrying outside the village, or a husband who was beaten or made a cuckold by his wife. This public mocking might be postponed till Carnival, when insult was licensed, and might be organised by societies like the Abbaye des Conards at Rouen or the Badia degli Stolti at Turin, which played prominent parts in Carnival. The victim, or his neighbour, or his effigy, might be taken through the streets mounted backwards on an ass, presumably to show that these breaches of the conventions of marriage turned the world upside down – and the beating of pots and pans provided an upside-down kind of music. The ritual might be used outside the marriage context, against preachers or landlords; in seventeenth-century France, tax-collectors were expelled from towns they visited in a kind of charivari. Alternatively, unpopular figures might be hanged or burned in effigy like 'Carnival'; indeed, a register – if it could be compiled – of everyone who was publicly destroyed in effigy between 1500 and 1800 would tell us a great deal about the popular culture of early modern Europe. Prominent on this list would be Judas, Machiavelli, Guy Fawkes, Cardinal Mazarin, Tom Paine, and, of course, the Pope.[44]

There is a sense in which every festival was a miniature Carnival because it was an excuse for disorder and because it drew from the same repertoire of traditional forms, which included processions, races, mock battles, mock weddings, and mock executions (above, p.122). The use of the term 'carnivalesque' is not intended to imply that Shrove Tuesday customs were the origin of all the others; the suggestion is simply that the major feasts of the year had rituals in common and that Carnival was an especially important cluster of such rituals. It is closer to the truth to think of the religious festivals of early modern Europe as little carnivals than to think of them as grave sedate rituals in the modern manner.

Social control or social protest?

So far, we have been looking at popular festivals primarily in terms of what they meant to the participants, but this approach is not the only one possible. Social anthropologists studying myths and rituals in many parts of the world have emphasised that these myths and rituals perform social functions, whether participants are aware of this or not. Can we say the same of early modern Europe? What, for example, were the functions of Carnival? Some functions of popular festivals seem obvious enough. They were entertainment, a welcome respite from the daily struggle to earn a living; they gave people something to look forward to. They celebrated the community itself, displaying its ability to put on a good show; and perhaps the mocking of outsiders (Jews at the Roman Carnival, peasants in that of Nuremberg) was, among other things, a dramatic expression of community solidarity. On the feast of St John the Baptist at Florence, there were rituals expressing the subordination of other communities to this capital city of an empire. Festivals were also an opportunity for different groups within the community to compete with one another, a competition which was often ritualised in the form of mock battles, like the battles on the bridges of Venice and Pisa or the football matches at Florence, but might also be expressed in the efforts of different parishes or guilds or quarters of the city to make a better display than their rivals. A priest of Provins in Champagne wrote in 1573 that the local processions expressed 'competition between churches' (*envye d'une église sur l'aultre*).⁴⁵

The ritual of charivari seems to have served the function of social control, in the sense that it was the means for a community, a village or urban parish, to express its hostility to individuals who stepped out of line and so to discourage other breaches of custom. To make spinsters pull a plough through the streets at Carnival was a way of encouraging them to find husbands. The rituals of public execution might also be regarded as a form of social control, to the extent that there was community consensus about the wickedness of the crime. Outside the face-to-face community the term 'social control' becomes misleading, and one needs to stop and ask which groups are using ritual to control which other groups. The ruling classes, who knew their Roman history, were well aware of the uses of 'bread and circuses', or of 'bread, bulls and work' (*pan, toros y trabajo*), the programme which the Spanish royal favourite Valenzuela put forward in 1674.⁴⁶ The official ritual at Tyburn expressed the attempt of the ruling classes to control ordinary people, while the unofficial rituals expressed protest against these attempts. The use of ritual in social conflict appears even more clearly in Palermo in 1647. An increase in the price of bread sparked off the conflict. A crowd went to burn the house of an unpopular official and succeeded in smashing the windows, an action which might be interpreted as the expression of their fury, but equally well as an attempt to put pressure on the government in an unofficial yet customary way. The crowd were headed off by some Carmelite friars, who walked up to them carrying the host, so that everyone had to fall to their knees. Here we see the use of religious ritual as a form of crowd control.[47]

These examples are obvious enough. Functional analysis is more interesting where it is more paradoxical, in other words when rituals which apparently express protest against the social order are interpreted as contributions to that order. A number of social anthropologists, notably the late Professor Max Gluckman, have advanced interpretations of this kind. In Zululand, just before the harvest, unmarried girls used to put on men's clothes, carry shields and assegais, sing bawdy songs and drive the cattle out, all activities normally confined to men. The Swazi insulted and criticised their king on the occasion of certain festivals. Gluckman explains this 'license in ritual', as he calls it, in terms of its social function. 'The lifting of the normal taboos and restraints obviously serves to emphasise them.' Apparent protests against the social order, these actions are in fact 'intended to preserve and even to strengthen the established order'. Gluckman goes so far as to suggest that where the social order is seriously questioned, 'rites of protest' do not occur. Similarly, Victor Turner, in a comparative study of rituals of status reversal, argues that the rituals lead to 'an ecstatic experience', an enhanced sense of community, followed by a 'sober return' to the normal social structure. 'By making the low high and the high low, they reaffirm the hierarchical principle.'[48]

Are these analyses of any relevance to early modern Europe? Surely they are. Just as Zulu girls put on men's clothes once a year, so did Venetian women. Just as the Swazi were licensed to criticise the authorities during certain festivals, so were the Spaniards. The world turned upside down was regularly re-enacted. Why did the upper classes permit this? It looks as if they were aware that the society they lived in, with all its inequalities of wealth, status and power, could not survive without a safety-valve, a means for the subordinates to purge their resentments and to compensate for their frustrations. They did not use the term 'safety-valve', because boilers were not equipped with these devices till the early nineteenth century, but they did make the same point by means of technologically simpler metaphors. Some French clerics defended the Feast of Fools in 1444 in these terms:

> We do these things in jest and not in earnest, as the ancient custom is, so that once a year the foolishness innate in us can come out and evaporate. Don't wine skins and barrels burst very often if the air-hole (*spiraculum*) is not opened from time to time? We too are old barrels. . .

In similar fashion an English visitor to Italy in the mid-seventeenth century explained the Roman Carnival to his own countrymen: 'all this is allowed the Italians that they may give a little vent to their spirits which have been stifled in for a whole year and are ready else to choke with gravity and melancholy'.[49] The safety-valve theory of festivals has much to recommend it. It draws attention to a number of features of Carnival which have received too little emphasis in the last few pages. For example, it helps explain the importance of violence, which, unlike food and sex, was not about to be restricted during Lent. Again, young men could openly express their desire for ladies of higher social status, and respectable ladies could walk the streets. Wearing masks helped liberate people from their everyday selves, conferring a sense of impunity like a cloak of invisibility in folktales.

Another point in favour of the theory is its suggestion of a controlled escape of steam. The expression of sexual and aggressive impulses was stereotyped and so channelled. Masks not only liberated their wearers from everyday roles but imposed new ones. In Rome, the constables, or *sbirri,* were on the streets in force to make sure that the revellers did not go too far; in spite of the proverb, it was not true that 'In Carnival, everything is permitted'. Hence the need for symbolism, the songs with double meanings, the aggression sublimated into ritual. The trial, execution and burial of 'Carnival' might be interpreted as a demonstration to the public that the time of ecstasy and licence was over and that they must make a 'sober return' to everyday reality. Comedies built round situations of reversal, like the judge in the stocks, and played during Carnival, frequently end in a similar way with a reminder to the audience that it is time to set the world the right way up again.[50]

In spite of the great value of 'safety-valve' or 'social control' theory, it will not do to interpret the Carnivals and other festivals of early modern Europe in these terms alone. Perhaps this is because Europe in this period was a group of societies more highly stratified than the Africa of Max Gluckman and Victor Turner; perhaps it is because anthropologists have been, until the later 1960s, concerned with consensus at the expense of conflict. At all events, in Europe between 1500 and 1800 rituals of revolt did coexist with serious questioning of the social, political and religious order, and the one sometimes turned into the other. Protest was expressed in ritualised forms, but the ritual was not always sufficient to contain the protest. The wine barrel sometimes blew its top.

The authorities were well aware of the problem on occasion, as is suggested by many edicts against carrying arms during Carnival, and, still more vividly, by a controversy at Palermo in 1648. 1647 had been, as we have just seen, a year of disturbances, which modern historians sometimes describe as a 'revolution'. The viceroy who was governing Sicily for the King of Spain arranged for the Carnival of 1648 to be more magnificent than usual in order to distract the people. However, some nobles disagreed with this policy and one of them expressed the fear that 'on the pretext of these assemblies of the people for these ridiculous spectacles, factious spirits would be able . . . to encourage some new riot'. The cardinal archbishop of Naples had called off the festival of St John the Baptist, for similar reasons, in 1647. Festivals meant that peasants came to town and that everyone took to the streets. Many people were masked, some were armed. The excitement of the occasion and the heavy consumption of alcohol meant that inhibitions against expressing hostility to the authorities or private individuals would be at their weakest. Add to this a bad harvest, an increase in taxes, an attempt to introduce, or to forbid, the Reformation; the resulting mixture could be explosive. There might be a 'switching' of codes, from the language of ritual to the language of rebellion. To move from the point of view of the authorities to that, more elusive, of ordinary people, it may well have been that some of those excluded from power saw Carnival as an opportunity to make their views known and so to bring about change.[51]

Riots may be regarded as an extraordinary form of popular ritual. Of course riots and rebellions are not just rituals; they are attempts at direct action, not symbolic action. However, rebels and rioters employed ritual and symbol to legitimise their action. As its name reminds us, the rebellion of the northern counties in England in 1536 took the form of a pilgrimage, the 'Pilgrimage of Grace', with the rebels marching behind a banner of the Five Wounds of Christ. In Normandy in 1639, the rebels marched behind the banner of St John the Baptist. Riots took over the rituals of charivari and Carnival in particular, because rituals of deposition, destruction and defamation – burning in effigy, for example – were suited to the protests which the rioters wanted to make. They did not stop at effigies; at Naples in 1585, the lynching of an unpopular official was preceded by a mock procession in which he was taken through the streets 'facing backwards and hatless' (*con le spalle voltate e senza berretta*), as if undergoing a charivari.[52]

Riots and rebellions frequently took place on the occasions of major festivals. In Basel they long remembered the massacre which took place on Shrove Tuesday 1376, which was known as *böse Fastnacht*, 'evil Carnival', just as Londoners remembered 'evil May Day' 1517, which turned into a riot against foreigners. At Bern in 1513, Carnival had turned into a peasant revolt. During the wars of religion in France, festivals were particularly likely to turn violent. At Romans in Dauphiné, the dances and masquerades organised by one of the 'kingdoms' for the Carnival of 1580 carried the message that 'the rich men of the town had enriched themselves at the expense of the poor', and the occasion turned into a massacre, first in town and then in the countryside, where the local gentlemen 'went hunting through the villages, killing the peasants like pigs'. Examples can easily be multiplied. At Dijon in 1630, the Carnival developed into a riot in which the wine-growers took the lead. The great revolt of Catalonia began on the day of one of the greatest of Spanish festivals, Corpus Christi. There was a serious riot in Madrid on Palm Sunday 1766. It is hardly surprising to find that members of the upper classes often suggested that particular festivals ought to be abolished, or that popular culture was in general need of reform. Their attempts to reform it are the subject of the next chapter.[53]

PART 3

Changes in Popular Culture

CHAPTER EIGHT

The Triumph of Lent: the Reform of Popular Culture

The first phase of reform, 1500–1650

One of the most famous Brueghel paintings is the *Combat of Carnival and Lent,* in which a fat man astride a barrel jousts with a thin old woman seated on a chair. The literal meaning of this painting is obvious enough, for mock battles between these two figures were a common part of Shrovetide festivities (above, p.185). About other possible meanings of the paintings there has been more debate. I am tempted to interpret 'Carnival', who belongs to the tavern side of the picture, as a symbol of traditional popular culture, and 'Lent', who belongs to the church side, as the clergy, who at that time (1559) were trying to reform or suppress many popular festivities. The reasons for this interpretation should become apparent in the course of the chapter.[1]

I should like to launch the phrase, 'the reform of popular culture', to describe the systematic attempt by some of the educated, (henceforth described as 'the reformers', or 'the godly'), to change the attitudes and values of the rest of the population, or as the Victorians used to say, to 'improve' them. It would be wrong to suggest that craftsmen and peasants were no more than 'passive receptacles' for reform; self-improvement took place, and godly artisans existed, like the 'mechanic preachers' of seventeenth-century England. However, the leadership of the movement was in the hands of the educated, usually the clergy.[2]

This reform movement was not monolithic, but took different forms from region to region and from generation to generation. Catholics and Protestants did not always oppose the same traditional practices or oppose those practices for the same reasons. Yet these variations should not prevent us from seeing the reform movement as a whole. The movement had two sides, negative and positive. The negative side, described in the first and third section of this chapter, was the attempt to suppress, or at least to purify, many items of traditional popular culture – the reformers may be regarded as 'puritans', at least in the literal sense that they were passionately concerned with purification. The positive side of the movement, discussed in the second section, was the attempt to take the Catholic and Protestant reformations to the craftsmen and peasants.

Both sides of the movement can be seen at their most clear-cut outside Europe, where missionaries from China to Peru faced the problem of preaching Christianity in an alien cultural setting. However, missionaries were at work in Europe too, facing problems in 'the dark corners of the land' which they sometimes compared to those of their colleagues working in the Indies. Jesuits who preached at Huelva, west of Seville, in the late sixteenth century declared that its inhabitants 'resembled Indians rather than Spaniards'. Sir Benjamin Rudyerd said in the House of Commons in 1628 that there were parts of northern England and of Wales 'which were scarce in Christendom, where God was little better known than amongst the Indians'.[3]

The reformers objected in particular to certain forms of popular religion, such as miracle and mystery plays, popular sermons, and, above all, religious festivals such as saints' days and pilgrimages. They also objected to a good many items of secular popular culture. A comprehensive list would reach formidable proportions, and even a short list would have to include actors, ballads, bear-baiting, bull-fights, cards, chap-books, charivaris, charlatans, dancing, dicing, divining, fairs, folktales, fortune-telling, magic, masks, minstrels, puppets, taverns and witchcraft. A remarkable number of these objectionable items could be found in combination at Carnival, so it is no surprise to find the reformers concentrating their attack at this point. In addition they banned – or burned – books, smashed images, closed theatres, chopped down maypòles, and disbanded abbeys of misrule.

This cultural reformation was not confined to the popular, for the godly disapproved of all forms of play. Yet one is left with the impression that it was popular recreations which bore the brunt of the attack. When the Italian Jesuit Ottonelli attacked actors, he distinguished the *comedianti*, who acted in private houses for the upper classes, from the *ciarlatani*, who acted in the market-place, and he reserved the full force of his disapproval for the latter.[4] All dancing came under fire, but some traditional dances, 'folk-dances', as we would call them, were singled out for particular condemnation.

What, according to the reformers, was wrong with popular culture? There were two essential religious objections, which Erasmus conveniently compresses into one sentence when describing as 'unchristian' the Carnival he witnessed in Siena in 1509. In the first place, Carnival is unchristian because it contains 'traces of ancient paganism' (*veteris paganismi vestigia*). In the second place, it is unchristian because on this occasion 'the people over-indulges in licence' (*populus . . . nimium indulget licentiae*).[5] These points are repeated by the godly over and over again, so that it may be worth considering them in a little more detail.

The first objection may be described as theological. The reformers disliked many popular customs because they were pagan survivals, 'superstitions' in the original meaning of the term. The idea that Carnival and other major festivals are pre-Christian survivals tends to be associated with Sir James Frazer, but in fact it goes back very much further. Many reformers were well read in the classics and remarked on the parallels between ancient festivals and modern ones. The Bavarian Lutheran Thomas Naogeorgus, St Carlo Borromeo, Archbishop of Milan, and a number of others compared the modern Carnival to the *Bacchanalia* of ancient times. Jean Deslyons, canon of Senlis, described the customary celebration of Twelfth Night as a renewal of paganism, 'the invocation of Phoebus by drawing lots and divining from beans'. The puritan divine Thomas Hall compared the English May Games to the ancient Feast of Flora. Pagan customs were worse than erroneous; they were diabolical. Pagan gods and goddesses were often believed to be demons. When St Carlo denounced plays as the liturgy of the Devil, he may have been speaking literally.[6]

Protestant reformers went further and described many official practices of the Catholic Church as pre-Christian survivals, comparing the cult of the Virgin Mary to the cult of Venus, and describing the saints as the successors of the pagan gods and heroes who had taken over their functions of curing illness and protecting from danger. St George, for example, was identified as a new Perseus, St Christopher as a second

Polyphemus. Joshua Stopford's *Pagano-Papismus*, 'or an exact parallel between Rome-pagan and Rome-christian in their doctrines and ceremonies', was an unusually elaborate comparison, but many of its points were, or became, commonplace.[7]

Magic too was denounced as a pagan survival. Were not Circe and Medea witches? Protestants accused Catholics of practising a magical religion, and Catholic reformers were concerned to purge popular culture of charms and spells. Maximilian van Eynatten, a canon of Antwerp who was in charge of censorship there, wrote a book on exorcism and suppressed a number of chap-books because of the references to magic contained in them; the famous *Four Sons of Aymon* was condemned in 1621 because of the divining practised by Maugis, uncle of the four heroes.[8] St Carlo saw the theatre as a form of dangerous magic; it was a theological commonplace that the Devil was a master of illusion. England apart, witches were hunted down in Protestant as well as Catholic countries not so much because they did harm as because they were heretics, adherents of a false religion, worshippers of pagan goddesses like Diana or Holde. Some of Margaret Murray's ideas as well as Frazer's go back to the godly of early modern Europe.

Some popular rituals were modelled on the Christian liturgy. This the reformers recognised, but it cut no ice with them. Rituals of this kind were denounced as irreverent, blasphemous, sacrilegious, as giving scandal, offending pious eyes and ears, profaning holy mysteries and making a mockery of religion. The traditional custom of electing boy bishops or abbots of the fools was interpreted by the godly as a mockery of the ecclesiastical hierarchy, and the boy bishop's sermon was described, in an English proclamation against the custom in 1541, as tending 'rather to the derision than to any true glory of God or honour of his saints'. Charivari was seen as a mockery of the sacrament of matrimony. The journeymen hatmakers, tailors, saddlers and other craftsmen of Paris, whose initiation rites included a form of service and the pouring of water over the head of the new recruit, had their rituals condemned in 1655 by a committee of doctors of theology who thought they were 'profaning holy baptism and holy mass'. The theologians could not see the difference between a mock baptism and a mockery of baptism (above, p.123).[9]

The popular sermon came under attack for similar reasons.

Erasmus once declared that a good preacher should play on the emotions of his audience by his words, not by distorting his face or gesticulating like a buffoon (*non scurrili corporis gesticulatione*), as some Italian friars did. One might think this comment no more than the reaction of a northerner to the more extravert, flamboyant body language of the south, but the many repetitions of the judgement to be found in the sixteenth and seventeenth centuries suggest that a change in the attitudes of the educated was taking place. Gian Matteo Giberti, Bishop of Verona, condemned preachers who 'tell ridiculous stories and old wives' tales in the manner of buffoons (*more scurrarum*), and make their congregation roar with laughter', and his condemnation was repeated by many church councils, often in virtually the same words. The Protestants agreed. The great puritan preacher William Perkins declared that 'it is not meet, convenient or laudable for men to move occasion of laughter in sermons'. An even more thoroughgoing condemnation of Popular preaching came from the printer Henri Estienne II, a convert to Calvinism. Estienne disliked preachers who made their audiences laugh or cry, preachers who inserted absurd or fabulous stories into their sermons, preachers who used coarse and colloquial language 'which they might have used in a brothel', and preachers who made ridiculous or blasphemous comparisons, like the one between Paradise and a Spanish inn.[10]

The popular religious drama was frequently attacked on similar grounds. Thus in 1534 the Bishop of Évora in Portugal prohibited plays without special permission, 'even if they represent the Passion of Our Lord Jesus Christ, or his Resurrection, or Nativity . . . because from these plays arise much that is unfitting (*muitos inconvenientes*), and they frequently give scandal to those who are not very firm in our holy Catholic faith, when they see the disorders and excesses of these plays'. A point frequently made against professional drama was that it was unfitting for actors of bad morals to represent the lives of the saints. Religious processions might be condemned if they included either animals or naked children (representing angels).[11]

The crucial point in all these examples seems to be the insistence of the reformers on the separation between the sacred and the profane. This separation now became very much sharper than it had been in the Middle Ages. In other words, the reform of popular culture was more than just another episode in the long war between the godly and the ungodly, it accompanied a major shift in religious mentality or sensibility. The godly were out to destroy the traditional familiarity with the sacred, because they believed that familiarity breeds irreverence.[12]

The second major objection to traditional popular culture was a moral one. Festivals were denounced as occasions of sin, more especially of drunkenness, gluttony and lechery, and as encouraging servitude to the world, the flesh, and the Devil – especially the flesh. It did not escape the godly that the maypole is a phallic symbol. Plays, songs and, above all, dances were condemned for awakening dangerous emotions and as incitements to fornication. Phillip Stubbes, the Elizabethan Puritan, attacked what he called 'the horrible vice of pestiferous dancing', providing participants with opportunities for 'filthy groping and unclean handling', and so acting as 'an introduction to whoredom, a preparative to wantonnesse, a provocative to uncleanness, and an introit to all kinds of lewdness'. Some dances were singled out for special denunciation. The Spanish Jesuit Juan de Mariana was particularly vehement against the *zarabanda,* and François de Caulet, Bishop of Pamiers in Languedoc, against *la volto,* 'the twirl'. What was wrong with *la volto* may be inferred from an ordinance of the seneschal, of Limoux, also in Languedoc, in 1666, prohibiting dances in which the boys threw the girls into the air, 'in such an infamous manner that what shame obliges us to hide most of all is uncovered naked to the eyes of those taking part and those passing by'.[13]

There were other moral arguments besides the one about indecency. For example, there was the point that games and festivals were occasions of violence. Thomas Hall quoted 'a common saying, that 'tis no festival unless there be some fightings', and a study of Carnival, in particular, bears this out (above, p.187). Stubbes attacked football in similar terms as 'a murthering play', or 'a friendly kind of fight'. Another of his points was that bear-baiting is wicked because it is cruel: 'God is abused when his creatures are misused'. In similar vein, Mariana condemned bull-fights because of the cruelty to the bulls. On the edge of morals and politics we find the argument that popular songs too often presented criminals as heroes. In 1537,

Robert Crowley wrote to Thomas Cromwell complaining about 'harpers' and 'rhymers' who praise robberies as 'valiantness'. The association between festival and revolt (above, p.203) was obvious enough, and so, for example, the famous Mère Folle society of Dijon was abolished in 1630 because of offences against the 'repose and tranquillity' of the town. [14]

Another moral argument against many popular recreations was the suggestion that they were 'vanities', displeasing to God because they wasted time and money. This is the burden of the attack on Carnival 'folly' which the Strasbourg lawyer Sebastian Brant added to the second, 1495 edition of his famous satire *The Ship of Fools*. In similar vein the English moralist Robert Crowley denounced alehouses as 'places of waste and excess', 'harbour for such men as live in idleness'. If the clergy disliked taverns for distracting people from church, the English government disliked them for distracting people from archery-practice. Similar arguments were used by Italian reformers. Archbishop Gabriele Paleotti of Bologna objected to plays partly because they encouraged schoolboys and apprentices to play truant, while an anonymous Italian *Discourse against Carnival,* published in 1607, criticises the 'superfluous expenses' of the season, and laments the lack of 'thrift, order, prudence'. [15]

In short, we find in this period two rival ethics or ways of life in open conflict. The ethic of the reformers was one of decency, diligence, gravity, modesty, orderliness, prudence, reason, self-control, sobriety, and thrift, or, to use a phrase made famous by Max Weber, 'this-wordly asceticism' (*innerweltliche Askese*). It was somewhat misleading of him to call it a 'Protestant ethic', since it could be found in Catholic Strasbourg, Munich and Milan as well as in Protestant London, Amsterdam and Geneva. It is tempting to call it 'the petty-bourgeois ethic' because it was to become characteristic of shopkeepers. The ethic of the reformers was in conflict with a traditional ethic which is harder to define because it was less articulate, but which involved more stress on the values of generosity and spontaneity and a greater tolerance of disorder. [16]

I have been describing the reform of popular culture as a general European movement, despite differences of religious belief. In the middle of the seventeenth century, the theatres were closed in Catholic Madrid as in Protestant London, and for similar reasons. It is natural for a western historian to be somewhat more hesitant about crossing the frontier of Orthodoxy, but there is reason to believe that a similar reform was in progress in Russia too.[17]

In 1551 a famous Russian church council, that of the *Stoglav* or 'hundred chapters', denounced the games of 'Greek origin and diabolical invention' which were played on the eve of St John the Baptist's day and during the Christmas season (above, p.193). The people were also forbidden to consult folk-healers or magicians. The *skomorokhi* were singled out for special denunciation because the men dressed as women and the women as men and because they kept bears, 'to seduce simple people'.[18]

However, the height of the Russian reform movement appears to have been in the middle of the seventeenth century and associated with the so-called 'philotheists' or 'zealots' like Archpriest Neronov and his disciple Archpriest Avvakum, whose autobiography has made him one of the best-known figures in seventeenth-century Russia. Tsar Alexis supported the zealots, and in 1648 issued an edict 'on the righting of morals and the abolition of superstition', against dancing, fiddlers, magic, masks, minstrels (*skomorokhi*), and the 'diabolical mare', a reference to the 'horse' which went from house to house during the twelve days of Christmas.[19]

How close was the parallel between eastern and western Europe? To help answer this question, it may be useful to compare the following passages, which describe the impact of reform at village level.

> I remember that being warned one feast day that wandering actors were playing a farce on a stage they had erected, I went there with some officers of the law. I climbed on to the stage, I tore the mask from the face of the leading actor, I took the fiddle away from the man who was playing and broke it, and made them come down from the stage, which I had the officers overturn.

> There came to my village dancing bears with drums and lutes, and I, though a miserable sinner, was zealous in Christ's service and I drove them out and I broke the buffoon's mask and the drums . . . and two great bears I took away – one I clubbed senseless but he revived and the other I let go into the open country.

These passages were both written in the middle of the seventeenth century. The first is by the curé of Nanterre, which was still a country village in those days; the second comes from the autobiography of Archpriest Avvakum. They give the impression that the troupes of wandering *bateleurs* and *skomorokhi* had much in common, and so had the reformers who were trying to suppress them.[20]

It is important to see the reform movement as a whole, but not at the price of making it seem monolithic; so it is time to say something about the variations. Avvakum was a reformer at the outset of his career, but he supported traditional popular religion against the liturgical reforms which were subsequently introduced by his old ally Nikon after Nikon became patriarch of Moscow.[21] Catholic and Protestant reformers were not equally hostile to popular culture, nor were they hostile for quite the same reasons. Catholic reform tended to mean modification; Protestant reform was more likely to mean abolition. Some arguments for reform are specifically Protestant, like the idea that festivals are relics of popery. Protestants usually want to abolish the feast-day as well as the feasting, and some oppose Lent as well as Carnival; Zwingli, for example, launched an attack on fasting. Some Protestants attacked all holy days other than Sunday, others were hostile to the very idea of a festival; to the idea, that is, that one time is holier than another. Many Protestants were equally radical in their attacks on holy images, which they considered 'idols' which had to be destroyed.[22] 'Ceremonies', like 'idols', were attacked as forms of exterior religion which came between God and man, and had to be abolished. Even chap-book romances might smell of popery. When *Pierre de Provence* was translated into German by a pupil of Luther's called Veit Warbeck, he carefully purged the text of its numerous references to the saints.

The Catholics, on the other hand, insisted that some times were holier than others, but this very insistence led them to object to the profanation of festival time – sacred time – by worldly activities. Catholic reformers were worried by the tendency of Carnival to encroach on Lent. Carlo Bascapè, Bishop of Novara, attacked the 'safety-valve' theory of recreation (above, p.202), arguing that it was impossible for someone to observe Lent with proper devotion if he had indulged in Carnival immediately before.[23] Catholic reformers denounced the tradition of dancing or performing plays in church (or even churchyard) because a church is a holy place; they were against people walking about during Mass, or selling articles in church porches, for the same reason. They forebade the laity to dress up as clergy in time of Carnival; this was blasphemous, because the clergy were holy people. For the same reason the clergy were forbidden to participate in popular festivals in the traditional manner, dancing and wearing masks like everyone else; they were forbidden to watch plays or attend bull-fights or even to gesticulate too violently in their sermons, and they were told to conduct themselves with the gravity and decorum appropriate to their sacred status. The famous cycles of tales about priest-tricksters like *Der Pfaffe vom Kalenberg* and *Il Piovano Arlotto* (above, p.156) ceased to be printed, for their heroes were all too obvious examples of the old-fashioned unreformed kind of parish priest.

As might have been expected, Catholic reformers of popular culture were less radical than Protestant ones. They did not attack the cult of the saints, but only its 'excesses', such as the cult of apocryphal saints, or the belief in certain stories about the saints, or the expectation of worldly favours, like cures or protection, from the saints. They wanted festivals purified but not abolished. They defended images in principle, while objecting to some particular examples. The difference between the two approaches might be symbolised, if not summed up, by what happened to St George. A chap-book life of St George, published in Augsburg in 1621, tells the story of his life and martyrdom without any reference to the dragon, which was presumably rejected as apocryphal. Pageants on St George's day were common in late medieval Europe; at Norwich, they featured St George, St Margaret and of course a dragon. The saints were abolished in 1552 because they 'savoured of popery', while the dragon, known affectionately as 'Old Snap', survived till 1835. Thus the reform of popular culture in Catholic Augsburg meant showing St George without the dragon; in Protestant Norwich it meant showing the dragon without St George.[24]

A division of the reformers into Catholic and Protestant is still too simple. Lutherans, for example, were more tolerant of popular traditions than Zwinglians and Calvinists were, and later generations did not always agree with their predecessors. To avoid over-simplification, it may be useful to sketch the history of the reform movement from 1500 to about 1650.

In the years around 1500, there were already a few prominent reformers like Sebastian Brant, who has been mentioned already, and his friend Johann Geiler of Kaisersberg, a priest at Strasbourg. Geiler objected to eating, drinking, dancing and gaming at church festivals, considering this 'the ruin of the common people' (*des gemeinen Volks Verderbnis*). He was particularly hostile to the local custom of the *Roraffe*. At Pentecost, a buffoon hidden behind a statue of this name in Strasbourg cathedral sang and clowned during the service. At much the same time, Girolamo Savonarola was trying to carry out similar reforms in Florence. A few days before the Carnival of 1496, he preached a sermon suggesting that 'the boys should collect alms for the respectable poor, instead of mad pranks, throwing stones and making floats'.[25]

These attacks on popular recreations were not exactly new in 1500. In the early fifteenth century, St Bernardino of Siena had denounced the custom of bringing in Yule, Jean Gerson the Feast of Fools, and Nicolas de Clamanges, church wakes: 'They keep vigils, but wicked and shameless ones. Some dance in the very churches and sing lewd songs, others . . . play at dice.' We can go back further. In the thirteenth century, Robert Grosseteste reproved clerics who organised 'plays which they call miracles and other plays which they call bringing in May or Autumn'. In the twelfth century, Gerhoh of Reichersberg attacked all religious plays. The Russian attacks on the *skomorokhi* followed Byzantine precedents, and so we can go on, backwards through time to the Fathers of the Church, like Augustine, who was shocked to find people dressing up in animal skins on New Year's Day, and Tertullian, who criticised Christian participation in the *spectacula* (the gladiatorial shows) and the *Saturnalia*. These condemnations by the Fathers were well-known and influential in the sixteenth and seventeenth centuries, and opponents of the theatre quoted Tertullian, mistranslating *spectacula* as 'plays'.[26]

In short, churchmen seem to have been condemning popular culture in much the same terms from the early days of Christianity onwards. This tradition of condemnation suggests that popular culture is remarkably resilient.[27] It also raises an obvious objection to the central thesis of this chapter, but to this objection it may be possible to find an answer.

The medieval reforms were essentially sporadic efforts by individuals. They were unlikely either to spread far or to last long, because of the nature of medieval communications. It was difficult for a reforming bishop to penetrate the more remote corners of his diocese often enough to make his intentions a reality there, and it was still more difficult for him to ensure that his reforms would outlive him. Hence the resilience of popular culture, and the fact that from Tertullian to Savonarola one finds a succession of reformers who make essentially the same complaints. In the course of the sixteenth century, however, sporadic efforts were replaced by a more concerted reform movement. There were more frequent attacks on traditional popular culture and there were more systematic attempts to purge it of both its 'paganism' and its 'licence'. This movement has, of course, a good deal to do with the Protestant and Catholic reformations, for the reform of the church, as it was understood at the time, necessarily involved the reform of what we call popular culture.

Luther, it is true, was relatively sympathetic to popular traditions. He did not object completely to images or to saints, and he was no enemy of Carnival or *Johannisnacht*. 'Let the boys have their game' was his attitude (*pueri etiam habeant suum lusum*). Still, he did object to the tales of Till Eulenspiegel and the Priest of Kalenberg because they glorified 'roguery'. In any case, the Lutherans were stricter than Luther. Andreas Osiander, who helped introduce the Lutheran reformation to Nuremberg, objected to the famous *Schembartlauf* and succeeded in having it abolished. The traditional Good Friday Passion Play also disappeared. The Bavarian Lutheran Thomas Naogeorgus mounted a general attack on popular festivals as relics of popery in his book *The Popish Kingdom*. In Lutheran Sweden, the bishops led the assault on 'idolatry and superstition' (*avguderi och vidskapelse*), with particular attention to magic and the cult of springs.[28]

Zwingli, Calvin, and their respective followers went much further than Luther in their opposition to popular traditions. Zwingli had all the images removed from Zürich churches in 1524, and they were not restored after his death in 1531. Calvin was opposed to plays and 'lewd songs' (*chansons deshonnêtes*) and from Scotland to Hungary, his followers were prominent among the opponents of popular festivals. In France in 1572, the Calvinist synod of Nîmes forbade even plays with biblical themes on the grounds that 'the Holy Bible was not given us to serve us as a pastime'. In Scotland, from the mid-1570s on, there was a sustained attack on the celebration of Christmas, Midsummer and other festivals with singing, dancing, bonfires and plays.[29]

The opposition of English Puritans to popular recreations is well known and well documented. Phillip Stubbes drew up a comprehensive indictment of Lords of Misrule, May Games, Christmas feasting, church ales, wakes, bear-baiting, cock-fighting, and dancing. It is an irony he would scarcely have appreciated that his *Anatomy of Abuses* (like the *Popish Kingdom*) is read today mainly by people who are interested in the popular recreations he condemned. J. Northbrooke's *Distraction of the Sabbath* and C. Fetherston's *Dialogue against Dancing* were contemporary works in a similar vein. These views had support in high places, notably from Edmund Grindal, Archbishop of York. As a result of pressure from Grindal and others, the popular religious drama disappeared in Elizabeth's reign. In Norwich the 'pageants', as they were often called, faded out around 1564; in Worcester, about 1566; in York, about 1572; in Wakefield and Chester, about 1575; in Chelmsford about 1576, and in Coventry about 1590.[30]

In the Dutch Republic, the attitudes of Calvinists were similarly strict, and the opposition to them was weaker. The synod of Edam (1586) forbade the use of church bells and organs to play 'thoughtless and worldly songs' (*lichtveerdige ende weereltlycke gesangen*). The synod of Doccum (1591) condemned 'bell-ringing to call young people together, erecting maypoles, hanging up garlands, and singing carnal songs and choruses underneath'. The synod of Deventer (1602) denounced, among other 'abuses', Shrove Tuesday plays and sword dances. The conflict between Carnival and Lent was still in progress in the mid-seventeenth century, when the Amsterdam preacher Petrus Wittewrongel sounded off against plays and maypoles, while another Dutch Calvinist, Walich Siewert, denounced the custom of filling children's shoes, on the feast of St Nicholas, 'with all sorts of sweets and nonsense' (*met allerley snoeperie ende slickerdemick*).[31]

On the Catholic side, the tradition of Geiler and Savonarola had its followers in the first half of the sixteenth century. There was Erasmus, much stricter than Luther where popular culture was concerned, and among active reformers there was Gian Matteo Giberti, the bishop of Verona. If examples before 1550 are isolated, this was no longer the case after the Council of Trent, which held its last and most decisive sessions in 1562 and 1563. In their attempts to counter the heresies of Luther and Calvin, the bishops assembled at Trent issued a number of decrees for the reform of popular culture. Although defending the tradition of placing images in churches, they declared:

> In the invocation of saints, the veneration of relics, and the sacred use of images, all superstition shall be removed, all filthy quest for gain eliminated, and all lasciviousness avoided, so that images shall not be painted or adorned with seductive charm, or the celebration of saints and the visitation of relics be perverted by the people into boisterous festivities and drunkenness, as if the festivals in honour of the saints are to be celebrated with revelry and with no sense of decency.[32]

A series of synods and provincial councils were held in Catholic Europe in the middle 1560s from Rheims to Prague, from Haarlem to Toledo, to put the Trent decrees into effect locally. Councils of this kind had often condemned the moral faults of the clergy or abuses in the administration of the sacraments; what was new in the 1560s was the concern with the reform of festivals and with the beliefs of the 'uneducated people' (*indocta plebs*). The Indexes of prohibited books issued in the later sixteenth century were mainly concerned with theological books in Latin, but they did ban some ballads and some chap-books, notably *Till Eulenspiegel* and *Reynard the Fox*. The Portuguese Index of 1624 prohibited a number of popular religious works like *The Testament of Jesus Christ*, *The Raising of Lazarus*, and special prayers to St Christopher and St Martin which were supposed to grant to anyone who recited them whatever they wanted, whether this was an escape from danger or 'Great vengeance on their enemies' (*grande vingança de inimigos*).[33]

In short, there was, from the 1560s onwards, an organised movement within the Catholic Church in support of individual reformers. We have already met St Carlo Borromeo,

Archbishop of Milan; Gabriele Paleotti, Archbishop of Bologna; and St Carlo's secretary and disciple Carlo Bascapè, who became Bishop of Novara. All three men set great store by the gravity and modesty of the clergy, and were declared enemies of taverns, of plays, and, above all, of Carnival. Gentler in his manner but a man of similar ideals was St François de Sales (styled 'Bishop of Geneva', but in practice Bishop of Annecy). With these bishops should be mentioned at least one Catholic layman, Maximilian, Duke of Bavaria, who took great personal interest in the work of reform in his territories in the early seventeenth century, prohibiting (amongst other things) magic, masquerades, short dresses, mixed bathing, fortune-telling, excessive eating and drinking, and 'shameful' language at weddings.[34]

An indicator of the impact of the reform movement on popular culture in Catholic as in Protestant Europe is the history of the religious drama. In parts of France and Italy it seems to have been on its way out about 1600. In Paris in 1548, the Fraternity of the Passion were forbidden to stage their customary mystery plays, (though it should be added that the Parlement of Paris allowed them to revive their performances more than twenty-five years later, in 1574 and again in 1577). According to the art-historian Giorgio Vasari, mystery plays had virtually ceased in Florence by the end of the 1540s. Curiously enough, texts of traditional religious plays continue to be printed in Florence until the end of the sixteenth century, but about 1625 they too disappear. In Milan, a provincial council forbade religious plays in 1566, a prohibition with no less a man than St Carlo to enforce it; in 1578, plays were denounced by the Archbishop of Bologna, and in 1583 the Council of Rheims forbade plays on feast-days altogether (*ludos theatrales . . . omnino prohibemus*). In 1601 the government of the Spanish Netherlands issued an edict against religious plays because they contained 'many useless things, dishonourable and intolerable, serving for nothing but to deprave and corrupt morals (*te corrumperen ende bederven alle goede manieren*), especially those of simple and good people, whereby the common people are shocked or led astray'.[35] In England, a revealing confrontation between the old attitudes and the new among the Catholic clergy occurred at Christmas 1594, in the castle of Wisbech in the Isle of Ely, where priests were imprisoned by the Elizabethan government. There were two groups or factions among the priests in Wisbech, seculars and Jesuits, respectively supporting traditional and Counter-Reformation Catholicism. At Christmas a hobby-horse was brought into the hall at Wisbech as part of the festivities. The Jesuit William Weston, leader of the Counter-Reformation Catholics, was shocked at this and other 'gross abuses', which he wanted to reform. The leader of the traditional Catholics, Christopher Bagshaw, was equally shocked at Weston's intolerance.[36]

If the clergy themselves sometimes objected to the reforms, it may be imagined that the laity did not always welcome them with enthusiasm. In Spain, the second rebellion of the Moriscos of the Alpujarras, which began in 1568, was their reaction to attempts to reform their popular culture by force, to prohibit their traditional costume, dances, and rituals. Elsewhere the opposition of the laity was expressed, appropriately enough, by a public, ritualised mocking of the reformers. In Nuremberg, where the opposition to the traditional *Schembartlauf* was led by the Lutheran pastor Andreas Osiander, the revellers took their revenge in 1539 in a truly carnivalesque manner. That year they made their float in the shape of a ship of fools, with Osiander himself, in his black gown, prominent among them, and they also attacked his house. In other words, their protest took the form of a somewhat eccentric charivari. In Bologna in 1578, the same year that Archbishop Paleotti had denounced plays, we have the first record of the burning of *La Vecchia*, 'the Old Woman', an image of Lent. Was Paleotti being guyed in the way Osiander had been? At Wells in 1607, a puritan clothier by the name of John Hole opposed the traditional custom of church ales. The May games in Wells were extremely elaborate that year, and the pageants included one of 'the holing game', a satire on John Hole and his friends. However, in these combats of Carnival and Lent, it was usually the godly who had the last word. Between 1550 and 1650, many traditional customs were abolished. The middle of the seventeenth century may be taken as ending a first phase in the reform of popular culture, a reform which arose out of the Catholic and Protestant reformations, was led in the main by the clergy, and justified primarily on theological grounds.[37] It was to be followed by a second phase in which the laity took the initiative.

The culture of the godly

The reform of popular culture has been presented so far in negative terms. Of course the reformers did have positive ideals, and in any case they knew that they had no chance of success if they did not offer the people something to replace the traditional festivals, songs, images which they were trying to abolish. Hence the godly tried to create a new popular culture, Luther, for example, made a collection of hymns, 'to give the young . . . something to wean them away from love-ballads and carnal verses, and to teach them something of value in their place'.[38] In this section I shall try to describe both the Catholic and the Protestant replacements. About reformed Orthodox culture there seems to be virtually no evidence, although it seems that the gap left by the banning of the *skomorokhi* was filled by the *kaleki*, itinerant professional singers of religious songs, or *stikhi*.

For the Protestants, a high priority was to make the Bible available to ordinary people in a language which they could understand. Luther made the point in his forceful way: 'One must ask the mother in the house, the children on the streets and the common man in the marketplace, and see from their own mouths how they speak, and translate accordingly.'[39] He published his New Testament in German in 1522, and the complete Bible in 1534, and his example was soon followed in other Protestant areas. Tyndale's New Testament was published in 1535; Laurentius Petri's Swedish Bible, known as 'Gustav Vasa's Bible', in 1541; the Geneva Bible in French in 1540 (better known in its revised version of 1588); the standard Czech Bible, the 'Kralice Bible', was produced in six volumes by a committee of ten scholars between 1579 and 1593; the standard Hungarian Calvinist Bible was first published in 1590; the standard Welsh translation was made by William Morgan, who died in 1604; the English Authorised Version, like the Kralice Bible the work of a committee, appeared in 1611.[40]

The publication of these vernacular Bibles was a major cultural event which greatly influenced the language and literature of the countries concerned. In France, the Huguenot minority came to speak what was called 'the patois of Canaan', an archaic French closer to the Geneva Bible than it was to the language of their Catholic compatriots. In Protestant Germany, the holy corner of the house came to be known as the *Bibel-Eck*. However, it would be quite wrong to imagine every family of Protestant craftsmen or peasants in our period owning or reading the Bible. It is true that by the eighteenth century, when such calculations begin to be possible, the literacy rate was much higher in Protestant Europe than it was in Catholic or in Orthodox Europe (below, p.251). Whether this high rate was cause or consequence of the Reformation is difficult to say – it was probably both. But not every Protestant could read, and not everyone who could read could afford to buy a Bible. Luther's New Testament of 1522 cost half a guilder at a time when this was the weekly wage of a journeyman carpenter, and Luther's complete Bible cost two guilders, eight groschen. Even in eighteenth-century Sweden, where adult literacy was over 90 per cent in some country districts, the evidence of inventories suggests that a Bible could be found only in one household in twenty.[41]

Protestant craftsmen and peasants must often have gained what knowledge of the Bible they possessed orally or at second hand. Readings from the Bible were an important part of both Lutheran and Calvinist services. Ordinary Protestants were particularly likely to know the Psalms, because they could be sung and had an important place in the reformed liturgies. Luther's most famous hymn, 'Our God he is a castle strong' (*Ein' feste Burg ist unser Gott*), is in fact an adaptation of Psalm 46, 'God is our refuge and strength'. The standard English version of the Psalms, 'Sternhold and Hopkins', went through nearly 300 editions between the mid-sixteenth and mid-seventeenth centuries. The standard Huguenot version was that of Marot and Beza, set to music by the composers Louis Bourgeois and Claude Goudimel. Other influential Calvinist versions included two in Dutch, by J. Utenhove (1566) and P. Marnix (1580); a Scottish translation associated with the Wedderburns, dating from the later sixteenth century; and one by A. Molnár (1607) in Hungarian. No doubt the Psalms owed part of their popularity to the identification of many Protestants with the people of Israel, engaged in a holy war with idolators. In Lyons in the 1560s, armed Huguenot craftsmen sang the Psalms in the streets, and when digging the foundations of their temple. In London in 1641 Puritans sang psalms to drown the Anglican services. Huguenots and Puritans sang psalms as they went into battle, in particular the 68th, 'Let God arise, let his enemies be scattered'. Cromwell's army sang a psalm in thanksgiving after their victory at Marston Moor. Protestants quoted psalms in their wills, they heard them sung in the heavens, they sang them at funerals, at weddings, at banquets, even in their dreams. A Swedish bishop complained that psalms were sung in alehouses, while the Consistory of Lausanne was shocked to hear in 1667 of some people who had been singing psalms while they danced. They were so much part of everyday life in some Calvinist areas that, when research into traditional folksongs got under way in nineteenth-century France, none could be found in the Cévennes. In this traditional Huguenot culture, the Psalms had taken over the functions of folksongs, and they were even used as lullabies.[42]

Central to Protestant popular culture was the catechism, a booklet containing elementary information about religious doctrine. Catechisms existed before the Reformation: what was new was to present the material in question-and-answer form, making it easy to spread – and test – religious knowledge. Famous examples are Luther's Small Catechism of 1529, Calvin's Catechism (especially in its revised version of 1542), and the Heidelberg Catechism of 1563. Luther's Little Catechism had been intended as a help for unlearned pastors, but it came to play a more direct part in the life of the laity. It was, as the Swedish bishop Laurentius Paulinus called it, 'the common man's Bible', 'a short summary of the entire Holy Scriptures'. In Sweden there were sermons on the catechism, and readings from the catechism at services, while the printed text was to be found in hymn-books. In the seventeenth century, the clergy began to go round from house to house in Sweden to test the laity on their knowledge of reading and of the catechism, a visitation known as *husförhör*. Elsewhere ability to answer the questions of the catechism correctly was sometimes made a condition of admission to the Lord's Supper, the central ritual of the Protestant churches. Sometimes the catechism was turned into verse to make memorisation easier, as in the case of Martin Rinckart's *Catechismus-Lieder,* published at Leipzig in 1645. It is not surprising to find that in some places catechisms were much more common than Bibles; in eighteenth-century Sweden, there was a catechism or hymn-book containing the catechism in every fifth or sixth house, whereas only one household in twenty contained the Bible.[43]

The message of the Psalms and the Catechism was driven home in a variety of other ways. Protestant culture was sermon culture. Sermons might last for hours and they might be a great emotional experience involving audience participation, with members of the congregation exclaiming, sighing or weeping. The existence of 'mechanick preachers' in England or the Cévennes showed that ordinary people might be attentive to the language and performing style of the preacher as well as his message; indeed, their culture predisposed them to be better connoisseurs of oral performances, whether by preachers, storytellers or ballad singers, than we are today. The laity could play a considerable part in 'prophesyings', public discussions about the meaning of Scripture. The literate laity could read controversial or devotional books. Calvin intended some of his treatises in French to be read by craftsmen, who were the largest social group in the Reformed church in his time; in the introduction to his treatises against the Anabaptists, he explains that the purpose of writing was to show those of the faithful who are *'rudes et sans lettres'* (presumably little-educated rather than illiterate) how dangerous the Anabaptists were.[44] Some devotional books became best-sellers. Arthur Dent's *The Plain Man's Pathway to Heaven* (1601) went through twenty-five editions in forty years, which suggests that this lively dialogue really did appeal to plain men; we know that it appealed to Bunyan, whose own *Pilgrim's Progress* (1678) not only went through twenty-two editions by 1699 but was read in other parts of Europe. In the Lutheran world, Johann Arndt's *True Christianity* and his *Garden of Paradise* were often reprinted up to the early nineteenth century.

Music, ritual and imagery all had their parts in Protestant popular culture, whatever the misgivings of the leaders. Luther allowed hymns other than the Psalms to be sung in church and wrote thirty-seven hymns himself. His example was followed by a number of pastors, notably Johannes Mathesius, Paul Gerhardt and Johannes Rist. In the process of writing they frequently employed the method of *Contrafaktur,* to use Luther's word for it; in plain English, 'counterfeiting', but in the sense of transposition or substitution, as in cases where hymns were modelled on folksongs and set to their tunes. Not all reformers approved of counterfeiting, but Luther practised it cheerfully. His Christmas hymn 'From heaven on high I come to you' (*Vom Himmel hoch da kom ich her*) follows a secular folksong in its first stanza, while another hymn, 'To me she's dear, the worthy maid' (*Sie ist mir lieb, die werde Magd*), was inspired by a love-song, transposed into religious terms by interpreting the maiden as the Church. One of the most famous examples of counterfeiting is a hymn by Johann Hesse, based on *Innsbruck ich muss dich lassen* (above, p.121).

> *O Welt ich muss dich lassen*
> *Ich fahr dahin mein Strassen*
> *Ins ewig Vaterland . . .*[45]

The religious music of Bach has its roots in Lutheran popular culture.

At Calvinist services, the Psalms were the only texts allowed to be sung, but that did not stop Calvinists writing hymns for singing outside. In a Scottish collection from the later sixteenth century, the counterfeiting is not too successful and the original secular songs sometimes show through, giving us not only an idea of the techniques of the reformers but also a rare glimpse of Scottish popular culture before the days of Knox. Here are three examples:

> *For lufe of one I mak my mone,*
> *Richt secreitly,*
> *To Christ Jesu . . .*
>
> *Quho is at my windo? quho, quho?*
> *Go from my windo, go, go!*
> *Lord, I am heir, ane wretchit mortall . . .*
>
> *Johne cum kis me now,*
> *Johne cum kis me now . . .*
> *The lord thy God I am,*
> *That Johne dois the call,*
> *Johne representit man,*
> *Be grace celestial . . .*

Much of traditional popular culture, as we have seen, consisted of parodies of official culture like mock trials and mock funerals. Here the wheel comes full circle and we find pious 'parodies' of the profane.[46]

In the early years of the Reformation, ritual and drama were pressed into the service of the Protestants. Carnivals were the occasion for mocking the Pope and his clergy at Wittenberg in 1521, at Bern in 1523, at Stralsund in 1525, and elsewhere. Satirical plays flourished in the 1520s and 1530s. At Basel in 1521, the citizens could see Gengenbach's *Totenfresser* (above, p.156). At Paris in 1523, they could see *The Farce of Theologastres,* a counterfeit of a miracle play in which 'Dame Faith', who is ill, finds that decretals and sermons do her no good, while the text of Holy Scripture cures her immediately. In Bern in 1525, people could see *The Indulgence-Seller,* a topical satire by the painter-poet Niklas Manuel. Thomas Naogeorgus adapted the traditional mystery play to Protestant purposes in his *Pammachius* (1538), which deals with a pope corrupted by power. In 1539, a play called *The Tree of Scripture* was performed at Middelburgh in the Netherlands; it attacked the clergy and 'superstition'. The first generation of reformers were well aware that 'into the common people things sooner enter by the eyes than by the ears: remembering more better that they see than that they hear', a point made by an Englishman in Henry VIII's reign who suggested an annual festival, with bonfires and processions, to commemorate the breach with Rome.[47]

In the long run, however, plays lost their importance for the Protestants, whether because their work was done, or the people more literate, or because the stricter reformers, who thought the drama essentially bad, managed to impose their will on the moderates. This history of the religious image in Protestant popular culture followed similar lines. In the first generation, the print was an important instrument of propaganda; one thinks of the Cranach studio and the *Passional of Christ and Antichrist* (above, p.137), but there were many other examples. After the early years, prints lost much of their importance. In Lutheran Europe, there was still a place for the devotional image: pictures of Luther, or illustrations of episodes from the Bible (the New Testament in particular), or emblems, like the illustrations in Arndt's *True Christianity* and *Garden of Paradise* which inspired a good many wall-paintings in German and Swedish churches, or even paintings of the Last Judgement or the pains of Hell. In Calvinist Europe, however, church walls were whitewashed and left bare. The roof, the pulpit or the funeral monuments might be decorated, but the vocabulary of ornament was reduced to a few simple terms: flowers, cherubs, reminders of mortality like hour-glasses and skulls, or moral emblems like the crane with a stone in its claw, symbolising vigilance. In both Lutheran and Calvinist areas, one often finds that the church or temple is decorated with texts. Luther recommended that the walls of cemeteries be painted not with images but with texts, such as 'I know that my Redeemer liveth'. One might find the Ten Commandments displayed on two boards, one at each side of the chancel arch, or a 'catechism altarpiece', inscribed with Commandments, Lord's Prayer and Creed, or texts from the Bible painted on the pulpit, or on the beams of the church roof; for 'Heaven and Earth shall pass away: but my words shall not pass away' (Luke 21). To a much greater degree than that of the Catholics, Protestant popular culture was a culture of the Word.[48]

There is less to say about reformed Catholic culture because it was less sharply distinct from the traditional popular culture to which the reformers objected. Catholic leaders no less than Protestants believed in counterfeiting – indeed, they had been practising it for centuries. In AD 601 Pope Gregory the Great advised Bishop Augustine, who was doing mission work in darkest England, that 'the temples of the idols in that country should on no account be destroyed'; the idols were to be destroyed, but the temples were to be converted into churches, 'and since they have a custom of sacrificing many oxen to devils, let some other solemnity be substituted in its place'. Gregory's basic principle was that 'it is certainly impossible to eradicate all errors from obstinate minds at one stroke, and whoever wishes to climb to a mountain top climbs gradually step by step and not in one leap'. This was the famous doctrine of 'accommodation', which explains how a pagan Midwinter festival could survive as Christmas and a Midsummer festival as the birthday of St John the Baptist. The doctrine underlay the practice of Catholic missionaries in the Indies in the sixteenth and seventeenth centuries, like the Jesuit Roberto de Nobili, who adapted Catholic rituals to the culture of the Brahmins of South India, justifying himself when challenged by quoting Pope Gregory.[49]

The same policy can be observed at work in early modern Europe. When the Muslims of Granada were converted – by force – at the end of the fifteenth century, the first archbishop of

Granada authorised these 'new Christians' to use their traditional songs in religious services. This policy can still be observed at the end of the seventeenth century. Bossuet, who was Bishop of Meaux as well as preacher at the court of Louis XIV, advised his clergy on the attitude they should take to bonfires on St John's Eve. 'Does the Church take part in these fires?' asked Bossuet – rhetorically:

> *Yes, because in a number of dioceses, and in this one in particular, a number of parishes light a fire which they call 'ecclesiastical'. What is the reason for lighting a fire in an ecclesiastical manner? To banish the superstitions practised at the fire of St John's Eve.*

Bossuet does not explain how exactly an ecclesiastical bonfire differs from an ordinary one, but the technique of accommodation is clear enough.[50]

To complicate matters in the early modern period, the Catholic reformers were fighting on two fronts: against the Protestants who wanted to reform too much, as well as against immorality and 'superstition'. Counter-Reformation culture bears the marks of both battles. It may be useful to describe three elements of this culture in order: reformed rituals, reformed images, and reformed texts.

Catholic reformers were well aware of the uses of ritual. They used ritual to convince ordinary people that the Protestants were wrong, or wicked, or both. Zwingli was burned in effigy at the Carnival of Lucerne in 1523, while Luther was regularly burned on St John's Eve in Catholic Germany until the beginning of the nineteenth century. Heretics recanted in public, or they were burned in public, as in the famous *autos-da-fe* at Valladolid and Seville at the beginning of the reign of Philip II; heretical books were burned in public, from Montpellier to Vilna. Savonarola turned his attack on Carnival into a kind of Carnival. His famous burning of 'vanities' at Florence was a deliberate substitute for the custom of lighting bonfires at Carnival and burning the floats, and on one occasion at least, 'Carnival' himself, 'in the form of a filthy and abominable monster', was added to the pyre, a mock execution in traditional style yet with a new meaning. In Milan, S. Carlo Borromeo not only forbade plays during Carnival, but organised processions as a substitute. The 'Forty Hours' devotion, which spread in the second half of the sixteenth century, and often involved magnificent effects of light and sound, also borrowed from secular festivals in order to take their place in the hearts of the faithful.[51]

The new rituals can be seen at their most dramatic in the missions which the Jesuits and others undertook in towns and in the countryside in the seventeenth century. In Brittany, for example, the missionaries organised a dialogue between the living and the damned and processions which acted out the Stations of the Cross. Even more theatrical were the missions in the Kingdom of Naples about the year 1650. Sermons had an important place in the mission, and might be preached in the evening or at dawn, so that working people had a chance to listen. They were often hell-fire sermons, in which the preacher might display a skull in order to strike to the hearts of his audience; 'it was often necessary for the preacher to leave off speaking for nearly a quarter of an hour, because of the groans and sobs of his listeners'. Even more important were the processions, mainly of men – we are in the south – including penitents 'with crowns of thorns on their heads, ropes round their necks, and in their hands bones, or death's heads, or little crucifixes, going through the streets barefoot and half naked', some of them carrying heavy crosses or beating themselves as they went. Then relics and statues would be carried past, followed by more of the laity, while the clergy brought up the rear, carrying basins full of prohibited books, love-songs and magical devices, material for another bonfire of vanities.[52]

Some mission preachers, like Le Nobletz or Maunoir in Brittany made use of visual aids, images to illustrate the life of St Martin, for example, or the Our Father, or the Holy Sacrament, or the pains of Hell.[53] Bossuet recommended his parish priests to attach images to the pulpit in order to make the congregation more attentive to the words of the preacher. Reformed Catholics, unlike reformed Protestants, continued to have a religion of images rather than a religion of texts, whether this was cause or consequence of the fact that Catholic areas were generally less literate than Protestant ones. Gregory the Great's suggestion that paintings were the books of the illiterate continued to have all its relevance. Reformers did not want to do without images altogether, although they might find specific popular religious images objectionable.

In place of what was reformed away, the Church offered

Catholics new saints and new images. St Ignatius Loyola, canonised in 1622, was usually shown as a bearded man holding an open book, the rule of his order, with his breast lettered IHS (Jesu Hominum Salvator – Jesus Saviour of Mankind). St Teresa of Avila, also canonised in 1622, was often represented in ecstasy, as in the famous sculpture by Bernini, her heart pierced by an angel with an arrow. In Central Europe, an important new arrival was John Nepomuk, who was already the object of a cult in the seventeenth century, although he was not canonised till 1729.[54] There were other important shifts in devotional emphasis. St Mary Magdalen became a more important figure than she had been before the Counter-Reformation, and so did St Joseph. St Joseph had been something of a comic figure in the later Middle Ages, 'Joseph the fool' (*Joseph le rassoté*), the holy cuckold. In the seventeenth century, however, the clergy seem to have been trying to persuade the faithful to take him more seriously. Fraternities dedicated to him were founded, and scenes of the Holy Family, in which he was included, tended to replace the traditional Virgin-and-child group. There was more emphasis on the cult of the Eucharist than there had been in the Middle ages; the rise of the 'Forty Hours' devotion is one indicator of this change.[55]

These shifts appear to have been the result of official Church policies. The cult of the Holy Family, like the cult of St Isidore the ploughman (canonised in 1622 along with St Ignatius and St Teresa) looks like a deliberate attempt to appeal to the ordinary layman. The canonisation of Ignatius, Teresa, and S. Carlo Borromeo emphasises the achievements of the Catholic Reformation. The cult of the Eucharist was a response to Protestant attacks on transubstantiation, the Mass, and the special position of the priesthood. Similarly, the new emphasis on St Mary Magdalen (usually represented as a weeping penitent), and the cult of St John Nepomuk (a priest who was murdered because he refused to reveal the secrets of confession) were responses to Protestant criticisms of the institution of confession and the sacrament of penance. In a famous essay, the anthropologist Malinowski described myths about the past as performing a function in the present, as the 'charter' of present institutions, legitimating them, justifying them. It certainly looks as if myths, rituals and images served the Counter-Reformation Church in that kind of way.[56]

It would have been odd if these appeals to the eye had not been accompanied by appeals to the ear. In fact vernacular hymns had been an important element of lay religious culture in the late Middle Ages, associated in particular with fraternities. In thirteenth-century Italy, the fraternities sang *laude*, hymns which were often pious counterfeits of the popular songs of the time. This practice continued into the early modern period. In an Italian miracle play about St Margaret, the heroine sings a *lauda* beginning:

> *O vaghe di Jesu, o verginelle*
> *Ove n'andate si leggiadre e belle?*
>
> (*O sweet ones of Jesus, a little maids/Where are you going, so fine and so pretty?*)

The tune is described as that of O *vaghe montanine e pastorelle*, 'O sweet mountain girls and shepherdesses'; this hymn (like the 'spiritual songs' of the Wedderburn collection) makes little attempt to disguise the original secular words. In Spain about the year 1500, the Franciscan Amborio Montesino wrote hymns which were 'spiritually counterfeited' (*contrahechos a lo divino*). Since love-poetry had borrowed from religious language, it was not difficult to turn it back to religious use, and praise the Virgin Mary instead of a worldly love. This tradition of hymn-writing continued after the Council of Trent. The Jesuit missionary Julien Maunoir composed 'spiritual canticles' to the Virgin, and others which 'contained all the principles of the faith', for use in the conversion of rural Brittany.[57]

Last, and probably least in Catholic culture, came the attempt to reach the literate laity through the Bible and other pious reading. Translations of the Bible were of course published in Catholic countries – the first printed Bible in German goes back to 1466. Catholic catechisms modelled themselves on Protestant ones (p.225 above). Those of the Jesuits Peter Canisius (1555) and Robert Bellarmine (1597) were often reprinted; more than seventy German editions of Canisius were published before 1800, while Bellarmine was translated into many European languages and dialects, including Basque, Bosnian, Croat, Furlan, Sicilian, Hungarian, Irish and Maltese. These catechisms were written in simple language and they were often illustrated, so it does look as if they were intended for the laity, rather than as works of reference for the clergy. In seventeenth-century France, the catechism was regularly taught to children in the *petites écoles*, on Sundays and on other holidays. Yet one has the impression, which a comparative study of inventories might confirm or refute, that the catechism played less of a part in the religious life of Catholic France than in that of Protestant Sweden.[58]

The same point might be made still more strongly about devotional books, although such books did exist. The *Imitation of Christ* was frequently reprinted in this period. The *Spiritual Combat* (1589), an anonymous work associated with the Italian priest Lorenzo Scupoli, went through at least twenty-three editions between 1609 and 1788 in France alone. In the mid-seventeenth century, when books were becoming cheaper, the synod of Chalons-sur-Marne suggested that the faithful should be encouraged to buy and read three books, and that these books should also be read aloud 'in the porch or at the entry to the church, every Sunday and on feast-days after Vespers.' The three books were the Catechism, the *Christian Pedagogue*, and a book called the *Pensez-y-bien*. The inventory of the stock of a Paris printer who died in 1698 mentions 450 copies of the *Imitation of Christ*, and 630 of the *Pensez-y-bien*. What was this famous *Pensez-y-bien*? It was a treatise on the art of making a good death. The reader is exhorted to imagine the hour of his death; to think about those things he would regret having done, if his hour had come; to reflect about those things he would like to have done, if he was now about to die. At the end of each paragraph, like a refrain, the italicised words, *Pensez-y-bien*.[59]

The second phase of reform, 1650–1800

The argument of the last two sections might be summarised as follows. In the late sixteenth and early seventeenth centuries there was a systematic attempt by members of the elite, mostly Catholic and Protestant clergy, to reform the culture of ordinary people. The reform had medieval precedents, but it was more effective in early modern Europe than in the Middle Ages because communications, from roads to books, were better than they had been. The reformers were no longer condemned to run on the spot, as they had been in the days of St Augustine and even St Bernardino, but could build on one another's work. The resilience of popular culture began to break down and important changes took place. How far and how fast these changes went, and how soon ordinary people made the new forms of Protestant and Catholic culture their own, these are difficult questions which cannot receive satisfactory answers until much more regional research has been carried out. My impression, based on the fragments of evidence assembled in the last few pages, is that a series of important changes had taken place by 1650, particularly in Protestant Europe and in the more urbanised regions. Near Bern and Zürich the reform of popular culture seems to have taken place about 1530, in Nuremberg the reformers had made an impression by 1540, in the province of Holland they seem to have won before 1600.[60]

In much of Catholic Europe, on the other hand, and in the more outlying parts of the continent, remote from major towns, major roads and major languages, the reformers won their victories only after 1650: in Protestant Wales and Norway, in Catholic Bavaria, Sicily, Brittany and Languedoc, not to mention eastern Europe. Yet the story to be told in this section is not just one of the gradual diffusion of unchanging ideals. These were years of a 'reformation within the reformation' (both Catholic and Protestant), and of the rise of groups of lay reformers who did not always want the same changes in popular culture as their clerical colleagues, or want changes for quite the same reasons.

The survival of 'pre-Reformation' Catholicism in outlying parts is not difficult to document. In some of these areas, for example, mystery plays were both late in coming and late in going. In the Bavarian highlands, the Passion plays of Oberammergau and other villages only began to be performed from 1634 on. Although they shocked some of the clergy – the Archbishop of Salzburg declared in 1779 that 'a stranger mixture of religion and profanity than the so-called Passion plays cannot be imagined' – they were not abolished till 1800, and the Oberammergau play was restored, in purified form, in 1810. In Sicily, mystery plays only became common in the mid-seventeenth century, and were still flourishing in the early nineteenth. In Brittany, too, plays of this kind were still being performed in the nineteenth century. A visitor to Finistère recorded, in 1765 or thereabouts, that he had seen people dancing in a chapel and a cemetery not far from Brest.[61]

It may be useful to look at one of these outlying parts in a little more detail: Languedoc. In late seventeenth-century Languedoc, there were two energetic reforming bishops, Nicholas Pavillon, Bishop of Alet, who modelled himself on S. Carlo Borromeo, and François-Étienne Caulet, Bishop of Pamiers, who modelled himself on Pavillon. It is clear from the papers of these two men that in the highlands of Languedoc the whole work of reform was still to be done. The two bishops record their horror at violent charivaris, indecent dances on feast-days, diviners, strolling players, and general ignorance of religion. Caulet was still having to forbid his clergy to frequent plays, dances and masquerades, as if the Catholic reformation had never happened. It was not only the mountains which separated the inhabitants of Alet and Pamiers from what was happening elsewhere; Pavillon noted the need for a catechism 'in the vulgar tongue' for his people, because they did not know French. No doubt this was why Bartholomé Amilha, who was appointed canon of Pamiers by Caulet, published his *Picture of the Life of a Perfect Christian* (1673) in Occitan. His verses are a lively exposition of the ideas of the reformers. He warns his readers, or listeners, of the dangers of dancing, gaming, frequenting those 'houses of iniquity' the taverns, and, above all, of the perils of Carnival.

Chrestias, pensen à la counsciença	*Christians, examine your consciences*
Duran aqueste Carnabal	*During this Carnival*
Soungen que cal fa penitenco	*Each think of penance*
Quiten la taberno é la bal,	*Leave the tavern and the dance,*
La mort es touto preparado	*Death is quite ready*
A fa calqu'autro mascarado.	*For another kind of masquerade.*

Amilha is also worried about the spread of Protestantism. Have you, he asks, read authors who 'smell of the faggot', Calvin's books or Marot's version of the Psalms?

Aurios legit d'auteurs que sentan le fagot,
Les libres de Calbin, o Salmes de Marot?

He also seems to expect his audience to take magic seriously:

As legit o gardat de libres de magio,
As foundat toun salut dessu l'astralougio . . .
As counsoultat Sourcie, Magicien, Debinaire,
Per la santat del fil, de la sor, o del fraire,
Per sabe le passat, o recouba toun be,
O couneisse l'partit que tu dibes abe. . .

(Have you read or kept magic books?
Have you founded your salvation on astrology? . . .
Have you consulted a sorcerer, magician or diviner
About the health of your son, your sister or your brother,
To know the past, or recover your goods,
Or to find out what match you are going to make? . . .)[62]

Whether their reforms survived Pavillon and Caulet seems impossible to say. Elsewhere in Languedoc, the godly still had their problems nearly a hundred years later. The Bishop of Lodève complained about an abbot of misrule in 1746, and his friend the parish priest of Montpeyroux, who used to refuse the sacraments to people who had taken part in dances, was the object of ritual mocking in 1740, when a band of masked men carried a mannequin dressed as a priest through the streets before beating it and burning it. The battle between Carnival and Lent was still going on.[63]

Yet it was not quite the same battle. Some of the reformers were going beyond the Council of Trent, or in a different direction, and were criticising popular devotion to the Virgin Mary and to the saints, hoping to replace this with a more biblical Christianity, purified from 'superstition'. This movement was associated particularly, but not exclusively, with the Jansenists, and in the late eighteenth century some of its leaders attempted to make far-reaching changes in popular religion in Austria and in Tuscany. In Austria, ritual was simplified, statues were removed, and some pilgrimage churches were closed altogether. In Tuscany, Scipione Ricci, who became Bishop of Pistoia and Prato in 1780, held a synod at which he suggested the transference of certain religious festivals to Sunday, recommended the laity to read the Bible, and criticised the devotion to the Sacred Heart. In both areas, this assault on traditional popular religion provoked peasant risings between 1788 and 1791, and Ricci was forced to resign.[64]

The changing views of Catholic reformers can be illustrated by their attitudes to images. In 1570 Johannes Molanus, a

Louvain theologian, published a treatise on religious images which sums up the position at the end of the Council of Trent. Molanus notes the need to avoid 'superstition' but he finds nothing wrong with the traditional images of 'the charity of St Martin' and of St Antony and his pig (above, p.155, 181). In 1673, however, the Archdeacon of Paris, on visitation in the diocese, ordered the churchwardens in one village 'to remove the St Martin from above the altar because he is on horseback, and to make him into a bishop, so that he is decent.' In other words, the traditional scene of the 'charity of St Martin' no longer seemed decent to a Counter-Reformation cleric; he was coming near to identifying the clerical with the sacred. An even more striking example of the Catholic reform of images and the widening gap between clerical and popular culture comes from the diocese of Orléans in 1682. In one village the bishop, on visitation, found an image of St Antony complete with his traditional pig. He immediately ordered the burial of the image-Catholics did not indulge in iconoclasm – because he considered it 'ridiculous and unworthy of this great saint'. The parishioners did not want to lose their image, and some of the women commented that the Bishop 'did not love the saints because he came from a race of Huguenots'. In more general terms the synod of Pistoia of 1786 criticised the cult of images, in particular the practice of giving different images of the same person different names, as if there were more than one Virgin Mary.[65]

It is not so easy to find Protestant areas which resisted the reform of popular culture until after 1650, but they did exist, particularly in the mountains. In Norway, for example, Catholic and even pagan beliefs survived into the eighteenth century. Crucifixes could still be seen, and the belief in the miracle-working powers of St Olav was still widespread. He was associated with a number of springs. In the Scottish Highlands, the war of the ministers against the traditional songs, dances and ballads seems to have been successful only in the eighteenth century; around the year 1700, a local gentleman, Martin Martin, was able to point to many survivals of Catholic and even of pre-Christian customs in the Western Isles.[66]

Another area where the reformers still found a good deal to do after 1700 was Wales, where many people cheerfully

continued to celebrate saints' days, carrying relics in procession
and holding races, football matches and cock-fights. Fairs,
fiddlers, folk-healers, harpers, interludes, storytellers and
wakes all flourished. This state of affairs was naturally a
challenge to the godly. Among the more energetic of them was
Griffith Jones, Nonconformist preacher, a tireless opponent of
wakes and fairs, and a great believer in Bible-reading, sermons,
hymns, and rural education by means of itinerant schoolmasters, known at the time as 'circulating schools'. Still more
famous was Howell Harris, leader of the Welsh Methodists in
Wesley's generation, (though he wouldn't admit to being a
Methodist) who, (said Whitefield),

> made it his business to go to wakes, etc. to turn people from such
> lying vanities. Many alehouse people, fiddlers, harpers etc
> (Demetrius-like) sadly cry out against him for spoiling their
> business.

Harris was also a vehement opponent of cock-fighting; a friend
wrote to him in 1738 that 'a captain of the cock-matches, who
heard you at Bettws, promises never to follow that wicked game
any longer'. As in the case of Languedoc, it is difficult to tell
how effective the Welsh reform movement was in any given
generation. One writer in 1802 suggested that the decline of 'the
national minstrelsy and customs of Wales' was sudden, recent,
and the work of 'fanatic' preachers, as he called them.

> In the course of my excursions through the Principality (he
> continued), I have met with several harpers and songsters who
> actually had been prevailed upon by these erratic strollers to
> relinquish their profession, from the idea that it was sinful.

Folktales and mining songs virtually disappeared. Thanks to the
efforts of the Calvinists and Methodists in the north, and the
Baptists and Congregationalists in the south, Welsh popular
culture became very much a chapel culture of hymns, sermons
and 'Thou Shalt Not on the wall'.[67]

The reformation within the Reformation in Protestant
Europe, parallel to Jansenism among the Catholics, was the rise
of 'Pietism'. In Germany this movement, led by Philipp Jakob
Spener, claimed to be going back to Luther, but it involved an
important shift of emphasis away from the reform of ritual and
belief, with which Luther had been much concerned, towards

inner or moral reform. The Scandinavians participated directly in the pietist movement, and the Welsh revival was parallel if not connected. In England in the 1690s, societies were founded for what was called the 'reformation of manners'. These societies promoted measures against fairs, gambling, masquerades, plays, taverns, whores, and 'obscene ballads'. The concern of the reformers for the 'profanation of the Lord's Day' links them to an earlier generation of Puritans, but the movement was essentially concerned with morals rather than theology, with 'licence' rather than 'superstition'. The ethic of respectability is more visible than before. The mid-eighteenth-century attack on English popular recreations by the Evangelicals should be placed in this tradition. In France, the Company of the Holy Sacrament, with its branches in Paris, Marseilles, Toulouse and elsewhere, was another society or pressure group for the reformation of manners, campaigning against Carnival and investigating the life and morals of diviners or rope-dancers.

A striking feature of this second phase of reform was the increasing part played in it by the laity. The Company of the Holy Sacrament was a mixed group of priests and laymen. In England, many laymen, from William III down to rural Justices of the Peace, took part, along with the clergy, in the movement for the reformation of manners, joining the local societies founded for the purpose or enforcing the ideals of the reformers on the Bench. Lay-preachers were prominent in the movements of religious revival in Britain and Scandinavia. In Norway one of them, Hans Hauge, not only burned fiddles and preached against folksongs, folktales and folk-dances, but also told his hearers to think for themselves about religion instead of simply listening to the clergy.[68]

Another difference between the first phase of reform and the second was the rising importance of secular arguments, including aesthetic considerations. Johann Christoph Gottsched, professor of poetry at Leipzig, launched an attack on the popular theatre of his day, the theatre of Hans Wurst and Harlequin, in the name not of morals but of good taste (*der gute Geschmack*). He complained that 'the common people always derive more enjoyment from foolery and foul abuse (*Narrenpossen und garstige Schimpfreden*) than from serious things'. He also objected to plays which broke the rules of Aristotle and to actors who took liberties with the text – in other words, extemporised in the traditional manner – for this resulted in pieces which were only good for the entertainment of 'the lowest of the mob' (*des untersten Pöbels*). Gottsched in fact succeeded in having Harlequin banished from the stage in 1737. His Viennese equivalent was Josef von Sonnenfels, whose letters on the Viennese theatre of the 1760s set off a brisk controversy, known as the *Hanswurst-Streit*. Like Gottsched, Sonnenfels found the popular theatre too scurrilous – indeed, he would have liked to censor gestures as well as texts – and his ideal was a theatre which observed the unities of time, place, and action in the manner of the classical drama of ancient Greece or seventeenth-century France.[69]

One of the most striking differences between the two phases of reform concerns the supernatural. Earlier reformers of popular culture, like Calvin and St Carlo Borromeo, had believed in the efficacity of the magic they denounced as diabolical; indeed, there would be a case for including the great witch-hunts, which reached their peak in the late sixteenth and early seventeenth centuries, in this movement of reform. However, a number of reformers of the second phase no longer took witchcraft seriously at all. In the diocese of Alet, Pavillon climbed to the top of a mountain to prevent the local people from burning a number of women they suspected of witchcraft. In the Dutch Republic, the Calvinist pastor Balthasar Bekker wrote a book to prove that the belief in witches was a foolish one.[70]

Changes in the meaning of words are sometimes sensitive indicators of much wider changes in attitude. In this context a term to watch is 'superstition'. In English and the romance languages the term had two basic meanings in the early modern period. Before 1650, the dominant meaning seems to be 'false religion', as in phrases like 'the Mahometan superstition'. The term is often used of magic and witchcraft in contexts suggesting that these rituals are efficacious but wicked. After 1650, however, the dominant meaning of the term came to be 'irrational fears' and the rituals associated with them, beliefs and practices which were foolish but harmless because they had no effect at all.[71] How fast the changes took place and among which social groups it is not easy to say. In England and France, witch-trials declined in the late seventeenth century because the magistrates no longer took witchcraft seriously; but in the small towns of south-west Germany they seem to have declined only because the magistrates no longer believed themselves capable of identifying the witches, and in Poland they did not decline at all until the next century. Whether there was a 'decline of magic' at the popular level before 1800 is of course another matter. The 'cunning folk' seem to have remained active enough in the nineteenth and even the early twentieth century in many parts of Europe, surviving the scepticism of the upper classes as they survived the witch-hunters. The resilience of popular culture should not be underestimated.[72]

The second phase of reform can be seen particularly clearly if one looks at eighteenth-century Spain, perhaps because traditional Spanish popular culture had been relatively little affected by the first phase, despite Mariana and Alcoçer. The movement began with Benito Feijoó, a Benedictine monk whose essays, collected together under the title of *The Universal Critical Theatre,* are a systematic critique of common errors, in particular the errors of the common people (*la plebe, la multitud,* or *el vulgo,* as he calls them). In his calm, moderate, cautious, rational way, Feijoó deals in turn with divining, 'supposed prophecies', magic, folk-healers, 'supposed miracles', and 'popular traditions'. He treats all these beliefs as irrationalities, credulities, 'extravagances'.[73]

In the next generation, a group of Spanish reformers put forward arguments – secular arguments – against bull-fights, against street ballads, and against the mystery plays of Calderón. Calderón's plays had already been attacked for 'mixing and confusing the sacred and the profane', but in 1762 the nobleman Nicolas Fernández de Moratín criticised them on more aesthetic grounds, in the manner of Gottsched and Sonnenfels, for breaking the rules laid down by reason and good taste, in other words the unities of time, place and action. The plays were condemned as irregular, capricious, extravagant. Moratín also attacked Lope de Vega, for corrupting the theatre and for writing 'barbarously, to please the people' (*barbaramente, por dar gusto al pueblo*). The public performance of *autos* on the feast of Corpus Christi was officially forbidden by Charles III in 1780.[74]

More political and moral arguments were advanced by Gaspar de Jovellanos and Juan Meléndez Valdés. Jovellanos thought that the theatre gave a bad example to the people by showing crime as successful instead of presenting instances of 'love of country, love of the sovereign, love of the Constitution'. Meléndez Valdés put forward similar arguments against street ballads in a speech of 1798. Bandits who murdered, raped, and resisted the forces of law and order were presented in a heroic light in broadside ballads, thus 'kindling in the imagination of the weak the desire to imitate them'. Other ballads were indecent and obscene; others corrupted the reason with their tales of 'supposed miracles and false devotions'. They should be suppressed, he said, and replaced by 'truly national songs' which would educate the common people, like the traditional ballads in praise of St James and the Cid.[75]

It must not be thought that mystery plays, street ballads, and bull-fights (which were also denounced by Jovellanos) disappeared from Spain at the end of the eighteenth century; there is plenty of evidence to the contrary. In Spain, as elsewhere, the reformers actually achieved very much less than they wanted. They may also be said to have achieved more than they wanted, in the sense that the reform movement had important consequences which they did not intend or even expect. The most obvious of these consequences was the widening of the split between the great and little traditions. The reformers did not want to create a separate purified culture of their own; they wanted to reach the people, to carry everyone with them. In practice, things worked out differently. The reforms affected the educated minority more quickly and more thoroughly than they affected other people and so cut the minority off more and more sharply from popular traditions. This split, together with other unplanned changes in popular culture, will be the subject of the next, and final, chapter.

CHAPTER NINE

Popular Culture and Social Change

The commercial revolution

The last chapter discussed a long and partially successful series
of attempts on the part of some members of the educated
minority to reform the culture of craftsmen and peasants.
However, it is clear enough that changes do not always take
place because someone wants them. In fact, between 1500 and
1800 European popular culture altered in ways which no one
intended, ways which no contemporary could have foreseen –
indeed, contemporaries were only partially aware of the changes
while they were going on. The major economic, social and
political changes of the period had their consequences for
culture, and so they need to be described here, however briefly
and schematically.

One of the most obvious of these changes was the growth in
population. In 1500 there were about 80 million people living in
Europe, a number which had more than doubled, to nearly 190
million, by 1800. Population growth led to urbanisation, for
there was less room on the land and some country people were
forced to migrate to towns in search of work. In 1500 there were
only four cities in Europe with populations of more than
100,000,* but by 1800, there were twenty-three. One of them,
London, had more than a million inhabitants.[1]

Less immediately visible to the naked eye than the rise of
towns but even more important was a sequence of economic
changes which may be summed up as the 'commercial
revolution', or the 'rise of commercial capitalism'. There was a
great expansion of trade within Europe and of trade between
Europe and the rest of the world. The international division of
labour was becoming sharper, with Western Europe
concentrating on manufactures (cutlery, paper, glass and
especially textiles), products which were exported to Eastern
Europe, Asia, Africa and America, while food and raw

*Istanbul, Naples, Paris and Venice.

materials such as iron, hides and cotton were imported in return. Certain towns and their regions specialised in particular products: Leiden in woollen cloth, Lyons in silk, Bologna in paper-making, and so on, and these industries were gradually shifting from production for the local market to production for a market which was national or even international.

With this commercial revolution went a communications revolution. More ships were built, more canals were dug, roads were improved, postal services became more frequent, and there was a greater use of money and credit. Agriculture, too, was transformed, at least in the neighbourhood of large towns; there was a shift from subsistence farming to farming for the growing urban market.

The scale of these economic changes should not be exaggerated. In 1800, less than 3 per cent of the population of Europe lived in towns of 100,000 people or more. The dominant form of industrial enterprise was the small workshop, not the factory, and production was only beginning to be mechanised at the end of the eighteenth century. But the changes were great enough to have serious social consequences.[2]

As the population rose, so did prices, particularly food prices. Prices tended to rise faster than wages, for an increase in wages had to be negotiated, and this meant economic polarisation; some of the rich were getting richer while some of the poor were becoming still poorer. The employers of wage labour profited: the merchants, the landowners who managed their estates themselves, and the better-off peasants and craftsmen. On the other hand, farm hands and journeymen, who received wages, were worse off than before, and smallholders, who supplemented their income by wage labour, often lost their independence.

Popular culture was, as we have seen, closely related to its environment, adapted to different occupational groups and regional ways of life. It was bound to change when its environment changed. How it changed is a subject historians are only beginning to investigate, and one would expect the story, when it is eventually told, to be a complex one, since different parts of Europe were caught up to a different degree in the economic changes. Here, as elsewhere in this book, I shall offer a simple model of a complex process, and argue that the commercial revolution led to a golden age of traditional popular culture (material culture, at least), before the combined commercial and industrial revolutions destroyed it.

In various parts of Western Europe, the impression of contemporaries (backed by the harder evidence of inventories) was that the peasantry were coming to own more material objects, and also better ones. In England the change seems to have come relatively early, in the reign of Elizabeth. In the past, a peasant and his family slept on the floor, and 'a mazer and a pan or two comprised all his substance'; but in the late sixteenth century, a farmer might have 'a fair garnish of pewter in his cupboard . . . three or four feather beds, so many coverlets and carpets of tapestry, a silver salt, a bowl for wine (if not a whole nest) and a dozen spoons to furnish up the suit'. Most spectacular of all, much of rural England was rebuilt in the late sixteenth and early seventeenth centuries. In Alsace, too, the sixteenth and seventeenth centuries were the great age of the art of the country craftsman, of the building and furnishing of half-timbered houses.[3]

In other parts of Western Europe, it seems to have been the eighteenth century which marked the decisive change. In Friesland, peasants acquired *schoorsteen kleden* (decorative cloths for the mantelpiece), curtains, mirrors, clocks, and silver spoons. In Artois, bowls and pots made of wood and crude earthenware were replaced by pewter and finer pottery. The inventory of the goods of Edme Retif, a farmer of Burgundy (and the father of Retif de la Bretonne), show that in 1764 he owned, among other things, twelve chairs, two large beds, silverware, and a prie-dieu. In Norway and Sweden, it is easy to find carved and painted chests and cupboards, bowls and plates of the eighteenth century, but difficult to find anything earlier which comes from a peasant's house. Norwegian rose-painting and Swedish painted hangings go back to the eighteenth century, when open fires (with the smoke let out through a hole in the roof) were replaced by stoves. Grandfather clocks made their appearance in farmhouses in eighteenth-century Sweden as in eighteenth-century Wales.[4]

The increase in the quantity (and perhaps quality) of the furniture and utensils in peasant houses of this period took place for two different reasons. In some regions, the richer peasants were prospering and this prosperity was translated into new standards of comfort. In England, it was the yeoman class which profited from the commercialisation of agriculture, built new houses and acquired 'a fair garnish of pewter'. In Alsace, the wine-growers were finding new markets at the time that they were building and furnishing new houses. In France, the end of Louis XIV's wars, and in Sweden, the end of Karl XII's wars, presumably meant an increase in prosperity. In Norway, the boom in timber exports (to Britain, among other places) led to a rise in the rural standard of living. In general, we may say that the peasant aristocracy, men like Edme Rétif, were now in a position to buy objects which they had previously made themselves.[5]

A second reason for the transformation in material culture can be found in the changing patterns of production. As the export market grew, regional specialisation in certain handicrafts became more pronounced than before. The pottery industry became important in Staffordshire, for example, and in Nevers. The tile industry of Leeuwarden, Haarlem, Amsterdam, Dordrecht and other centres in the Netherlands was at its height between 1600 and 1800; the tiles, painted with ships, windmills, tulips, soldiers and many other motifs, were popular in England and in Germany as well as at home. In the eighteenth century, Dalarna in Sweden became a centre for the production of painted furniture, which was sold in the market at Mora. In 1782, 484 professional craftsmen were recorded as having been at work in the district of Gudbrandsdal in Norway, an area like Dalarna famous for its painted furniture. Popular art was available as never before.[6]

The rise of the market meant increased demand, and to cope with demand, the process of production was standardised. There could be no question of producing objects for the special requirements of the individual customer, as had been traditional. In the course of the eighteenth century, the designs of Dutch tiles were simplified to a few rapid strokes, and semi-mechanical methods like the use of stencils came in. It was only a matter of a generation or two before the hand-made artifact would begin to yield to the standardised, machine-made, mass-produced artifact. The rise of the market also eroded local material culture. In the countryside near Edinburgh in the late eighteenth century, the better-off farmers or 'gudemen' were buying Wedgwood pottery and Manchester-made clothes, not to mention fire-shovels and curtains of printed cotton. These were the first signs of the destructive power of the commercial revolution – but the process which was to destroy traditional popular culture first made possible some of its finest achievements.[7]

Meanwhile, Eastern Europe remained outside many of these trends. In many regions the peasants had been enserfed in the course of the sixteenth century, so the profits from higher food prices did not go to them. In the Balkans, the chimneyless one-room dwelling continued to prevail, making painted decorations out of the question, and people owned relatively few material objects. As late as 1830, a Serbian rural household is said to have owned on average only fifty pieces of furniture and utensils, about ten per head.[8]

The rise of the market, or the widening of the market, affected performances as well as artifacts. If the decline of fairs must have been a blow to the wandering entertainers who performed there, the growth of large towns will have provided them with compensating opportunities. How far urban popular entertainment changed between 1500 and 1800 is a difficult question. It has recently been argued that eighteenth-century England witnessed a 'commercialisation of leisure' in the sense that businessmen began to regard leisure activities as a good investment and in the sense that facilities actually grew. Whether there were, say, more puppet-shows in eighteenth-century London than there had been in the previous century it is difficult to be sure, since such an informally-organised entertainment leaves few documentary traces; but there certainly were new entertainments, and more formally-organised ones, and an increasing use of advertisements to tell the public what was going on. Thomas Topham, the strong-man, gave 'exhibitions' of his powers in London and elsewhere in the 1730s and 1740s, lifting weights, bending iron pokers, and pulling against a horse. Jack Broughton opened his boxing-ring in Oxford Street in 1743, charged for admission and advertised when matches would take place. Horse-races were already advertised in the newspapers by the 1720s, and by 1800, according to J. H. Plumb, 'racing was a complex industry involving thousands of workers and an investment that ran into hundreds of thousands of pounds'. The most striking case of the commercialisation of popular culture is the circus, which goes back to the later eighteenth century; Philip Astley founded his circus at Westminster Bridge in 1770. The elements of the circus, performers such as clowns and acrobats, are, as we have seen, traditional; what was new was the scale of the organisation, the use of a building as a setting for the performance rather than a street or square, and the role of the entrepreneur. Here as elsewhere in the eighteenth-century economy, large-scale enterprises were driving out small ones.[9]

One might have expected the English to be the pioneers of this early industrial revolution in entertainment, but there are some continental parallels. At the time that the professional boxer was making his appearance in England, we find the professional bull-fighter emerging in Spain. If Daniel Mendoza was a popular hero in England, the same could be said of Pedro Romero, or Pepe Hillo, or of Romero's great rival, Costillares. About 1780 it was said that the whole of Madrid was divided into the two factions of *Costillaristas* and *Romeristas*. A new type of popular hero made his appearance in the eighteenth century: the sports idol. It may be suspected, although documentation is lacking to establish the point, that popular festivals in Italy became increasingly commercialised between 1500 and 1800. When Montaigne visited Loreto in 1581, he found this little village (and major pilgrimage centre) full of shops, 'richly furnished' with candles, rosaries and holy images, for all the world like Lourdes or Assisi today. Montaigne was disappointed by the Roman Carnival, but foreigners like him kept on going; indeed, it might be argued that in the seventeenth and eighteenth centuries, Carnival at Rome or Venice was as much for the visitors, the pilgrims or tourists, as for the local inhabitants. Festivals certainly made a much-needed contribution to the economy of those two cities, and a contemporary estimated that 30,000 people visited Venice for the Carnival of 1687.[10] In short, there was a gradual shift taking place away from the more spontaneous and participatory forms of entertainment towards more formally-organised and commercialised spectator sports, a shift which was, of course, to go much further after 1800.

In the larger towns, the process of social change seems to have enriched popular culture. In the countryside, particularly in outlying regions, the same process led to cultural impoverishment. At the end of the eighteenth century the Committee of the Highland Society investigated popular poetry in order to make

up their minds about the authenticity of Ossian (above, p.17).
They discovered that traditional popular poetry was
disappearing, as a result of 'the change of manners in the
Highlands, where the habits of industry have now superseded
the amusement of listening to the legendary narrative or heroic
ballad'. It is not clear from that sentence whether they really
regretted the change or not, but one of their informants was a
good deal more downright. Hugh M'Donald, a tacksman from
the island of Uist, summed up the process of commercialisation
and 'the change of manners' as follows:

> The noblest virtues have been ruined, or driven into exile, since the
> love of money has crept in amongst us; and since deceit and
> hypocrisy have carried mercenary policy and slavish, sordid avarice
> into our land.[11]

The uses of literacy

The most obvious example of the commercialisation of popular
culture has not yet been mentioned: the printed book. By 1500,
presses had been set up in more than 250 centres and some
40,000 editions run off, making about twenty million copies at a
time when the population of Europe was little more than eighty
million. Book production continued to increase from 1500 to
1800. In France in the sixteenth century, for example, the peak
was just under 1,000 titles (or a million copies) a year; in the
seventeenth century, the peak was just over 1,000; and in the
eighteenth century there was a steady but dramatic increase to a
peak of 4,000 titles a year.[12]

What difference did this flood of printed books make to
craftsmen and peasants? Could they read them? It is no easy
matter to calculate literacy rates before the collection of
(relatively) reliable statistics on the subject by governments in
the middle of the nineteenth century – apart from Sweden and
Finland, where the Church made careful investigations and kept
full records.* Historians have usually had to make do with
calculating the proportion of signatures to marks among the
witnesses to wills, in marriage registers or contracts, or in other
official documents like tax assessments or the Protestation Oath
of loyalty to the English Parliament in 1642. The ability to sign

---

*During the *husförhor*, people would be examined on their reading abilities and given
one of three marks, for reading 'accurately', 'to some extent', or 'not at all'.

one's name should not be confused with the ability to read fluently, but there is some evidence that the two skills are correlated and that 'the level of signatures runs below but closely parallels reading skills'.[13]

Using this kind of evidence, historians have concluded that a substantial minority of ordinary people in early modern Europe were in fact able to read; that more of them could read in 1800 than in 1500; that craftsmen were generally much more literate than peasants, men than women, Protestants than Catholics, and Western Europeans than Eastern Europeans. For all these assertions there is precise but fragmentary evidence. So far as the structure of literacy is concerned, it has been discovered that about 65 per cent of the craftsmen were literate, compared to about 20 per cent of the peasants, in Narbonne and the surrounding countryside in the late sixteenth century; and that in late seventeenth-century France taken as a whole, about 14 per cent of brides signed the marriage register, less than half as many as their grooms (about 29 per cent). The Scandinavians, the Dutch and the British – all West European Protestants – had the best literacy records in early modern Europe. In 1850 Russia had 10 per cent adult literacy, Italy and Spain 25 per cent, compared to England's 70 per cent, Scotland's 80 per cent, and Sweden's 90 per cent.[14]

As for changes over time, there were striking increases in literacy in the first half of our period, 1500–1650, for example in parts of Italy and England. In Venice about 1450, 61 per cent of a sample of witnesses could sign their names, but the proportion had increased to 98 per cent by 1650. In Durham about 1570, 20 per cent of the lay witnesses before the consistory court were literate (but less than 20 per cent of the craftsmen, and virtually no peasants at all); by about 1630 the figure had climbed to 47 per cent. In other parts of Europe, it was the second half of the period, 1650–1800, which showed dramatic rises in literacy. In France as a whole, the average literacy rate for men rose from 29 per cent about 1690 to 47 per cent about 1790; in England, it rose from 30 per cent in 1642 to 60 per cent in the second half of the eighteenth century. More limited regional studies sometimes tell a more striking story. In Amsterdam, the literacy rate for men was 57 per cent in 1630, but had risen to 85 per cent by 1780. In Marseilles, it was 50 per cent between 1700 and 1730, but rose to 69 per cent by 1790. In Normandy, it rose from 10 per cent to over 80 per cent in the course of the eighteenth century. In parts of Sweden, where the evidence is fullest and most direct, the rise is the most remarkable of all. In Möklinta parish, for example, 21 per cent of men and women could read in 1614, but 89 per cent by 1685–94; in Skellefteå parish, in 1724, 43 per cent of the men and women born in 1644 or before could read, but 98 per cent of those born in 1705 or later. In Härnösand diocese, literacy was 50 per cent in 1645 but 98 per cent in 1714.[15]

This rise in literacy was the result of spreading educational facilities, and the spread of educational facilities was part of the movement for the reform of popular culture described in the previous chapter. Secular-minded reformers were ambivalent about popular literacy. They distrusted much of traditional oral culture, as we have seen, but they also feared that education might make the poor discontented with their station in life and encourage the peasants to leave the land. Some, like Voltaire, thought that the majority of children should not be taught to read and write at all; others, like Jovellanos, that the peasants should learn the three Rs but no more.[16]

The godly had more faith in literacy, which they saw as a step on the road to salvation. In Scotland, for example, John Knox wanted a school set up in every parish (although it was long before this wish could be translated into reality, even in the Lowlands). In England (Lawrence Stone has argued), there was an 'educational revolution' between 1560 and 1640, encouraged by the foundation of schools by the godly, and there was a rise in literacy in the later eighteenth century due in part to an increase in Sunday schools. It was thanks to the Puritans that schools were established in market towns in Wales under the 'Act for the Propagation of the Gospel', and thanks to the Nonconformists that 'circulating schools' carried literacy into the countryside in the eighteenth century. In Sweden, the Church mounted the campaign which led to the breakthrough into majority literacy about 1700. In France, the godly (the Compagnie du Saint Sacrement, Jean-Baptiste de la Salle and the Frères Chrétiens) helped the growth in educational facilities noticeable from the late seventeenth century onwards.[17]

However, we must not assume that the consequences of literacy were what the godly assumed they would or should be. What did the literate craftsmen and peasants read in the early modern period? Did they have access to books at all? There are at least three problems hiding behind that apparently simple word 'access', and they need to be taken in turn.

The first problem is that of physical access: could books reach craftsmen and peasants? There was no serious problem for townsmen, who could find books for sale in St Paul's Churchyard in London, at the Pont-Neuf in Paris, at the Puerta del Sol in Madrid, and in many other places, often pinned up on a string in the street (which is why the Spanish still call popular reading-matter *literatura de cordel*, 'literature of the string'). For the majority of the population, who lived in the countryside, there was more of a distribution problem, but not an insoluble one. Books and other printed matter, such as broadsheets, could be bought at fairs, or from itinerant ballad-singers or chapmen. An Englishman in 1611 defined a chapman as 'a paltry pedlar, who in a long pack or maund (which he carries for the most part open and, hanging from his neck, before him) hath almanacs, books of news, or other trifling wares to sell'.[18] It was because of this neck-bag that the French called chapmen *colporteurs*. These chapmen would provision themselves with material from booksellers in towns and then make their way from village to village. Little is known about them before the early nineteenth century, but at that point French villages were served by *colporteurs* who came for the most part from the Haut Comminges in the Pyrenees, worked in small teams and specialised either in summer or in winter distribution.[19] For obvious reasons the books which the chapmen carried with them, the 'chap-books', were small, booklets rather than true books in the modern sense, often only 32, 24 or even 8 pages long. Such booklets were already being produced in Italy and Spain in the early sixteenth century, and they can be found in most parts of Europe by the eighteenth.[20]

A second problem is that of economic access: could craftsmen and peasants afford printed matter? In a period when the price of paper accounted for a higher proportion of the cost of production than it does today, small books were cheap books. In France in the seventeenth and eighteenth centuries they were printed on paper of low quality, bound in blue paper of the kind used to wrap sugar-loaves (hence the name 'Bibliothèque Bleue'), and sold for one or two sous apiece at a time when an urban worker's average wage was from fifteen to twenty sous a week and the normal price of bread was two sous a pound. Almanacs cost 3 sous, *c.*1700. In Sweden, chap-books have become known as *skillingtryck*, 'shilling literature', because at the end of the eighteenth century they cost a Swedish *skilling*, the smallest coin in circulation. In England in the seventeenth century, almanacs cost twopence and broadsheets a penny; in the eighteenth century, when the standardised 24-page chap-book made a regular appearance, that cost a penny too. It does look as though broadsides and chap-books were within the means of some craftsmen and peasants, and the testimony of inventories is that in Lyons and Grenoble in the eighteenth century, a minority of craftsmen owned a few more substantial books.[21]

A final problem is that of linguistic access: were broadsides and chap-books written simply enough for men and women with little more than basic literacy? Anyone who takes the trouble to read some of these chap-books today will find that their language is usually simple, the vocabulary relatively small, the constructions unsophisticated. They are unlikely to have presented serious problems of comprehension even for people who read slowly and with difficulty. Serious linguistic problems were only likely to occur in regions remote from centres of chap-book production (usually areas of low literacy) like eastern Europe or southern Italy. The Bibliothèque Bleue can have meant little in Lower Brittany or in Languedoc, where French was still a foreign language.

In short, printed matter was accessible to a good many craftsmen and peasants in this period, even if we cannot say whether a 'good many' was more or less than 50 per cent, let alone calculate – given their fragility – how many broadsides and chap-books there were. The survival rate of early seventeenth-century English newspapers (which were not only fragile, but numbered), has been estimated at only 0.013 per cent.[22] The fact that thousands of broadsides and chap-books have survived from the period 1500–1800 should allow us to assume the importance of this material and pass on to the still more elusive question of its significance. In other words, what kind of impact did it have on traditional popular culture? What were the consequences of increasing literacy?

To a modern reader, the parallel between broadsides or chap-books and the 'mass culture' of the contemporary world is likely to be striking. He will notice the increasing standardisation of format, he will be sensitive to the devices for attracting buyers, like sensational titles or the (frequently false) claim that a narrative is 'full', 'faithful', 'true' or 'new'. The fact that executions or royal visits were sometimes described in print before they happened is reminiscent of our modern 'pseudo-event'. We are aware of the presence of the entrepreneur (the Bindoni family in sixteenth-century Venice, the Oudot family in seventeenth-century Troyes, the Dicey family in eighteenth-century London), the businessman who was making popular literature into a commodity.[23] Yet it is not easy to say how much difference these changes made to performers and to their audiences.

For the professional singer or storyteller, the printed sheet or booklet could mean a welcome extension to his repertoire, or a supplementary income from selling texts. Already in 1483 'Bernardino the charlatan' was buying a poem called *La Sala de Malagigi* twenty-five copies at a time from a Florentine printer, presumably to sell after his performance.[24] In the long run, however, the book was both a dangerous competitor and a treacherous ally. It was a dangerous competitor because the purchaser of the printed text could dispense with the performance altogether; he lost his incentive to stand in the square for an hour at a time, listening to an itinerant singer. The spread of literacy and the decline of the epic occurred together in Western Europe, while illiteracy and the epic survived together in Sicily, in Bosnia, in Russia. The book was a treacherous ally because the fixing of texts in print affected the nature of the performance, encouraging the repetition, as opposed to the re-creation, of a song or story. It has been suggested that literacy stunts the capacity to improvise, just as it removes some of the incentive. The hypothesis is difficult enough to test at the best of times, and impossible for this period; but if true, it would furnish another explanation of the apparent importance of blind ballad-singers, suggesting that their immunity from print preserved their creative powers. It is likely, then, that print encouraged a division of labour between the performer, who now sang whatever publishers fed him, and the author of new songs and stories. The author, who might never see his public and did not have to perform what he had composed, was emancipated from oral tradition and the pressures of the audience, and could invent, or plagiarise, whatever he chose. But this new freedom was a dangerous gift for all but the most talented; most of us need the support of a tradition. It is hardly surprising that new broadside ballads rarely equal their traditional predecessors.[25]

What of the growing reading public? Did the printed book revolutionise their attitudes and values? Thanks to the spread of literacy in the Third World in recent years, this question has become a highly topical one, to which sociologists often give a positive answer. In Nigeria in the 1950s, there was a rise of popular pamphlets, written in English, a black Bibliothèque Bleue (with the town of Onitsha as its Troyes), which was often concerned to convert its readers to new values, such as hard work, thrift, achievement, sophistication, and progress. In a study of the Middle East (based on interviews), an American sociologist argued that print (together with other mass media and underlying social changes, notably urbanisation) produces a new kind of personality, the 'mobile personality', as he calls it. The new kind of man or woman is characterised by a high capacity for empathy (the result of the variety of their vicarious experiences), and a willingness to accept change, to move from one place to another, or to express their own opinions about society; in a word, modernity.[26]

No such spectacular changes are visible in early modern Europe, where urbanisation was not taking place at the same speed as in Nigeria or the Middle East today, while the world to which literacy gave access included no industrial societies to take as a model. We cannot interview the dead or measure their capacity for empathy, but the attitudes to Turks or Jews or witches expressed in this period suggest that it cannot have been very great (above, p.167). In an ingenious attempt to test the modernisation hypothesis, one historian has compared the bequests of literate and illiterate New Englanders in the eighteenth century. He found that the two groups gave the same proportion of their wealth to charity, and that both groups made bequests to members of their family or village rather than to outsiders, and gave to the poor or to the church rather than to schools. In short, the attitudes of the literate were traditional.[27] The content of popular printed matter does not suggest any violent break in continuity. Much that was printed had already formed part of the repertoire of performers within the oral tradition and bears the marks of this origin: ballads and dialogues, mock sermons and mystery plays. Perhaps one should invoke the force of inertia here, but the continuity may be due to the uses of printed matter, not so much for private, silent reading as for reading aloud to less literate neighbours or relatives. A historian who sits down to read through a series of chap-books published between 1500 and 1800 is likely to be impressed by the overwhelming importance of tradition; the same genres, the same texts. Officials who arrested chapmen on the road and turned out their packs made the same discovery. As late as 1812, a German chapman was found to be carrying, among his thirty-six books, one on the interpretation of dreams, the life of Genoveva of Brabant, the romance of the four sons of Aymon, and the jests of Till Eulenspiegel. A French chapman arrested in 1825 had twenty-five books including a dream-book, *The Four Sons of Aymon, Pierre de Provence,* and *Puss in Boots.*[28] Almanacs, one of the most popular types of book in the period, changed little from year to year or even from century to century, but offered the same astrological, medical, agricultural, and religious instruction.[29] One begins to wonder whether print did not preserve and even diffuse traditional popular culture rather than destroy it. How many ballads would there have been for collectors to record from 'oral tradition' in the nineteenth century, had it not been for the existence of broadsides?[30]

A second look does not destroy the first impression but qualifies it. Old themes did not go out between 1500 and 1800, but new themes did come in. Cultural changes, in this case as in others, were not so much 'substitutive' as 'additive'. New kinds of popular hero joined the traditional saint, knight, ruler and outlaw. The hussar was a new form of knight; the smuggler, a new kind of outlaw; the entrepreneur, a new kind of hero altogether. Conduct books were current in chap-book form by the eighteenth century, and (like Nigerian popular literature), told the reader how to write a good letter or how to approach the opposite sex, listing appropriate compliments like 'I prize your chaste love above all the wealth of India'.[31] More important, it is possible to see in the chap-books and in other kinds of source evidence of two gradual but important changes in popular attitudes, in Western Europe at least. They may be summed up in two clumsy but useful abstractions:

secularisation and politicisation.

'Secularisation' is no more easy to define than 'religion'. Perhaps we should distinguish two senses of the term, a strong and a weak. In the strong sense, secularisation could be defined as the rejection of religion. The historian who talks about this process must of course be able to point to an age of faith from which the falling-off took place. French historians have recently been giving the problem of *déchristianisation*, as they call it, a good deal of attention. Since there were Bretons in the seventeenth century who were said not to know how many gods there were, while Protestants were forced to conform or leave France in 1685, it is clear that the high point of Catholic orthodoxy in France must have come late, perhaps in the years 1720–50. Yet in the 1790s, when the pressures to conform were relaxed by the revolutionary government, a substantial proportion of the population stopped making their Easter duties, especially in Paris and other large towns. We do not know how spontaneous this withdrawal was, nor what it meant to the craftsmen and peasants involved. Perhaps it was a rejection of organised religion, a popular Deism like that of the free-thinking artisans of London and Vienna in the 1790s. Perhaps it was a rejection of official Catholicism by families of former Protestants or by people who resented the clergy's attack on traditional beliefs and customs.[32]

Secularisation in the weak sense might be defined as the expression of hopes and fears in increasingly worldly terms, the decline of the supernatural, or what Max Weber called the 'disenchantment of the world' (*Die Entzauberung der Welt*). The chap-books offer some positive evidence about this change. In England, some stories read like a secular substitute for works of devotion. Defoe's *Robinson Crusoe* and *Moll Flanders*, both current in cheap and abbreviated form in the eighteenth century, may each be interpreted as a secularised pilgrim's progress with the achievement of wealth and status as a sign or salvation or even in place of salvation. Another chap-book, *Hocus Pocus*, often reprinted, exposed the tricks of jugglers and conjurers, showing that they did not employ magic but only sleight of hand. Such examples suggest that changes in the culture of the learned – notably that complex of changes summed up in the phrase 'the Scientific Revolution' – were making some impact on popular culture.[33] A recent study of eighteenth-century

French almanacs suggests that they were less concerned with the supernatural than seventeenth-century almanacs had been. The story of Bonhomme Misère, in its eighteenth-century chap-book form, reads as if references to the supernatural had been rather clumsily cut out. Misère has his wish granted after a visit from 'deux particuliers nommés Pierre et Paul', who are never identified as the saints they originally were.[34]

Hopes and fears which had traditionally been expressed in religious terms now needed another mode of expression and increasingly found it in the political.

Politics and the people

Another important shift in popular attitudes between 1500 and 1800 may be described as the 'politicisation' of popular culture, or the spread of political consciousness. How can we tell whether ordinary people were politically conscious or not? There are two problems here, one conceptual and one empirical. What is politics? For the early modern period it may be appropriate to define it as 'affairs of state', not local issues but the concerns of rulers, in other words the succession, war, taxation, and economic and religious problems in so far as they forced themselves on the attention of governments. Political consciousness might be defined as awareness of these problems and their possible solutions, involving a 'public opinion', and a critical (though not necessarily a hostile) attitude to the government. The empirical problem is the historian's notorious inability to subject the dead to an opinion poll, and the danger of arguing from negative evidence when we know so little about the craftsmen and peasants of the time; we do not know what they usually talked about in taverns, in the market-place, or at home. All that can be done is to combine the evidence of popular movements and popular literature, and to see if a pattern emerges. That pattern looks remarkably like the growth of political consciousness. In Western Europe at least, between the Reformation and the French Revolution, craftsmen and peasants were taking an increasing interest in the actions of governments and feeling a greater sense of involvement with politics than before.

When Luther appealed to the princes and the nobles of the 'German nation', a theological debate became political. Rulers had to decide what attitude to adopt towards the Reformation. Luther also appealed to 'Herr Omnes', as he called him, to the 'common man', and his opponents had to do the same. In the 1520s many pamphlets were published to persuade ordinary people that Luther was right, or wrong, and satirical prints drove the messages home. Luther himself was well aware of the propaganda value of the print. 'On all the walls (he once wrote), on every sort of paper and playing cards, priests and monks are to be so portrayed that the people are disgusted when they see or hear of the clergy.' The response of the German peasants to the debate was, of course, their great rebellion of 1525. Luther never intended the peasants to rebel, and condemned them when they did, but their resentment against clerical landlords was surely encouraged by his propaganda campaign, and it seems that they interpreted Luther's insistence on the 'freedom of a Christian man' as referring not so much to spiritual freedom as to freedom from serfdom. Many of their grievances were traditional, but the spiritual legitimation of their revolt was new, allowing them to attack landlords and princes in the name of a higher authority. It even became possible to criticise the emperor. In a popular song of 1546, 'Germany' tells the emperor to his face that he is 'treacherous and false' for laying waste the German land (in other words, for attacking the Protestants) when he should be campaigning against the Turk.[35]

In Germany, the debate over the Reformation died down in the mid-sixteenth century, but its consequences for popular culture continued to be felt elsewhere. In France and in the Netherlands in the 1560s and 1570s, groups of nobles, rebelling in the name of liberty and true religion (Calvinist this time) against their respective rulers, appealed, as Luther had done, to the people.

In the Netherlands, the League of the Nobility, dismissed contemptuously as 'these beggars', made the name their own and staged a kind of political drama, a banquet in which they carried begging-bowls. In the streets of Antwerp and Brussels, 'Long live the Beggars' (*Vive le Geus*) became a popular cry. Beggar songs were soon circulating on broadsheets, denouncing King Philip and his governor the Duke of Alba as tyrants and the Pope as Antichrist, and commenting on current events in the war which followed, including the capture of Brill, the siege and relief of Leiden, and the assassination of the rebel leader,

William the Silent. These songs were supplemented by pamphlets, prints, medals and badges, like the crescent inscribed *Liever Turcx dan Paus*, 'sooner Turk than Pope'.[36]

In France, too, songs and prints made ordinary people more aware of the issues at stake in the civil war, a three-way conflict between the militant Huguenots, the militant Catholics organised into the 'Catholic League', and a centre group supported by Catherine de' Medici and her son Henri III. Like the Beggars, the Huguenots produced songs and prints in support of their cause, like the print of *Le Renversement de la Grand Marmite*, where the overturned pot is the Church of Rome, out of which fall cardinals, bishops, etc. The Catholic League struck back with prints showing the Huguenots as monkeys and Henri III as a devil or a hermaphrodite.[37]

As in Germany, these appeals to the people had more radical results than the leaders had intended. What was happening cannot be described simply in terms of the 'impact' of the ideas of the learned on a passive body of ordinary people; the people were assimilating the new ideas to their own experiences, their own needs. In Ghent in the late 1570s, a committee of eighteen was set up with the support of the craft-guilds which pressed for the immediate introduction of the Calvinist reformation, and in March 1579 there was an attack on the houses of the rich by a crowd chanting *Papen blot, ryckemans goet*, 'the rich man's goods, the Pope's blood'. In Paris ten years later, the supporters of the Catholic League erected barricades in the streets, drove out Henri III, and set up a committee of sixteen, which, like the Ghent committee, claimed to speak for craftsmen and shopkeepers. These popular urban movements alarmed the noble leaders of revolt. The committee at Ghent was suppressed by William the Silent; that at Paris, by the Duke of Mayenne.[38] Peasant attitudes, too, were changing. Already in 1562, some nobles complained to the Calvinist synod of Nîmes about the egalitarian doctrines of their peasants. In Provence in 1578, Catholic and Protestant peasants combined to burn châteaux and massacre nobles. In 1594, an assembly of rebellious peasants at Bergerac ended with the cries of 'Liberté!' and 'Vive le Tiers Etat!'[39]

In France, the civil wars came to an end in the 1590s; in the Netherlands, a truce with Spain was signed in 1609; but Central Europe was soon to become involved in the Thirty Years' War

(1618–48), in which fighting was again accompanied by political pamphlets, prints and songs, mocking or praising the princes, their councillors and their generals. Catholic prints showed the Protestant Frederick of Bohemia wandering homeless after he had been driven from his kingdom; Protestants mocked cardinal Khlesl, adviser to the Emperor Ferdinand II, singing (to the tune of *O du armer Judas*) 'O ich armer Khlesl/Was hab ich getan', or parodying *O Welt ich muss dich lassen* (above, p.227) with *O Wien ich muss dich lassen*. Traditional prophecies about the 'Lion of the North' were applied to Gustav Adolf of Sweden and circulated widely in print.[40]

The outbreak of the Thirty Years' War also coincides with the appearance of a new medium for expressing, or forming, political attitudes, the *coranto* or newspaper, which it may be useful to define as a printed sheet or sheets concerned with current events and published (this was the innovation) at regular and short intervals. The first newspaper centre was Amsterdam, where the sheets were published in Dutch, German, French and English. They tended to come out once or twice a week. The 'lame messenger' (a common phrase of the time for the news) was gathering speed.[41]

There is much to be said for the view that between 1618 and 1648, more western Europeans were interested in politics than ever before. Affairs of state were impinging more on people's lives, and information about politics was circulating more widely than it had been. In the Dutch Republic, there was a stream of pamphlets, prints and songs concerned with such current events as the conflict between Prince Maurice, William the Silent's son and successor, and Jan van Oldenbarnevelt, who was executed for 'treason' in 1618. In Italy, it was remarked in 1621 that 'even the barbers and even more vile artisans (*gli altri più vili artefici*) were discussing reason of state in their workshops and meeting-places', and this testimony is made plausible by the fact that weekly newspapers were founded in no less than six Italian cities between 1636 and 1646.[42]

In England and in France in the 1640s there was not so much a stream of pamphlets as a flood. In France the Fronde, a rebellion against the rule of Cardinal Mazarin, involved the publication of some 5,000 *mazarinades*, some of them news-sheets, others satires. Some were written in a vigorous and simple verse which anyone could understand. At a quarter or half a sou each, these *mazarinades* were much cheaper than the chap-books of the Bibliothèque Bleue, lending colour to the claim made by one of them that everybody was against Mazarin:

> Il n'est de trou ni de taverne
> Où chaque artisan ne le berne,
> Chaque compagnon de métier,
> Gaigne-petit et savetier
> Jusque aux vendeuses de morues
> En font des comptes dans les rues.
>
> (There's no tavern or other den where every craftsman is not mocking him, every journeyman, cheap-jack and cobbler. Even the fishwives criticise him in the streets).[43]

Popular political consciousness is still more evident in the English Civil War. That English peasants or craftsmen had participated in earlier political events can be seen from the Pilgrimage of Grace or the Elizabethan Puritan movement or the broadside ballads commenting on the Spanish Armada, but when the opponents of Charles I appealed, like the opponents of Philip II and Henri III, to the people, they became involved to an unprecedented extent. Huge petitions were organised – 15,000 people signed the Root and Branch Petition, 30,000 people the petition for justice against Strafford. The political term 'demonstration' only came into use in England in the early nineteenth century, but it is difficult to find a more appropriate term to describe the behaviour of the crowds who escorted Burton, Bastwick and Prynne into London in triumph after their release from prison in 1640, or assembled at Westminster shouting 'no bishops' or 'no popish lords' during the three 'December Days' of 1641. To quote an unsympathetic contemporary comment, 'there was a kind of discipline in disorder, tumults being ready at command, upon a watch-word given'. There was a vast increase in political information. Between 1640 and 1663 the bookseller George Thomason collected nearly 15,000 pamphlets and over 7,000 newspapers, including sermons, speeches in the House of Commons, tracts advocating social reform, tracts condemning social reform, and news, whether 'Joyful News from Shrewsbury' or 'Horrible News from Hull'. Political songs and prophecies were legion, and about 150 political prints have survived from the year 1641 alone.[44]

As in the Netherlands and in France in the sixteenth century, so more radical views emerged in the course of the English Civil War. The Levellers expressed the view that 'the laws ought to be equal' and that 'the people' (meaning small-holders, whether yeomen or craftsmen) ought to choose parliaments, on the grounds that 'all power is originally and essentially in the whole body of the people'. It is difficult to say how much support the Levellers enjoyed or even how widely their views were known, but even more difficult to resist the conclusion that the English in the mid-seventeenth century were the most politically conscious society in Europe.[45]

In the second half of the period, political texts and images became more and more a part of their everyday life, rather than a response to extraordinary conditions like a civil war. The restoration of Charles II was not sufficient to suppress the new concern with political issues. At the time of their bid to exclude James, Duke of York, from the succession, the Whigs organised petitions, published ballads and prints, and laid on political processions on the scale of a Lord Mayor's Show. The fact that the term 'mob' came into use in English in the late seventeenth century may reflect upper-class awareness – and fear – of popular political consciousness. In eighteenth-century England, ballads and pamphlets remained important political media, and a sermon by the controversial Tory divine Henry Sacheverell sold 40,000 copies in a few days (ten times as many as Luther's pamphlet *To the Christian Nobility*, sold in Germany nearly two hundred years before). Popular political rituals reached their high point at the end of the 1760s with the demonstrations of support for John Wilkes. Sacheverell had been represented in Staffordshire pottery, Admiral Vernon on medals (plate 11); the ugly face of Wilkes appeared on spoons, jugs, pipes and buttons. Prints now appeared often enough to make the print-shop a political institution, with crowds pressing their noses against the windows to see the latest comment on the issues of the day, from the South Sea Bubble to the American Revolution. One print, *The Funeral Procession of Miss Americ Stamp*, sold 16,000 copies.[46]

If anything made politics part of ordinary life for ordinary people in eighteenth-century England, at least in the towns, that thing was surely the newspaper, encouraged by the Licensing Act of 1695 which abolished pre-publication censorship. There were soon a number of newspapers to choose from: *The Observator,* a Whig paper which came out twice a week from 1702 on; *The Rehearsal,* a Tory paper founded by Charles Leslie in 1704; and *The Review,* edited by Defoe, published two or three times a week from 1704 to 1713. As in the case of chap-books, we need to ask whether these papers were accessible to craftsmen and other workers, but the answer seems to be 'yes'. One testimony worth taking seriously is Leslie's own, that although 'the greatest part of the people . . . cannot read at all', yet 'they will gather about one that can read, and listen to an *Observator* or *Review* (as I have seen them in the streets)'. As for the problem of expense – a newspaper cost 2d at this period – it could be solved in the ways described by a Swiss visitor to London in 1726:

> Most craftsmen begin the day by going to the coffee-house to read the news there. I have often seen shoe-blacks and other people of that kind club together to buy a newspaper for a *liard* every day and to read it together.

They had good reason to be interested in 1726, because it was then that *The Craftsman,* an opposition paper, began to appear. Three years later, *The Craftsman* itself summed up the situation with the words, 'we are become a nation of statesmen'. If this was true, words fail the historian who has to describe the situation in the 1760s, when many more newspapers were bought.[47]

If there was another nation of 'statesmen' in Europe at this time, it was surely the Dutch Republic. Amsterdam long remained what it had become in the 1620s, a great centre of news and newspapers, and the long-lived *Oprechte Haarlemsche Courant* was founded at Haarlem in 1656. The tradition of the pamphlet and the political print, established during the revolt against Spain, was not allowed to lapse. During the wars with France, Louis XIV was satirised as a tyrant and a bigot in much the same way as Philip II had been. The lynching of the de Witt brothers in 1672 and the bursting of the 'Bubble' in 1720 were commemorated in scores of prints; the artists included the gifted Romeyn de Hooghe. In Scandinavia, although the urban population was small, newspapers independent of the government can be found from the mid-eighteenth century onwards. Denmark had the *Kobenhavske Post-Tidener* (1749), founded by E. H. Berling and still going (under the name *Berlingske Tidende*) to this day; Sweden had the *Tidningar* (1758); and Norway the *Efterretninger* (1765). Sweden had a tradition of popular participation in politics, since the peasants were represented in the Riksdag, and were coming to play a more important part there in the early eighteenth century, under such leaders as Per Larsson and Olof Håkansson, their spokesmen in the 1720s and 1730s respectively. Ballads and prints about domestic political issues were in circulation. On the fall of Baron Görtz, a German who was employed by Charles XII to raise money for his wars, a broadside expressed the general feeling of rejoicing:

Du har allt ont påfunnit	*You have done all kinds of ill*
Det du betala skall . . .	*And you shall pay for it . . .*
Mästerligt har du jagat	*Skilfully have you hunted*
Efter silver och gull.	*After silver and gold.*

Denmark and Norway had their Görtz in the late eighteenth century in J. F. Struensee, who was physician to King Christian VII, the queen's lover, and the real ruler of the two kingdoms until he fell from power in 1772. An English visitor to Setran in Norway some years later observed in a peasant's cottage 'a print of the unfortunate Struensee in prison, tormented by the Devil: those prints were, I presume, circulated and greedily received by the common people at the time of his fall'. The later eighteenth century was also the time of two risings which suggest that the Norwegian peasants were becoming more politically conscious, the *Strilekrig* of 1765, when the Bergen area rebelled against a new tax, and the Lofthus rising of 1786, directed initially against a factory-owner who had reduced wages but spreading to involve several provinces. Thus in Scandinavia and the Netherlands as well as in Britain the liberal-democratic systems established in the nineteenth century had some basis in the popular political culture of the century before.[48]

Elsewhere in Europe it is more difficult to find evidence of political consciousness among craftsmen and peasants before about 1790, when the situation was suddenly transformed following the French Revolution. In fact the ice had begun to thaw, or at least to crack, a little earlier in France. In Paris about 1780, an observer remarked that pamphlets attacking ministers were being hawked openly in the streets, and that the conversation in the cafés was mainly about politics. After 1789, French popular culture became politicised. Popular newspapers appeared, and one of them, Hébert's *Père Duchesne,* written in a vigorously colloquial style, is said to have reached a circulation of a million copies. Catechisms and almanacs became political. In 1791, the *Almanach de Père Duchesne,* describing itself as an 'ouvrage bougrement patriotique', commented on the events of the previous year; in 1792 the *Almanach de la Mère Gérard* put the rights of man and the rights of the citizen into *vaudevilles,* popular verses.[49]

The illiterate could follow what was going on not only by listening to speeches or readings but also by looking at images. Political prints, like the famous print of the peasant carrying a nobleman and a priest on his back (Plate 19), now joined the pious images produced at Épinal and elsewhere. There were political plates and political fans. The plates, manufactured at Nevers in particular, carried inscriptions like *Vive la Liberté, Vive le Tiers État* (Plate 18) the fans carried pictures of General Lafayette and of the fall of the Bastille. New rituals were devised, some of them modelled on traditional popular rituals. The planting of the liberty tree was a political version of the planting of the maypole. At Rheims, on 14 July 1794, Bastille day was commemorated in a carnivalesque form, with the siege and capture of a mock castle filled with straw men.[50]

As in the England of the 1640s, so in the France of the 1790s popular participation in political debate led to the emergence of radical views. In fact the *sans-culottes* had not a little in common with the Levellers. Both groups believed in the sovereignty of the 'people', in the sense of the small property owners; both groups believed in equality of rights; both groups derived most of their support from craftsmen; and both groups failed to impose their views on the leaders of the revolution. One difference between them is surely significant: the *sans-culotte* militants were better-organised and more concerned for the political education of their supporters in popular societies and in general assemblies. As for the French peasants, they seem to have been made more politically conscious by the Revolution. Their hostility to landlords, especially townsmen, was expressed more openly than before: 'il y a assez longtemps que ces bougres de bourgeois nous menaient'.[51]

The news of the French Revolution made considerable impact on other parts of Europe, encouraging ordinary people to think that their grievances too could be remedied. It is no surprise to find this happening in the Dutch Republic and in England, where a lively political culture had long been in existence. In the Netherlands, pamphlets were smuggled in from France and societies formed to read them; the old Republic was overthrown; and sympathisers with the Revolution began to wear French-style caps of liberty, to plant liberty trees and to dance round them. In England, Tom Paine's comments on the Revolution, the *Rights of Man*, rapidly became a best-seller, and may have sold 200,000 copies in 1793 alone. Radical societies were founded to reform Parliament and to give every adult male the vote.[52]

More significant, because less precedented, was the impact of the French Revolution on Austria, Italy and Spain. In Austria, so the minister of police sadly observed in 1790, 'the unsuitable material presented in various newspapers, which are so cheap that even the lowest classes are buying them, is having a very mischievous effect on their readers'. Even the peasants had their own paper, the *Bauernzeitung* or 'Peasant News', published in Graz. They heard about the abolition of feudalism in France and demanded the abolition of their own feudal dues. An innkeeper from Graz called Franz Haas led a campaign for wider political representation, and a nobleman from the same area commented in 1792 that 'the common people here speak quite loudly now'. In Vienna in 1792 there was a rising of unemployed journeymen, under the influence of the Revolution.[53]

In Spain and Italy the situation was more complicated, because there, as in western France, ordinary people rose against the French Revolution and its local supporters. The execution of Louis XVI was followed by anti-French demonstrations in Barcelona, part of a crusade against the Revolution organised by the friars and drawing on traditional xenophobia. However, people were doing more than just following the lead of the friars. A letter describing Madrid in 1795 remarks on the popular concern with what was happening in France: 'ordinary porters are buying newspapers'. By their opposition to the Revolution the Spanish peasants, like the peasants of western France, were expressing their hostility to the local bourgeoisie, who supported it. A similar interpretation may be given of events in Italy in 1799. In Tuscany, there were riots against the French army of occupation and the destruction of liberty trees; in Calabria, more anti-French riots and attacks on the 'Jacobins', the Revolution's local supporters. In both cases, as in Spain and the Vendée, the local clergy helped organise the riots, which they interpreted as a defence of the faith; but the rioters were expressing not only their devotion to the Church but also their hostility to foreigners and to the rich.[54] The period 1500–1800 certainly ends with a bang.

The episodes described in the last few pages are well-known, but it is not usual to consider them together. When we do, they begin to look like one enormous movement, the political education of the common man. There is a good deal to be said for such an interpretation. I do not mean to suggest that political consciousness increased steadily and cumulatively throughout the period, or that there was a kind of relay race in which the Germans passed the baton to the Dutch, the Dutch to the British, the British to the French. The political education of ordinary people was an informal education by events and so it was necessarily intermittent; for example, the generation of Frenchmen who lived through the wars of religion were forced to be politically conscious in a way their sons and grandsons were not. However, the centralisation of states and the growth of armies (trends which were more steady than intermittent) meant that politics was affecting the lives of ordinary people more directly and more visibly than before. European governments were making increasing demands on their subjects between 1500 and 1800, taking more away from them in taxes and taking more of them away to serve in the army. In the sixteenth century, armies might contain tens of thousands of men, but two million men passed through the French army between 1700 and 1763, while Russia had nearly half a million men under arms in 1796[55]. Rulers taxed their subjects more heavily to pay for these armies, and employed more officials, partly to collect the new taxes. Craftsmen and peasants had good reason to be more aware of the state by the end of the eighteenth century than they had been three hundred years before.

The other major factor making for continuous, cumulative change was the press. The prints and pamphlets of one generation drew on earlier ones. The newspapers let people know that they were not alone, that other regions and even nations were fighting in the same cause. Lofthus, the Norwegian peasant leader, perhaps the first whose appeal extended beyond the borders of a single province, was known by contemporaries as 'a second Washington'. If 1648 was, like 1848, a year of European revolutions (or at least, of revolts), this may have been in part because the different rebels knew about one another. In the second half of the period, newspapers and political prints became permanent institutions and gave some craftsmen, at least, access to a more continuous political education. Contemporaries realised this, whether they approved or disapproved of the trend. In the reign of Charles II, the official censor, Sir Roger L'Estrange, declared his dislike of newspapers for precisely this reason, that to read the paper 'makes the multitude too familiar with the actions and counsels of their superiors, too pragmatical and censorious, and gives them not only a wish but a kind of colourable right and licence to the meddling with the government'. Conservatives were in a dilemma. To prevent their radical opponents from monopolis- ing the media they had to produce newspapers themselves – as L'Estrange produced *The Observator* – and by doing this, they made a contribution to the changes they disliked. The organisation of demonstrations and riots against the French Revolution (in England, Spain and Italy) is likely to have had a similar effect in the long run.[56]

The withdrawal of the upper classes[57]

In 1500 (so it was suggested in Chapter 2), popular culture was everyone's culture; a second culture for the educated, and the only culture for everyone else. By 1800, however, in most parts of Europe, the clergy, the nobility, the merchants, the professional men – and their wives – had abandoned popular culture to the lower classes, from whom they were now separated, as never before, by profound differences in world view. One symptom of this withdrawal is the change in the meaning of the term 'people', which was used less often than before to mean 'everyone', or 'respectable people', and more often to mean 'the common people'.[58] The next few pages are an attempt to elucidate this withdrawal thesis, to answer the questions, Who withdrew? From what did they withdraw? In what parts of Europe? and Why?

The clergy, the nobility and the bourgeoisie had their own reasons for abandoning popular culture. In the case of the clergy, withdrawal was part of the Catholic and Protestant reformations. In 1500 the majority of the parish clergy were men of a similar social and cultural level to their parishioners. The reformers were not satisfied with this situation and demanded a learned clergy. In Protestant areas the clergy tended to be university graduates, and in Catholic areas after the Council of Trent, priests began to be trained at seminaries; in Orthodox areas there was no perceptible change. In addition, Catholic reformers emphasised the dignity of the priesthood; St Carlo Borromeo told his clergy to preserve their gravity and decorum wherever they were. The old-style parish priest who wore a mask and danced in church at festivals and made jokes in the pulpit was replaced by a new-style priest who was better-educated, higher in social status, and considerably more remote from his flock.[59]

For the nobles and the bourgeoisie, the Reformation was less important than the Renaissance. The nobles were adopting more 'polished' manners, a new and more self-conscious style of behaviour, modelled on the courtesy-books, of which the most famous was Castiglione's *Courtier*. Noblemen were learning to exercise self-control, to behave with a studied nonchalance, to cultivate a sense of style, and to move in a dignified manner as if engaging in a formal dance. Treatises on dancing also multiplied and court dancing diverged from country dancing. Noblemen stopped eating in great halls with their retainers and withdrew into separate dining-rooms (not to mention 'drawing-rooms', that is, 'withdrawing-rooms'). They stopped wrestling with their peasants, as they used to do in Lombardy, and they stopped killing bulls in public, as they used to do in Spain. The nobleman learned to speak and write 'correctly', according to formal rules, and to avoid the technical terms and the dialect words used by craftsmen and peasants.[60] These changes had their social function. As their military role declined, the nobility had to find other ways of justifying their privileges: they had to show they were different from other people. The polished manners of the nobility were imitated by officials, lawyers and merchants who wanted to pass for noblemen. The withdrawal of all these groups from popular culture was the more complete because it included their wives and daughters, who had long performed the function of mediators (above, p.28). It is difficult to measure the development of women's education between 1500 and 1800 because so much of it was informal, at home rather than in schools. However, the multiplication of treatises on their education, from Juan Luis Vives, *The Education of a Christian Woman* (1529), to Francesco Algarotti, *Newtonianism for Ladies* (1737) suggests that more and more upper-class women were sharing the culture of their husbands.[61]

This separation of upper-class and lower-class cultures can be seen most clearly in those parts of Europe where their imitation of the court meant that the local upper classes literally spoke a different language from ordinary people. In Languedoc, for example, the nobility and bourgeoisie adopted French, which separated them (or expressed their separation) from the craftsmen and peasants who spoke only Occitan. In Wales, the gentry began to speak English and to withdraw their patronage from the traditional bards, so that the order of bards became extinct. In the Scottish Highlands, in Adam Ferguson's day, Gaelic became, as he put it, 'a language spoken in the cottage, but not in the parlour, or at the table of any gentleman'. In Bohemia, the great nobles were mainly Germans, who had been given their estates after the battle of the White Mountain in 1620. They, and the court of Vienna, set the tone; by 1670, the Jesuit Bohuslav Balbín could note bitterly that 'if anyone in Bohemia is heard speaking Czech, he is thought to have harmed his reputation'. Anyone, that is, who was anyone; Czech was for peasants. In eighteenth-century Norway, educated people spoke Danish, the language of the court in Copenhagen; Holberg, a Bergen man, wrote his plays in Danish. Similarly, in Finland educated people spoke Swedish and abandoned their own language to craftsmen and peasants; two languages for two cultures.[62]

It was not just the language of ordinary people that the upper classes rejected, but their whole culture. The change of attitude that marked their withdrawal from participation in popular festivals has been discussed in detail in Chapter 8; clergy, nobility and bourgeoisie alike were coming to internalise the ethos of self-control and order. Thus – to take two examples almost at random – a Dutch poet, describing a country fair, chooses a mock-heroic style to express his attitude of amused detachment from the proceedings, while a French writer, later in the eighteenth century, found the Paris Carnival an embarrassment even to watch, for 'all these diversions show a folly and a coarseness which makes the taste for them resemble that of pigs'.[63] It was not simply the popular festival that the upper classes were rejecting, but also the popular world-view, as the examination of changing attitudes to medicine, prophecy and witchcraft may help to show.

The old rivalry between the university-trained physician and the unofficial healer seems to have acquired more intellectual content in the age of the scientific revolution, as a few examples may suggest. In 1603 an Italian physician, Scipione Mercurio, published a book on 'popular errors' in the field of medicine, making a sharp distinction between educated people, who patronise real physicians like himself, and 'ordinary people' *(persone volgari)* who run to the piazza (running was itself an offence against decorum) to take the advice of charlatans, mountebanks, and 'evildoers who are popularly known as witches'. In 1619 a French physician, the Sieur de Courval, launched a similar attack on charlatans, provoking a reply from no less a member of that profession than Tabarin (above, p.95). Another contribution to this debate was Sir Thomas Browne's *Pseudodoxia Epidemica,* a study of 'received tenets and commonly-presumed truths, which examined proved but vulgar and common errors'. Sir Thomas was a physician and it was his medical practice which gave him the opportunity to observe the 'erroneous disposition of the people', whose 'uncultivated understandings' made them credulous and so easily deceived by 'saltimbancoes, quacksalvers and charlatans', as well as by 'fortune-tellers, jugglers, geomancers'. At this point the terms 'charlatan', 'mountebank' and 'quack' seem to have acquired the pejorative overtones they have kept ever since.[64]

It was recently remarked by a student of the subject that 'only when intelligent and educated men ceased to take prophecy seriously were the Middle Ages truly at an end'. But when was this? That depends on the kind of prophecy. During the seventeenth century, learned and popular attitudes diverged. In the sixteenth century, the prophecies current in the name of 'marvellous Merlin' had been taken seriously enough to be reprinted in France and Italy; after 1600, 'Merlin's drunken prophecies', as the Puritan William Perkins called them, were neglected. The abbot Joachim of Fiore followed Merlin into oblivion, although a serious scholar like the Jesuit Papebroch still found him interesting in the later seventeenth century. Other forms of prognostication were undermined. In his letter on comets, Pierre Bayle rejected the idea that comet signified future disasters as a popular error; and argued that comets were natural phenomena and nothing more. The Dutch scholar van Dale and his French populariser Fontenelle undermined the credibility of the oracles of the ancient world. Only the prophecies of the Bible continued to be taken seriously by the learned. Thus one might speak of the 'reform of prophecy' in the seventeenth century, of educated men growing increasingly sceptical of the non-biblical prophecies and trying, like Newton, to put the study of biblical prophecies on a firmer basis. From the end of the seventeenth century, there are signs of a declining interest in prophecy, of a greater willingness to scoff. When in 1679 a minister at Lydgate, Yorkshire, raised the topic of the millennium, his congregation asked him to concern himself with 'more profitable subjects'; when in 1688 the Dutch stateman Coenraad van Beuningen began to neglect his affairs for the interpretation of the Apocalypse, this was treated as one of the indications that he had lost his reason. It was almost as natural for educated men to scoff at prophecies in 1800 as it had been for them to take prophecies seriously three hundred years before. Meanwhile, chap-books reprinted old prophecies, like Mother Shipton's, as if nothing had happened, and popular prophets continued to arise; Joanna Southcott's *Strange Effects of Faith* was published in 1801.[65]

The growing split between learned and popular culture is still more obvious in the case of witches. Belief in the power and maleficence of witches seems to have been almost universal in the first half of our period. Indeed, the late sixteenth and early seventeenth centuries marked the height of the European 'witch-craze', when there were more trials and executions of people accused of witchcraft then ever before. From about 1650, however, the number of trials began to decline, at least in Western Europe. This was not because ordinary people had stopped accusing one another of witchcraft but because the learned had stopped believing in it. If they did not reject the idea of witchcraft altogether, then they were increasingly sceptical about specific accusations. In France, the magistrates of the Parlement of Paris stopped taking witchcraft accusations seriously about 1640, followed somewhat later by the magistrates in the provinces. In seventeenth-century Essex, the gentry on the Grand Jury would reject presentments for witchcraft with a verdict of *ignoramus*, although the local villagers were still ducking witches. The clergy as well as the educated laity were changing their minds. In 1650, for example, Cardinal Barberini wrote to the inquisitor of Aquileia about a witchcraft case that it was 'full of holes *(molto diffectuoso)*, because virtually nothing that he has confessed has been verified', a criterion which the judges had not exactly worried about in earlier trials. The difference in attitude which could be found between an educated pastor and his flock in the eighteenth century emerges clearly from a story of Boswell's. When Johnson and he visited the Hebrides, a minister told them that

> the belief of witchcraft, or charms, was very common, insomuch that he had many prosecutions before his session . . . against women, for having by these means carried off the milk from people's cows. He disregarded them; and there is not now the least vestige of that superstition. He preached against it; and in order to give a strong proof to the people that there was nothing in it, he said from the pulpit, that every woman in the parish was welcome to take the milk from his cows, provided she did not touch them.[66]

This withdrawal from popular culture did not take place in any one generation, but at different times in different parts of Europe. The process has never been described in the detail it deserves, but here there is space only for treating a few examples impressionistically, looking at a few regions where the withdrawal took place early and at others where it came relatively late.

In Italy, the literary and social ideals formulated in the 1520s by Bembo and Castiglione implied a rejection of popular culture, and there is evidence for increasing separation between the amusements of the poor and those of the rich in Florence and in Rome in the late sixteenth century. However, the process of withdrawal was much less clear-cut in Italy than it was in France or England; even in the eighteenth century, many educated Italians continued to share popular beliefs about magic and witchcraft.[67]

In France there seems to have been a gradual but steady process of withdrawal between 1500 and 1800. In Paris in the early sixteenth century, the amateur actors of the Basoche left the streets and squares for indoor performances in the Parlement for a more exclusive audience. In the mid-sixteenth century, the poets of the Pléiade rejected popular literary forms like *rondeaux*, *ballades* and *virelais* for something closer to the classical norms. By the early seventeenth century, the new aristocratic ideal of the 'man of honour' (*honnête homme*), in the style of Castiglione's courtier, was making the old romances of chivalry obsolete. Warriors like Ogier the Dane and Reynaud de Montauban were, after all, rough diamonds, lacking the polish now required of the gentleman. They were abandoned to the Bibliothèque Bleue, to be replaced by a new kind of aristocratic hero, less impulsive and more self-controlled, who figures in the plays of Racine and the romances of Madame de Lafayette. The formulation of the linguistic and literary ideals of French classicism by Vaugelas and Boileau implied the rejection of most traditional popular songs as irregular and barbarous; Boileau uses the Pont-Neuf, where the ballad-singers performed, as a symbol of what should be avoided in good poetry. Louis XIV's withdrawal from Paris to Versailles helped widen the gap between courtly and popular culture; unlike his father, Louis did not attend popular festivals in Paris like the bonfires on St John's Eve. The Italian comedians, once popular at court, now seemed too undignified for cultivated eyes and ears, and they were relegated to the fairs. The late seventeenth century was also the time of the spread of Jansenism among the parish clergy, now trained increasingly in seminaries, and they began to distance themselves from the 'superstitions' of their flocks. At much the same time, the magistrates of the parlements ceased taking witchcraft seriously. The split widened still further in the eighteenth century. Nobles had usually lived on their estates and taken part in the business and pleasure of the local community; in the eighteenth century, more of them were deserting the country for the town, becoming outsiders in their own regions. Educated southerners not only spoke French instead of Occitan, they learned to purify it of regional expressions, to judge by the success of *Les Gasconismes Corrigés* (1766), a book which told them not to say 'Carnaval' but 'Mardi Gras', not 'montagnols' but 'montagnards', not 'soir' but 'nuit', and so on. By the end of the eighteenth century, Rousseau could mock the idea that 'One has to dress differently from the people, speak, think, act, live differently from the people'.[68]

In England, too, the withdrawal of the upper classes came relatively early. In Elizabeth's reign the references made by educated men to minstrels and their ballads became more and more patronising as the literary ideals of the Renaissance made their impact. Sir Philip Sidney, who found *Chevy Chase* moving, still regretted its 'rude style', as he called it. Puttenham's *Art of English Poesie* (1581) makes an explicit distinction between 'vulgar poesie', created by 'instinct of nature' (including anything from the songs of the Indians of Peru to traditional English ballads) and 'artificial poesie', created by the educated. There is no doubt that he preferred the latter; 'artificial' was a term of praise at this time. The gentleman-essayist Sir William Cornwallis wrote about popular culture with a mixture of curiosity, detachment and contempt:

> pamphlets, and lying stories and news, and two penny poets I would know them, but beware of being familiar with them: my custom is to read these, and presently to make use of them, for they lie in my privy . . . I have not been ashamed to adventure mine ears with a ballad-singer . . . to see earthlings satisfied with such coarse stuff . . . to see how thoroughly the standers by are affected, what strange gestures come from them, what strained stuff from their poet.

By the early seventeenth century, the public theatres, where Shakespeare had been played to noblemen and apprentices alike, were no longer good enough for the upper classes, and private theatres were established where a seat cost sixpence. The Elizabethan jig, a satirical song-and-dance act, had been popular with everyone, but for the dramatists writing for the new private theatres, 'jig' became a pejorative term referring to a 'low' form of art. In England as in France, the upper classes were increasingly frequenting dancing-masters to learn more dignified dances. The English gentry were becoming better-educated; in the late sixteenth and early seventeenth centuries, they went to Oxford and Cambridge in increasing numbers. They were coming to spend more time in London, where they could observe the manners of the court, or in provincial capitals like York and Norwich, and this, no less than their university education, was cutting them off (culturally speaking) from their tenants. On their own estates they gave up entertaining those tenants to meals in the great hall, the traditional occasions for performances by minstrels and buffoons. Buffoons were becoming unfashionable; Charles I was the last king of England to have a court fool. Like the French nobility, the English gentry abandoned the romance of chivalry to the lower classes. From the mid-seventeenth century on, *Guy of Warwick* and *Bevis of Hampton* were reprinted only in chap-book form. In the late seventeenth century, educated people were coming to think of the belief in witches as a characteristic of 'such as are of the weakest judgment and reason, as women, children, and ignorant and superstitious persons'. In the eighteenth century, Lord Chesterfield recommended his son to avoid 'common proverbs', which were 'proofs of having kept bad and low company'.[69]

In the northern and eastern parts of Europe, the withdrawal of the upper classes from popular culture seems to have come rather later than it did in France and England. In Denmark, for example, ballads and chap-books seem to have been part of the culture of the gentry until the end of the seventeenth century, when they were abandoned under the influence of French models of behaviour. As the Danish Boileau, T. C. Reenberg, put it in his *Art of Poetry*,

Det der nu er	*What to the kitchen now is banned*
Fordömt til Borgestuer	*And alehouses and stalls,*
Er fordum bleven läst og hört	*Was once with pleasure read and heard*
Med Lyst af ädle Fruer.	*By dames in princely halls.*

The new ideals were expressed with force and wit by Ludvig Holberg, another admirer of Boileau and French classicism, whose poems and plays often make fun of the literature and beliefs of the people. His play *Heexerie eller Blind Alarm* ridicules the belief in witches, and his burlesque epic *Peder Paars* mocks the enthusiasm for *Ogier the Dane* and other romances of chivalry.[70]

Further east, the change seems to have occurred later still. The Polish gentry continued to read chap-books like *Melusine* and *Magelona* until the middle of the eighteenth century, when they were replaced by imported western fiction like Richardson and Fielding, Lesage and Prévost. Witch-trials reached their peak in Poland when they were already declining in Western Europe, and it was well into the eighteenth century before they began to die out. In Hungary too the eighteenth century seems to have been the time that the aristocracy and gentry withdrew from popular culture; they began to read Richardson and Rousseau, to prefer modern German and Italian music to that of the traditional bagpipers, who had had an honoured place in noble households in the seventeenth century. How complete the withdrawal had become by the end of the period may be illustrated from a story told by Zoltan Kodály. One day in 1803, the poet Benedek Virág heard someone singing a folksong outside his window; he did not catch the ending, so he asked his friend Kazinczy about it. It did not occur to him to approach the peasant himself. 'Kazinczy lived seven days' journey away yet Virág asked him to supply the words of a song he could quite easily have found out for himself by going outside his own gate.'[71]

In Scotland, too, the eighteenth century seems to have been the time the upper classes withdrew from popular culture. Scott described the process in terms much like Reenberg, as the decline of minstrel poetry from 'the courts of princes and halls of nobles' to 'the frequenters of the rustic ale-bench'. In Edinburgh, respectable people abandoned the taverns where they had been accustomed to drink alongside craftsmen and shopkeepers. In the countryside near Edinburgh, the mummers fell out of favour with the gentry, as one gentleman remembered:

> As their rhymes were mere unmeaning gibberish, and their demeanour exceedingly boisterous, the custom became intolerable; so that . . . they were generally hooted at and forbid in every decent family, and in the end they dwindled away into nothing; though, in some few cases they were to be seen as far down as the year 1800 or lower.

The local dialect was rejected as provincial and incorrect. 'Scotticisms', like 'Gasconisms', were corrected, and the readers of James Beattie's book on the subject were warned never to say 'clattering' when they meant 'chattering', or 'dubiety', when they meant 'doubt'. It may easily be imagined how educated people now regarded bagpipe music and traditional ballads. Adam Smith may be taken as a spokesman for the new attitudes, themselves becoming old-fashioned by 1780, when an interviewer asked him about his literary tastes, and received this trenchant reply:

> It is the duty of a poet to write like a gentleman. I dislike that homely style which some think fit to call the language of nature and simplicity and so forth. In Percy's *Reliques* . . . a few tolerable pieces are buried under a heap of rubbish. [72]

It is likely that the Russian nobles were among the last in Europe to abandon their popular traditions, in spite of Peter the Great's attempts to 'westernise' them. (His liking for buffoons and buffoonery suggests that he was not altogether westernised himself.) It has been argued that the aristocratic audience for the *lubok*, the illustrated chap-book, disappeared in the seventeenth century, and the use of French by the upper nobility suggests a conscious withdrawal from popular culture. However, it is unlikely that this withdrawal was complete by 1800. Readers of *War and Peace* and other Russian novels will remember that noblemen kept dwarves and buffoons in their households and that noblewomen venerated icons and holy fools just like the peasants. In his memoirs the nobleman Aksakov recalled that his grandfather used to go to sleep listening to *skazki*, folktales, told him by their serf-housekeeper. As for merchants and officials, around the year 1800 they were still meeting in the evenings to listen to traditional ballads. [73]

The withdrawal from popular culture took place at different speeds in different parts of Europe, but the main trend seems clear enough. Similarly, the essential explanation seems clear enough, whatever the local nuances, interesting as it would be to have these brought out; it was, surely, that learned culture changed so rapidly between 1500 and 1800, the age of the Renaissance, the Reformation and Counter-Reformation, the Scientific Revolution, and the Enlightenment (and each of these terms is short-hand for a movement which was not only complex but changing all the time). European popular culture was far from static for these three hundred years, but it did not, indeed could not, change so fast. As we have seen, there were all sorts of contacts between learned culture and popular culture. Chapmen distributed books and pamphlets by Luther and Calvin, Voltaire and Rousseau; peasant painters imitated the baroque and rococo styles with the help of engravings. However, this was not enough to prevent the gap between learned and popular culture widening, for oral and visual traditions could not absorb rapid change, or, to vary the metaphor, they were resilient to change, accustomed to taking the new and transforming it into something very like the old (above, p.147). A rapidly changing popular culture, supposing anyone had wanted it, would have been impossible in early modern Europe, which lacked the institutional and economic basis for it. Even if the necessary schools could have been founded and the schoolmasters paid, many craftsmen and peasants could not have afforded to do without the contributions made by the labour of their children. In the nineteenth century, the growth of towns, the spread of schools, and the development of the railways, among other factors, made rapid change in popular culture possible, indeed inevitable; that is why this study of traditional popular culture ends around the year 1800.

From withdrawal to discovery

As the gap between the two cultures gradually widened, so some educated men began to see popular songs, beliefs and festivals as exotic, quaint, fascinating, worthy of collection and record.

The earlier collectors had what might be described as the 'pre-split mentality'. They thought of the ballads and proverbs which they transcribed and published as a tradition which belonged to everyone, not just to the common people. This is the attitude, for example, of Heinrich Bebel and Sebastian Franck. Bebel was the son of a Swabian peasant but became a well-known humanist, professor at the university of Tübingen. In 1508 he published a collection of German proverbs and an anthology of funny stories, both translated into Latin. In both collections he drew on oral tradition, and many of his stories are set in his native Suabia. He has therefore been presented as a

Renaissance 'folklorist', a description which is somewhat misleading. Bebel offers his proverbs as examples of traditional German wisdom, without suggesting that they belong to the peasants in particular. His jest-book includes what we would call 'folktales', but for Bebel they were just 'tales'. Similar points may be made about Sebastian Franck, who also published a collection of German proverbs (this time, in the original language) and also a *Weltbuch,* a description of the peoples of the world and their beliefs, customs, and ceremonies. Franck too has been described as a folklorist, but he does not make the distinction between learned and popular culture any more than Bebel does. He believed that his proverbs expressed the wisdom of mankind, and his *Weltbuch* describes different nations without distinguishing social groups within them. In the German-speaking world the interest in popular culture as distinct from learned culture seems to go back no further than Friedrich Friese, who published a study of 'the remarkable ceremonies of the peasants of Altenburg' in 1703.[74]

The Scandinavian 'forerunners' of the folklorists were, like Bebel and Franck, unconscious of any split between learned and popular culture, no doubt because the split came late to those parts. Anders Vedel, for example, who was tutor to the great astronomer Tycho Brahe, published a collection of a hundred Danish ballads in 1591. The preface, addressing Queen Sophia, recommends the ballads as 'historical antiquities', valuable 'documents' which tell about 'early kings and battles'. There is no suggestion that these songs belong to the common people; they are described as 'Danish songs' (*Danske viser*), not as 'folksongs' (*folkeviser*), a term which came into use only in the nineteenth century. Again, King Gustav Adolf of Sweden has been described as appointing a 'folklore commission'. Thanks to the advice of Johan Bure, a distinguished antiquary and the king's former tutor, Gustav did indeed appoint a commission to tour Sweden and look for runes, ballads, coins, costumes, tools, and methods of agriculture and fishing. However, the inclusion of runes and coins in the list suggests that what Bure and his successor Johan Hadorph were interested in were Swedish antiquities rather than specifically popular antiquities. They were in the tradition of Flavio Biondo and William Camden, not in that of Herder. A more difficult case to interpret is that of the clergyman and scholar Peder Syv, who reprinted Vedel's ballad collection in 1695 plus a historical introduction and a hundred more texts. He also wrote a treatise *On the Errors of the Vulgar* (including, for example, the belief in magical formulae). It looks as though he rejected popular culture, like his contemporary Holberg, but did not see the old ballads as part of it.[75]

After about 1650 it is possible to find scholars in England, France and Italy who distinguish between learned culture and popular culture, reject popular beliefs, but find them a fascinating object of study. John Aubrey is an obvious example. His attitude was that 'old customs and old wives-fables are gross things: but yet ought not to be quite rejected: there may be some truth and usefulness be elicited out of them: besides, 'tis a pleasure to consider the errors that enveloped former ages: as also the present'.[76] The scholar-clergy of the late seventeenth and early eighteenth centuries saw popular culture in a similar perspective. They collected information about customs and 'superstitions', disapproved of much of what they collected, but continued to collect it all the same. A famous example of the type was Jean-Baptiste Thiers, the son of an innkeeper who became a country priest and a would-be reformer of popular religion. He wrote one treatise arguing for the reduction of feast-days, another attacking the profanation of churches by the hawkers who established themselves in the porches, and a third, his most famous, on superstitions, which provides far more detail than a plain condemnation could require. The same can be said of Henry Bourne, a curate at All Saints, Newcastle, who published in 1725 a book (in English) called *Antiquitates Vulgares*, 'popular antiquities', concerned with 'ceremonies and opinions, which are held by the common people'. The tone is critical, distinguishing 'which may be retained, and which ought to be laid aside'; but the wealth of detail on fairies, May Day, wakes, harvest suppers and the rest made the book useful to generations of later folklorists who lacked Bourne's reforming zeal. Most important of all these scholar-clerics, from the European point of view, was L. A. Muratori, a priest of rigorist views and an antiquary whose appointment as librarian to the Duke of Modena gave him the leisure and the access to books he needed. Muratori wrote a fascinating essay on the power of fantasy in which he suggested that witches and their victims suffered alike from an excess of imagination. His greatest work is a collection of essays on Italian antiquities, including 'the

seeds of superstition in the dark ages in Italy', from trial by
ordeal to the Yule log ritual. Concerned to refute what he called
'the ridiculous traditions of the ignorant vulgar', Muratori was
also concerned to reconstruct them.[77]

While these clergymen studied the history of popular
religion, a few of the laity were interesting themselves in popular
poetry. Like Puttenham (above, p.277), Montaigne distinguished between popular and artistic poetry; unlike him, he
appreciated both:

> Poetry which is popular and quite natural has an innocence and
> grace comparable to the greatest beauties of artistic poetry, as can be
> seen in the *villanelles* of Gascony and in the songs which have been
> brought back from nations which have no knowledge of any science
> or even of writing.

Montaigne could see beauties in popular songs which Du
Bellay, for example, could not. During his visit to Italy,
Montaigne took great interest in an illiterate peasant woman
who extemporised verses (above, p.105); he defended itinerant
actors against their critics and suggested that they should receive
some measure of civic support. These attitudes are, of course,
related to his critique of the 'civilisation' of his own day. The
case of Malherbe is more difficult to interpret. Malherbe was no
apologist for savagery; he was a court poet whose main concern
was to purify the literary language and to write verses which
were polished and correct. In a sense he belongs with Boileau to
the movement of withdrawal from popular culture described in
the last section. Yet one day a colleague found Malherbe lying
on his bed singing a folksong, *D'où venez-vous Jeanne?* 'I
would rather have written that song', Malherbe told him, 'than
all the works of Ronsard.' When people asked Malherbe (as they
often did), about points of French usage, he would send them to
his 'masters' in language, the dockers of Port-au-Foin. His ideal
in language and literature was a natural simplicity; a simplicity
which, like the grace of Castiglione's courtier, usually takes a
good deal of hard work to achieve. If a popular song happened
to exemplify his ideals, Malherbe praised it; he was not
interested in the popular as such. What a traditional
ballad-singer – or the dockers of Port-au-Foin – would have
made of Malherbe's poems is difficult to imagine.[78]

Folktales as well as popular songs appealed to some

intellectuals in seventeenth-century France. At the court of Louis XIV, fairy stories were in fashion. Some writers even published their own versions: Mme D'Aulnoy, Mlle Lheritier, and the senior government official Charles Perrault (though he did not put his name on the title-page of the first edition). In the next generation, the tradition was continued by the Comte de Caylus, who founded the 'Pedlar's Academy', and published stories collected from women who told them while they were shelling peas. Perrault and the others did not take folktales altogether seriously, or at least they did not want to admit that they did; yet they found the stories fascinating. It is as if educated people were beginning to feel they needed an escape from the disenchanted world, the Cartesian intellectual universe they now inhabited. It was precisely the unscientific, the marvellous, which attracted them in folktales, as it attracted the historians of 'superstition'.[79]

The attitude of Joseph Addison to popular literature is midway between that of Malherbe and Perrault. In three essays in *The Spectator* of 1711 he surprised his readers by discussing two ballads, *Chevy Chase* and *The Two Children in the Wood*. Addison, like other writers of his day, believed that good literature obeyed universal rules, and so he discusses *Chevy Chase* as 'an heroic poem', comparing it to the *Aeneid*. What impresses him in particular is the 'majestic simplicity' of the poem, in contrast to what he calls the 'Gothic manner in writing', in other words the metaphysical and baroque styles; he comes near to presenting these ballads as examples of classicism. At the same time Addison confesses, however apologetically, to a general interest in popular literature:

> When I travelled, I took a particular delight in hearing the songs and fables that are come from father to son, and are most in vogue among the common people of the countries through which I passed; for it is impossible that anything should be universally tasted and approved by a multitude, though they are only the rabble of a nation, which hath not in it some peculiar aptness to please and gratify the mind of man.

It is this 'particular delight' which was to become so fashionable later in the eighteenth century, and with it the view, expressed here with some hesitation, that the values of ordinary people ought not to be rejected either. Civilisation had its price.

Similarly Thomas Blackwell, in a study of Homer published in 1735, suggested that Homer was lucky to have lived at a time when manners were 'unaffected and simple', and when the language was not 'thoroughly polished in the modern sense'. Robert Lowth, lecturing on the sacred poetry of the Hebrews, suggested that it was both less polished and more sublime than the poetry of the Greeks.[80]

Herder knew about some of these predecessors and learned from them. His *Volkslieder* takes its epigraphs from Addison, Sidney and Montaigne. Yet, if we look back over the three hundred years discussed in this book, the change in the attitudes of educated men seems truly remarkable. In 1500, they despised the common people, but shared their culture. By 1800 their descendants had ceased to participate spontaneously in popular culture, but they were in the process of rediscovering it as something exotic and therefore interesting. They were even beginning to admire 'the people', from whom this alien culture had sprung.

The Discovery of the People: Select Studies and Anthologies, 1760–1846

Publications in parts are mentioned in the year in which the first part came out

1760	J. Macpherson, *Fragments of Ancient Poetry*
1762	J. Macpherson, *Fingal*
1763	H. Blair, *A Critical Dissertation on the Poems of Ossian*
1765	T. Percy, *Reliques of Ancient Poetry*
1766	H. G. Porthan, *De Poesi Fennica*
1770	M. I. Chulkhov, *Sobranie Raznykh Pesen*
1774	A. Fortis, *Viaggio in Dalmazia*
1775	S. Johnson, *A Journey to the Western Islands*
1776	D. Herd, *Ancient and Modern Scottish Songs*
1776	G. A. Bürger, *Herzensausguss über Volkspoesie*
1776	V. F. Trutovsky, *Sobranie Russkich Prostych Pesen*
1777	J. Brand, *Observations on Popular Antiquities*
1778	J. G. Herder, *Volkslieder*
1780	J. J. Bodmer, *Altenglische und Altschwäbische Ballade*
1782	J. K. A. Musäus, *Volksmärchen der Deutschen*
1783	J. Pinkerton, *Select Scottish Ballads*
1789	C. Ganander, *Mythologia Fennica*
1789	C. Brooke, *Reliques of Irish Poetry*
1790	N. A. Lvov, *Sobranie Narodnykh Russkikh Pesen*
1791	J. Ritson, *Pieces of Ancient Popular Poetry*
1800	'Otmar', *Volkssagen*
1801	J. Strutt, *Sports and Pastimes of the People of England*
1802	W. Scott, *Minstrelsy of the Scottish Border*
1802	Chateaubriand, *Génie du Christianisme*
1804	K. Danilov, *Drevnie Rossiyskie Stikhotvoreniya*
1806	A. von Arnim/C. Brentano, *Des Knaben Wunderhorn*
1807	J. Görres, *Die Deutsche Volksbücher*
1808	W. Grimm, *Uber die Entstehung der Altdeutschen Poesie*
1810	F. L. Jahn, *Deutsches Volkstum*
1812	J. Grimm/W. Grimm, *Kinder- und Haus-Märchen*

1812   W. Abrahamson, etc, *Udvalgte Danske Visen*
1814   A. Afzelius/E. Geijer, *Svenska Folkviser*
1814   V. S. Karadžić, *Malo Prostonarodna Pesnaritsa*
1817   G. Renier Michiel, *Origine delle Feste Veneziane*
1818   M. Placucci, *Usi e Pregiudizi de' Contadini della Romagna*
1818   A. Czarnocki, *O Słowiańszczyźnie przed Chreścijaństwem*
1822   F. L. Čelakovský, *Slowanské Národnj Pjsne*
1824   C. Fauriel, *Chants Populaires de la Grèce Moderně*
1828   A. Durán, *Romancero*
1830   L. Gołębiowski, *Lud Polski*
1832   E. Geijer, *Svenska Folkets Historie*
1835   E. Lönnrot, *Kalevala*
1836   F. Palacký, *Geschichte von Böhmen*
1839   Villemarqué, *Barzaz Breiz*
1841   P. C. Asbjørnsen/J. Moe, *Norske Folk-Eventyr*
1841   N. Tommaseo, *Canti Popolari*
1846   J. Erdélyi, *Népdalok és Mondák*
1846   J. Michelet, *Le Peuple*

Select Publications illustrating the Reform of Popular Culture, 1495–1664

1495 S. Brant, *Das Narrenschiff* (second edn)
1540 H. Sachs, *Gespräch mit der Fastnacht*
1553 T. Naogeorgus, *Regnum Papisticum*
1556 G. Paradin, *Le Blason des Danses*
1559 F. de Alcoçer, *Tratado del Juego*
1566 H. Estienne, *Apologie pour Herodote*
1577 J. Northbrooke, *A Treatise against Dicing*
1578 G. Paleotti, *Scrittura*
1579 C. Borromeo, *Memoriale*
1579 J. Northbrooke, *Distractions of the Sabbath*
1582 C. Fetherston, *Dialogue against Dancing*
1583 P. Stubbes, *Anatomy of Abuses*
1584 R. Scot, *Discovery of Witchcraft*
1594 C. Bascapè, *Contra gli Errori . . . avanti la Quaresima*
1606 C. Bascapè, *Settuagesima*
1607 Anon., *Discorso contra il Carnevale*
1608 J. Savaron, *Traité contre les Masques*
1609 C. Noirot, *L'Origine des Masques*
1633 W. Prynne, *Histriomastix*
1640 G. D. Ottonelli, *Della Christiana Moderatione del Teatro*
1655 P. Wittewrongel, *Oeconomia Christiana*
1655 G. Hall, *Triumph of Rome*
1660 T. Hall, *Funebria Florae*
1664 J. Deslyons, *Discours . . . contre le Paganisme des Rois*

Notes

Prologue

1 On definitions of culture, A. L. Kroeber and C. Kluckhohn, *Culture: a critical review of concepts and definitions*, (1952), new edn, New York, 1963.
2 A. Gramsci, 'Osservazioni sul folclore' in *Opere*, 6, Turin, 1950, pp. 215f.
3 See Bibliography under G. Cocchiara, A. Dundes, A. van Gennep, G. Ortutay, etc.
4 See Bibliography under M. Bakhtin, C. Baskervill, D. Fowler, A. Friedman, V. Kolve, M. Lüthi, etc.
5 Particularly helpful on the issues raised in this book has been the work of G. Foster, C. Geertz, M. Gluckman, C. Lévi-Strauss, R. Redfield, V. Turner, E. Wolf.
6 For successful examples of quantitative approaches in this field, see Bollème (1969) and Svärdström (1949), on French almanacs and Swedish paintings respectively.

1 The Discovery of the People

1 The most useful single book on the discovery is Cocchiara (1952). For *Volkslied* and other terms in the cluster, in German, see, appropriately enough, J. Grimm and W. Grimm (eds), *Deutsches Wörterbuch*, Leipzig, 1852, etc.
2 J. G. Herder, 'Über die Wirkung der Dichtkunst auf die Sitten der Völker' (1778), in his *Sämtliche Werke*, ed. B. Suphan, 8, Hildesheim, 1967. On him, R. T. Clark, *Herder*, Berkeley and Los Angeles, 1955, esp. Ch.8.
3 J. Grimm, *Kleinere Schriften*, 4, Hildesheim, 1965, pp. 4, 10n.
4 On Percy, Friedman (1961a), Ch. 7; on the reception of the *Reliques* in Germany, H. Lohre, *Von Percy zu Wunderhorn*, Berlin, 1902, Part 1.
5 A. A. Afzelius and E. G. Geijer (eds), *Svenska Folkviser*, Stockholm, 1814, p. x. On Afzelius, Jonsson, pp. 400f.; on Geijer, J. Landqvist, *Geijer*, Stockholm, 1954; on both, E. Dal, *Nordisk Folkeviseforskning siden 1800*, Copenhagen, 1956, Ch. 10.
6 C. Fauriel (ed.), *Chants Populaires de la Grèce Moderne*, 1, Paris, 1824, pp. xxv, cxxvi; on him, M. Ibrovac, *C. Fauriel*, Paris, 1966, esp. Part 1.

7 V. Knox, *Essays Moral and Literary*, 2nd edn, London, 1779, essay 47.

8 L. Tieck, *Werke*, 28 vols, 1828–54, 15, p. 21; on him, B. Steiner, *L. Tieck und die Volksbücher*, Berlin, 1893, esp. pp. 76f.

9 Notably J. K. A. Musäus (ed.), *Volksmärchen der Deutschen* (1782), and 'Otmar' (ed.), *Volkssagen*, Bremen, 1800.

10 G. von Gaal (ed.), *Märchen der Magyaren*, Vienna, 1822; on him, L. Dégh (ed.), *Folktales of Hungary*, London, 1965, p. xxvi.

11 W. Hone, *Ancient Mysteries Described*, London, 1823; F. J. Mone, (ed.), *Altteutsche Schauspiele*, Quedlinburg/Leipzig, 1841.

12 Arnim q. by H. U. Lenz, *Das Volkserlebnis bei L. A. von Arnim*, Berlin, 1938, p. 123; for Chateaubriand see his *Génie du Christianisme*, Paris, 1802, Part 3, Ch. 6.

13 Clark (note 2), pp. 51f.

14 J. W. von Goethe, *Italienische Reise*, ed. H. von Einem, Hamburg, 1951, pp.484f.

15 J. Strutt, *Sports and Pastimes of the People of England*, London, 1801; G. Renier Michiel, *Origine delle Feste Veneziane*, Venice, 1817; I. M. Snegirov, *Ruskie Prostonarodnye Prazdniki*, Moscow, 1838. On the discovery of the people in Russia, P. Pascal, *Civilisation Paysanne en Russie*, Lausanne, 1969, pp. 14f.

16 On Trutovsky, G. Seaman, *History of Russian Music*, 1, Oxford, 1967, pp. 88f.; *Grove's*, article 'Folk Music: Austrian'; K. Lipiński, *Piesni Polskie i Ruskie Ludu Galicyjskiego*, Lwów, 1833.

17 E. G. Geijer, *Svenska Folkets Historia*, Stockholm, 1832 on; Palacký published his first volume in German in 1836 as *Geschichte von Böhmen*, but continued it in Czech as *Dějiny Národu Ceského*. On Michelet and the people, see Boas, pp. 65f., and C. Rearick, *Beyond the Enlightenment: Historians and Folklore in Nineteenth-Century France*, Bloomington/London, 1974, pp. 82f.

18 In 1860 S. J. Kraszewski published *Die Kunst der Slaven*; in 1861, William Morris founded the firm of Morris, Marshall, Faulkner and Co.; in 1867 Eilert Sundt published a study of domestic industry in Norway, and some farm buildings were re-erected on a piece of land outside Oslo. The idea of an open-air museum of farmhouses was put forward by a Swiss scholar, C. V. de Bonstetten, in 1799.

19 A. Fortis, *Viaggio in Dalmazia*, 2 vols, Venice, 1774, esp. 1, pp. 43f.; on him, G. F. Torcellan, 'Profilo di A. Fortis' in his *Settecento Veneto*, Turin, 1969, pp. 273f.; S. Johnson, *A Journey to the Western Islands of Scotland* (1775), and J. Boswell, *Journal of a Tour to the Hebrides* (1785), both ed. R. W. Chapman, repr. Oxford, 1970, esp. Johnson, pp. 27f., 90, and Boswell, pp. 250f.

20 On Spanish 'populism', C. Clavería, *Estudios sobre los Gitanismos del Español*, Madrid, 1951, pp. 21f., and J. Ortega y Gasset, *Papeles sobre Velázquez y Goya*, Madrid, 1950, pp. 282f.; but

Ortega's assumption that this aristocratic enthusiasm was uniquely Spanish will not stand up to comparative research. The quotation from Blanco White, *Letters from Spain*, 2nd edn, London, 1825, p. 237.

21   J. G. Herder, *Ideen zur Philosophie der Geschichte*, 4 vols, Riga/Leipzig, 1784–91, Part 3; 'manners, customs . . .' q. from W. Thoms, defining the term 'folklore' which he had just invented in 1846, repr. in A. Dundes (ed.), *The Study of Folklore*, Englewood Cliffs, 1965, pp. 4f.; on folksongs as invention rather than discovery, Bausinger, p. 14.

22   'Chodakowski', q. *Grove's*, article 'Folk Music: Polish'.

23   T. Percy (ed.), *Hau Kiou Choaan*, 4, London, 1761, p. 200. Percy made the translations for this volume himself – from the Portuguese.

24   H. Honour, *Neoclassicism*, Harmondsworth, 1968, sees late eighteenth-century artists and writers as rejecting the baroque and rococo styles in the name of classicism. This certainly happened, but the rules of classicism were themselves being rejected at the same time and sometimes by the same people.

25   On Gottsched, below, p.240; on Bodmer, M. Wehrli, *J. J. Bodmer und die Geschichte der Literatur*, Frauenfeld/Leipzig, 1936; Goethe q. R. Pascal, *The German Sturm und Drang*, Manchester, 1953, p. 242.

26   On Ossian, J. S. Smart, *James Macpherson*, London, 1905, and D. S. Thomson (1952).

27   H. Blair, *A Critical Dissertation on the Poems of Ossian*, (1763), 2nd edn, London, 1765, esp. pp. 2, 21, 63; on Herder as collector, L. Arbusow, 'Herder und die Begründung der Volksliedforschung', in E. Keyser (ed.), *Im Geiste Herders*, Kitzingen, 1953.

28   On Rousseau in this context, Cocchiara (1952), pp. 135f.; examples of Norwegian peasants in porcelain by Claus Rasmussen Tvede in Kunstindustri-Museet, Bergen.

29   J. Horák, 'Jacob Grimm und die slawische Volkskunde', in *Deutsche Jahrbuch für Volkskunde*, 9 (1963).

30   Cocchiara (1952), pp. 231f.; L. L. Snyder, *German Nationalism* (1952), 2nd edn, Port Washington, 1969, Chs 2, 3.

31   J. Lundqvist, *Geijer*, Stockholm, 1954, Ch. 6.

32   On Porthan, M. G. Schybergson, *H. G. Porthan*, Helsinki, 1908 (in Swedish), esp. Ch. 4; the 'Finnish intellectual' (Söderhjelm) q. Wuorinen, p. 69.

33   On Lönnrot, J. Hautala, *Finnish Folklore Research 1828–1918*, Helsinki, 1969, Ch. 2, and M. Haavio, 'Lönnrot' in *Arv*, 1969–70.

34   On Poland, H. Kapełuś/J. Krzyżanowski (eds), *Dzieje Folklorystyki Polskiej*, Wrocław, etc., 1970; on Willems, J. E. F. Crick, *J. F. Willems*, Antwerp, c. 1946; Scott, 1, p. 175.

35   Arnim/Brentano, p. 886; cf. R. Linton, 'Nativistic Movements'

in *American Anthropologist*, 45 (1943), and J. W. Fernandez, 'Folklore as an Agent of Nationalism', repr. in I. Wallerstein (ed.), *Social Change: the Colonial Situation*, New York, 1966.

36 Wilson.

37 On France, P. Bénichou, *Nerval et la Chanson Folklorique*, Paris, 1970, esp. Ch. 1; F. Gourvil, *T. C. H. Hersart de la Villemarqué*, Rennes, 1959.

38 On Grégoire, M. de Certeau *et al.*, *Une Politique de la Langue*, Paris, 1975, esp. pp. 12f., 141f.; on Finistère, J. de Cambry, *Voyage dans le Finistère*, 3 vols, Paris, 1799.

39 H. Mackenzie (ed.), *Report of the Committee . . . appointed to Inquire into the . . . Authenticity of . . . Ossian*, Edinburgh, 1805; on the Celtic Academy, Durry; the Academy's questionnaire repr. in Van Gennep, 3, pp. 12f., and in de Certeau; pp. 264f., cf. S. Moravia, *La Scienza dell'Uomo nel '700*, Bari, 1970, pp. 187f.

40 For the Italian questionnaire, G. Tassoni (ed.), *Arti e Tradizioni Popolari: le Inchieste Napoleoniche sui Costumi e le Tradizioni nel Regno Italico*, Bellinzone, 1973; M. Placucci, *Usi e Pregiudizi dei Contadini di Romagna* (1818), repr. in P. Toschi (ed.), *Romagna Tradizionale*, Bologna, 1952; on Placucci, G. Cocchiara, *Popolo e Letteratura in Italia*, Turin, 1959, pp. 118f.

41 'Otmar' was J. Nachtigall; 'Chodakowski' was A. Czarnocki; 'Merton' was W. Thoms; 'Kazak Lugansky' was V. I. Dal; 'Saintyves' was the publisher E. Nourri; and 'Davenson' hides the classical scholar H. I. Marrou.

42 'Otmar' (note 9), p. 22.

43 Scott 1, p. 175; Arnim, p. 861.

44 M. B. Landstad, q. O. J. Falnes, *National Romanticism in Norway*, New York, 1933, p. 255.

45 Mackenzie (note 39), p. 152; cf. D. S. Thomson (1952).

46 Lönnrot q. F. P. Magoun (ed.), *The Kalevala*, Cambridge, Mass., 1963, preface. Cf. Jonsson, pp. 675f. on forgeries, pp. 801f. on ballad editing in Sweden.

47 Wilson, p. 76.

48 Percy, 1, p. 11; Fowler, p. 249.

49 Pinkerton was exposed in 1784 by the acute and irascible scholar Joseph Ritson, on whom see B. H. Bronson, *J. Ritson, Scholar at Arms*, 2 vols, Berkeley, 1938. On Arnim and Brentano, F. Rieser, *Des Knaben Wunderhorn und Seine Quellen*, Dortmund, 1908, esp. pp. 45f.

50 Schoof; cf. A. David/M. E. David, 'A Literary Approach to the Brothers Grimm', in *Journal of the Folklore Institute*, 1 (1964).

51 Seaman (note 16), p. 88; on folk-music collecting in Sweden, Jonsson, pp. 323f.

52 Simpson (1966), p. xvi; W. Chappell, (ed.), *A Collection of*

National English Airs, 1, London, 1838, preface.
53   On the romantic reconstruction of the Carnival of Cologne by F. F. Wallraf, Klersch, pp. 84f.; on Nuremberg, Sumberg, p. 180; on Nice, Agulhon (1970), pp. 153f.
54   S. Piggott, *The Druids*, London, 1968, Ch. 4; T. Parry, *A History of Welsh Literature*, Oxford, 1955, pp. 301f. Prys Morgan, of the University College of Swansea, gave a paper on the Welsh discovery/invention of their past at the Past and Present conference in 1977.
55   H. N. Fairchild, *The Noble Savage*, New York, 1928, Ch. 13.
56   Boswell (note 19, above) p. 246.
57   Chapters 8 and 9 are an attempt to set out the most important of these changes.
58   Coirault, 5th exposé; Boas, Ch. 4; and for a sophisticated defence of the idea of collective creation, Jakobson/Bogatyrev.
59   J. G. Herder, *Sämtliche Werke*, ed. B. Suphan, 25, Hildesheim, 1967, p. 323.

2 Unity and Variety in Popular Culture

1   On the Tiv, P. Bohannan, 'Artist and Critic in a Tribal Society', in M. W. Smith (ed.), *The Artist in Tribal Society*, London, 1961.
2   On the 'ballad community' in parts of Europe, Entwistle, pp. 7f.; in north-east Scotland, Buchan (1972), pp. 18f.
3   Redfield, pp. 41-2.
4   On Ferrara, E. Welsford, *The Court Masque*, Cambridge, 1927, p. 100; on Paris, P. de L'Estoile, *Mémoires-Journaux*, 12 vols, Paris, 1875–92, 2, p. 106; on Nuremberg, Sumberg, p. 59. Beerli (1956) notes that sixteenth-century Bern had two carnivals, a week apart, for the nobles and the peasants, but this seems exceptional.
5   On France, Davis (1975), pp. 99f., 111f.
6   On Poliziano and Pontano, G. Cocchiara, *Le Origini della Poesia Popolare*, Turin, 1966, pp. 29f.; on Malherbe, below, p.284; on Hooft, Wirth, p. 164; on Queen Isabella, Entwistle, p. 28; on Ivan and Sophia, notes 8 and 12 below.
7   On the *visböcker* (some of which are printed in Noreen/Schück) Jonsson, pp. 31f., and E. Dal, *Nordisk Folkeviseforskning siden 1800*, Copenhagen, 1956, Ch. 26.
8   On Zan Polo, Lea, 1, pp. 247f.; on Tarleton, Baskervill (1929), pp. 95f.; on Tabarin, Bowen, pp. 185f.; on Ivan, G. Fletcher, *The Russe Commonwealth* (1591), ed. A. J. Schmidt, Ithaca, 1966, p. 147 (cf. Jakobson (1944), p. 63).
9   On Gouberville, E. Le Roy Ladurie, *Le Territoire de l'Historien*, Paris, 1973, p. 218; on German broadsheets, Coupe, p. 19; on French

almanacs, Bollême (1969), pp. 15, 27; on Swedish healers, Tillhagen (1962), p. 1; on the Finnish *kåsor*, N. Cleve, 'Till Bielkekåsornas Genealogi' in *Fataburen* 1964, a reference I owe to the kindness of Maj Nodermann.

10   Grazzini q. R. J. Rodini, *A. F. Grazzini*, Madison etc., 1970, p. 148; J. Aubrey, *Brief Lives*, Oxford, 1898, 'Corbet'; *Fataburen* 1969 (special issue on Swedish wedding customs), pp. 142, 152.

11   For English attitudes to the 'many-headed monster', Hill (1974), Ch. 8.

12   On the Cracow area, Wyczański; noblewomen who compiled *visböcker* printed in Noreen/Schück include Barbro Banér and Queen Sophia (the Swedish wife of a late sixteenth-century king of Denmark).

13   E. Obiechnina, *Culture, Tradition and Society in the West African Novel*, Cambridge, 1975, pp. 35f.

14   A. Gramsci, 'Osservazioni sul Folclore' in his *Opere*, 6, Turin, 1950, pp. 215f.

15   Kodály, p. 20.

16   On stratification within the peasantry, Lefebvre (1924), pp. 321f.; P. Goubert, *Beauvais et le Beauvaisis de 1600 à 1730*, Paris, 1960; Blickle, pp. 84f.

17   P. Jeannin, 'Attitudes Culturelles et Stratifications Sociales' in L. Bergeron (ed.), *Niveaux de Culture et Groupes Sociaux*, Paris/The Hague, 1967, pp. 67f.

18   Bødker, articles 'drängvisor', 'pigvisor'.

19   Johnson (Ch. 1, note 19), pp. 38f.

20   Barley (1967) pp. 746f. (cf. C. Fox, *The Personality of Britain*, Cardiff, 1932); on the Alpujarras, F. Braudel, *The Mediterranean*, 1, Eng. trans., London, 1972, p. 35.

21   *Grove's*, article 'Folk Music: Norway', etc.

22   J. Hansen, *Zauberwahn, Inquisition und Hexenprozess*, Bonn, 1900, pp. 400f., followed by Trevor-Roper, pp. 30f.; contrast Cohn (1975), p. 225.

23   Cipolla, pp. 73f.; J. J. Darmon, *Le Colportage de Librairie en France sous le Second Empire*, Paris, 1972, pp. 30f.; Vovelle (1975).

24   On shepherd culture in France, Louis, pp. 151f.; in central Europe, Jacobeit; in Hungary, Fél/Hofer, pp. 23f.; in Poland, W. Sobisiak in *Burszta*, 2, pp. 186f.; on their music, *Grove's*, article 'bagpipe'; on their songs, Erk/Böhme, nos 1471–1596.

25   S. Paolucci, *Missioni de' Padri della Compagnia di Giesù nel Regno di Napoli*, Naples, 1651, pp. 21f.

26   Examples of eighteenth-century Iberian shepherd art in Hansen, pp. 138, 150.

27   For the proverb, Amades (1950–1), p. 1030 (cf. Hornberger, p. 16); for the magic, Jacobeit, pp. 367f.

28   Hornberger, pp. 85f.; Jacobeit, pp. 328f.; on *autos del*

nacimiento in Spain, Rael, Ch. 1.
29 Hornberger, pp. 38f.; Jacobeit, pp. 173f.; on Brie, Mandrou (1968), pp. 500f.
30 On woodlanders, M. Devèze, *La Vie de la forêt française au 16e siècle*, 1, Paris, 1961, pp. 130f.; on Russia, J. H. Billington, *The Icon and the Axe*, New York, 1966, pp. 16f.; on the Balkans, Stoianovich.
31 Karadžić, q. Wilson, pp. 33, 24; on Cossack songs, Stief (Ch. 4) and Ralston, pp. 41f.
32 On miners' culture, Heilfurth (1959, 1967), Schreiber (1962), Sébillot (1894); on their language, Avé-Lallemant, 3, pp. 113f.
33 T. C. Smout, *A History of the Scottish People 1560–1830*, new edn, London, 1972, p. 169; F. Rodriguez Marín, *Cantos Populares Españoles*, 5 vols, Seville, 1882–3, no. 7581; the painting, from a MS. in Vienna, in J. Delumeau, *Civilisation de la Renaissance*, Paris, 1967, facing p. 20.
34 On guild honour and social outcasts, Danckert.
35 On craftsman culture, Krebs; G. Fischer, *Volk und Geschichte*, Kulmbach, 1962; E. P. Thompson (1963), pp. 830f. Rituals of German guilds described in F. Friese, *Ceremonial-Politica*, Leipzig, 1708–16. On clothing, P. Cunnington/C. Lucas, *Occupational Costume in England from the Eleventh Century to 1914*, London, 1967, pp. 82, 111.
36 On English weaver culture, G. C. Homans, 'The Puritans and the Clothing Industry in England', in his *Sentiments and Activities*, London, 1962; T. Deloney, *Jack of Newbury*, London, 1596; J. Collinges, *The Weavers' Pocket-Book*, London, 1675; R. C., *The Triumphant Weaver*, London, 1682; E. P. Thompson (1963), Ch. 9; M. Vicinus, 'Literary Voices in an Industrial Town' in H. J. Dyos/M. Wolff (eds), *The Victorian City*, London, 1973. On the silk-workers of Lyons, M. Garden, *Lyon et le Lyonnais au 18e siècle*, Paris, 1970, pp. 242f.; German weaver songs in Schade, pp. 79f.; Dutch weaver songs discussed in Wirth, pp. 316f.
37 On shoemaker culture, Garden (note 36), pp. 244f.; Schade, pp. 75f.; Friese (note 35), pp. 341f.; Bødker, p. 278; T. Deloney, *The Gentle Craft*, London, 1597–8.
38 On Portugal, D'Azevedo, pp. 19f., 27f., 36f.; on the Cévennes, E. Le Roy Ladurie (1966), p. 349; on Vienna, E. Wangermann, *From Joseph II to the Jacobin Trials*, 2nd edn, Oxford, 1969, pp. 17f.
39 M. H. Dodds and R. Dodds, *The Pilgrimage of Grace*, 1, Cambridge, 1915, p. 92; Soboul (1966), p. 49.
40 On journeyman culture, Hobsbawm (1959), Ch. 9; M. Crubellier, *Histoire Culturale de la France, 19e-20 Siècles*, Paris, 1974, pp. 91f.; Hauser (1899), Ch. 3; E. Coornaert, *Les Compagnonnages en France*, Paris, 1966, esp. pp. 35f., 178f.; on the Griffarins, Davis (1975), pp. 4f.

41   T. Gent, *The Life of Mr T. Gent*, London, 1832, p. 16; Krebs, pp. 42, 68f.; German songs in Schade, pp. 135f., 247; the Hungarian song in T. Klaniczay (ed.), *Hét Evszázad Magyar Versei*, 1, 2nd edn, Budapest, 1966, p. 68.

42   G. Tassoni, 'Il Gergo dei Muratori di Viadana', in *Lares*, 20 (1954); D. Knoop/G. P. Jones, *The Genesis of Freemasonry*, Manchester, 1947; J. M. Roberts, *The Mythology of the Secret Societies*, London, 1972, Ch. 2; for Manole the Mason, Amzulescu, no. 164, and Ortutay (1968), pp. 107f.

43   Hauser (1899), Ch. 2; S. R. Smith, 'The London Apprentices as Seventeenth-Century Adolescents' in *P&P*, 61 (1973); *The Honour of the Taylors*, London, 1687.

44   On London shows, D. M. Bergeron, *English Civic Pageantry 1558–1642*, London, 1971, Ch. 2; on Pasquino, R. Silenzi/F. Silenzi, *Pasquino*, Milan, 1932.

45   J. M. Yinger, 'Contra-Culture and Sub-Culture' in *American Sociological Review*, 25 (1960); M. Clarke, 'On the Concept of Sub-Culture' in *British Journal of Sociology*, 25 (1974).

46   On the culture of English itinerants, Hill (1972), Ch. 3.

47   On soldier culture, Rehnberg, and A. Corvisier, *L'Armée Française*, Paris, 1964, Part 4, Ch. 5; on soldiers' language, Avé-Lallemant, 3, pp. 119f.; for the concept 'total institution', E. Goffman, *Asylums*, New York, 1961; songs quoted from Kohlschmidt, nos 17, 30 (cf. Erk-Böhme, nos 1279–1433); on Arnim and 'Das heisse Afrika', F. Rieser, *Des Knaben Wunderhorn und seine Quellen*, Dortmund, 1908, p. 197.

48   *Grove's*, article 'Shanty'; Davids – a reference which (as the reader may have guessed) I owe to Professor C. R. Boxer; J. Leyden (ed.), *The Complaynt of Scotland*, Edinburgh, 1801, p. 62; Braga (1867b), p. 145; K. Weibust, *Deep Sea Sailors*, Stockholm, 1969; R. D. Abrahams, *Deep the Water, Shallow the Shore: Essays on Shantying in the West Indies*, Austin/London, 1974, pp. xiii, 10.

49   Dress: Cunnington/Lucas (note 35), p. 58; for maritime terms in nine European languages, J. H. Röding, *Allgemeines Wörterbuch der Marine*, 4 vols, Hamburg/Halle, 1794-8; E. Ward, *The London Spy*, 1, London, 1706, pp. 281f.

50   Rituals: Henningsen *passim;* Hasluck, pp. 342f.; Art: H. J. Hansen (ed.), *Art and the Seafarer*, Eng. trans., London, 1968. Literacy: Vovelle (1973), pp. 378f. On maritime culture, in the fifteenth and sixteenth centuries, J. Bernard, *Navires et Gens de Mer à Bordeaux*, Paris, 1968, esp. Chs 3, 4, a reference for which I am indebted to Peter Lewis.

51   Sébillot (1901); F. Alziator, 'Gli Ex-Voto del Santuario di Nostra Signora di Bonaria', in his *Picaro e Folklore*, Florence, 1959; Schrijnen, 2, pp. 125f.; S. Klonowicz, *The Boatman*, Eng. trans., Cambridge

Springs, 1958, lines 1021f.

52 Pulci's glossary in Camporesi, pp. 179f.; for Elizabethan England, Salgádo, pp. 62f.; 210f.; for France, Sainéan; for Spain, Salillas; for Germany, Avé-Lallemant, 3 and 4.

53 C. García, *La Desordenada Codicia de los Bienes Agenos*, Paris, 1619, Chs 7, 8, 13; on Paris, F. de Calvi, *Histoire Générale des Larrons*, Paris, 1631, Book 1, Ch. 17; on London, Aydelotte, pp. 95f.; on literary stereotypes, E. von Kraemer, *Le Type de Faux Mendiant dans les Littératures Romanes*, Helsinki, 1944.

54 On 'Counter-Culture', Yinger (note 45); *Grove's*, article 'Folk Music: Jewish'; P. Bénichou, *Romancéro Judeo-Español de Marruecos*, Madrid, 1968; Wilson, p. 399.

55 J. Caro Baroja, *Los Moriscos del Reino de Granada*, Madrid, 1957, pp. 108f.; Gallego, pp. 59f.; M. Ladero Quesada, *Granada*, Madrid, 1969, pp. 68f., 163f.

56 J. P. Clébert, *The Gypsies*, Eng. trans., London, 1963, esp. pp. 96f.; C. Clavería, *Estudios sobre los Gitanismos del Español*, Madrid, 1951 pp. 7f.; the quotation from J. de Quiñones, *Discurso contra los Gitanos*, Madrid, 1631, f. 11.

57 S. Ardener (ed.), *Perceiving Women*, London, 1975 (esp. contributions by the Ardeners and C. Hardman); *Journal of American Folklore*, the special issue on 'Women and Folklore', 1975; on Galicia, K. Lipiński (ed.), *Pieśni Polskie . . .*, 1833; on Serbia, Karadžić (1824–33), Book 1, introduction; on women's work songs in Scotland, Collinson, pp. 67f.; on literacy in Amsterdam, Hart; in France, Fleury/Valmary; on books for women, L. B. Wright, pp. 109f., and Schotel (1873–4), 2, Ch. 7; on women and ecstatic religion, Bost (1921), p. 25, and K. V. Thomas, 'Women in the Civil War Sects' in *P&P*, 13 (1958) (cf. I. M. Lewis, *Ecstatic Religion*, Harmondsworth, 1971, pp. 75f.).

58 C. Sauvageon, q. Bouchard, p. 352.

59 P. Smith in J. Thirsk (ed.), *Agrarian History of England and Wales*, 4, Cambridge, 1967, pp. 767f.; Bernard (note 50), p. 753, on Breton ship-names; on Scandinavia, C. Nordmann, *Grandeur et Liberté de la Suède*, Paris/Louvain, 1971, pp. 120f.; on Lithuania, M. Mosvidius, *Catechismus* (1547), facsimile edn, Heidelberg, 1923, preface; S. Herberstein, *Description of Moscow* (1557), Eng. trans., London, 1969, p. 36.

60 On regional variation (with Yugoslav examples), Bosković-Stulli; on border ballads, Reed.

61 C. von Sydow, *Selected Papers on Folklore*, Copenhagen, 1948, esp. pp. 11f., 44f.

62 Svärdström (1957), p. 3; P. Bogatyrev, *The Functions of Folk Costume in Moravian Slovakia*, Eng. trans., The Hague/Paris, 1971, p. 54.

63   K. Liestøl, p. 15; S. Resnikow, 'The Cultural History of a Democratic Proverb', in *Journal of English and Germanic Philology*, 36 (1937).

64   Motif-Index J. 1700f; Christensen.

65   Nygard (cf. Vargyas, pp. 129f.); Child 95, Motif-Index D. 1855.2.

66   A. Fortis, *Viaggio in Dalmazia*, 1, Venice, 1774, p. 66; Hansen, p. 158.

67   On the 'tradition area', Motif-Index, introduction; N. N. Martinovitch, *The Turkish Theatre*, New York, 1933; M. Marriott, 'The Feast of Love', in M. Singer (ed.), *Krishna*, Honolulu, 1966; on the concept 'Indo-European', S. Poliakov, *The Aryan Myth*, Eng. trans., London, 1974, pp. 194f.

68   R. Dorson (ed.), *Studies in Japanese Folklore*, Bloomington, 1963, gives a first impression; G. P. Murdock, 'World Ethnographic Sample', in *American Anthropologist*, 59 (1957); cf. C. Kluckhohn, 'Recurrent Themes in Myth', in H. A. Murray (ed.), *Myth*, New York, 1960.

69   S. Erixon (ed.), *Atlas över Svensk Folkkultur* 1, Uddevalla, 1957; on ballad provinces, Seemann *et al.*, p. xviii (cf. Entwistle, pp. 21f., who distinguishes four ballad areas, Nordic/Romance/Balkan/Russian); M. J. Herskovits, *The Human Factor in Changing Africa*, New York, 1962, pp. 56f.

70   On settlement patterns, C. T. Smith, *An Historical Geography of Western Europe before 1800*, London, 1967, Ch. 5; on houses, F. Braudel, *Capitalism and Material Life*, 1, London, 1974 edn, pp. 192f.; on literacy, Fleury/Valmary and Cipolla, esp. pp. 113f.

71   On border cultures, Angyal; Reed; J. Mavrogordato (ed./trans.), *Digenes Akritas*, Oxford, 1956; H. Inalcik, *The Ottoman Empire*, London, 1973, pp. 6f.

72   P. Chaunu, 'Le Bâtiment dans l'Economie Traditionelle' in J. P. Bardet (ed.), *Le Bâtiment*, 1, Paris/The Hague, 1971, pp. 9f.; J. C. Peristiany (ed.), *Honour and Shame*, London, 1965; cf. Agulhon (1966), and Bennassar.

73   J. Swift, 'An Argument against Abolishing Christianity in England' in *Prose Works*, ed. H. Davis, 2, Oxford, 1939, p. 27.

74   J. Meier, *Kunstlied und Volkslied in Deutschland*, Halle, 1906; H. Naumann, *Primitive Gemeinschaftskultur*, Jena, 1921.

75   Redfield, p. 42: for other statements of the two-way flow theory, see Baskervill (1920), Haan (1950), Entwistle Chs 7, 8, and Crubellier (note 40), pp. 125f.

76   Hoskins (1963); Hauglid; Svärdström (1949, 1957).

77   J. Addison, *Remarks on Several Parts of Italy*, London, 1705, p. 104; A. F. Grazzini, *Rime Burlesche*, ed. C. Verzone, Florence, 1882, p. 240.

78   Chambers (1933), pp. 82, 149; E. Warner, 'Pushkin in the Russian Folk-Plays', in J. J. Duggan (ed.), *Oral Literature*, Edinburgh/London, 1975; Straeten, pp. 169f.
79   On Sicily, Pitrè (1889), 1, pp. 121f.; on France, Mandrou (1964), pp. 40, 131f.
80   E. P. Thompson, 'Anthropology and the Discipline of Historical Context', in *Midland History*, 1 (1971–2), p. 52.
81   E. Welsford, *The Court Masque*, Cambridge, 1927, pp. 20f.; cf. F. Sieber, *Volk und Volkstümliche Motiven im Festwerk des Barocks*, Berlin, 1960.
82   T. Klaniczay, *Zrínyi Miklós*, Budapest, 1964, pp. 127f.; J. Playford, *The Dancing Master*, London, 1652.
83   On Gay, F. Kidson, *The Beggars' Opera*, Cambridge, 1922; on Perrault, Soriano, pp. 479f.; Friedman (1961a) is concerned with 'the influence of popular on sophisticated poetry' in England 1600–1800.
84   Sébillot (1883), esp. the introduction.
85   G. Bronzini, *Tradizione di Stile Aedico dai Cantari al Furioso*, Florence, 1966, discusses Ariosto's debt to popular traditions; for a chap-book version of Ariosto, British Library 1071.c.63.(32); for shepherds and pastoral, Hornberger, p. 207.
86   Ginzburg (1966); Cohn (1975); Kieckhefer.
87   P. Goubert, *The Ancien Regime*, Eng. trans., London, 1973, pp. 261f.; D. Macdonald, *Against the American Grain*, New York, 1972, pp. 3f.
88   On Croce, Guerrini; on Sachs, Balzer; on Deloney, Roberts; J. Timoneda, *El Sobremesa y Alivio de Caminantes*, Valencia, 1564 (cf. Ch. 5, note 34).

3 An Elusive Quarry

1   Perceptive comments on these problems in Hobsbawm (1959), p. 2, Samuel, and M. de Certeau, *L'Écriture de l'Histoire*, Paris, 1975, esp. Ch. 5.
2   On Guadix, Gallego; on South Kyme, N. J. O'Conor, *Godes Peace and the Queenes*, Cambridge, 1934.
3   R. Tarleton, *Jests* (posthumous, London, 1611); F. Andreini, *Bravure*, Venice, 1607; C. dell' Altissimo, *I Reali di Francia* (posthumous, Venice, 1534); S. Tinódi, *Cronica*, 1554; O. Maillard, *Sermones de Adventu*, Lyons, 1503; G. Barletta, *Sermones*, Brescia, 1497.
4   Fuller could not have seen Tarleton but expands the comment in his epitaph, quoted by W. Camden, *Remains*, London, 1605, Part 2, p. 58: 'Hic situs est cuius vox, vultus, actio possit/Ex Heraclito reddere Democritum'.

5   F. Flamini, *La Lirica Toscana del Rinascimento*, Pisa, 1891, p. 187n.
6   On sermons, cf. pp. 132 below.
7   On Villon, Ziwès; P. Guiraud, *Le Jargon de Villon*, Paris, 1968.
8   Bakhtin; Sébillot (1883); M. Beaujour, *Le Jeu de Rabelais*, Paris, 1969, pp. 18f.; J. Paris, *Rabelais au Futur*, Paris, 1970, p. 45.
9   C. García, *La Desordenada Codicia de los Bienes Agenos*, Paris, 1619; on G. B. Basile, B. Croce, *Saggi sulla letteratura Italiana del 1600*, Bari, 1911; cf. R. M. Dorson, 'The Identification of Folklore in American Literature' in *Journal of American Folklore*, 70 (1957).
10   On the roof damage, J. Huizinga, *The Waning of the Middle Ages*, Harmondsworth, 1965 edn, p. 13.
11   Moser-Rath (1964, 1968); M. Michael, *Die Volkssage bei Abraham a Sancta Clara*, Leipzig, 1933.
12   J. W. Blench, *Preaching in England*, Oxford, 1964, Ch. 3.
13   A. P. Moore, *The Genre Poissard and the French stage of the Eighteenth Century*, New York, 1935.
14   On Eulenspiegel, J. Lefebvre (1968), Ch. 5.
15   On the Peasants' War ballads, Liliencron, nos 374f., esp. 380, 383, 384; the *London Magazine*, q. Brewer, p. 159.
16   On the Bibliothèque Bleue, Mandrou (1964), who argues that the chap-books reflect the values of the peasant audience. Some doubts about the audience raised by Bollème (1965) and by H. J. Martin, *Livre, Pouvoirs et Société*, Paris, 1969, pp. 955f.; some doubts about the reflection raised by Ginzburg (1966), pp. xif.
17   B. H. Bronson, 'Folksong and Live Recordings', repr. in Bronson (1969); Lord, pp. 19, 23, 79, 109, 136.
18   Doubts raised by B. H. Bronson, 'Mrs Brown and the Ballad', repr. in Bronson, 1969; her reliability defended by Buchan (1972), Ch.19; on Die Frau Viehmännin, Schoof, pp. 62f.; H. V. Velten, 'Perrault's influence on German Folklore' in *Germanic Review*, 5 (1930); Friedman (1961a), p. 53.
19   On the evidence of confessions, Ginzburg (1966), p. xi; Trevor-Roper, pp. 42f.; Thomas (1971), pp. 516f.
20   Contrast the interpretations of risings in seventeenth-century France in Porchnev, Mousnier, and R. Mandrou. 'Vingt Ans Après', in *Revue Historique*, 242 (1969), pp. 29f.
21   For the text of the Code Paysanne, A. de la Borderie, *La Révolte du Papier Timbré*, Saint-Brieuc, 1884, pp. 93f.; discussion in Mousnier, pp. 141f.; E. B. Bax, *German Society at the close of the Middle Ages*, London, 1894, pp. 54f.
22   Blickle, esp. pp. 37, 157; Franz (1963), pp. 73f.
23   P. Goubert/M. Denis (eds), *1789: les Français ont la Parole*, Paris, 1964, pp. 29f., 225.
24   Ginzburg (1966), p. 9; Thomas (1971), esp. Ch. 17; Macfarlane,

302   *Popular Culture in Early Modern Europe*

Chs 10–16.

25   On the idea of cultural 'brokers', E. Wolf, 'Aspects of Group Relations in a Complex Society', in *American Anthropologist*, 58 (1956); for the Sheale MS., T. Wright (ed.), *Songs and Ballads*, London, 1860.

26   B. Cellini, *Autobiography*, trans. G. Bull, Harmondsworth, 1956; G. C. Croce, *Descrizione della Vita*, Bologna, 1600; J. Bunyan, *Grace Abounding*, London, 1966; S. Bamford, *Early Days*, new edn, London, 1893.

27   E. Panofsky, *Meaning in the Visual Arts*, New York, 1955, Ch. 1.

28   On clothes, P. Bogatyrev, *Functions of Folk Costumes in Moravian Slovakia*, Eng. trans., The Hague/Paris, 1971, and H. Kuper, 'Costume and Identity' in *Comparative Studies in Society and History*, 15 (1973); on houses, P. Bourdieu, 'The Berber House', in M. Douglas (ed.), *Rules and Meanings*, Harmondsworth, 1973, pp. 98f.; B. H. Kerblay, *L'Izba*, Lausanne, 1973, esp. pp. 42f.

29   M. Bloch, *Les Caractères Originaux de l'Histoire Rurale Française*, Paris, 1964 edn, p. xii.

30   For the visual arts, Adhémar and Hansen, *passim*.

31   Wossidlo 139b is a story collected in 1919 from a man of 75 who had it from his father, who was born in 1793. On the reliability of oral tradition, see J. Vansina, *Oral Tradition*, Eng. trans., London, 1965.

32   Another pioneer was Nils Andersson (1864–1921), in Sweden, on whom see O. Anderson, *Spel Opp I Spelmänner*, Stockholm, 1958. Some nineteenth-century collectors had taken a serious interest in folk-tunes, as Ludwig Lindeman did in Norway, but recording them accurately was a problem before 1900.

33   On Rybnikov and Russian *byliny*, Chadwick, introduction; on Parry, Lord; B. A. Rosenberg, *The Art of the American Folk Preacher*, New York, 1970; on French diviners, M. Bouteiller, *Sorciers et Jeteurs de Sort*, Paris, 1958; on Yugoslav healers, Kemp; on Scandinavia, see *Arv*, 18–19 (1962–3).

34   Cf. W. C. Sturtevant, 'Anthropology, History and Ethno-History', in *Ethno-History*, 13 (1966); what Bloch calls the 'regressive method' Sturtevant calls 'up-streaming'. Cf. J. Vansina, *Oral Tradition*, London, 1965, and Phythian-Adams (1975).

35   On continuity at the village level, Bouchard; P. Goubert, *The Ancien Régime*, Eng. trans., London, 1973, pp. 42f.; E. R. Cregeen, 'Oral Tradition and Agrarian History in the West Highlands' in *Oral History*, 2, no.1. Recent studies by Alan Macfarlane, Peter Clark and Margaret Spufford suggest that there was considerable geographical mobility in Essex, Kent and Cambridgeshire in the sixteenth and seventeenth centuries; I assume that these areas were untypical because of their proximity to London. I. Opie/P. Opie, *The Lore and Language of Schoolchildren*, Oxford, 1959, p. 2.

36   Chambers (1933): Brody. For other examples of making ends meet, Davis (1975), pp. 104f. (on charivari in France), and Soriano, pp. 148f.

37   R. M. Dawkins, 'The Modern Carnival in Thrace' in *Journal of Hellenic Studies*, 6 (1906); for German plays, Keller.

38   M. Bloch, 'Pour une Histoire Comparée des Sociétés Européennes', trans. in his *Land and Work in Medieval Europe*, London, 1967; Nygard.

39   E. E. Evans-Pritchard, *Witchcraft Oracles and Magic among the Azande*, Oxford, 1937, an inspiration to Thomas (1971); M. Marwick, *Sorcery in its Social Setting*, Manchester, 1965.

40   On rites of reversal, M. Gluckman, *Customs and Conflict in Africa*, Oxford, 1956, and M. Marriott (Ch. 2, note 67); on the Berber house, Bourdieu (note 28 above).

41   Foster (1960): G. Balandier, *Daily Life in the Kingdom of the Kongo*, Eng. trans., London, 1968. Cf. N. Wachtel, *La Vision des Vaincus*, Paris, 1971, on Peru. Now available in English (*The Vision of the Vanquished*, Hassocks 1977)

4 The Transmission of Popular Culture

No references are given for information found in standard biographical dictionaries.

1   Schoof, pp. 62f.

2   C. von Sydow, *Selected Papers on Folklore*, Copenhagen, 1948, pp. 12–16.

3   Duchartre/Saulnier, pp. 44f., 88f.; Mistler (esp. the contribution by Blaudez).

4   On the Norwegian craftsmen, Anker, esp. Chs 6, 8; on the men of Dalarna, Svärdström (1949, 1957); I have benefited much from discussions with Peter Anker and Maj Nodermann on these points.

5   On blacksmiths, Hansen, pp. 18, 106, 118–19.

6   On minstrels, Salmen; in France, Petit de Julleville; in Spain, Menéndez Pidal (1924); in England, Fowler, pp. 96f.; in Hungary, Leader, Ch. 2; in Russia, Zguta.

7   V. Turner, *The Forest of Symbols*, Ithaca/London, 1967, esp. Chs 6, 10.

8   On charlatans, T. Garzoni, *La Piazza Universale*, Venice, 1585, Chs 103–4; their speeches imitated by Ben Jonson in *Volpone* (Act 2, scene 1).

9   On the *skomorokhi*, Zguta.

10   On English news-writers, Shaaber, Ch. 10; F. C. Brown, *Elkanah Settle*, 1910; on bards, T. Parry, *A History of Welsh Literature*, Oxford, 1955, pp. 133f., and D. S. Thomson (1974), Ch. 1.

11   Rosenfeld (1939), Ch. 1. P. Slack, 'Vagrants and Vagrancy in

England' in *Economic History Review*, 27 (1974), p. 364, notes a fortune-teller, a minstrel, a morris-dancer and two conjurors among the vagrants recorded at Salisbury in the early seventeenth century.

12   A. de Rojas, *El Viaje Entretenido* (1603), Madrid, 1901 edn, pp. 149f.; cf. A. D. Shergold, *A History of the Spanish Stage*, Oxford, 1967, Ch. 6.

13   On Languedoc, Le Roy Ladurie (1966) p. 130; on France, P. Coirault, *Formation de Nos Chansons Folkloriques*, 1, Paris, 1953, pp. 63f.; on Italy, Levi, pp. 6f., and Buttitta, pp. 149f.; on Serbia, Lord (cf. Cronia, introduction); on Russia, A. Rambaud, *La Russie Epique*, Paris, 1876, pp. 435f.; on Spain, Caro Baroja (1969), pp. 46f., 179f., and Varey, pp. 109f., 232f.; on Germany, Riedel.

14   Salmen, pp. 52, 55; E. Munhall, 'Savoyards in French Eighteenth-Century Art' in *Apollo*, 87 (1968), a reference I owe to Erica Langmuir; the quotation from H. Swinburne, *Travels in the Two Sicilies*, 1, London, 1783, p. 377.

15   Danckert, pp. 221f.

16   On beggars in England, Aydelotte, pp. 43f.; on France, J. P. Gutton, *La Société et les Pauvres*, Paris, 1971, pp. 184f.

17   On Palermo, L. Vigo (ed.), *Canti Popolari Siciliani*, Catania, 1857, pp. 56f.; C. E. Kany, *Life and Manners in Madrid 1750–1800*, Berkeley, 1932, pp. 62f.; Karadžić q. Wilson, pp. 24, 111.

18   D. O'Sullivan, *Carolan*, London, 1958.

19   On French schoolmasters, Vovelle (1975), p. 127; on Missus a Deo, A. Battistella, *Il S. Officio e la Riforma Religiosa in Bologna*, Bologna, 1905, p. 13.

20   Hefele, esp. pp. 19f.; on Caracciolo, Erasmus, *Opera*, V. Leiden, 1704 (repr. Hildesheim, 1962), cols 985–6; Maillard q. H. Lasswell/N. Leites, *Studies in Rhetoric*, New York, 1925, p. 4.

21   Diderot to Sophie Volland, 5 September 1762, in P. France (ed. trans.), *Diderot's Letters*, London, 1972, p. 119.

22   J. F. V. Nicholson, *Vavasor Powell*, London, 1961 (cf. Hill (1974), pp. 34f.); on England, esp. Bunyan, Tindall; on France, Bost (1921), pp. 16f.

23   On England, Chambers (1903); on the French 'Abbeys', Davis (1975), Ch. 4; on Spain, Very; on Florence, D'Ancona (1891), 1, pp. 400f.; on Siena, Mazzi; on Nuremberg, Sumberg.

24   On the Netherlands, Straeten.

25   On Meistergesang, A. Taylor (1937), and G. Strauss, *Nuremberg in the Sixteenth Century*, New York, 1966, pp. 264f.

26   Davis (1975), Ch. 4; Tilliot; H. G. Harvey.

27   On Mrs Brown, Buchan (1972), Ch. 7; on France, L. Petit de Julleville, *Les Mystères*, 1, repr. Geneva 1968, Ch. 9; on Italy, D'Ancona (1891) 1, pp. 258f.

28   Coirault, pp. 63f., discusses eight eighteenth-century *chanteurs*.

29   On Pèri, Lazzareschi; on Fullone, Pitrè (1872); on Croce, Guerrini.

30   On the shanachie, Jackson (1936); on Wales, T. G. Jones, p. 218; on Naples, J. J. Blunt, *Vestiges of Ancient Manners . . .*, London, 1823, p. 290; J. W. von Goethe, *Italienische Reise* (ed. H. von Einem, Hamburg, 1951), 3 October 1786.

31   O. Andersson, 'Folk-Musik', in S. Erixon/A. Campbell (eds), *Svensk Bygd och Folkkultur*, 1, Stockholm, 1946, pp. 108f.; Burdet, pp. 108f.; on Calabria, H. Swinburne, *Travels in the Two Sicilies*, 1, London, 1783, p. 114; on Scotland, Collinson, pp. 113f.; on Russia, H. M. Chadwick/N. Chadwick, *The Growth of Literature*, 3 vols, Cambridge, 1932–40, 2, pp. 286f.

32   On Böhm, Cohn (1957), pp. 226f.; on Bernardo, D. Weinstein, *Savonarola and Florence*, Princeton 1970, pp. 324f.; on Bandarra, D'Azevedo, pp. 7f.; cf. Manning, pp. 38f., on London c. 1640.

33   On England, Thomas (1971), Ch. 8, and Macfarlane, Ch. 8; on Sweden, Tillhagen (1962, 1969); on Spain, S. de Covarrubias, *Tesoro de la Lengua Castellana* (1611), repr. Barcelona, 1943, s. v. *Saludadores*, on Sicily, Blunt (note 30), p. 165; on France, F. Lebrun, *Les Hommes et la Mort en Anjou aux 17e et 18e Siecles*, Paris/The Hague, 1971, p. 405n.; on Lucerne, Schacher, pp. 98f.

34   On Northern Italy (Friuli), Ginzburg (1966), pp. 45f., 56f., 82f., 96, 151, 123f.; on Sweden, Tillhagen (1962, 1969).

35   On Ramírez, L. P. Harvey; on Fagerberg, Edsman; on folk healers today, A. Kiev, *Curanderismo*, New York/London, 1968, esp. Ch. 8.

36   Christie, p. 178.

37   On 'tale occasions', L. Dégh, *Folktales and Society*, Blooming-ton/London, 1969, Ch. 6; G. Massignon, *Contes Traditionnels des Teilleurs de Lin du Trégar*, Paris, 1965, introduction. N. Du Fail, *Propos Rustiques* (1547), Paris 1928 edn, Ch. 5.

38   The 'wakes' and 'church-ales' are best documented from the attempts to suppress them, on which see pp. 217 below.

39   On the cultural functions of the English inn, F. G. Emmison, *Elizabethan Life: Disorder*, Chelmsford, 1970, Ch. 18 (on Essex); E. K. Chambers, The Elizabethan Stage, 2, Oxford, 1923, pp. 379f. (on London); S. Rosenfeld (1960), p. 76 (on the Queen's Arms at Southwark); D. Lupton, *London and the County Carbonadoed* (1632), q. J. Thirsk/J. P. Cooper (eds), *Seventeenth-Century Economic Documents*, Oxford, 1972, p. 348 (on paintings); Spufford, pp. 231, 246 (on the godly at inns). (S. Rosenfeld (1960), p.76 (on the Queen's Arms at Southwark).

40   On Poland, J. Burszta, *Wieś i Karczma*, Warsaw, 1950, a reference for which I am grateful to Keith Wrightson; on the French *cabaretier*, Bercé (1974a), pp. 297f.; on innkeepers and the peasants'

war, E. B. Bax, *The Peasant War in Germany*, London, 1899, pp. 77, 111, 113, 116 (cf. below, p.268 for the role of innkeeper Franz Haas of Graz in the riots of 1790).

41　G. F. Lussky, 'The Structure of Hans Sachs' *Fastnachtspiele*' in *Journal of English and Germanic Philology*, 26 (1927); on dancing in Swiss taverns, Burdet, pp. 65f.; on France, A. P. Moore, *The Genre Poissard and the French Stage of the Eighteenth Century*, New York, 1935, pp. 284f.; *Don Quixote*, 2, Chs 25–6 (cf. Varey, pp. 232f.); Machiavelli to Vettori, 10 December 1513.

42　On piazza S. Marco, a vivid description in T. Coryate, *Crudities*, 1, Glasgow 1905 edn, pp. 409f. (Coryate was there in 1608); on the Pont-Neuf, F. Boucher, *Le Pont-Neuf*, 2, Paris, 1926, pp. 149f.

43　Cf. P. Bohannan/G. Dalton (eds), *Markets in Africa*, Evanston, 1962, pp. 15f.

44　N. Staf, *Marknad och Möte*, Stockholm, 1935; E. Mentzel, *Geschichte der Schauspielkunst in Frankfurt*, Frankfurt, 1882, pp. 48f.

45　Brockett; M. Lister, *A Journey to Paris*, London, 1699, pp. 175f.

46　C. Walford, *Fairs Past and Present*, London, 1883; H. Morley, *Memoirs of Bartholomew Fair*, London, 1859; S. Rosenfeld (1960); on the godly at fairs, Spufford, p. 261.

47　On individuality in oral tradition, Lord, pp. 63f., and M. Azadovsky, *Eine Sibirische Märchenerzählerin*, Helsinki, 1926.

48　On Tarleton, Bradbrook; on Carolan, O'Sullivan (note 18), pp. 74f.; on the Sicilian *sfida*, Pitrè (1872), pp. 109f.

49　P. Barry in M. Leach/T. Coffin (eds), *The Critics and the Ballad*, Carbondale, 1961.

50　'Otmar', *Volkssagen*, Bremen, 1800, pp. 42f.; M. Panić-Surep, *Filip Višnjić*, Belgrade, 1956 (in Serbo-Croat); on Fiorillo, Lea, pp.91, 93; on Stranitzky, Rommel, pp. 206f.; the Scots examples from Collinson, pp. 208f.; on the visual arts, Svärdström (1949), p. 12 and Hauglid, p. 17.

51　Vuk q. Wilson, p. 396.

52　Sharp, pp. 13f.; on 'preventive censorship', Jakobson/Bogatyrev.

5 Traditional Forms

1　On the dance, see esp. Guilcher, Louis, Sachs, and the various national folk-music articles in *Grove's*.

2　A. Fortis, *Viaggio in Dalmazia*, 1, Venice, 1774, pp. 93f.

3　On sword-dances, Louis, pp. 275f.

4　Sachs, pp. 367, 99.

5　This eighteenth-century text in L. W. Forster (ed.), *Penguin Book of German Verse*, Harmondsworth, 1957, p. 56.

6　Cronia, p. 114.

7　Menéndez Pidal (1938), p. 44.

8   *Io son lo Gran Capitano della Morte*: sixteenth-century Italian chap-book in British Library, C.57.i.7.(36).
9   Child 117; S. Tinódi, *Cronica* (1554), repr. Budapest 1881; Cristoforo 'Altissimo', *I Reali di Francia*, Venice, 1534.
10   F. Flamini, *La Lirica Toscana del Rinascimento*, Pisa, 1891, p. 72.
11   F. G. Emmison, *Elizabethan Life: Disorder*, Chelmsford, 1970, Ch. 4.
12   Forster (note 5), p. 76.
13   On the idea of the 'game', Kolve, pp. 12f.
14   For Italian examples, see the volume cited in note 8; for French, Viollet-le-Duc, nos 49, 62; for German, H. Sachs, *Werke,* 2 vols, Weimar, 1960, 1, pp. 323f., 368f.
15   The Italian term for all three kinds of play was simply *rappresentazioni sacre*, 'sacred shows'.
16   *Saint Hareng*, repr. Paris 1830 (cf. Viollet-le-Duc nos 23, 37); Haberdyne's sermon in Salgãdo, pp. 381f.
17   Kuiper, no. 239; on the genre, Werner, Mehring.
18   On this genre, García de Diego.
19   Coupe, p. 126; George, p. 85; Ovsyannikov (1968), plate 31.
20   Coupe, pp. 214f.; C. Lévi-Strauss, *La Pensée Sauvage*, Paris, 1962, p. 26.
21   On the relation between genre and meaning, E. D. Hirsch, jr, *Validity in Interpretation*, New Haven/London, 1967.
22   Kodály, q. Szabolcsi, p. 173.
23   On wandering, W. Tappert, *Wandernde Melodien* (1865), 2nd edn, Leipzig, 1890; on stereotyping of variations, Collinson, pp. 174f.
24   H. Swinburne, *Travels in the Two Sicilies*, 1, London, 1783, p. 379.
25   Elschek.
26   H. Mackenzie (ed.), *Report of the Committee . . . appointed to inquire into the . . . Authenticity of . . . Ossian*, Edinburgh, 1805, p. 19.
27   Scott 1, p. 8; *Scottish Tragic Ballads* (published anonymously), London, 1781, p. xx; J. H. Jones.
28   Ortutay (1968), p. 125; cf. Motif-Index E.631.0.1., 'twining branches grow from graves of lovers'.
29   Webber, appendix 2.
30   C. Lévi-Strauss, *Mythologiques*, 4 vols, Paris, 1964–70.
31   Lord, p. 4.
32   Daur, *passim*.
33   Bolte/Polívka, 1, pp. 165f.; P. Delarue, M. L. Tenèze (ed), *Le Conte Populaire Français*, 2, Paris, 1964, pp. 245f.
34   G. F. Straparola, *Le Piacevoli Notti*, 2 vols, Venice, 1550–55; J.

308 *Popular Culture in Early Modern Europe*

Timoneda, *El Sobremesa y Alivio de Caminantes*, Valencia, 1564 (cf.
J. W. Childers, *Motif-Index of the Cuentos of Juan Timoneda*,
Bloomington, 1948).
35 Propp, pp. 31f.; Motif-Index, *passim*.
36 The helper: Straparola (note 34), 3.1, 3.2, 3.3, 4.3, 5.1, 7.5, 11.1;
the test: Straparola, 3.2, 3.4, 5.1, 10.3.
37 Bolte, 1, pp. 165f.
38 J. U. Surgant, *Manuale Curatorum* (1503 edn, s.1.), Part 1,
Ch. 16; J. Aubrey, *Brief Lives*, Oxford, 1898, 'Charles Cavendish';
W. Nicholls, *A Defence of the Doctrine and Discipline of the Church
of England*, Eng. trans., London, 1725, Part 2, Ch. 14; B. A.
Rosenberg, *The Art of the American Folk Preacher*, New York, 1970,
pp. 48, 53f.
39 Surgant (note 38), Part 1, Ch. 8; *Sermones Dormi Secure*,
Rutlingen, 1484 (there are 25 editions by 1520 in the British Library
alone).
40 On the card, Rosenberg (note 38), pp. 29, 91–3, and G. R. Owst,
Literature and Pulpit in Medieval England, 2nd edn, Oxford, 1961,
p. 99; a criticism of extended metaphors in sermons in J. Eachard,
Works, 11th edn, London, 1705, pp. 38f.
41 E. C. Cawte, A. Helm, and N. Peacock, *English Ritual Drama*,
London, 1967; Sokolov, pp. 499f.; Rael, Ch. 1.
42 F. Andreini, *Le Bravure del Capitano Spavento*, Venice, 1607; cf.
Spezzani.
43 On *lazzi*, Petraccone, pp. 63f., 191f., 263f.
44 O. Szentpál, 'Formanalyse der ungarische Volkstänze', in *Acta
Ethnographica*, 7 (1958); *Grove's*, article 'Folk Music: Czech'.
45 G. E. Lessing, *Laokoön*, 1766.
46 Amades (1947), 2, p. 150.
47 On the battle-scene, Landsverk; a reference I owe to the kindness
of Marta Hoffmann.
48 Olrik (1908); Shklovsky q. Oinas/Soudakoff, p. 156.
49 Luther used the term 'antithesis' for the *Passional* in a letter of 7
March 1521; cf. Coupe, pp. 204f., and G. Fleming, 'On the Origin of
the *Passional Christi und Antichristi*' in *Gutenberg Jahrbuch* (1973).
50 George, pp. 4, 25; Kunzle, p. 3.
51 Buchan (1972), pp. 88f., Olrik (1908), pp. 135f.
52 Contrast, for example, Clemet Håkansson's Three Magi (now in
Nordiska Museet, Stockholm) with that of Gentile da Fabriano (now
in the Uffizi, Florence).
53 P. Bénichou, *Romancéro Judeo-Español de Marruecos*, Madrid,
1968, p. 111.
54 This variant of the ballad in J. M. Serrat's record, *Chansons
Traditionnelles* (sung in Catalan), coll. 'Le Chant du Monde', LDX
74491.

55 Propp; Lévi-Strauss (note 30); cf. A. Dundes, *The Morphology of North American Indian Folktales*, Helsinki, 1964; Schenda (1965–6); and T. Todorov, *Grammaire du Décaméron*, The Hague/Paris, 1969.

56 D'Ancona (1872) contains 43 plays of which 8 deal with saintly women, of which 6 take this form; Viollet-le-Duc contains 64 plays of which 24 centre on married couples.

57 F. Scala, *Il Teatro delle Favole Rappresentative*, Venice, 1611, no. 1.

58 Buchan (1972), p. 121.

59 Lord, p. 36.

60 Lord, p. 78; cf. Gesemann (1926), pp. 65f.

61 A. Fortis, *Viaggio in Dalmazia*, 1, Venice, 1774, p. 92; M. Martin, *A Description of the Western Islands of Scotland* (1703), ed. D. J. Macleod, Stirling, 1934, p. 95; Mackenzie (note 26), p. 148; T. Pennant, *A Tour in Wales*, 2, London, 1781, p. 92; R. Steffen (ed.), *Norska Stev*, Oslo, 1899.

62 M. de Montaigne, *Journal de Voyage en Italie*, Paris 1955 edn, p. 175; Pitrè (1872), pp. 109f.

63 'Altissimo' (note 9); on the *commedia*, Nicoll, pp. 24f., Petraccone, pp. 52f., 69f.; on Asia today, J. R. Brandon, *Theatre in Southeast Asia*, Cambridge, Mass., 1967, Ch. 7; J. L. Peacock, *Rites of Modernisation*, Chicago/London, 1968, pp. 61f. T. Coryat, *Crudities*, Glasgow 1905 edn, 1, pp. 409f.

64 Nicholls (note 38), p. 333; J. Bunyan, *Works*, 1, London, 1692, the preface by E. Chandler and J. Wilson; cf. Tindall, Ch. 8, and J. Downey, *The Eighteenth-Century Pulpit*, Oxford, 1969, pp. 164f. On Mrs Brown, Buchan (1972), Ch. 7.

65 L. P. Harvey.

66 Rosenberg (note 38), pp. 55f.; on a nineteenth-century storyteller, Pitrè (1889), 1, p. 203.

67 Karadžić q. Wilson, p. 169; Román q. L. P. Harvey, p. 96; F. Yates, *The Art of Memory*, London, 1966; an example of the use of this art by an Italian singer in 1435 in O. Bacci, *Prosa e Prosatori*, Milan, n.d. (*c.* 1907), pp. 99f.

68 The quotation, from Perrucci (1699), in Petraccone, p. 94; on the concept 'improvisation', Astakhova; I have also benefited from discussions with Ruth Finnegan on this point.

69 On the British ballad, J. H. Jones; Friedman (1961b); and Buchan (1972), Ch. 7. For a similar controversy about Spanish ballads, Webber; Beattie; and Norton/Wilson, pp. 55f. On Sweden, and Ingierd Gunnarsdotter, Jonsson, pp. 278f. (cf. A. Noreen (ed.), *K. Bibliotekets Visbok i 4:o*, Uppsala, 1915, nos 42, 46, 51). On the lack of distinction between memorisation and creation in France, Coirault, pp. 621f.

70 Gesemann (1926), p. 96.

310   *Popular Culture in Early Modern Europe*

71 T. Coffin in M. Leach/T. Coffin (eds), *The Critics and the Ballad*, Carbondale, 1961, p. 247; G. Allport/L. Postman, 'The Basic Psychology of Rumour' in W. schramm (ed.), *Mass Communications*, 2nd edn, Urbana, 1960.
72 A. Warburg, *Gesammelte Schriften*, 2 vols, Leipzig/Berlin, 1932 (see index, 'Antike: Bildmotive'); E. R. Curtius, *European Literature and the Latin Middle Ages*, Eng. trans., New York, 1953; E. H. Gombrich, *Art and Illusion*, London, 1960, esp. Chs 2 and 5.
73 W. J. Ong, 'Oral Residue in Tudor Prose Style' in *Proceedings of the Modern Language Association*, 80 (1965).
74 Wolf/Hofmann, numbers 5a and 98 and p. 327; A. Rambaud, *La Russie Epique*, Paris, 1876, p. 292.
75 F. Fleuret (ed.), *Cartouche et Mandrin*, Paris, 1932, plates ii, vi.

6 Heroes, Villains and Fools

1 O. E. Klapp, *Heroes, Villains and Fools: the changing American Character*, Englewood Cliffs, 1962, p. 17.
2 On St Martin, Jürgensen; on St Nicholas, Meisen (1931); on Bevis, Greve; on the Turks, P. Belon, *Observations*, Paris, 1553, Book 3, Ch. 42, and C. de Bruin, *Reizen*, Delft, 1668, p. 125.
3 On the saints, H. Delehaye, *Les Légendes Hagiographiques*, Brussels, 1905; on Alexander, G. Cary, *The Medieval Alexander*, Cambridge, 1956.
4 M. Luther, *Works*, 53, ed. U. S. Leupold, Philadelphia, 1965, pp. 214f.; J. Crespin, *Histoire des Martyrs*, 3 vols, Toulouse, 1885–9; W. Haller, *Foxe's Book of Martyrs and the Elect Nation*, London, 1963, esp. Ch. 4; for Sacheverell, below, p.264.
5 Quotations from broadside ballads in the British Library, C.40.m.10(172) and C.22.f.6(168).
6 Ditfurth (1869), no. 24 (cf. nos 10, 12, etc.); on the king as conqueror and judge, P. Goubert, *L'Ancien Régime*, 2, Paris, 1973, pp. 27f.
7 Bercé (1974a), pp. 391, 492, 608, 636; P. Goubert/M. Denis (eds), *1789: Les Français ont la Parole*, Paris, 1964, pp. 41–2, 48, 204, 217; on Henri IV, Reinhard.
8 On Maximilian, Waas, pp. 89, 136–7, 150; on Mátyás, Komorovský, pp. 69f.; on Olav, Bø, Ch. 6.
9 On James V, Percy, 2, p. 67; Dr David Stevenson of the University of Aberdeen informs me that in the seventeenth century the phrase 'the gudeman of Ballengight' was a cryptic way of referring to the King of Scotland. The story about Ivan from S. Collins, *The Present State of Russia*, London, 1671, pp. 52f. I have not seen A. Veselovsky, *Skazki ob Ivane Groznom*, Leningrad, 1938.
10 On the battle of Frankenhausen, Eberhardt, pp. 97f.; on the

Russian 'true tsar', J. Billington, *The Icon and the Axe,* New York, 1966, pp. 198f.
11 On Philip II as Pharaoh, Kuiper, no. 145; on Henri II, Bordier, p. 209; on Henri III as Herod, Blum, pp. 250f.; on Tsar Maximilian, Sokolov, pp. 499f., and Billington (note 10), pp. 97, 665.
12 On Louis XIII, Porchnev, pp. 135f., 279; on Louis XIV, F. Gaiffe, *L'Envers du Grand Siècle,* Paris, 1924, p. 12, and Bercé (1974a), p. 609; on Henry VIII, M. H. Dodds/R. Dodds, *The Pilgrimage of Grace,* 1, Cambridge, 1915, p. 69; on George II, Wearmouth, p. 24; on George III, George, Ch. 7.
13 Bercé (1974a), pp. 300f.; cf. Koht (1926), Ch. 12, on Norway, and A. Giraffi, *Le Rivolutioni di Napoli,* Venice, 1647, pp. 16, 19, on Naples.
14 Norwegian examples in Koht (1926), pp. 226f., and Anker, p. 209.
15 For pictures of these incidents, L. Réau, *Iconographie de l'Art Chrétien,* Vol. 3, 3 parts, Paris 1958–9, under the relevant saints.
16 I. Meiners, *Schelm und Dümmling in Erzählungen des Deutschen Mittelalters,* Munich, 1967; G. Folena (ed.), *Motti e Facezie del Piovano Arlotto,* Milan, 1953.
17 On Staffordshire pottery, C. Lambert and E. Marx, *English Popular Art,* London, 1951, p. 75; on Russian statuettes, Ovsyannikov (1970), pp. 31, 33; for French farces. Viollet-le-Duc, nos 18–22, 24, 26, 32; for Italian stories, Rotunda, K.1354.2.2, K.2111.3, Q.424.3; cf. Koht (1926), Ch. 10 and pp. 251f., on Norway.
18 On Marko, Karadžić, q. Djurić, p. 315; on Orlando, G. Lippomano in 1577, q. D'Ancona (1913), p. 35.
19 R. Johnson, *The Seven Champions of Christendom,* London, 1596 (a work which went through at least twenty-six editions by 1770).
20 Ditfurth (1874), nos 6, 8, 13–15; 'Larwood and Hotten', *The History of Signboards,* London, 1866, pp. 54f.; on Vernon, Perceval, nos 54, 68–9.
21 The quotation from Fél/Hofer, p. 367; for a hussar on a broadside, Arnim/Brentano, pp. 253f.; for examples of soldiers in art, Hauglid, p. 48, Uldall, fig. 21; discussion in A. Corvisier, *L'Armée Française,* Paris, 1964, pp. 98f.
22 D. Boughner, *The Braggart in Renaissance Comedy,* Minneapolis, 1954, esp. Ch. 1; for the Italian tales, Rotunda, T.72, U.34; on 1525, Zins, p. 186; on Mecklenburg, Wossidlo.
23 'I eat all', in W. Brückner (ed.), *Populäre Druckgraphik Europas,* Munich, 1969, fig. 104; A. Taylor (1921); Motif-Index, X.310–19; Guershoon, nos 40, 132; Hill (1972), index under 'lawyers'.
24 Mousnier, pp. 115f.; Bercé (1974a), pp. 484, 625f.; cf. the Norwegian evidence in Koht (1926), pp. 167f., 238f.

25   The usurer in H. E. Rollins, *A Pepysian Garland,* Cambridge, 1922, no. 5; Mompesson in George, p. 12; on eighteenth-century France and England, Cobb, pp. 246f., Rudé (1964), Chs 1, 7, and E. P. Thompson (1971, 1975); on Wales, T. Parry, *A History of Welsh Literature,* Oxford, 1955, pp. 267f.
26   Motif-Index X.372; Chambers (1933), index under 'doctor'; Keller, nos 6, 48, 82, 85, etc.; D'Ancona (1891), 1, p. 578.
27   On the entrepreneur, T. Deloney, *Jack of Newbury,* London, 1596 (at least fifteen editions by the end of the seventeenth century); T. Deloney, *The Gentle Craft,* London, 1597 (more than twenty editions by the end of the eighteenth century); H. B. Wheatley (ed.), *The History of Dick Whittington,* London, 1885, introduction; D. Piper, 'Dick Whittington and the Middle-Class Dream of Success', in R. Browne/M. Fishwick, *Heroes of Popular Culture,* Bowling Green, 1972.
28   E. Gordon Duff (ed.), *The Dialogue . . . between the Wise King Solomon and Marcolphus,* London, 1892; A. Zenatti (ed.), *Storia di Campriano Contadino,* Bologna, 1884.
29   'Champfleury', *De La Littérature Populaire en France,* Paris, 1861: there are fourteen known editions of this tale before 1800. For *Bonde Lyckan,* painted on a board in an eighteenth-century Norwegian cottage (now in Oslo, Norsk Folkemuseum no. 81), Landsverk, p. 52, and Koht (1926), pp. 261f.
30   D. Merlini, *Saggio di Ricerche sulla Satira contra il Villano,* Turin, 1894; *Rappresentazione di Biagio Contadino,* Florence, 1558; H. Sachs, *Heinz in Nürnberg; Frottola d'un Villan dal Bonden che se voleva far Cittadin in Ferrara,* (Venice, no date but sixteenth century).
31   On the saints, Réau (note 15); a play on Susanna in Keller, no. 129, and ballads in Noreen/Schück; a Danish chap-book on Griselda went through at least thirteen editions, 1528–1799.
32   On women as witches, Thomas (1971), pp. 568f., Midelfort, pp. 182f., Monter, pp. 118f.; on their deceitfulness, Motif-Index f.585.1, K.443.9 (cf. *Le Malizie delle Donne,* Venice, c. 1520, and other works in that genre).
33   Hobsbawm (1959, 1969) are the classic studies of outlaws in English; cf. Domokos, Eeckaute, Fuster, and Y. Castellan, *La Culture Serbe au Seuil de l'Indépendance,* Paris, 1967, pp. 125f.
34   On Pugachev, Avrich, Ch. 4, and Pascal (1971); on Jánošik, Melicherčík; on Diego Corrientes, Caro Baroja (1969), Ch. 17, and C. Bernaldo de Quiros/L. Ardila, *El Bandolerismo,* Madrid, 1931; on Angiolillo, B. Croce, *La Rivoluzione Napoletana del 1799,* Bari, 1912, appendix; on Kidd, Bonner.
35   On Rob Roy, *The Highland Rogue,* London, 1743, pp. 20f.; on Turpin, *The Genuine History of the Life of Richard Turpin,* London, 1739; on Diego Corrientes, Caro Baroja (1969), p. 368; on Angiolillo,

Croce (note 34).

36   The chap-book on Ianot Poch in British Library, 11450.e.25 (3); on Kidd, Bonner, pp. 86f.; on unfavourable popular attitudes to outlaws, A. Blok, 'The Peasant and the Brigand', in *Comparative Studies in Society and History*, 14 (1972).

37   R. Schwoebel, *The Shadow of the Crescent*, Nieuwkoop, 1967, pp. 19f., 166f., 213; Hartmann, 2, nos 110-114; J. Caro Baroja, *Los Moriscos del Reino de Granada*, Madrid, 1957, pp. 131f., 176; J. G. Wilkinson, *Dalmatia and Montenegro*, London, 1848, p. 337.

38   J. Trachtenberg, *The Devil and the Jews*, New Haven, 1943; C. Schwoebel, *La Légende du Juif Errant*, Paris, 1877; Coupe, p. 132; V. Newall, 'The Jew as a Witch Figure' in V. Newall, (ed.), *The Witch Figure*, London/Boston, 1973; Liliencron, nos 439-443; on Judas, *The Lost and Undone Son of Perdition*, Wotton-under-Edge, n.d. (cf. Bollème (1971), p. 224).

39   Trevor-Roper; Cohn (1975), p. 259, discusses projection; on Baba Yaga, Ralston, pp. 161f.; on French Protestants, J. Estèbe, *Tocsin pour un Massacre*, Paris, 1968, pp. 190f., and Davis (1975), Ch. 6; on English Catholics, C. Wiener, 'The Beleaguered Isle' in *P&P*, 51 (1971), and R. Clifton, 'The Popular Fear of Catholics during the English Revolution' in *P&P*, 52 (1971); T. Adorno *et al.*, *The Authoritarian Personality*, New York, 1950.

40   On Charles V and Henri IV in folktales, Bercé (1976), pp. 36, 62, and Bercé (1974a), p. 608.

41   For the term 'crystallisation', Schmidt (1963), pp. 306f.; cf. K. L. Steckmesser, 'Robin Hood and the American Outlaw', in *Journal of American Folklore*, 79 (1966).

42   On Ratsey (executed 1605), S. H. Atkins (ed.), *The Life and Death of Gamaliel Ratsey*, London, 1935, introduction; on Whittington, note 27 above.

43   E. M. Butler, *The Fortunes of Faust*, Cambridge, 1952, pp. 7f.; C. Dédéyan, *Le Thème de Faust dans la Littérature Européenne*, 1, Paris, 1954.

44   M. Bloch, *The Royal Touch*, Eng. trans., London, 1973; for King Olav, Bø, Ch. 4.

45   On Razin, Avrich, p. 121; I have not seen A. N. Lozonova, *Narodnye Pesni o Stepane Razine*, Saratov, 1928.

46   On St Peter, Martin of Arles, *De Superstitionibus*, Paris 1517 edn; on St George, Ferté, p. 340; cf. T. Naogeorgus, *Regnum Papisticum*, 1553, p. 156, on ducking St Urban; on St Christopher, Amades (1952), p. 22.

47   On the plague, Wilson, p. 22, following Karadžić; for the inscription *Crédit est Mort* in an inn at Lyons, T. Coryat, *Crudities* (1611), Glasgow 1905 edn, 1, p. 213.

48   Ardener (Ch. 2, note 57).

49　Pastor F. J. Wille, q. Koht (1926), p. 52; Amades (1950–1), p. 1135.
50　Strobach, nos 1–3, 16–19; Coupe, p. 144; *Pericles*, Act 2, scene 1.
51　Lüthi (1970), pp. 11f.; Guershoon, nos 88, 1143; Jente, nos 72, 353.
52　Hobsbawm (1959), p. 24; contrast Meličerčik and other East European scholars who present outlaws as rebels against 'feudalism'.
53　Franz (1933), pp. 157ff.; Mousnier, p. 117; Thompson (1971); Bø, Ch. 6.
54　On 1525, Blickle, pp. 127f., 135f., 186f.; on Gaismair, F. Seibt, *Utopica*, Düsseldorf, 1972, pp. 82f.; Gaismair's plan printed in Franz (1963), pp. 285f.; 'When Adam delved' as slogan in Germany in 1525, Zins, p. 186.
55　Böhm and Bockelson q. Cohn (1957), pp. 228, 265; Seibt (note 53), pp. 182f.; on fatalism, cf. Kaplow, p. 166, comparing poor Parisians of the eighteenth century with the 'culture of poverty' described by the anthropologist Oscar Lewis.
56　On Essex, Samaha, p. 73; on class consciousness (and the lack of it), Hobsbawm (1971), p. 9; on 'limited good', Foster (1965); on witches, below, p. 274; on the Vivarais, Le Roy Ladurie (1966), pp. 607f.
57　On Turkish villagers, D. Lerner, *The Passing of Traditional Society*, Glencoe, 1958, p. 132; the proverb in Guershoon, no. 149.
58　On material insecurity, Galarneau, and Thomas (1971), pp. 5f.; G. Correas, *Vocabulario de Refranes*, Madrid 1924 edn, pp. 44, 300; Jente, no. 42; on the fourteen helpers, Schreiber (1959).

7 The World of Carnival

1　A. Fortis, *Viaggio in Dalmazia*, 1, Venice, 1774, p. 57.
2　H. Swinburne, *Travels in the Two Sicilies*, 1, London, 1783, p. 67.
3　Bringéus, *Arbete och Redskap*, Lund, 1973, pp. 250f., 265, 287.
4　R. Caillois, *L'Homme et le Sacré*, Paris 1963 edn, p. 125; T. Gray, *Correspondence*, ed. P. Toynbee/L. Whibley, 1, Oxford, 1935, p. 127. (Gray had not in fact passed a year in Turin.)
5　On Prato, R. Dallington, *A Survey of Tuscany*, London, 1605, p. 16; on Barcelona, J. Townsend, *A Journey Through Spain*, 1, London, 1791, pp. 106f.; on Provence, C. de Ribbe, *La Société Provençale à la Fin du Moyen Age*, Paris, 1898, pp. 165f.
6　For contrasted definitions, E. R. Leach, 'Ritual' in D. Sills (ed.), *International Encyclopaedia of the Social Sciences*, 13, New York, 1968, pp. 521f. The Scots singer in Mackenzie (Ch. 1, note 39), p. 54.
7　Chambers (1903), 1, pp. 174f.; on May (not Robin), cf. J. Frazer, *The Magic Art*, 2, London, 1911, pp. 52f.

8 On St John, Lanternari; on wild men, Bernheimer.
9 C. Kluckhohn, 'Myths and Rituals' in *Harvard Theological Review*, 35 (1942); G. S. Kirk, *Myth*, Cambridge, 1970, Ch. 1; on the pig, Gaignebet (1974), pp. 57f.; on the goose, Arnim/Brentano, p. 608.
10 'no sharp distinction': cf. Bakhtin, pp. 7f.
11 J. Taylor, 'Jack a Lent' in his *Works*, London, 1630, p. 115; S. Collins, *The Present State of Russia*, London, 1671, p. 22.
12 S. Slive, *Frans Hals*, 1, London, 1970, p. 37; he does not say how he acquired this information.
13 J. W. von Goethe, *Italienische Reise*, ed. H. von Einem, Hamburg, 1951, p. 492; Townsend (note 5), pp. 39f.
14 R. Lassels, *The Voyage of Italy*, Paris, 1670, p. 195.
15 H. Swinburne, *Travels through Spain*, London, 1779, p. 228.
16 Caro Baroja (1965), pp. 53f., 83f.
17 Davis (1975), pp. 114f.; Sumberg, p. 59.
18 Sumberg, *passim*; Singleton; C. Noirot, *L'Origine des Masques* (1609), repr. in Leber, pp. 50f.; cf. Vaultier (1946), pp. 60f.
19 On Rome, Clementi; on Lille, Cottignies, no. 40; on Britain, F. P. Magoun, *History of Football*, Bochum, 1938, Ch. 9; on France, Vaultier (1965), pp. 45f.; C. M. Ady, *The Bentivoglio of Bologna*, London, 1937, p. 172.
20 On mock sieges, Pitrè (1889), 1, pp. 23f.; on mock lawsuits, H. G. Harvey, pp. 19f., and Vaultier (1946), pp. 68, 75; on mock sermons, Caro Baroja (1965), p. 35; on mock ploughings, Keller, no. 30, Coupe, p. 176; on mock weddings, Caro Baroja (1965), pp. 90f.
21 For mock battles, Gaignebet (1972); Toschi (1955), on Bologna; on Venice, B. T. Mazzarotto, *Le Feste Veneziane*, Florence, 1961, pp. 31f.; on Madrid, Caro Baroja (1965), p. 110.
22 For two brilliant but questionable attempts to interpret Carnival, Bakhtin (esp. pp. 197f.) and Gaignebet (1974).
23 The Koenigsberg sausage in Bakhtin, p. 184n.; on conceptions, J. Dupâquier's table in J. Le Goff/P. Nora (eds), *Faire de l'Histoire*, 2, Paris, 1974, p. 86 (but he does not take the movable feast of Carnival into his calculations). The song from A. F. Grazzini, *Rime Burlesche*, ed. C. Verzone, Florence, 1882, pp. 164f.; the phallus mentioned by I. Fuidoro, *Giornali di Napoli*, 1, Naples, 1934, p. 209.
24 Caro Baroja (1966), p. 84.
25 On Venice, Dallington (note 5), p. 65; on London, Taylor (note 11); on Seville, Blanco White, *Letters from Spain*, 2nd edn, London, 1822, p. 237.
26 O. Odenius, 'Mundus Inversus' in *Arv*, 10 (1954), is a useful guide to the rich literature on the subject; cf. Cocchiara (1963) and Grant.
27 Hill (1972), p. 186.

28   On Heilbronn, H. W. Bensen, *Geschichte des Bauernkriegs in Ostfranken*, Erlangen, 1840, p. 158, a reference for which I am grateful to Henry Cohn of the University of Warwick; on Norfolk, Hill, 'Many-headed monster' (1965), repr. in Hill (1974); on the Vivarais, Le Roy Ladurie (1966), pp. 607f.

29   On Cockaigne, Cocchiara (1956) and (for Hungary), Tassy; the French text in Cottignies, no. 55. I have not seen E. M. Ackermann, *Schlaraffenland*, Chicago, 1944.

30   I. Donaldson, *The World Upside Down: Comedy from Jonson to Fielding*, Oxford, 1970.

31   G. B. Spagnuoli, 'Mantuanus', *Fasti*, Strasbourg, 1518, Book 2.

32   Sumberg, pp. 159, 162, and fig. 45.

33   For fertility (besides Wilhelm Mannhardt and Sir James Frazer) are Rudwin (1920), Toschi (1955), pp. 166f.; against are van Gennep, von Sydow (Chapter 4, note 2), Caro Baroja (1965).

34   The quotations from Tilliot, p. 29, and J. Chandos, *In God's Name*, London, 1971, pp. 39f. Cf. Chambers (1903), 1, pp. 274f., and Kolve, pp. 135.

35   On the twelve days of Christmas in England, H. Bourne, *Antiquitates Vulgares*, Newcastle, 1725, pp. 147f.; on the riding of Yule, A. G. Dickens, 'Tudor York', in P. M. Tillott, (ed.), *Victoria County History: the City of York*, London, 1961, p. 152; on *La Befana*, Pola, p. 87.

36   On Russia, G. Fletcher, *Of the Russe Commonwealth* (1591), ed. A. J. Schmidt, Ithaca, 1966, p. 142, and A. Olearius, *Travels* (1647), Eng. trans., Stanford, 1967, p. 241; on Spain, Caro Baroja (1965), pp. 139f.

37   On Hock Tuesday at Coventry, Phythian Adams (1972), pp. 66f.; on May games, Chambers (1903), 1, pp. 174f., and P. Stubbes, *Anatomy of Abuses*, London, 1583, pp. 94f.; on London, P. J. Grosley, *Londres*, Lausanne, 1770, p. 321; on Italy, Pola, 3, pp. 334f., 431f., and Toschi (1955), pp. 16f., 44f.; Covarrubias q. Palencia/Mele, p. 45.

38   On England, Kolve; on Spain, Very, and Varey/Shergold.

39   E. Jolibois, *La Diablerie de Chaumont*, Chaumont, 1838; on Florence, Guasti; on Estonia, Baltasar Russow, q. I. Paulson, *The Old Estonian Folk Religion*, The Hague, 1971, pp. 103f.; cf. Kohler, pp. 130f., on Germany.

40   Lewis Morris, q. T. G. Jones, p. 155; J. Houel, *Voyage Pittoresque*, 4 vols, Paris, 1782–7, 3, p. 17: Bourne (note 35), p. 229.

41   On Bologna, L. Frati, *La Vita Privata di Bologna dal Secolo 13 al 17*, Bologna, 1900, pp. 161f.; on London, H. Morley, *Memoirs of Bartholomew Fair*, London, 1885; on St Martin's day, Jürgensen, Kohler, pp. 141f., Schotel (1868), and at Groningen, E. H. Waterbolk, 'Deux Poèmes Inconnus de Rodolphe Agricola' in

Humanistica Lovaniensia (1972), p. 47. (I am grateful to Prof. Waterbolk for sending me a copy of this article.)

42 J. Boswell, *Life of Johnson*, ed. G. B. Hill/L. F. Powell, 4, Oxford, 1934, p. 188; on Savonarola, L. Landucci, *Diario*, Florence, 1883, pp. 176f.; 'backwards on an ass', F. Platter, *Beloved Son Felix*, Eng. trans., London, 1961, p. 121.

43 On the unofficial rituals of execution, P. Linebaugh, 'The Tyburn Riot' in Hay, pp. 66f., and M. Foucault, *Surveiller et Punir*, Paris, 1975, pp. 61f.; J. R. Moore, *Defoe in the Pillory*, New York 1973 edn, pp. 3f.

44 The definition is that of R. Cotgrave, *A Dictionary of the French and English Tongues*, London, 1611. Recent studies of charivari include Pinon; Davis (1975), Ch. 4, on France; E. P. Thompson (1972), on England. On the tax-collector, Bercé (1974a), p. 180.

45 C. Haton, *Mémoires*, 2, Paris, 1857, p. 722; cf. Heers (1971).

46 Bennassar, p. 124, with a good discussion of the functions of festivals.

47 Hay, p. 62n., objects to the concept 'social control'; on Palermo, A. Pocili, *Delle Rivoluzioni della Città di Palermo*, Verona, 1648, p. 16.

48 M. Gluckman, 'Rituals of Rebellion in South-East Africa' repr. in his *Order and Rebellion in Tribal Africa*, London, 1963; M. Gluckman, *Custom and Conflict in Africa*, Oxford, 1956, Ch. 5; V. Turner, *The Ritual Process*, London, 1969, Ch. 5.

49 The *Oxford English Dictionary*, article 'safety-valve', notes that William Hone used this metaphor about popular festivals in 1825; the 1444 text (to which attention was drawn by Bakhtin) tr. from H. Denifle (ed.), *Chartularium Universitatis Parisiensis*, 4, Paris, 1897, pp. 652f.; on Rome, Lassels (note 14), p. 188.

50 Donaldson (note 30).

51 On Palermo, V. Avria, q. Pitrè (1889), 1, p. 10; the term 'code switching' I owe to Ranajit Guha of the University of Sussex; on Naples, A. Giraffi, *Le Rivoluzioni di Napoli*, Venice, 1647, p. 7; on festival and revolt, Bercé (1976), Cobb, pp. 18f., Davis (1975), pp. 97, 131, and P. Weidkuhn, 'Fastnacht, Revolte, Revolution' in *Zeitschrift für Religions–und Geistesgeschichte*, 21 (1969).

52 M. H. Dodds and R. Dodds, *The Pilgrimage of Grace*, 1, Cambridge, 1915, pp. 129, 213; on Normandy, Mousnier, p. 111; on Naples, R. Villari, *La Rivolta Antispagnuola a Napoli*, Bari, 1967, pp. 42f.

53 On Bern, Beerli (1953), p. 369; on the wars of religion, Davis (1975), Ch. 6; on Romans, Le Roy Ladurie (1966), pp. 393f.; cf. Bercé (1976), pp. 75f.; the quotations from E. Piemond, *Mémoires*, ed. J. Brun-Durand, Valence, 1885, pp. 88f.; on Dijon, Porchnev, pp. 135f.

8 The Triumph of Lent

1   On the painting, Gaignebet (1972), and O. Stridbeck, 'The Combat of Carnival and Lent' in *JWCI* (1956).

2   Davis (1974), p. 309, criticises the 'passive receptacles' approach. This chapter is in the tradition of Delumeau and Bercé (1976), but moving from the reform of popular Catholicism to that of popular culture as a whole.

3   On Huelva, A. Domínguez Ortiz, *The Golden Age of Spain*, Eng. trans., London, 1971, p. 323n.; Rudyerd q. Hill (1974), p. 19.

4   Ottonelli q. Lea, 1, p. 311.

5   Erasmus, 'Supputatio Errorum in Censuris Beddae' in his *Opera*, IX, Leiden, 1706 (repr. Hildesheim 1962), col. 516.

6   J. Deslyons, *Discours contre le Paganisme des Rois*, Paris, 1664, p. 41; T. Hall, *Funebria Florae*, London, 1660, p. 7; on S. Carlo, Taviani, pp. 13, 17, 24f.

7   J. Stopford, *Pagano-Papismus*, London, 1675.

8   On Eynatten, van Heurck, pp. 5f.

9   The condemnation of 1655 printed in Leber, pp. 472f.

10   Erasmus, 'Ecclesiastes' in his *Opera*, 5 Leiden, 1704 (repr. Hildesheim, 1962) col. 985; Giberti q. A. Grazioli, *G. M. Giberti*, Verona, 1955; cf. Schannat, index under 'fabulosa et vana non immiscenda concionibus'; W. Perkins, *The Whole Treatise of the Cases of Conscience*, London, 1632, p. 344; H. Estienne, *Apologie pour Hérodote* (1566), Chs 34–36.

11   The Bishop of Evora q. Braga (1867a), p. 48.

12   On the older mentality, J. Huizinga, *The Waning of the Middle Ages*, Harmondsworth 1965 edn, pp. 151f.

13   P. Stubbes, *Anatomy of Abuses*, London, 1583, pp. 98f.; cf. Perkins (note 10); Doublet (1895a), pp. 369f.; Dejean, p. 32n.

14   Hall (note 6), p. 10; on Mère Folle, Tilliot, pp. 111f.

15   S. Brant, *Das Narrenschiff* (2nd edn, Strasbourg, 1495), section 110b; R. Crowley, *Select Works*, London, 1872, p. 8; P. Prodi, *Il Cardinale G. Paleotti*, 2, Rome, 1967, p. 210; the *Discorso* repr. in Taviani, pp. 65f.

16   M. Weber, *The Protestant Ethic and the Spirit of Capitalism*, Eng. trans., London, 1930; cf. Hill (1964), and E. P. Thompson (1963, pp. 350f.; 1967).

17   As Wiertz remarks, little research has been done on popular religion in Orthodox Europe; he gives references to what there is.

18   E. Duchesne (ed.), *Le Stoglav*, Paris, 1920, pp. 242f.; cf. Zguta, p. 302.

19   Pascal (1938), pp. 35f., 54f., 49f.; cf. Zguta, pp. 306f.

20   Unpublished memoirs of Beurrier, curé of Nanterre from 1637 on, q. Ferté, p. 292; Avvakum, *Autobiography*, Eng. trans., London,

1963, pp. 47–8, referring to events of the 1640s.

21   R. O. Crummey, *The Old Believers and the World of Antichrist*, Madison, 1970, pp. 8f., discusses the Russian schism as a split between the elite and the people.

22   For a case-study of English iconoclasm, Phillips; it is a pity that David Freedberg's work on Dutch iconoclasm remains unpublished.

23   Bascapè repr. in Taviani, pp. 45f.

24   *Rueff von dem Heyligen Ritter S. Gergen*, Augsburg, 1621; C. Hole, *English Folk Heroes*, London, 1947, pp. 27f.

25   On Geiler, L. Dacheux, *Un Réformateur Catholique à la Fin du 15e Siècle*, Paris/Strasbourg, 1876, p. 67n.; on Savonarola, L. Landucci, *Diario*, ed. J. Del Badia, Florence, 1883, p. 124.

26   I. Origo, *The World of St Bernardino*, London, 1963, p. 166; on Gerson and Clamanges, P. Adam, *La Vie Paroissiale en France au 14e Siècle*, Paris, 1964, pp. 264f.; Grosseteste q. Baskervill (1920), p. 43; earlier examples in Chambers (1903), 2, Appendix N.

27   I take the term 'resilience' from R. Hoggart, *The Uses of Literacy*, Harmondsworth 1958 edn, p. 264.

28   On Protestantism and popular culture, a bibliographical essay in Brückner (1974), pp. 23f.; on Luther, Clemen (1938), Klinger, Kohler. On Osiander, Roller, pp. 140f. and Sumberg, pp. 176f. T. Naogeorgus, *Regnum Papisticum*, no place, 1553. On Lutheran Sweden, Granberg.

29   On Zwingli and popular culture, Trümpy (cf. C. Garside, *Zwingli and the Arts*, New Haven/London, 1966). On Dutch Calvinism, Wirth, pp. 120f., 173f.; on Scottish Calvinism. T. C. Smout, *A History of the Scottish People*, London 1972 edn, pp. 78f.

30   Dickens (Ch. 7, note 32); Gardiner; E. Grindal, *Remains*, Cambridge, 1843, pp. 141f.

31   Wirth, pp. 174f.; R. D. Evenhuis, *Ook dat was Amsterdam*, 2, Amsterdam, 1967, pp. 116f.

32   Council of Trent, 25th session, in E. C. Holt (ed.), *A Documentary History of Art*, 2, New York, 1958, pp. 64f.

33   For the decrees of German councils, Schannat; for Spanish councils, Saenz; for S. Carlo Borromeo's councils, P. Galesinus (ed.), *Acta Ecclesiae Mediolanensis*, Milan, 1582; for a sample of French councils, T. Gousset (ed.), *Les Actes de la Province Ecclésiastique* de Reims, 4 vols, Reims, 1842–4, esp. Vols 3, 4; on censorship, F. H. Reusch, (ed.), *Die Indices Librorum Prohibitorum des 16. Jahrhunderts*, Tübingen, 1886, esp. pp. 242, 315, 384; on Eulenspiegel, C. Sepp, *Verboden Lectuur*, Leiden, 1889, p. 261; on the 1624 Index, Braga (1867a), pp. 107f.

34   Delumeau, pp. 256f.; on Bavaria, F. Stieve, *Das Kirchliche Polizeiregiment in Bayern unter Maximilian I*, Munich, 1876.

35   In Cioni's bibliography, mention is made of more than 200

editions of religious plays between 1600 and 1625; after 1625, the number is negligible. The 1601 edict q. Straeten, p. 67.
36   C. Bagshaw, *A True Relation* (1601), repr. in T. G. Law, *A Historical Sketch of the Conflict between Jesuits and Seculars*, London, 1889, esp. p. 18, a reference for which I am grateful to John Bossy.
37   On the revolt of the Alpujarras, J. Elliott, *Imperial Spain*, London, 1964, pp. 228f.; on Nuremberg, Roller, pp. 140f., Sumberg, pp. 176f.; on Bologna, Toschi (1955), p. 143; on Wells, Sisson, pp. 157f.
38   M. Luther, preface to the Wittenberg hymn-book of 1524, in his *Werke*, 35, Weimar, 1923, p. 474.
39. M. Luther, *Sendbrief am Dolmetschen*, in *Werke*, 30, Part 2, Weimar, 1909, pp. 632f.
40   S. L. Greenslade (ed.), *The Cambridge History of the Bible*, Cambridge, 1963, Chs 3, 4.
41   On the cost, Greenslade (note 38), p. 95; on Sweden, Pleijel (1955), pp. 9f., 16f.
42   There were at least 288 editions of Sternhold and Hopkins, 1547–1640. On the psalms in Huguenot culture, Bost (1912), Douen, Le Roy Ladurie (1966) Eng. trans. p. 271, and Davis (1975), p. 4; in Puritan culture, Manning, pp. 32, 244f.; in Swedish culture, Olsson.
43   On the term 'catechism' (used of oral instruction by Augustine, of a book from Luther on), J. Geffcken, *Der Bildercatechismus des 15. Jahrhunderts*, Leipzig, 1855; on Germany, Strauss, pp. 38f.; on Sweden, Pleijel (1955, pp. 17f.; 1965, pp. 64f.) and Johansson (1969), pp. 42f.; two of the books most frequently reprinted in England before 1640 were Nowell's catechism and Egerton's catechism.
44   On Calvin's reading public, F. M. Higman, *The Style of John Calvin*, Oxford, 1967, Appendix A.
45   For Luther's hymns, see his *Werke* (note 36), pp. 411f.; for Lutheran hymns, Wackernagel, esp. Vols 3–5.
46   'Go from my window' is sung by Merrythought in Beaumont's *Knight of the Burning Pestle* (1613), Act 3, Scene 5. For the Scottish collection, D. Laing (ed.), *A Compendious Book of Psalms and Spiritual Songs*, Edinburgh, 1868; for Calvinist songs of battle, Bordier, Kuiper, and H. J. van Lummel (ed.), *Nieuw geuzenlied-Boeck*, new edn, Utrecht, 1892.
47   'An Englishman', probably Richard Morison; S. Anglo, 'An Early Tudor Programme for Plays and other Demonstrations against the Pope', in *JWCI* 20 (1957).
48   On Lutheran iconography, Christie, Haebler, Lieske, Scharfe (1967; 1968), and Svärdström (1949), pp. 93f. There seems to be nothing comparable on Calvinist temples; but there is a fine example of a pulpit with floral decoration in the temple at Kolozsvár (Cluj) in Transylvania, and of a ceiling painted with emblems (the crane among

them) in the village church of Körösfö nearby.

49   Gregory q. Bede, *Ecclesiastical History*, Eng. trans., Harmondsworth, 1955, Book 1, Ch. 30; R. de Nobili, *Première Apologie* (1610), French trans., Paris, 1931, esp. p. 67.

50   On Granada, Domínguez Ortiz (note 3), p. 323; J. B. Bossuet, *Catéchisme du Diocèse de Meaux*, Paris, 1690, pp. 363f.; cf. Lanternari.

51   On Savonarola, Landucci (note 25), pp. 124, 163; cf. Manzoni, p. 216. On the Forty Hours, below, note 55.

52   S. Paolucci, *Missioni de'Padri della Compagnia di Giesù nel Regno di Napoli*, Naples, 1651, pp. 19f., 23, 42f.

53   H. Le Gouvello, *Le Vénérable Michel Le Nobletz*, Paris, 1898, pp. 187f.

54   E. Mâle, *L'Art Religieux . . . après le Concile de Trente*, Paris, 1951, pp. 100f.; cf. Amades (1947), 2, figs 218–19.

55   On St Joseph, Huizinga (note 12), p. 164, and Mâle (note 52), pp. 309f.; on the Forty Hours, M. S. Weil, 'The Devotion of the Forty Hours and Roman Baroque Illusions', in *JWCI* 37 (1974).

56   Compare Mâle's examples with B. Malinowski, *Magic, Science and Religion*, New York, 1954, pp. 101, 107, 144.

57   D'Ancona (1872), 2, p. 129; Wardropper, p. xxvi; A. Boschet, *Le Parfait Missionaire, ou la Vie du R. P. Julien Maunoir*, Paris, 1697, esp. p. 96.

58   C. Sommervogel, *Bibliothèque de la Compagnie de Jésus*, Vols 1 and 2, Brussels/Paris, 1890–1, articles 'Bellarmine' and 'Canisius'; on the catechism in France, Dhotel, and J. R. Armogathe in *Images du Peuple*.

59   The catalogues of the British Library and the Bibliothèque Nationale list twenty-three editions of Scupoli between them. On the synod of Chalons and the printer of Paris, H. J. Martin, *Livre, Pouvoirs et Société*, Paris, 1969, pp. 956f., 706.

60   On the Bern area, Trümpy; on Holland, Wirth; on Nuremberg, Sumberg. On Lutheran Germany, a more sceptical view in Strauss.

61   On Bavaria, L. G. Séguin, *The Country of the Passion-Play*, London, 1880, p. 175; on Sicily, Pitrè (1876), pp. 7f.; on Brittany, F. M. Luzel (ed.), *Sainte Tryphine*, Quimperlé, 1863, p. vii; on Finistère, J. de Cambry, *Voyage dans le Finistère*, 3 vols, Paris, 1799, 3, p. 176.

62   On Languedoc, Dejean and Doublet (1895a, b); B. Amilha, *Le Tableu de la Bido del Parfet Crestia*, Toulouse, 1673, esp. pp. 231f.

63   Fabre/Lacroix, pp. 161, 168.

64   On Austria, E. Wangermann, *From Joseph II to the Jacobin Trials*, 2nd edn, Oxford, 1969, p. 31; on Italy, J. Carreyre, 'Synode de Pistoie' in *Dictionnaire de Théologie Catholique*, 12, Paris, 1935; for the popular reaction, Turi, pp. 7f.; for a South Italian Jansenist

reformer, cf. de Rosa, pp. 34f., 49, 73, 126. On the connexion with Jansenism, contrast A. Adam, *Du Mysticisme à la Révolte*, Paris, 1968, pp. 285f., with E. Appoli, *Le Tiers Parti Catholique au 18e Siècle*, Paris, 1960, pp. 330f.

65 J. Molanus, *De Picturis et Imaginibus Sacris*, Louvain, 1570, esp. Chs 1, 16, 26, 59 (Antony) and 71 (Martin); the archdeacon q. Ferté, p. 104n.; for the bishop of Orléans at Sennely, Bouchard, p. 299.

66 On Norway, Bø, Ch. 4; on Scotland T. C. Smout, *A History of the Scottish People 1560–1830*, London 1972 edn, p. 80; cf. M. Martin, *A Description of the Western Islands of Scotland* (1703), ed. D. J. Macleod, Stirling, 1934.

67 E. Saunders, *A View of the State of Religion in the Diocese of St David's*, London, 1721, esp. p. 36; T. Rees, *History of Protestant Nonconformity in Wales*, 2nd edn, London, 1883, esp. pp. 313f., 348; on Howell Harris, G. Whitefield, q. Walsh, p. 220; the writer in 1802 was E. Jones, *The Bardic Museum;* on the disappearance of Welsh folklore, T. G Jones, pp. 161, 218.

68 On the English reformation of manners, Bahlman (but cf. Malcolmson, Chs 6 and 7, suggesting that a 'systematic and sustained attack' on popular recreations did not begin till the mid-eighteenth century); on Scandinavia, Pleijel (1965), pp. 19f., and (on Hauge) Koht (1926), Ch. 23; on France, Allier (1909, 1914).

69 J. C. Gottsched, *Versuch einer Critische Dichtkunst* (1730), in his *Werke*, Berlin/New York, 1973, esp. Part 2, Ch. 11; J. von Sonnenfels, 'Briefe über die Wienerische Schaubühne', in his *Gesammelte Schriften*, 10 vols, Vienna, 1783–7, 5, pp. 189f.; Rommel, pp. 384f.

70 On Pavillon, Dejean, esp. p. 31n.; on Bekker, W. P. C. Knuttel, *B. Bekker*, The Hague, 1906.

71 On England, *O. E. D.*, article 'superstition'; on Italy, G. Cocchiara, *Sul Concetto di Superstizione*, Palermo, 1945; on France, J. B. Thiers, *Traité des Superstitions*, Paris, 1704, esp. Ch. 9; for the classical background, A. Momigliano, 'Popular Religious Beliefs and the Late Roman Historians' in Cuming/Baker.

72 On France, Mandrou (1968), Part 3; on England, Thomas (1971), esp. p. 570; on Germany, Midelfort; on Poland, Baranowski.

73 B. G. Feijoó, *Teatro Critico Universal*, 8 vols, Madrid, 1733, esp. 1, essay 1; 2, essays 3–5; 3, essays 1, 6; 5, essay 16.

74 'Mixing and confusing', q. A. A. Parker, *The Allegorical Drama of Calderón*, Oxford/London, 1943, p. 20; N. Fernández de Moratín, *Desengaños al Teatro Español*, Madrid, 1762, pp. 10f., 21; Very, pp. 106f.

75 G. de Jovellanos, 'Memoria para el Arreglo de la Policía de los Espectáculos' (1790) in his *Pbras Escogidas*, Madrid, 1955, 2, p. 29; J. Meléndez Valdés, *Discursos Forenses*, Madrid, 1821, pp. 167f. (cf. A.

Gonzalez Palencia, 'Meléndez Valdés y la Literatura de Cordel', repr. in his *Entre Dos Siglos*, Madrid, 1943).

9 Popular Culture and Social Change

1 R. Mols, 'Population in Europe' in C. Cipolla (ed.), *The Fontana Economic History of Europe*, 2, London, 1974; F. Braudel, *Capitalism and Material Life*, Eng. trans., London, 1973, Ch. 1.
2 Braudel (note 1), *passim;* cf. C. T. Smith, *An Historical Geography of Western Europe*, London, 1967, Ch. 10.
3 On England, Harrison (1577) q. Hoskins; cf. Barley (1961, 1967); on Alsace, Riff (1945), pp. 4f.
4 On Friesland, de Vries (who notes the beginning of these developments in the seventeenth century); on Artois, Le Roy Ladurie (1975), p. 415; N. Rétif de la Bretonne, *La Vie de Mon Père*, ed. G. Rouger, Paris, 1970, pp. xxx–xxxi; on Norway, Anker, Ch. 8; on Sweden, Svärdström (1949).
5 On England, Hoskins (1963); on Alsace, Riff (1945); on Norway, Koht (1926), pp. 205f.
6 On the Netherlands, Korf; on Sweden, E. Heckscher, *An Economic History of Sweden*, Eng. trans., Cambridge, Mass., 1954, pp. 189f.; on Norway, Kloster.
7 On the Netherlands, Korf; on Lothian, G. Robertson, *Rural Recollections*, Irvine, 1829, pp. 102f.
8 Stoianovich.
9 Plumb (1973); P. Egan, *Boxiana*, London, 1812, pp. 48f. (on Broughton).
10 J. M. Cossio, *Los Toros*, 1, Madrid, 1945, pp. 584f.; Montaigne, *Journal*, Paris 1955 edn, p. 141; on Venice, M. Misson, *Nouvelle Voyage d'Italie*, The Hague, 1691, 1, pp. 193f.
11 Mackenzie (Ch. 1, note 39), p. 10; ibid., Appendix, p. 47.
12 H. J. Martin in J. Cain *et al.*, *Le Livre Français*, Paris, 1972, esp. pp. 48f., 59; on printing and the people, Davis (1975), Ch. 7.
13 The standard survey of European literacy is Cipolla. Among the more important contributions since are Furet/Sachs, Johansson (1969, 1973), Lockridge, Neuburg, Schofield (1973), Vovelle (1975). Quotation from Lockridge, p. 7; cf. Schofield (1973), and Furet/Sachs, pp. 715f.; contrast the views of Neuburg, p. 96.
14 On Narbonne, Le Roy Ladurie (1966), p. 333; on France, Fleury/Valmary; the 1850 figures in Cipolla, Table 24.
15 On Venice, Cipolla, pp. 58f.; on Durham, M. James, *Family Lineage and Civil Society*, Oxford, 1975, pp. 105f.; on France, Fleury/Valmary; on England, Stone (1969) and Schofield (1973); on Amsterdam, Hart; on Marseilles, Vovelle (1973), pp. 378f.; on Sweden, Johansson (1969, 1973).

16   G. de Jovellanos, *Obras Escogidas*, Madrid, 1955, 1, p. 71.
17   Stone (1964); Hill (1974); T. Parry, *A History of Welsh Literature*, Oxford, 1955, pp. 257f.; Johansson (1969, 1973); Poutet; Laget.
18.   R. Cotgrave, *A Dictionary of the French and English Tongues*, London, 1611, article 'Bissouart'.
19   On chapmen, Neuburg, Ch. 5; Schenda (1970), Ch. 4; J. J. Darmon, *Le Colportage de Librairie en France sous le Second Empire*, Paris, 1972, pp. 30f.
20   On England, J. Ashton; on France, Bollème (1969, 1971) and Mandrou (1964); on the Northern Netherlands, Schotel (1873–4); on the Southern Netherlands, van Heurck; on Denmark, Jacobsen, 13; on Spain, Caro Baroja (1969); on Russia, Ovsyannikov (1968).
21   On French prices, Mandrou (1964), p. 18; on English prices, J. Ashton, p. viii; a Swedish *skilling* was a 48th of a riksdaler, see Heckscher (note 6), p. 198. On Lyons, Garden (Ch. 2, note 36), pp. 459f.; on Grenoble, Solé.
22   Dahl (1946), p. 23.
23   Fehr; Shaaber; on the 'pseudo-event', D. Boorstin, *The Image*, New York, 1962, Chs 1–2 (an Elizabethan example in Shaaber, p. 294). On the Oudot family, Mandrou (1964), pp. 30f.; on the Dicey family, Shepard (1973), pp. 28f.
24   E. Nesi (ed.), *Il Diario della Stamperia di Ripoli*, Florence, 1903, pp. 97, 114.
25   On the stunting of improvisation, Lord, Ch. 6.
26   On Nigeria, E. Obiechnina, *An African Popular Literature*, revised edn, Cambridge, 1973; on the Middle East, D. Lerner, *The Passing of Traditional Society*, Glencoe, 1958.
27   Lockridge, esp. pp. 33f. Margaret Spufford's critique of this argument remains unpublished.
28   Schenda (1970), pp. 250, 253.
29   Bollème (1969), Bosanquet (1917, 1930) and Svensson (1967).
30   Shepard (1973), p. 45.
31   *The Academy of Compliments* (London, Aldermary Church-yard, no date), pp. 10–11.
32   Le Bras, 1, pp. 267f.; Delumeau, pp. 293f.; B. Plongeron, *Conscience Religieuse en Révolution*, Paris, 1969, Ch. 2; Vovelle (1973).
33   It is hard to be precise because it is hard to treat chap-books, often undated, as a time series, apart from almanacs.
34   Bollème (1969); Champfleury, *De la littérature populaire en France*, Paris, 1861.
35   Luther (letter, 2 June 1525), q. George, p. 3; the song of 1546 in Liliencron, no. 522; cf. Erk-Böhme, nos 262–97; Blickle, pp. 127f.; Gravier, pp. 175f.; Schottenloher, pp. 59f., 81f.
36   For the songs, Kuiper, Lummel (Ch. 8, note 46); for the

pamphlets, Knuttel; the badge reproduced in K. Haley, *The Dutch in the Seventeenth Century*, London, 1972, fig. 20.
37 For the songs, Bordier; for the prints, Adhémar, Blum.
38 H. G. Koenigsberger, 'The Organisation of Revolutionary Parties in France and the Netherlands', repr. in his *Estates and Revolutions*, Ithaca/London, 1971; T. Wittman, *Quelques Problèmes Relatifs à la Dictature Révolutionnaire des Grandes Villes de Flandre*, Budapest, 1960; J. H. Salmon, 'The Paris 16' in *Journal of Modern History*, 44 (1972), who points out that the 16 was originally dominated by the upper classes but that they withdrew.
39 J. H. Salmon, *French Society in Crisis*, London, 1975, pp. 139, 209, 287; Le Roy Ladurie (1966) p. 393.
40 For the broadsheets, Coupe; for the songs, Erk-Böhme, nos 303–16 and Ditfurth (1882): nos 3, 4 (on Khlesl); for the prophecies, R. Haase, *Das Problem der Chiliasmus und der Dreissig Jährige Krieg*, Leipzig, 1933.
41 Dahl (1939, 1946).
42 L. Zuccoli (1621), in B. Croce/S. Caramella (eds), *Politici e Moralisti del '600*, Bari, 1930, p. 25.
43 M. N. Grand-Mesnil, *Mazarin, La Fronde et la Presse*, Paris, 1967; *Le Pernonisme Berné*, Paris?, c. 1650, p. 2. (British Library 1492m 17(10)).
44 Manning, esp. Chs 1, 4; the comment from D. Digges, q. Manning, p. 91; on prints, George, pp. 14f.; on pamphlets and papers, *A Catalogue of the Pamphlets . . . collected by G. Thomason*, London, 1908, and J. Frank, *The Beginnings of the English Newspaper, 1620–1660*, Cambridge, Mass., 1961.
45 On the Levellers, Hill (1972), Ch. 7.
46 For ballads, Rollins (1929–32), and Perceval; for Wilkes, Rudé (1974), pp. 222f., and Brewer, Ch. 9; for prints, George, pp. 65f.
47 Plumb (1968); Brewer, Ch. 8; the Swiss visitor was C. de Saussure, *Lettres et Voyages*, Lausanne, etc. 1903 cdn, p. 167. A *liard* was a quarter of a sou and should refer to the contribution of each individual rather than the price of the paper.
48 On Dutch prints, J. van Kuyk, *Oude Politieke Spotprenten*, The Hague, 1940, pp. 21f.; on Swedish peasant leaders, E. Ingen, *Bonden i Svensk Historie*, 2, Stockholm, 1948, pp. 24f.; the Görtz ballad in Hildeman, pp. 80f.; on Struensee, W. Coxe, *Travels into Poland, Russia, Sweden*, 3, London, 1790, p. 168; the risings described by Koht (1926), Chs 21, 22.
49 The observer is S. Mercier, *Tableau de Paris*, 1, Paris, 1782, pp. 68f., 90; on Père Duchesne, J. Godechot, in C. Bellanger *et al.* (eds), *Histoire Générale de la Presse Française*, 1, Paris, 1969, pp. 456f.; on political almanacs, Soboul (1966), pp. 217f.
50 For the plates, 'Champfleury', *Histoire des Faïences Patriotiques*

sous la Révolution, Paris, 1867; for a Frenchman selling the fans at Bilbao in 1790, R. Herr, *The Eighteenth-Century Revolution in Spain*, Princeton, *1958, p. 251*; on Rheims, M. Crubellier, *Histoire Culturelle de la France*, Paris, 1974, p. 43 (cf. Ozouf (1976, esp. Ch. 9) and Tiersot).

51   Soboul (1958); P. Bois, *Paysans de l'Ouest*, Le Mans, 1960, pp. 594f.

52   P. J. Blok, *History of the People of the Netherlands*, 5, Eng. trans., New York/London, 1912, Chs 12–16; E. P. Thompson (1963), pp. 89f., 104f.

53   E. Wangermann, *From Joseph II to the Jacobin Trials*, 2nd edn, Oxford, 1969, pp. 32, 47, 77f., 81; L. Schmidt (1971), no. 31.

54   Godechot; Herr (note 50), p. 294; Turi; G. Cingari, *Giacobini e Sanfedisti in Calabria nel 1799*, Messina/Florence, 1957, esp. pp. 283f.

55   A. Corvisier, *L'Armée Française*, Paris, 1964, p. 151; G. Rudé, *Europe in the Eighteenth Century*, London, 1972, p. 216.

56   L'Estrange q. in the article on him in the *Dictionary of National Biography*. The paper he founded is distinct from the Whig *Observator* of the early eighteenth century.

57   This withdrawal thesis has been put forward several times in different national contexts, though never (so far as I know) discussed at any length or on a comparative basis. On Spain, Juan Valera, discussed in Caro Baroja (1969), pp. 24f.; for England, F. R. Leavis, *The Common Pursuit*, Harmondsworth 1962 edn, p. 188; for Germany, E. Cohn, *Gesellschaftsideale und Gesellschaftsroman*, Berlin, 1921, p. 98; for Denmark, R. Paulli in Jacobsen, 13, pp. 171f.; for Russia, R. Jakobson (1944); for France, Davis (1975), p. 265.

58   For French usage, C. Faure de Vaugelas, *Remarques sur la Langue Française*, Paris, 1647, preface; W. Bahner, 'Le Mot et la Notion du "peuple" dans l'Oeuvre de Rousseau', in *Studies on Voltaire*, 55 (1967); *Images du Peuple*, Part 1; and see now H. Payne, *The Philosophes and the People*, New Haven, 1976. For England, *O.E.D.*, article 'vulgar', notes the new meaning 'ill-bred' which joined the traditional meanings of 'vernacular' and 'ill-educated'. For German, Stieler's definition of 1691, q. W. Conze, in H. U. Wehler (ed.), *Moderne Deutsche Sozialgeschichte*, Cologne/Berlin, 1966, p. 113.

59   On the Catholic clergy, Delumeau, pp. 72f., 271f.

60   On wrestling, B. Castiglione, *Il Cortegiano* (1528); on self-control, N. Elias, *Über den Prozess der Zivilisation*, 1, Basel, 1939; cf. R. zu Lippe, *Naturbeherrschung am Menschen*, 2 vols, Frankfurt, 1974 (esp. on the dance).

61   R. Kelso, *Doctrine for the Lady of the Renaissance*, Urbana, 1956, lists 891 treatises on the subject.

62   On Languedoc, P. Wolff, *Histoire de Toulouse*, Toulouse,

1958, pp. 212f., 236; on Wales, T. Parry, *A History of Welsh Literature*, Oxford, 1955; on Scotland, A. Ferguson q. Mackenzie (Ch. 1, note 39) p. 65; on Bohemia, R. J. Kerner, *Bohemia in the Eighteenth Century*, New York, 1932, pp. 344f.; B. Balbín, *Dissertatio Apologetica*, Prague, 1775, p. 7; on Norway, O. J. Falnes, *National Romanticism in Norway*, New York, 1933; on Finland, Wuorinen, esp. p. 44.

63 L. Rotgans, *Boerekermis*, Amsterdam, 1708, esp. pp. 10–11, 29; S. Mercier, *Tableau de Paris*, 8 vols, Paris, 1782–4, 5, Ch. 431.

64 P. Talpa, *Empiricus sive Indoctus Medicus*, Antwerp, 1563, p. 9; S. Mercurio, *De Gli Errori Popolari d'Italia*, Venice, 1603, esp. Book 4; T. Browne, *Pseudodoxia Epidemica*, London, 1646, esp. Ch. 3; Courval's *Les Tromperies des Charlatans Découvertes* repr. in Tabarin, *Oeuvres*, 2, Paris, 1858, with Tabarin's reply. Cf. Davis (1975), pp. 258f.

65 M. Reeves, *The Influence of Prophecy in the Later Middle Ages*, Oxford, 1969, p.508; P. Hazard, *La Crise de la Conscience Européenne*, Paris, 1935, Part 2, Ch. 2; Haase (note 40); C. W. Roldanus, *C. van Beuningen*, The Hague, 1931; E. Labrousse, *P. Bayle*, 2, The Hague, 1964; and on England, Thomas (1971), pp. 427f.; B. Capp, *The Fifth Monarchy Men*, London, 1972 (esp. conclusion); F. Manuel, *Isaac Newton Historian*, Cambridge, 1963, pp. 144f.; and on Joanna Southcott, E. P. Thompson (1963), pp. 382f.

66 Trevor-Roper, pp. 97f.; Caro Baroja (1961), Ch. 4; Mandrou (1968), Chs 7–9; Macfarlane, pp. 57, 88; Thomas (1971), Chs 18, 22; Midelfort, Ch. 6. Barberini q. Ginzburg (1966), p. 137: the minister q. Boswell (Ch. 1, note 19) p. 266.

67 For Florentine examples, Guasti, p. 72; for Roman examples, J. Delumeau, *L'Italie de Botticelli à Bonaparte*, Paris, 1974, p. 328; on the eighteenth century, F. Venturi, 'Enlightenment versus the Powers of Darkness' in his *Italy and the Enlightenment*, London, 1972; L. Parinetto, *Magia e Ragione*, Florence, 1974.

68 J. Du Bellay, *Défense et Illustration de la Langue Française*, (1549), esp. Book 2, Ch. 4; on language, J. Lough, *An Introduction to Seventeenth-Century France*, London, 1954, pp. 244f.; on the clergy, M. De Certeau, *L'Ecriture de l'Histoire*, Paris, 1975, pp. 207f.; M. Desgrouais, *Les Gasconismes Corrigés*, Toulouse, 1766; Rousseau q. Bahner (note 58), p. 122.

69 Friedman (1961a), Chs 1–2; W. Cornwallis, *Essays*, London, 1600, 'Of the Observation and Use of Things'; on the jig, Baskervill (1929), p. 111; on fools, Welsford, Ch. 7; R. S. Crane, 'The Vogue of Guy of Warwick', in *Proceedings of the Modern Language Association*, 30 (1915), esp. pp. 167f.; J. Webster, *The Displaying of Supposed Witchcraft*, London, 1677, p. 323; Chesterfield to his son, 25 July 1741.

70   Reenberg q./trans. R. C. A. Prior, *Ancient Danish Ballads*, 3 vols, London, 1860, 1 p. viii; cf. R. Paulli in Jacobsen 13, pp. 228f.

71   P. Cazin, *Le Prince-Evêque de Varmie*, Paris, 1940, p. 131, on romances in Poland; on witches, Baranowski. B. Szabolcsi, *A Concise History of Hungarian Music*, London, 1964, pp. 37, 43; Kodály, p. 16.

72   Scott, 1, p. 13; on mummers, Robertson (note 7), pp. 118f.; J. Beattie, *Scotticisms*, 1787; J. Rae, *Life of Adam Smith* (1895), repr. New York, 1965, p. 369; general discussion in D. Craig, *Scottish Literature and the Scottish People 1680–1830*, London, 1961, Chs 1–2.

73   On the 'alienation' of Russian nobles from their traditional culture, M. Raeff, *Origins of the Russian Intelligentsia*, New York, 1966, pp. 74f.; on Peter the Great's buffoons, Welsford, pp. 182f.; on the audience for the *lubok*, Ovsyannikov (1968), p. 17; on traditional survivals, R. Pipes, *Russia under the Old Regime*, London, 1975, p. 187; S. T. Aksakov, *A Russian Gentleman*, Eng. trans., London, 1917, p. 289; and Chadwick, p. xiii.

74   For the view I am opposing, E. Schmidt; H. Bebel, *Proverbia Germanica*, ed. W. H. D. Suringar, Leiden, 1879; H. Bebel, *Facetien*, ed. G. Bebermayer, Leipzig, 1931; S. Franck, *Weltbuch*, 2 vols, Frankfurt 1567; S. Franck, *Sprichwörter*, 2 vols, Frankfurt, 1541; F. Friese, *Historische Nachricht von der Merkwürdigen Ceremonien der Altenburgischen Bauern* (1703), repr. Schmölln, 1887; on Friese, G. Fischer, *Volk und Geschichte*, Kulmbach, 1962.

75   For the view I am opposing, Hustvedt; P. Syv (ed.), *Udvalde Danske Viser*, Copenhagen, 1695, repr. Vedel's preface and adds his own; on Sweden, Jonsson, pp. 35f., and Svensson (1955).

76   J. Aubrey, 'Remains' in *Three Prose Works*, Fontwell, 1972, p. 132; on him, R. Dorson, *The British Folklorists*, London, 1968, pp. 4f.

77   J. B. Thiers, *Traité des Superstitions*, Paris, 1704; H. Bourne, *Antiquitates Vulgares*, Newcastle, 1725 (on him, Dorson, *The British Folklorists*, London, 1968, pp. 10f.); L. A. Muratori, *Dissertazioni sopra le Antichità Italiane*, 3 vols, Milan, 1751; on him, S. Bertelli, *Erudizione e Storia in L. A. Muratori*, Naples, 1960.

78   Montaigne, *Essais*, 1, Ch. 54; on Malherbe, G. Tallemant des Réaux, *Historiettes*, ed. A. Adam, 1, Paris, 1960, p. 119.

79   On the fashion, M. E. Storer, *La Mode des Contes de Fées*, *(1685–1700)*, Paris, 1928; on Caylus, A. P. Moore, *The Genre Poissard and the French Stage of the Eighteenth Century*, New York, 1935, pp. 96f.

80   *The Spectator*, no. 70; Friedman (1961a), Ch. 4; T. Blackwell, *An Enquiry into the Life and Writings of Homer*, London, 1735; R. Lowth, *De Sacra Poesia Hebraeorum*, Oxford, 1753.

Select Bibliography

This bibliography contains (i) modern anthologies of source material, which are marked with an asterisk, and (ii) a selection of books and articles on popular culture, 1500–1800, published before October 1976. Every work cited in abbreviated form in the notes is cited in full here, but some books cited in full in the notes are not in the bibliography, and some books cited in the bibliography are not in the notes. One important kind of source is omitted from this bibliography: the collections of Western European broadsides and chap-books in the British Library, bound in volumes but catalogued by the titles of individual items.

Abbreviations

AESC	*Annales: Économies, Sociétés, Civilisations*
Child	F. J. Child (ed.), *The English and Scottish Popular Ballads* (1882), new edn, 5 vols, New York, 1965
FFC	*Folklore Fellows Communications*
Funk and Wagnall	*Funk and Wagnall's Standard Dictionary of Folklore, Mythology and Legend*, ed. M. Leach, 2 vols, New York, 1949–50
JWCI	*Journal of the Warburg and Courtauld Institutes*
Motif-Index	S. Thompson (ed.), *Motif-Index of Folk Literature*, revised edn, 6 vols, Copenhagen, 1955–8
P&P	*Past and Present*

A. Ademollo, *Il Carnevale di Roma nei Secoli 17 e 18*, Rome, 1883
J. Adhémar *et al.*, *Imagerie Populaire Française*, Milan, 1968
*A. N. Afanasiev (ed.), *Narodnye Russkie Skazki*, 8 vols, 1855–63; a selection trans. as *Russian Fairy Tales*, London, 1946
M. Agulhon (1966), *La Sociabilité Méridionale*, Aix
M. Agulhon (1970), *La République au Village*, Paris
*R. Allier (1909) (ed.), *La Compagnie du Très Saint Sacrement à Marseille*, Paris
R. Allier (1914), *La Compagnie du Très Saint Sacrement à Toulouse*, Paris

J. Amades (1934), *Gegants, Nans i Altres Entremesos*, Barcelona
J. Amades (1947), *Xilografies Gironines*, 2 vols, Girona
*J. Amades (1950–1) (ed.), *Folklore de Catalunya*, 2 vols, Barcelona
J. Amades (1952), *Els Ex-Vots*, Barcelona
J. Amades (1966), *Danzas de Moros y Christianos*, Valencia
*A. I. Amzulescu (ed.), *Balade Populare Romîneşti*, 3 vols, Bucharest, 1964
*A. D.'Ancona (1872) (ed.), *Sacre Rappresentazioni*, 3 vols, Florence
A. D'Ancona (1891), *Origini del Teatro Italiano*, 2 vols, Turin
A. D'Ancona (1913), *Saggi di Letteratura Popolare*, Livorno
W. Anderson, *Kaiser und Abt*, Helsinki, 1923
A. Angyal, 'Die Welt der Grenzfestungen' in *Süd-Ost Forschungen*, 16 (1957). (On the Turkish-Habsburg frontier)
P. Anker, *Folkekunst i Norge*, Oslo, 1975
*A. von Arnim/C. Brentano (eds), *Des Knaben Wunderhorn* (1806). (References are to the Munich 1957 edn)
*J. Ashton (ed.), *Chap-books of the Eighteenth Century*, London, 1882
J. W. Ashton, 'Folklore in the Literature of Elizabethan England' in *Journal of American Folklore*, 70 (1957)
A. M. Astakhova, 'Improvisation in Russian Folklore' (1966), trans. in Oinas/Soudakoff
H. M. Atherton, *Political Prints in the Age of Hogarth*, Oxford, 1974
F. C. B. Avé-Lallemant, *Das Deutsche Gaunerthum*, 4 vols, Leipzig, 1858–62
P. Avrich, *Russian Rebels*, London, 1973
R. Axton, *European Drama of the Early Middle Ages*, London, 1974. (900–1400)
F. Aydelotte, *Elizabethan Rogues and Vagabonds*, Oxford, 1913, repr. London, 1967
J. Lucio D'Azevedo, *A Evolução do Sebastianismo*, Lisbon, 1918

*K. Badecki (ed.), *Polska Komedja Rybałtowska*, Lwów, 1931
D. W. R. Bahlman, *The Moral Revolution of 1688*, New Haven, 1957
M. Bakhtin, *Rabelais and His World* (1965), Eng. trans., Cambridge, Mass., and London, 1968
J. Balys, 'Estonian Folklore and Mythology' in *Funk and Wagnall*
J. Balys, 'Latvian Folklore and Mythology' in *Funk and Wagnall*
J. Balys, 'Lithuanian Folklore and Mythology' in *Funk and Wagnall*
B. Balzer, *Bürgerliche Reformationspropaganda*, Stuttgart, 1973. (On H. Sachs)
B. Baranowski, *Procesy Czarownie w Polsce w 17 i 18 Wieku*, Lodz, 1952
M. Barbeau, 'French Folklore' in *Funk and Wagnall*
M. W. Barley (1961), *The English Farmhouse and Cottage*, London

M. W. Barley (1967), 'Rural Housing in England' in J. Thirsk (ed.), *Agrarian History of England and Wales*, 4, Cambridge

P. Barry, 'The Part of the Folk Singer in the Making of Folk Ballads' in M. Leach/T. Coffin (eds), *The Critics and the Ballad*, Carbondale, 1961

B. Bartók, *Hungarian Folk Music* (1924), Eng. trans., Oxford, 1931

C. R. Baskervill (1920), 'Dramatic Aspects of Medieval Folk Festivals in England' in *Studies in Philology*, 17

C. R. Baskervill (1923–4), 'Mummers' Wooing Plays in England' in *Modern Philology*, 21

C. R. Baskervill (1929), *The Elizabethan Jig*, Chicago, repr. New York, 1965

H. Bausinger (1967) (ed.), *Masken zwischen Spiel und Ernst*, Tübingen

H. Bausinger (1968), *Formen der 'Volkspoesie'*, Berlin

B. Beattie, 'Oral-Traditional Composition in the Spanish *Romanceros* of the Sixteenth Century' in *Journal of the Folklore Institute*, 1 (1964)

C. A. Beerli (1953), *Le Peintre Poète Nicolas Manuel*, Geneva

C. A. Beerli (1956), 'Quelques Aspects des Jeux, Danses et Fêtes a Berne pendant la première moitié du 16e siècle' in J. Jacquot (ed.), *Les Fêtes de la Renaissance*, 1, Paris

N. Belmont, *Mythes et Croyances dans l'Ancienne France*, Paris, 1973

B. Bennassar, *L'Homme Espagnol*, Paris, 1975

Y. M. Bercé (1974a), *Histoire des Croquants*, 2 vols, Geneva/Paris

*Y. M. Bercé (1974b) (ed.), *Croquants et Nu-Pieds*, Paris

Y. M. Bercé (1976), *Fête et Révolte*, Paris

*A. E. Berger (ed.), *Lied-, Spruch-, und Fabeldichtung im Dienste der Reformation*, Leipzig, 1938

D. M. Bergeron, *English Civic Pageantry, 1558–1642*, London, 1971

R. Bernheimer, *Wild Men in the Middle Ages*, Cambridge, Mass., 1952

P. Blickle, *Die Revolution von 1525*, Munich/Vienna, 1975

A. Blum, *L'Estampe Satirique en France Pendant les Guerres de Religion*, Paris, n.d.

O. Bø, *Heilag-Olav i Norsk Folketradisjon*, Oslo, 1955

G. Boas, *Vox Populi*, Baltimore, 1969

L. Bødker, *Folk Literature (Germanic)*, Copenhagen, 1965

G. Bollême (1965), 'Littérature Populaire et Littérature de Colportage au 18e siécle' in F. Furet (ed.), *Livre et Société*, 1, Paris

G. Bollème (1969), *Les Almanacs Populaires au 17e et 18e Siècles*, Paris/The Hague

*G. Bollème (1971) (ed.), *La Bibliothèque Bleue*, Paris

J. Bolte/G. Polívka, *Anmerkungen zu den Kinder- und Hausmärchen der Brüder Grimm*, 5 vols, Leipzig, 1913–32

W. H. Bonner, *Pirate Laureate: the Life and Legends of Captain Kidd*, New Brunswick, 1947

*H. L. Bordier (ed.), *Le Chansonnier Huguenot de 16e Siècle*, Paris, 1870

E. F. Bosanquet (1917), *English Printed Almanacs . . . to the year 1600*, London

E. F. Bosanquet (1930), 'English 17th-Century Almanacs' in *The Library*

M. Bosković-Stulli, 'Regional Variations in Folktales' in *Journal of the Folklore Institute*, 3 (1966)

J. Bossy, 'The Counter-Reformation and the People of Catholic Europe' in *P&P* 47 (1970)

C. Bost (1912) *Les Prédicants Protestants des Cévennes*, 2 vols, Paris

C. Bost (1921), 'Les prophètes du Languedoc en 1701 et 1702' in *Revue Historique* 136–7

G. Bouchard, *Le Village Immobile: Sennely-en-Sologne au 18e Siècle*, Paris, 1972

B. C. Bowen, *Les Caractéristiques Essentielles de la Farce Française*, Urbana, 1964

M. C. Bradbrook, *The Rise of the Common Player*, London, 1962. (England 1300–1600)

T. Braga (1867a), *Historia da Poesia Popular Portugueza*, Porto

*T. Braga (1867b) (ed.), *Cancioneiro Popular*, Coimbra

T. Braga (1886), *O Povo Portuguez*, 2 vols, Lisbon

*T. Braga (1906–9) (ed.), *Romanceiro Geral Portuguez*, 3 vols, 2nd edn, Lisbon

J. Brewer, *Party Ideology and Popular Politics at the Accession of George III*, Cambridge, 1976

K. M. Briggs, *The Anatomy of Puck*, London 1959

O. G. Brockett, 'The Fair Theatres of Paris in the 18th Century' in M. J. Anderson, (ed.), *Classical Drama and its Influence*, London, 1965

A. Brody, *The English Mummers and Their Plays*, London, 1970

B. H. Bronson (1959), *The Traditional Tunes of the Child Ballads*, 3 vols, Princeton

B. H. Bronson (1969), *The Ballad as Song*, Berkeley and Los Angeles

W. Brückner (1958), *Die Verehrung des Heiligen Blutes in Walldürn*, Frankfort

W. Brückner (1966), *Bildnis und Brauch*, Berlin

W. Brückner (1968), 'Popular Piety in Central Europe' in *Journal of the Folklore Institute*, 5

W. Brückner (1974) (ed.), *Volkserzählung und Reformation*, Berlin

D. Buchan (1968), 'History and Harlaw', in *Journal of the Folklore Institute*, 5

D. Buchan (1972), *The Ballad and the Folk*, London

*D. Buchan (1973) (ed.), *A Scottish Ballad Book,* London

J. Burdet, *La Danse Populaire dans le Pays de Vaud,* Basle, 1958

J. Burszta (ed.), *Kultura Ludowa Wielkopolska,* 3 vols, Poznań, 1960 –7

E. M. Butler, *The Fortunes of Faust,* Cambridge, 1952

A. Buttitta, 'Cantastorie in Sicilia' in *Annali del Museo Pitrè,* 8–10 (1957–9)

*P. Camporesi (ed.), *Il Libro dei Vagabondi,* Turin, 1973

J. Caro Baroja (1961), *The World of the Witches,* Eng. trans., London, 1964

J. Caro Baroja (1965), *El Carnaval,* Madrid

*J. Caro Baroja (1966) (ed.), *Romances de Ciego,* Madrid

J. Caro Baroja (1969), *Ensayo sobre la Literatura de Cordel,* Madrid

*V. Castañeda/A. Huarte (eds), *Colección de Pliegos Sueltos,* Madrid, 1929

*V. Castañeda (ed.), *Nueva Colección de Pliegos Sueltos,* Madrid, 1933

E. Catholy, *Fastnachtspiel,* Stuttgart, 1966

*N. K. Chadwick (ed.), *Russian Heroic Poetry,* Cambridge, 1932

E. K. Chambers (1903), *The Medieval Stage,* 2 vols, Oxford

E. K. Chambers (1933), *The English Folk-Play,* Oxford

M. Cherniavsky (1961), *Tsar and People: Studies in Russian Myths,* New Haven

M. Cherniavsky (1966), 'The Old Believers and the New Religion' in *Slavic Review,* 25

*A. Christensen (ed.), *Molboernes Vise Gerninger,* Copenhagen, 1939

S. Christie, *Den Lutherske Ikonografi i Norge inntil 1800,* 2 vols, Oslo, 1973

A. Cioni (ed.), *Bibliografia delle Sacre Rappresentazioni,* Florence, 1961

C. M. Cipolla, *Literacy and Development in the West,* Harmondsworth, 1969

S. Cirac Estapañán, *Los Procesos de Hechicerías en la Inquisición de Castilla la Nueva,* Madrid, 1942

V. E. Clausen, *Det folkelige Danske Traesnit i Etbladstryk, 1650–1870,* Odense, 1971

O. Clemen (1937), *Die Volksfrömmigkeit des Ausgehenden Mittelalters,* Dresden/Leipzig

O. Clemen (1938), *Luther und die Volksfrömmigkeit seiner Zeit,* Dresden/Leipzig

F. Clementi, *Il Carnevale Romano,* Rome, 1899

R. Cobb, *The Police and the People: French Popular Protest 1789–1820,* Oxford, 1970

G. Cocchiara (1952), *Storia del Folklore in Europa,* Turin

G. Cocchiara (1956), *Il Paese di Cuccagna,* Turin

G. Cocchiara (1963), *Il Mondo alla Rovescia,* Turin

N. Cohn (1957), *The Pursuit of the Millennium,* new edn, London, 1970

N. Cohn (1975), *Europe's Inner Demons,* London

P. Coirault, *Recherches sur Notre Ancienne Chanson Populaire Traditionnelle,* 5 parts, Paris, 1933

F. Collinson, *The Traditional and National Music of Scotland,* London, 1966

F. Cottignies, *Chansons et Pasquilles,* ed. F. Carton, Arras, 1965

W. A. Coupe, *The German Illustrated Broadsheet in the Seventeenth Century,* 2 vols, Baden-Baden, 1966

D. Cressy, 'Literacy in Preindustrial England' in *Societas,* 4 (1974)

*A. Cronia (ed.), *Poesia Popolare Serbo-Croata,* Padua, 1949

G. J. Cuming/D. Baker (eds), *Popular Beliefs and Practice,* Cambridge, 1972

F. Dahl (1939), 'Amsterdam – Earliest Newspaper Centre of Western Europe' in *Het Boek,* 25

F. Dahl (1946), *Dutch Corantos, 1618–1650,* The Hague

W. Danckert, *Unehrliche Leute,* Bern/Munich, 1963

A. Daur, *Das Alte Deutsche Volkslied,* Leipzig, 1909

*H. Davenson (ed.), *Le Livre des Chansons,* Neuchâtel, 1946

C. A. Davids, 'Het Nederlandse Zeemanslied in de 17de en 18de Eeuw' in *Mededelingen van de Nederlandse Vereniging voor Zeegeschiedenis* 23 (1974)

N. Z. Davis (1974), 'Some Tasks and Themes in the Study of Popular Religion' in C. Trinkaus/H. Oberman (eds), *The Pursuit of Holiness,* Leiden

N. Z. Davis (1975), *Society and Culture in Early Modern France,* London

E. Dejean, *Un Prélat Indépendant au 17e Siècle: Nicolas Pavillon,* Paris, 1909

J. Delumeau, *Le Catholicisme entre Luther et Voltaire,* Paris, 1971

J. C. Dhotel, *Les Origines du Catéchisme Moderne,* Paris, 1967

L. M. van Dis, *Reformatorische Rederijkersspelen,* Haarlem, n.d.

*F. W. von Ditfurth (1869) (ed.), *Einhundert Historische Volkslieder des Preussischen Heeres von 1675 bis 1866,* Berlin

*F. W. von Ditfurth (1874) (ed.), *Die Historische Volkslieder des Oestreichischen Heeres,* Vienna

*F. W. von Ditfurth (1882) (ed.), *Die Historische-Politische Volkslieder des Dreissig-Jährigen Krieges,* Heidelberg

V. Djurić, 'Prince Marko in Epic Poetry' in *Journal of the Folklore Institute,* 3 (1966)

S. Domokos, 'Zur Geschichte der Räuberballaden' in *Acta Litteraria,*

3 (1960)

*G. Doncieux (ed.), *Le Romancéro Populaire de la France*, Paris, 1904

G. Doublet (1895a), 'Un Diocèse Pyrénéen sous Louis XIV' in *Revue des Pyrénées*, 7

G. Doublet (1895b), *Un Prélat Janséniste, F. de Caulet*, Paris/Foix

O. Douen, *Clement Marot et le Psautier Huguenot*, 2 vols, Paris, 1878–9

O. Driesen, *Der Ursprung des Harlekin*, Berlin, 1904

P. L. Duchartre, *L'Imagerie Populaire Russe et les Livrets Gravés, 1629–1885*, Paris, 1961

P. L. Duchartre/R. Saulnier, *L'Imagerie Populaire*, Paris, 1925

L. Dumont, *La Tarasque*, Paris, 1951

A. Dundes/A. Falassi, *La Terra in Piazza: an Interpretation of the Palio of Siena*, Berkeley and Los Angeles, 1975

M. J. Durry, 'L'Académie Celtique et la Chanson Populaire', in *Revue de Littérature Comparée*, 9 (1929)

P. van Duyse, *De Rederijkkamers in Nederland*, 2 vols, Ghent, 1900–2

H. Eberhardt, 'Der Kyffhäuserberg in Geschichte und Sage' in *Blätter für Deutsche Landesgeschichte*, 96 (1960)

C. M. Edsman (1967), 'A Swedish female folk healer', in Edsman (ed.), *Studies in Shamanism*, Stockholm

D. Eeckaute (1965), 'Les Brigands en Russie au 17e and 19e Siècles', in *Revue d'Histoire Moderne*, 12

O. Elschek, 'The Problem of Variation in 18th-Century Slovak Folk Music', in *Studia Musicologica*, 7 (1965)

W. J. Entwistle, *European Balladry*, Oxford, 1939

S. Erixon (1938), *Folklig Möbelkultur i Svenske Bygder*, Stockholm

S. Erixon (1939), 'Turwächter und Prangerfiguren' in *Folk-Liv*, 3

*L. Erk/F. M. Böhme (eds), *Deutsche Liederhort*, 3 vols, Leipzig, 1893–4

A. Espinosa, 'Spanish Folklore', in *Funk and Wagnall*

D. Fabre/J. Lacroix, *La Vie Quotidienne des Paysans de Languedoc au 19e Siècle*, Paris, 1973

H. Fehr, *Massenkunst im 16. Jahrhundert*, Berlin, 1924

E. Fél/T. Hofer/K. Csilléry, *Hungarian Peasant Art*, Budapest, 1958

E. Fél/T. Hofer, *Saints, Soldiers, Shepherds*, Budapest, 1966

R. de Felice, 'Paura e Religiosità popolare nello stato della Chiesa alla fine del 18 secolo' in his *Italia Giacobina*, Naples, 1965

J. Ferté, *La Vie Religieuse dans les Campagnes Parisiennes 1622–96*, Paris, 1962

R. Finnegan, 'Literacy v. Non-Literacy: the Great Divide?' in R. Horton/R. Finnegan (eds), *Modes of Thought*, London, 1973

M. Fleury/P. Valmary, 'Les Progrès de l'Instruction Elémentaire de Louis XIV à Napoleon III', in *Population*, 1 (1957).

G. M. Foster (1960), *Culture and Conquest: America's Spanish Heritage*, Chicago

G. M. Foster (1965), 'Peasant Society and the Image of Limited Good' in *American Anthropologist*, 67

J. Fournée, *Enquête sur le Cult Populaire de St Martin en Normandie*, Nogent, 1963

D. C. Fowler, *A Literary History of the Popular Ballad*, Durham, N.C., 1968

G. Franz (1933), *Der Deutsche Bauernkrieg*, Munich/Berlin, 7th edn, 1965

*G. Franz (1963) (ed.), *Quellen zur Geschichte des Bauernkrieges*, Munich

A. B. Friedman (1961a), *The Ballad Revival*, Chicago, 1961

A. B. Friedman (1961b), 'The Formulaic Improvisation Theory of Ballad Tradition', in *Journal of American Folklore*, 74

Funk and Wagnall's Standard Dictionary of Folklore, Mythology and Legend, ed. M. Leach, 2 vols, New York, 1949–50

F. Furet/W. Sachs, 'La Croissance de l'Alphabétisation en France' in *AESC*, 29 (1974)

J. Fuster, *El Bandolerisme Català:* Vol. 2, *La Llegenda*, Barcelona, 1963

C. Gaignebet (1972), 'Le Combat de Carnaval et de Carême' in *AESC*, 27

C. Gaignebet (1974), *Le Carnaval*, Paris

C. Gaignebet (1975), 'Le Cycle Annuel des Fêtes à Rouen au milieu du 16e siècle' in J. Jacquot (ed.), *Les Fêtes de la Renaissance*, 3, Paris

C. Galarneau, 'La Mentalité Paysanne en France sous l'Ancien Régime' in *Revue de L'Histoire de l'Amérique Française*, 14 (1960)

A. Gallego y Burín/A. Gámir Sandoval, *Los Moriscos del Reino de Granada*, Granada, 1968

A. N. Galpern, 'Late Medieval Piety in Sixteenth-Century Champagne', in C. Trinkaus/H. Oberman (eds), *The Pursuit of Holiness*, Leiden, 1974

P. García de Diego, 'El Testamento en la Tradición' in *Revista de Dialectología y Tradiciones Populares*, 9–10 (1953–4)

H. C. Gardiner, *Mysteries' End*, New Haven, 1946

A. van Gennep, *Manuel de Folklore Française*, 3 vols, Paris, 1937–43

M. D. George, *English Political Caricature*, Vol. 1, Oxford, 1959

*G. Gesemann (1925) (ed.), *Erlangenski Rukopis*, Sremski Karlovci (Carlowitz)

G. Gesemann (1926), 'Kompositionsschema und Heroisch-Epische Stilisierung' in his *Studien zur Südslavischen Volksepik*, Reichenberg

C. Ginzburg (1966), *I Benandanti*, Turin

C. Ginzburg (1972), 'Folklore, Magia, Religione' in R. Romano/C. Vivanti (eds), *Storia d'Italia*, 1, Turin

C. Ginzburg (1976), *Il Formaggio e le Vermi*, Turin

J. Godechot, 'Caractères Généraux des Soulèvements Contre-Révolutionnaires' in *Homenaje a J. Vicens Vives*, 2, Barcelona, 1967

A. González Palencia/E. Mele, *La Maya*, Madrid 1944

G. Granberg, 'Kyrkan och Folktron' (1948) repr. in A. B. Rooth (ed.), *Folkdikt och Folktro*, Lund, 1971

H. Grant, 'El Mundo al Reves' in *Hispanic Studies in Honour of J. Manson*, Oxford, 1972. (In English).

M. Gravier, *Luther et L'Opinion Publique*, Paris, 1942

R. Greve, *Studien über den Roman Buovo d'Antona in Russland*, Berlin, 1956

*J. Grimm/W. Grimm (eds), *Kinder- und Hausmärchen* (1812)

Grove's Dictionary of Music and Musicians, 5th edn, ed. E. Blom, 9 vols, London, 1954

*S. Grundtvig (ed.), *Danmarks Folkeviser i Udvalg*, Copenhagen, 1882

*C. Guasti (ed.), *Le Feste di S. Giovanni Battista in Firenze*, Florence, 1884

O. Guerrini, G. C. *Croce*, Bologna, 1879

A. Guershoon, *Certain Aspects of Russian Proverbs*, London, 1941

J. M. Guilcher, *La Tradition Populaire de Danse en Basse-Bretagne*, Paris/The Hague, 1963

T. W. R. de Haan (1950), *Volk en Dichterschaap*, Assen

T. W. R. de Haan (1965) (ed.), *Volkskunst der Lage Landen*, 3 vols, Amsterdam/Brussels

H. C. von Haebler, *Das Bild in der Evangelischen Kirche*, Berlin, 1957

T. Hampe, *Die Fahrenden Leute in der Deutschen Vergangenheit*, Leipzig, 1902

M. Harmon/G. Cocchiara/A. M. Marabotti, 'Folk Art' in *Encyclopaedia of World Art*, 5, London, 1971

H. J. Hansen (ed.), *European Folk Art*, Eng. trans., London, 1968

S. Hart, 'Enige Statistische Gegeuens inzake Analfabetisme te Amsterdam in de 17e en 18e eeuw' in *Amstelodanum*, 55 (1968)

*A. Hartmann (1880) (ed.), *Das Oberammergauen Passionspiel*, Leipzig

*A. Hartmann (1907–13) (ed.), *Historische Volkslieder*, Munich

H. G. Harvey, *The Theatre of the Basoche*, Cambridge, Mass., 1941

L. P. Harvey, 'Oral Composition and the Performance of Novels of Chivalry in Spain' in J. J. Duggan (ed.), *Oral Literature*, Edinburgh/London, 1975

F. W. Hasluck, *Christianity and Islam under the Sultans*, 2 vols, Oxford, 1929

R. Hauglid (ed.), *Native Art of Norway*, Oslo, 1965

H. Hauser (1899), *Ouvriers du Temps Passé*, Paris

H. Hauser (1909), *Études sur la Réforme Française*, Paris

D. Hay (1975) (ed.), *Albion's Fatal Tree: Crime and Society in 18th-Century England*, London

J. Heers (1971), *Fêtes, Jeux et Joutes dans les Sociétés d'Occident à la Fin du Moyen Age*, Montreal

J. Heers (1973), 'Les Métiers et les Fêtes Médiévales en France du Nord et en Angleterre' in *Revue du Nord*, 55

H. Hefele, *Hl Bernardin von Siena und die Franziskanische Wanderpredigt in Italien*, Freiburg, 1912

*G. Heilfurth (1959) (ed.), *Bergreihen*, Tübingen

G. Heilfurth (1967), *Bergbau und Bergmann in der Deutschsprachigen Sagenüberlieferungen Mitteleuropas*, Marburg

H. Henningsen, *Crossing the Equator*, Copenhagen, 1961

E. van Heurck, *Les Livres Populaires Flamands*, Antwerp n.d. (c.1931)

*K. I. Hildeman et al. (eds), *Politisk Rimdans*, Stockholm, 1960

C. Hill (1958), *Puritanism and Revolution*, London

C. Hill (1964), *Society and Puritanism in Pre-Revolutionary England*, London

C. Hill (1965), 'The Many-Headed Monster in Late Tudor and Early Stuart Political Thinking', reprinted in Hill (1974)

C. Hill (1972), *The World Turned Upside Down: Radical Ideas during the English Revolution*, London

C. Hill (1974), *Change and Continuity in Seventeenth-Century England*, London

E. J. Hobsbawm (1959), *Primitive Rebels*, new edn, Manchester, 1971

E. J. Hobsbawm (1969), *Bandits*, London

E. J. Hobsbawm (1971), 'Class Consciousness in History' in I. Mészaros (ed.), *Aspects of History and Class Consciousness*, London

M. Hodgart (1950), *The Ballads*, new edn, London, 1962

*M. Hodgart (ed.), *The Faber Book of Ballads*, London

M. Hoffmann, *En Gruppe Vevstoler på Vestlandet*, Oslo, 1958

*J. Horák (ed.), *Slovenske L'udove Balady*, Bratislava, 1956

T. Hornberger, *Der Schäfer*, Stuttgart, 1955

W. G. Hoskins, 'The Rebuilding of Rural England', repr. in his *Provincial England*, London, 1963

W. G. Hoskins, *The Midland Peasant*, London, 1957. ('Excursus' on peasant houses 1400–1800)

*J. Hrabák (ed.), *Staročeské Drama*, Prague, 1950

S. B. Hustvedt, *Ballad Criticism in Scandinavia and Great Britain during the Eighteenth Century*, New York, 1916

*G. O. Hyltén-Cavallius/G. Stephens (eds), *Sveriges Historiska och Politiska Visor*, 1, Örebro, 1853

Images du Peuple au 18e Siècle, Paris, 1973

K. Jackson (1936), 'The International Folktale in Ireland', in *Folklore*, 47
K. Jackson (1961), *The International Popular Tale and Early Welsh Tradition*, Cardiff
W. Jacobeit, *Schafhaltung und Schäfer*, Berlin, 1961
*J. P. Jacobsen *et al.* (eds), *Danske Folkebøger*, 14 vols, Copenhagen, 1915–36
R. Jakobson (1944), 'On Russian Fairy Tales', reprinted in Jakobson, *Selected Writings*, 1966
R. Jakobson, *Selected Writings*, 4, The Hague/Paris, 1966
R. Jakobson/P. Bogatyrev, 'Die Folklore als eine Besondere Form des Schaffens', repr. ibid
S. P. Jakobson, 'Slavic Folktales', in *Funk and Wagnall*
*R. Jente (ed.), *Proverbia Communia*, Bloomington, 1947. (803 Dutch proverbs from a fifteenth-century collection)
A. Jobst, *Evangelische Kirche und Volkstum*, Stuttgart, 1938
E. Johansson (1969), *Kvantitativa Studier av Alphabetiseringen i Sverige*, Umeå
E. Johansson (1973), *Literacy and Society in a Historical Perspective*, Umeå
E. Jolibois, *La Diablerie de Chaumont*, Chaumont, 1838
J. H. Jones, 'Commonplace and Memorisation in the Oral Tradition of the English and Scottish Popular Ballads' in *Journal of American Folklore*, 74 (1961)
T. G. Jones, *Welsh Folklore and Folk-Custom*, London, 1930
B. R. Jonsson, *Svensk Balladtradition*, 1, Stockholm, 1967
W. Jürgensen (1910), *Martinslieder*

J. Kaplow, *The Names of Kings: the Parisian Labouring Poor in the Eighteenth Century*, New York 1972
R. Kapp, *Heilige und Heiligenlegende in England*, Halle/Saale, 1934
V. S. Karadžić (ed.), *Srpske Narodne Pjesme*, 4 vols (1824–33)
*V. S. Karadžić (ed.), *Srpske Narodne Prilovetke*, (1853), Eng. trans. as *Hero Tales and Legends of the Serbians*, London, 1914
I. Katona, *Historische Schichten der Ungarische Volksdichtung*, Helsinki, 1964 (*FFC* no. 194)
M. Keen, *The Outlaws of Medieval Legend*, London, 1961
*A. Keller (ed.), *Fastnachtspiele*, 3 vols, Stuttgart, 1853–8
P. Kemp, *Healing Ritual*, London, 1935. (On Yugoslavia)
R. Kieckhefer, *European Witch-Trials: their Foundations in Popular and Learned Culture, 1300–1500*, London, 1976
J. Klersch, *Die Kölnische Fastnacht*, Cologne, 1961
E. Klingner, *Luther und der Deutsche Volksaberglaube*, Berlin, 1912

R. Kloster, 'Handverksbygden og bygdehandverkeren', repr. in Svensson (1968)

W. P. C. Knuttel (ed.), *Catalogus van de Pamfletten Verzameling Berustende in de Koninklijke Bibliotheek*, 9 vols, The Hague, 1889–1920

Z. Kodály, *Folk Music of Hungary* (1952), Eng. trans., London, 1971

E. Kohler, *Martin Luther und der Festbrauch*, Cologne/Graz, 1959

*W. Kohlschmidt (ed.), *Das Deutsche Soldatenlied*, Berlin, 1935

H. Koht (1926), *Norsk Bondereising*, repr. Oslo, 1975. (The French trans., *Les Luttes des Paysans en Norvège*, Paris, 1929, is much abbreviated)

H. Koht (1929), 'The Importance of the Class Struggle in Modern History', in *Journal of Modern History*

V. Kolve, *The Play called Corpus Christi*, Stanford, 1966

J. Komorovský, *Král Matej Korvín v L'udovej Prozaickej Slovesnosti*, Bratislava, 1957

D. Korf, *Dutch Tiles*, Eng. trans., London, 1963

W. Krebs, *Alte Handwerksbräuche*, Basel, 1933

H. Kügler, 'Friedrich der Grosse' in L. Mackensen (ed.), *Handwörterbuch des Deutsche Märchens*, 2, Berlin, 1940

*E. T. Kuiper (ed.), *Het Geuzenliedboek*, 2 vols, Zutphen, 1924

D. Kunzle, *The Early Comic Strip*, Berkeley and Los Angeles, 1973

M. Laget, 'Pétites Écoles en Languedoc au 18e Siècle' in *AESC*, 26 (1971)

H. Landsverk, 'Fra Biletverda i Folkekunsten' in *By og Bygd*, 18 (1952–3)

V. Lanternari, 'La Politica Culturale della Chiesa nelle Campagne: la Festa di S. Giovanni' in *Società*, 11 (1955)

P. Laslett, *The World We have Lost*, London, 1965

M. W. Latham, *The Elizabethan Fairies*, New York, 1930

E. Lazzareschi, *Un Contadino Poeta: Giovan Domenico Pèri d'Arcidosso*, 2 vols, Rome, 1909–11

K. M. Lea, *Italian Popular Comedy*, 2 vols, Oxford, 1934

N. A. M. Leader, *Hungarian Classical Ballads and their Folklore*, Cambridge, 1967

*C. Leber (ed.), *Collection des Meilleures Dissertations*, 9, Paris, 1826

G. Le Bras, *Études de Sociologie Religieuse*, 2 vols, Paris, 1955–6

F. Lebrun, *Les Hommes et la Mort en Anjou aux 17e et 18e Siècles*, Paris/The Hague, 1971

G. Lefebvre (1924), *Les Paysans du Nord pendant la Révolution Française*, repr. Bari, 1959

G. Lefebvre (1932), 'La Révolution Française et les Paysans', repr. in his *Études sur la Révolution Française*, Paris, 1954

G. Lefebvre (1934), 'Foules Révolutionnaires', repr. ibid

J. Lefebvre (1964), 'Le Jeu de Carnaval de Nuremberg' in J. Jacquot (ed.), *Le Lieu Théâtral à la Renaissance*, Paris

J. Lefebvre (1968), *Les Fols et la Folie*, Paris

J. Lefebvre (1975), 'Vie et Mort du Jeu de Carnaval à Nuremberg' in J. Jacquot (ed.), *Les Fêtes de la Renaissance*, 3, Paris

E. Le Roy Ladurie (1966), *Les Paysans de Languedoc*, 2 vols, Paris; abbreviated Eng. trans., Urbana, 1974

E. Le Roy Ladurie (1971), 'Mélusine Ruralisée' in *AESC*, 26

E. Le Roy Ladurie (1975), 'De la Crise Ultime à la Vraie Croissance' in G. Duby/A. Wallon (eds), *Histoire de la France Rurale*, Paris

E. Levi, *I Cantari Leggendari del Popolo Italiano*, Turin, 1914

R. Lieske, *Protestantische Frömmigkeit im Spiegel der Kirchlichen Kunst des Herzogtums Württemberg*, Munich/Berlin, 1973

*A. Liestøl (ed.), *Norske Folkeviser*, Oslo, 1964

K. Liestøl, *Scottish and Norwegian Ballads*, Oslo, 1946

*R. von Liliencron (ed.), *Die Historische Volkslieder der Deutschen vom 13. bis 16. Jahrhundert*, 4 vols, Leipzig, 1865–9

A. L. Lloyd, *Folksong in England* (1967), new edn, London, 1969

K. A. Lockridge, *Literacy in Colonial New England*, New York, 1974

C. G. Loomis, *White Magic: an Introduction to the Folklore of Christian Legend*, Cambridge, Mass., 1948

R. S. Loomis, 'Celtic Folklore' in *Funk and Wagnall*

A. B. Lord, *The Singer of Tales* (1960), new edn, New York, 1966

A. Lottin, *Vie et Mentalité d'un Lillois sous Louis XIV*, Lille, 1968

M. Louis, *Le Folklore et la Danse*, Paris, 1963

*D. S. Low (ed.), *The Ballads of Marko Kraljević*, Cambridge, 1922

L. Lowenthal, *Literature, Popular Culture and Society*, Englewood Cliffs, 1961

M. Lüthi (1947), *Das Europäische Volksmärchen*, new edn, Bern, 1960

M. Lüthi (1970), *Volksliteratur und Hochliteratur*, Bern/Munich

D. Macdonald, 'Masscult and Midcult', in his *Against the American Grain*, New York 1962

A. Macfarlane, *Witchcraft in Tudor and Stuart England*, London, 1970

R. W. Malcolmson, *Popular Recreations in English Society 1700–1850*, Cambridge, 1973

R. Mandrou (1964), *De la Culture Populaire au 17e et 18e Siècles*, Paris

R. Mandrou (1968), *Magistrats et Sorciers en France au 17e Siècle*, Paris

B. Manning, *The English People and the English Revolution, 1640–1649*, London, 1976

*L. Manzoni (ed.), *Libro di Carnevale*, Bologna, 1881

C. Mazzi, *La Congrega dei Rozzi di Siena nel Secolo 16*, Florence, 1882

*A. Medin/L. Frati (eds), *Lamenti Storici*, 4 vols, Bologna, 1887–94

G. Mehring, 'Das Vaterunser als Politische Kampfsmittel' in *Zeitschrift des Vereins für Volkskunde*, 19 (1909)

J. Meier, *Kunstlied und Volkslied in Deutschland*, Halle, 1906

K. Meisen (1931), *Nikolauskult und Nikolausbrauch im Abendlande*, Düsseldorf

K. Meisen (1962–3), 'St Michael in der Volkstümliche Verehrung des Abendlandes' in *Rheinische Jahrbuch für Volkskunde*, 13–14

A. Meličerčik, *Jánošíkovská Tradícia na Slovensku*, Bratislava, 1952

R. Menéndez Pidal (1924), *Poesia Juglaresca y Juglares*, Madrid

R. Menéndez Pidal (1938) (ed.), *Flor Nueva de Romances Viejos*, 16th edn, Buenos Aires, 1967

H. C. E. Midelfort, *Witch Hunting in Southwestern Germany 1562–1684*, Stanford, 1972

*M. Milá y Fontanals (ed.), 'Romancerillo Catalan', in his *Observaciones sobre la Poesia Popular*, Barcelona, 1853

J. Mistler *et al.*, *Epinal et L'Imagerie Populaire*, Paris, 1961

E. W. Monter, *Witchcraft in France and Switzerland*, Ithaca/London, 1976

*E. Moser-Rath (1964) (ed.), *Predigtmärlein der Barockzeit*, Berlin

E. Moser-Rath (1968), 'Literature and Folk Tradition', in *Journal of the Folklore Institute*, 5

R. Mousnier, *Fureurs Paysannes*, Paris, 1967. Eng. trans. as *Peasant Uprisings*, London, 1971

R. Muchembled, 'Sorcellerie, Culture Populaire et Christianisme au 16e Siècle' in *AESC*, 28 (1973)

V. E. Neuburg, *Popular Education in 18th-Century England*, London, 1971

A. Nicoll, *The World of Harlequin*, Cambridge, 1963

*H. G. Nielsen (ed.), *Danske Viser fra Adelsvisebøger og Flyveblader, 1530–1630*, Copenhagen, 1912

M. Nodermann, *Nordisk Folkkonst*, Stockholm, 1968

*A. Noreen/H. Schück (eds), *1500– och 1600–talens Visböcker*, 12 parts, Stockholm/Uppsala, 1884–1927

*F. J. Norton/E. M. Wilson (eds), *Two Spanish Verse Chap-Books*, Cambridge, 1969

H. O. Nygard, *The Ballad of Heer Halewijn*, Helsinki/Knoxville, 1958 (*FFC* no. 169)

F. J. Oinas/S. Soudakoff (eds), *The Study of Russian Folklore*, The Hague/Paris, 1975

A. Olrik (1908), 'Epic Laws of Folk Narrative', trans. in A. Dundes (ed.), *The Study of Folklore*, Englewood Cliffs, 1965

*A. Olrik (1939) (ed.), *A Book of Danish Ballads*, Princeton/New York

B. Olsson, 'Psalmboken som Folkbok' (1942), repr. in Pleijel (1967)

G. Ortutay (1959a), 'Principles of Oral Transmission in Folk Culture' in *Acta Ethnographica*, 8

G. Ortutay (1959b), 'Das Ungarische Volksmärchen' in *Acta Litteraria*, 2

*G. Ortutay (1968) (ed.), *Magyar Népballadák*, Budapest

Y. Ovsyannikov (1968), *The Lubok: 17th–18th Century Russian Broadsides*, Moscow

Y. Ovsyannikov (1970), *Russian Folk Arts and Crafts*, Moscow

M. Ozouf (1971), 'Les Cortèges Révolutionnaires et la Ville' in *AESC*, 26

M. Ozouf (1975), 'Space and Time in the Festivals of the French Revolution' in *Comparative Studies in Society and History*, 17 (1975)

M. Ozouf (1976), *La Fête Revolutionnaire*, Paris

*V. Pandolfi (ed.), *La Commedia dell'Arte*, 6 vols, Florence, 1957–61

P. Pascal (1938), *Avvakum et les Débuts du Raskol*, Paris

*P. Pascal (1971), *La Révolte de Pougatchëv*, Paris

*M. Perceval (ed.), *Political Ballads Illustrating the Administration of Sir Robert Walpole*, Oxford, 1916

*T. Percy (ed.), *Reliques of Ancient Poetry* (1765), new edn, 3 vols, London, 1891

L. Petit de Julleville, *Les Comédiens en France au Moyen Age*, Paris, 1885

*E. Petraccone (ed.), *La Commedia dell'Arte*, Naples, 1927

R. Petrović, 'The Oldest Notation of Folk Tunes in Yugoslavia', in *Studia Musicologica*, 7 (1965)

H. G. Pfander, *The Popular Sermon of the Medieval Friar in England*, New York, 1937

J. Phillips, *The Reformation of Images: Destruction of Art in England 1535–1660*, Berkeley and Los Angeles, 1973

C. Phythian-Adams (1972), 'Ceremony and the Citizen: the Communal Year at Coventry 1450–1550' in P. Clark/P. Slack (eds), *Crisis and Order in English Towns*, London

C. Phythian-Adams (1975), *History and Folklore*, London

*E. Picot (ed.), *Recueil Général des Sotties*, 3 vols, Paris, 1902–12

R. Pinon, 'Qu'est-ce qu'un Charivari?' in *Festschrift für G. Heilfurth*, Göttingen, 1969

G. Pitrè (1872), *Studi di Poesia Popolare*, repr. Florence, 1957

G. Pitrè (1876), *Della Sacre Rappresentazioni Popolari in Sicilia*, Palermo

G. Pitrè (1889), *Usi e Costumi del Popolo Siciliano*, 4 vols, Palermo

H. Pleijel (1955), *The Devotional Literature of the Swedish People*, Lund

H. Pleijel (1958), *Das Luthertum im Schwedischen Volksleben*, Lund

H. Pleijel (1965), *Husandakt, Husaga, Husförhör*, Stockholm

H. Pleijel *et al.* (1967), *Våra Äldsta Folkböcker*, Lund

J. H. Plumb (1968), 'Political Man' in J. L. Clifford (ed.), *Man versus Society in 18th-Century England*, Cambridge

J. H. Plumb (1973), *The Commercialisation of Leisure in 18th-Century England*, Reading

G. C. Pola Falletti-Villafalletto, *Associazioni Giovanili e Feste Antichi*, 4 vols, Turin, 1939–42

B. Porchnev, *Les Soulèvements Populaires en France de 1623 à 1648* (1948), French trans., Paris, 1963

Y. Poutet, 'L'Enseignement des Pauvres dans la France du 17e Siècle', in *Dix-Septième Siècle*, 90–1 (1971)

V. Propp, *Morphologie du Conte* (1928), French trans., Paris, 1970

J. B. Rael, *The Sources and Diffusion of the Mexican Shepherd's Plays*, Guadalajara, 1965

W. Ralston, *The Songs of the Russian People*, London, 1872

R. Redfield, *Peasant Society and Culture*, Chicago, 1956

J. Reed, *Border Ballads*, London 1973

J. Reglà, *El Bandolerisme Català: 1, La Historia*, Barcelona, 1962

M. Rehnberg, *Vad Skall Vi Göra med de Blanke Gevär*, Stockholm, 1967

M. Reinhard, *La Légende de Henri IV*, Paris, 1936

K. V. Riedel, *Der Bänkelsang*, Hamburg, 1963

A. Riff (1945), *L'Art Populaire et l'Artisanat Rural en Alsace*, Strasbourg

A. Riff (1963) (ed.), *Art Populaire d'Alsace*, Strasbourg/Paris

A. Rigoli (ed.), *Scibilia Nobili e Altre Storie*, Parma, 1965

W. E. Roberts, 'Folklore in the Novels of Thomas Deloney' in W. E. Richmond (ed.), *Studies in Folklore*, Bloomington, 1957

A. Rodríguez-Moñino (ed.), *Diccionario Bibliográfico de Pliegos Sueltos Poeticos (Siglo XVI)*, Madrid, 1970

H. U. Roller, *Der Nürnberger Schembartlauf*, Tübingen, 1965

H. E. Rollins (1919), 'The Black-Letter Broadside Ballad' in *Proceedings of the Modern Language Association*

*H. E. Rollins (1929–32) (ed.), *The Pepys Ballads*, 8 vols, Cambridge, Mass.

J. Romeu (1948), *El Mito de 'El Conte Arnau'*, Barcelona

*J. Romeu (1957) (ed.), *Teatre Hagiogràfic*, Barcelona

O. Rommel, *Die Alt-Wiener Volkskomödie*, Vienna, 1952

H. F. Rosenfeld, *Der hl Christophorus*, Leipzig, 1937

S. Rosenfeld (1939), *Strolling Players and Drama in the Provinces 1660–1765*, Cambridge

S. Rosenfeld (1960), *The Theatre of the London Fairs in the Eighteenth*

Century, Cambridge
V. Rossi, 'Un Cantastorie Ferrarese del Secolo 16' in *Rassegna Emiliana*, 2 (1889–90)
D. P. Rotunda, *Motif-Index of the Italian Novella in Prose*, Bloomington, 1942
*L. Rouanet (ed.), *Colección de Autos, Farsas y Coloquios del Siglo 16*, 4 vols, Barcelona/Madrid, 1901
G. Rudé (1959), *The Crowd in the French Revolution*, Oxford
G. Rudé (1964), *The Crowd in History, 1730–1848*, New York
G. Rudé (1974), *Paris and London in the Eighteenth Century*, London
M. Rudwin (1920), *The Origin of the German Carnival Comedy*, London
M. Rudwin (1931), *The Devil in Legend and Literature*, Chicago/London

C. Sachs, *A World History of the Dance*, Eng. trans., London, 1938
*J. Saenz (ed.), *Collectio Maxima Conciliorum Omnium Hispaniae*, Rome, 1755, Vols 5, 6
*J. Sahlgren (ed.), *Svenska Folkböcker*, 8 vols, Stockholm, 1946–56
M. Sahlin, *Études sur la Carole Médiévale*, Uppsala, 1940
L. Sainéan, *L'Argot Ancien, 1455–1850*, Paris, 1907
*G. Salgãdo (ed.), *Cony-Catchers and Bawdy Baskets*, Harmondsworth, 1972
P. Salies, 'Imagerie Populaire et Confréries Toulousaines' in *Gazette des Beaux-Arts*, 1962
R. Salillas, *El Delincuente Español*, 2 vols, Madrid, 1896–8
W. Salmen, *Der Fahrende Musiker im Europäischen Mittelalter*, Kassel, 1960
*S. Salomone-Marino (1875) (ed.), *Storie Popolari in Poesia Siciliana*, Bologna
S. Salomone-Marino (1924), *Costumi ed Usanze dei Contadini di Sicilia*, Palermo
J. Samaha, 'Sedition amongst the "inarticulate" in Elizabethan England', in *Journal of Social History* 8 (1975)
R. Samuel, 'People's History' in his *Village Life and Labour*, London, 1975
R. Saulnier/A. Aynaud, 'Prototypes de L'Imagerie Populaire' in *Arts et Traditions Populaires*, 1 (1953)
J. Schacher, *Das Hexenwesen im Kanton Luzern*, Lucerne, 1947
*O. Schade (ed.), *Handwerkslieder*, Leipzig, 1864
*J. F. Schannat (ed.), *Concilia Germaniae*, 11 vols, Cologne, 1759–90. (Esp. Vols 5–10)
G. Schanz, *Zur Geschichte der Deutschen Gesellen-Verbände*, Leipzig, 1877
M. Scharfe (1967), 'Bildzeugnisse Evangelischer Frömmigkeit' in M.

Scharfe *et al.*, *Volksfrömmigkeit*, Stuttgart

M. Scharfe (1968), *Evangelische Andachtsbilder*, Stuttgart

E. Schaumkell, *Der Kultus der hl Anna am Ausgang des Mittelalters*, Freiburg/Leipzig, 1893

R. Schenda (1965–6), 'Italienische Volkslesestoffe im 19. Jahrhundert' in *Archiv für Geschichte des Buchwesens, 7*

R. Schenda (1970), *Volk ohne Buch*, Frankfurt

D. F. Scheurleer (ed.), *Van Varen en van Vechten*, 3 vols, The Hague, 1914

E. Schmidt, *Deutsche Volkskunde im Zeitalter des Humanismus*, Berlin, 1904

L. Schmidt (1955) (ed.), *Masken in Mitteleuropa*, Vienna

L. Schmidt (1963), *Die Volkserzählung*, Berlin

*L. Schmidt (1965) (ed.), *Le Théâtre Populaire Européen*, Paris

*L. Schmidt (1971) (ed.), *Historische Volkslieder aus Österreich*, Vienna

G. Schochet, 'Patriarchalism, Politics and Mass Attitudes in Stuart England', in *Historical Journal*, 12 (1969)

C. Schoebel, *La Légende du Juif Errant*, Paris, 1877

R. Schofield (1968), 'The Measurement of Literacy in Pre-Industrial England' in J. Goody (ed.), *Literacy in Traditional Societies*, Cambridge

R. Schofield (1973), 'Illiteracy in Pre-Industrial England' in Johansson (1973)

W. Schoof, *Zur Entstehungsgeschichte der Grimmschen Märchen*, Hamburg, 1959

G. D. J. Schotel (1862–4), *Geschiedenis der Rederijkers in Nederland*, 2 vols, Amsterdam

G. D. J. Schotel (1868), *Het Oud-Hollandsch Huisgezin der 17e Eeuw*, Haarlem

G. D. J. Schotel (1873–4), *Vaderlandsche Volksboeken*, 2 vols, Haarlem

K. Schottenloher, *Flugblatt und Zeitung*, Berlin, 1922

G. Schreiber *et al.* (1959), *Die Vierzehn Nothelfer*, Innsbruck

G. Schreiber (1962), *Der Bergbau in Geschichte, Ethos und Sakralkultur*, Berlin/Opladen

J. Schrijnen, *Nederlandsche Volkskunde*, 2nd edn, 2 vols, Zutphen, 1930

W. Scott, *Minstrelsy of the Scottish Border*, ed. T. F. Henderson, 3 vols, Edinburgh, 1902

P. Sébillot (1883), *Gargantua dans les Traditions Populaires*, Paris

P. Sébillot (1894), *Les Travaux Publics et les Mines dans les Traditions et les Superstitions de Tous les Pays*, Paris

P. Sébillot (1901), *Le Folklore des Pêcheurs*, Paris

*E. Seemann *et al.* (eds), *European Folk Ballads*, Copenhagen, 1967

J. P. Seguin, *L'Information en France de Louis XII à Henri II*, Geneva, 1961

M. A. Shaaber, *Some Forerunners of the Newspaper in England*, Philadelphia, 1929

C. Sharp, *English Folksong: some Conclusions*, London, 1907

L. Shepard (1969), *John Pitts*, London

L. Shepard (1973), *The History of Street Literature*, Newton Abbot

C. M. Simpson (1941–2), 'Tudor Popular Music' in *Huntington Library Quarterly*, 5

C. M. Simpson (1966), *The British Broadside Ballad and its Music*, New Brunswick

*C. S. Singleton (ed.), *Canti Carnascialeschi del Rinascimento*, Bari, 1936

C. Sisson, *Lost Plays of Shakespeare's Age*, (1936), repr. London, 1970

A. Soboul (1958), *Les Sans-Culottes Parisiens en l'An II*, Paris, abbreviated Eng. trans., Oxford, 1964

A. Soboul (1966), 'Classes Populaires et Rousseauisme', repr. in his *Paysans, Sans-Culottes et Jacobins*, Paris

A. Soboul (1970), *La Civilisation et la Révolution Française*, Paris

Y. M. Sokolov, *Russian Folklore* (1938), Eng. trans. repr. Detroit, 1971

J. Solé, 'Lecture et Classes Populaires à Grenoble' in *Images du Peuple*

*F. L. von Soltau (ed.), *Ein Hundert Deutsche Historische Volkslieder*, Leipzig, 1836

M. Soriano, *Les Contes de Perrault: Culture Savante et Traditions Populaires*, Paris, 1968

A. Spamer (ed.), *Die Deutsche Volkskunde*, 2 vols, Leipzig/Berlin, 1934–5

P. Spezzani, 'L'Arte Rappresentativa di Andrea Perrucci e la Lingua della Commedia dell'Arte' in G. Folena (ed.), *Lingua e Strutture del Teatro Italiano del Rinascimento*, Padua, 1970

M. Spufford, *Contrasting Communities*, Cambridge, 1974

C. Stief, *Studies in the Russian Historical Song*, Copenhagen, 1953

T. Stoianovich, 'Material Foundations of Pre-Industrial Civilisation in the Balkans', in *Journal of Social History*, 4 (1970–1)

L. Stone (1964), 'The Educational Revolution in England, 1560–1640' in *P&P*, no. 28

L. Stone (1969), 'Literacy and Education in England, 1640–1900' in *P&P*, no. 42

E. van der Straeten, *Le Théâtre Villageois en Flandre*, 2 vols, Brussels, 1881

G. Strauss, 'Success and Failure in the German Reformation' in *P&P*, no. 67 (1975)

*H. Strobach, *Bauernklagen: Untersuchungen zum Sozialkritischen Deutschen Volkslied*, East Berlin, 1964

D. Subotić, *Yugoslav Popular Ballads*, Cambridge, 1932

S. L. Sumberg, *The Nuremberg Schembart Carnival*, New York, 1941
S. Svärdström (1949), *Dalmålningarna och deres Förlagor*, Stockholm
S. Svärdström (1957), *Masterpieces of Dala Peasant Painting*, Stockholm
S. Svensson (1955), 'Gustaf Adolf und die Schwedische Volkskunde' in *Festschrift für W. E. Peuckert*, Berlin.
S. Svensson (1967), 'Almanackan', in H. Pleijel (1967)
S. Svensson (1968) (ed.), *Nordisk Folkkunst*, Stockholm
B. Szabolcsi, 'Folk Music, Art Music, History of Music', in *Studia Musicologica*, 7 (1965)
J. Szöverffy, 'History and Folk Tradition in East Europe' in *Journal of the Folklore Institute*, 5 (1968)

F. Tassy, 'Il Paese di Cuccagna', in *Acta Litteraria*, 2 (1959)
*F. Taviani (ed.), *La Commedia dell'Arte e la Società Barocca*, Rome, 1970
A. Taylor (1921), 'The Devil and the Advocate', in *Proceedings of the Modern Language Association*, 36
A. Taylor (1931), '*Edward*' and '*Sven i Rosengård*', Chicago
A. Taylor (1937), *The Literary History of Meistergesang*, New York/London
A. Taylor (1949), 'Germanic Folklore', in *Funk and Wagnall*
R. Taylor, *The Political Prophecy in England*, New York, 1911
J. Tazbir, 'Die Gesellschaftliche Funktion des Kultus des Heiligen Isidor des Pflügen in Polen', in *Acta Polonica Historica*, 20 (1969)
K. V. Thomas (1964), 'Work and Leisure in Pre-Industrial Society' in *P&P*, no. 29
K. V. Thomas (1971), *Religion and the Decline of Magic*, London
E. P. Thompson (1963), *The Making of the English Working Class*, London
E. P. Thompson (1967), 'Time, Work-Discipline and Industrial Capitalism', in *P&P*, no. 38
E. P. Thompson (1971), 'The Moral Economy of the English Crowd', in *P&P*, no. 50
E. P. Thompson (1972), 'Rough Music', in *AESC*, 27
E. P. Thompson (1973–4), 'Patrician Society, Plebeian Culture', in *Journal of Social History*, 7
E. P. Thompson (1975), 'The Crime of Anonymity', in D. Hay *et al.* (eds), *Albion's Fatal Tree*, London
R. Thompson, 'Popular Reading and Humour in Restoration England' in *Journal of Popular Culture* (1976)
D. S. Thomson (1952), *The Gaelic Sources of Macpherson's Ossian*, Edinburgh/London
D. S. Thomson (1974), *An Introduction to Gaelic Poetry*, London
*R. J. E. Tiddy, *The Mummer's Play*, Oxford, 1923

J. Tiersot *Les fêtes et les Chants de la Révolution Française*, Paris, 1908

C. H. Tillhagen (1962), *Folklig Läkekonst*, 2nd edn, Stockholm

C. H. Tillhagen (1969), 'Finnen und Lappen als Zauberkundige' in *Festschrift für G. Heilfurth*, Göttingen

J. B. du Tilliot, *Mémoires pour Servir à l'Histoire de la Fête des Fous*, Lausanne/Geneva, 1741

W. Y. Tindall, *John Bunyan, Mechanick Preacher*, New York, 1934

K. Togeby, *Ogier le Danois dans les Littératures Européennes*, Copenhagen, 1969

P. Toschi (1935), *La Poesia Popolare Religiosa in Italia*, Florence

P. Toschi (1955), *Origini del Teatro Italiano*, Turin

P. Toschi (1964), *La Legenda di S. Giorgio nei Canti Popolari Italiani*, Rome

J. Trachtenberg, *The Devil and the Jews*, New Haven, 1943

H. R. Trevor-Roper, *The European Witch-Craze*, Harmondsworth, 1969

R. C. Trexler (1972), 'Florentine Religious Experience: the Sacred Image', in *Studies in the Renaissance*, 19

R. C. Trexler (1974), 'Ritual in Florence: Adolescence and Salvation in the Renaissance', in C. Trinkaus/H. A. Oberman (eds), *The Pursuit of Holiness*, Leiden

T. F. Troels-Lund, *Dagligt Liv i Norden i det Sekstende Aarhundrede*, 14 vols, Copenhagen/Oslo, 1908–10

H. Trümpy, 'Die Reformation als Volkskundliches Problem' in *Festschrift für G. Heilfurth*, Göttingen, 1969

G. Turi, *Viva Maria: la Reazione alle Riforme Leopoldine, 1790–99*, Florence, 1969

P. D. Ukhov, 'Fixed Epithets in the Byliny', in Oinas/Soudakoff

K. Uldall, *Dansk Folkekunst*, Copenhagen, 1963

J. E. Varey, *Historia de los Títeres en España*, Madrid, 1957

J. E. Varey/N. D. Shergold, 'La Tarasca de Madrid', in *Clavileño*, 4 (1953)

L. Vargyas, *Researches into the Medieval History of Folk Ballad*, Budapest, 1967

R. Vaultier (1946), *Les Fêtes Populaires à Paris*, Paris

R. Vaultier (1965), *Le Folklore pendant la Guerre de Cent Ans*, Paris

A. Vecchi, *Il Culto delle Immagine nelle Stampe Popolari*, Florence, 1968

F. G. Very, *The Spanish Corpus Christi Procession*, Valencia, 1962

*M. Viollet-le-Duc (ed.), *Ancien Théâtre Français*, 3 vols, Paris, 1854

B. Vogler, 'La Législation sur les Sépultures dans l'Allemagne Protestante', in *Revue d'Histoire Moderne et Contemporaine*, 22 (1975)

M. Vovelle (1973), *Piété Baroque et Déchristianisation en Provence au 18e Siècle*, Paris

M. Vovelle (1975), 'Y a-t-il eu une Révolution Culturelle au 18e Siècle? L'Education Populaire en Provence', in *Revue d'Histoire Moderne et Contemporaine*, 22

J. de Vries, 'Peasant Demand Patterns and Economic Development: Friesland 1550–1750' in W. N. Parker/E. L. Jones (eds), *European Peasants and their Markets*, Princeton, 1975

G. E. Waas, *The Legendary Character of the Emperor Maximilian*, New York, 1941

*P. Wackernagel (ed.), *Das Deutsche Kirchenlied*, 5 vols, Leipzig, 1864–7

J. Walsh, 'Methodism and the Mob in the 18th Century' in Cuming/Baker

*B. W. Wardropper (ed.), *Cancionero Espiritual*, Oxford, 1954

R. F. Wearmouth, *Methodism and the Common People*, London, 1945

R. H. Webber, *Formulistic Diction in the Spanish Ballad*, Berkeley and Los Angeles, 1951

E. Welsford, *The Fool* (1935), repr. London, 1968

R. M. Werner, 'Das Vaterunser als Gottesdienstliche Zeitlyrik' in *Vierteljahrschrift für Litteraturgeschichte*, 5 (1892)

B. Widén, 'Literacy in the Ecclesiastical Context' in Johansson (1973)

P. Wiertz, 'Zur Religiösen Volkskultur der Orientalischen und Orthodoxen Kirchen' in E. von Ivánka, *et al.* (eds.), *Handbuch der Ostkirchenkunde*, Düsseldorf, 1971

D. Wilson, *The Life and Times of Vuk Stefanović Karadžić*, Oxford, 1970

L. C. Wimberley, *Folklore in the English and Scottish Ballads*, Chicago, 1928

S. Windakiewicz, *Teatr Ludowy w Dawnej Polsce*, Kraków, 1904

H. F. Wirth, *Der Untergang des Niederländischen Volksliedes*, The Hague, 1911

R. Wohlfeil (ed.), *Reformation oder Frühbürgerliche Revolution*, Munich, 1972

*F. J. Wolf/C. Hofmann (eds), *Primavera y Flor de Romances*, 2 vols, Berlin, 1856

*R. Wossidlo (ed.), *Herr und Knecht: Anti-Feudale Sagen aus Mecklenburg*, Berlin, 1960

L. B. Wright, *Middle-Class Culture in Elizabethan England*, Chapel Hill, 1935

*T. Wright (ed.), *Songs and Ballads*, London, 1860

J. H. Wuorinen, *Nationalism in Modern Finland*, New York, 1931

*D. Wuttke (ed.), *Fastnachtspiele des 15. und 16. Jahrhunderts*,

Stuttgart, 1973
A. Wycański, 'Alphabétisation et Structure Sociale en Pologne au 16e Siècle' in *AESC*, 29 (1974)

R. Zguta, 'Skomorokhi' in *Slavic Review*, 31 (1972)
H. Zins, 'Aspects of the Peasant Rising in East Prussia in 1525', in *Slavonic and East European Review*, 38 (1959–60)
A. Ziwès, *Le Jargon de Maître François Villon, Paris, 1960*

Popular culture: a supplementary bibliography

This bibliography is selective. It concentrates on studies of early modern Europe published since 1976 (when the first edition of this book was sent to press), but includes a few general discussions of popular culture or historical studies of other regions or periods.

L. Allegra (1981), 'Il parroco: un mediatore fra alta e bassa cultura', *Storia d'Italia Annali* 4, Turin, 897–947
S.D. Amussen (forthcoming), 'The Gendering of Popular Culture in Early Modern England', in Harris
B. Ankarloo and G. Henningsen (1990, eds), *Early Modern European Witchcraft*, Oxford
A. Appadurai (1986, ed), *The Social Life of Things*, Cambridge
A.A. Arantes (1981), *O que ě cultura popular*, S. Paulo
M. Aris (1987), 'Alternative Voices from Bhutan', *Past and Present* 115, 131–64.

P. Bailey (1987), *Leisure and Class in Victorian England*, second edition
M.M. Bakhtin (1929), *Problems of Dostoyevsky's Poetics*, English trans. Manchester
M.M. Bakhtin (1981), *The Dialogic Imagination*, Austin
M.G. Baylor (1989), 'On the Front between the Cultures: Thomas Müntzer on Popular and Learned Culture', *History of European Ideas* 11, 523–36
J. Beauroy, et al. (1976, eds), *The Wolf and the Lamb: Popular Culture in France from the Old Regime to the 20th Century*, Saratoga
W. Bergsma (1990), 'Slow to hear God's Holy Word? Religion in Everyday Life in Early Modern Friesland', in *Experiences and Explanations*, ed. L. Laeyendecker et al, Ljouwert, 59–78
M. Bertrand (1985, ed.), *Popular Traditions and Learned Culture in France*, Saratoga
F. Bethencourt (1987), *O imaginário da magia: feiticeiras, saludadores e nigromantes no séc. xvi*, Lisbon

M. Boiteux (1977), 'Le carnaval annexé', *Annales E.S.C.* 32, 356–77

P. Bourdieu (1982), 'The Uses of the People', English trans in his *In Other Words*, Cambridge, 1990, 150–5

T. Brennan (1988), *Public Drinking and Popular Culture in 18th-Century Paris*, Princeton

J. Brewer and J. Styles (1980, eds), *An Ungovernable People*, London

R. Briggs (1989), *Communities of Belief*, Oxford

P. Brown (1981), *The Cult of the Saints*, London

W. Brückner, P. Blickle and D. Breuer (1985, eds), *Literatur und Volk im 17.Jahrhundert*, Wiesbaden

P. Burke (1979), *Dutch popular culture in the 17th century*, Rotterdam

P. Burke (1981), 'The Classical Tradition and Popular Culture', in Vovelle, 237–44

P. Burke (1981), 'The Bibliothèque Bleue in Comparative Perspective', *Quaderni del '600 francese*, 59–66

P. Burke (1982), 'A Question of Acculturation', in Zambelli, 197–204

P. Burke (1984), 'Popular Culture between History and Ethnology', *Ethnologia Europea* 14, 5–13

P. Burke (1986), 'Revolution in Popular Culture', in *Revolution*, ed. R. Porter and M. Teich, Cambridge, ch.10

P. Burke (1987), *Historical Anthropology of Early Modern Italy*, Cambridge

P. Burke (1988a), 'Popular Piety', in *The Counter-Reformation: a Guide to Research*, ed. J. O'Malley, St Louis, 113–32

P. Burke (1988b), 'Bakhtin for Historians', *Social History* 13, 85–90

P. Burke (1990), 'Popular Culture Reconsidered', in *Mensch und Objekt*, ed. G. Jaritz, Krems, 181–92

P. Burke (1992a), 'We, the People: Popular Culture and Identity in Modern Europe', in *Modernity and Identity*, ed. S. Lash and J. Friedman, Oxford, 293–308

P. Burke (1992b), 'Learned Culture and Popular Culture in Renaissance Italy', *Pauvres et riches: Mélanges offerts à Bronislaw Geremek*, ed. M. Aymard et al., Warsaw, 341–9

E.B. Burns (1980), *The Poverty of Progress*, Berkeley

B. Bushaway (1982), *By Rite: Custom, Ceremony and Community in England 1700–1880*, London

H. Buszello, 'The Common Man's View of the State', in *The German Peasant War*, ed R. Scribner and G. Benecke, ch.9

E. Cameron, *The Reformation of the Heretics: the Waldenses of the Alps 1480–1580*, Oxford

P. Camporesi (1980), *Bread of Dreams*, English trans Cambridge 1989

P. Camporesi (1981), 'Cultura popolare e cultura d'elite fra medioevo ed età moderna', *Storia d'Italia Annali* 4, 81–157

P. Camporesi (1983), *The Incorruptible Flesh*, English trans Cambridge 1987

B. Capp (1979), *Astrology and the Popular Press*, London

B. Capp (1985), 'Popular Literature', in Reay, ch.6

B. Capp (1989a), 'Popular Culture and the English Civil War', *History of European Ideas* 10, 31–41

B. Capp (1989b), 'John Taylor the Water-Poet: a Cultural Amphibian in 17th-century England', *History of European Ideas* 11, 537–44

E. Casale (1982), *Il villano dirozzato*, Florence

R. Chartier (1981), 'La culture populaire en question', *Histoire*, 8, 85–96

R. Chartier (1984), 'Culture as Appropriation: Popular Cultural Uses in Early Modern France', in Kaplan, ch.9

R. Chartier (1987), *The Cultural Uses of Print in Early Modern France*, Princeton

R. Chartier (1989), *The Cultural Origins of the French Revolution*, Princeton

Louis Châtellier (1993), *La religion des pauvres: Les missions rurales en Europe et la formation du catholicisme moderne, xvie–xixe siècles*, Paris

T. Cheesman (1989–90), 'The Return of the Transformed Son: a Popular Ballad Complex and Cultural History, Germany 1500–1900', *Oxford German Studies*, 18–19, 59–91

W.A. Christian (1981a), *Apparitions in Late Medieval and Renaissance Spain*, Princeton

W.A. Christian (1981b), *Local Religion in 16th-Century Spain*, Princeton

P. Clark (1978), 'The Alehouse and the Alternative Society', in *Puritans and Revolutionaries*, ed. D. Pennington and K.V. Thomas, Oxford, 47–72

P. Clark (1983), *The English Alehouse*, London

S. Clark (1983), 'French historians and Early Modern Popular Culture', *P&P* 100, 62–99

S. Clark (1991), 'The Rational Witch-Finder', in Pumfrey 222–48

T.V. Cohen (1988), 'The Case of the Mysterious Coil of Rope: Street Life and Jewish persona in Rome in the Middle of the Sixteenth Century', *Sixteenth-Century Journal* 19, 209–22

P. Collinson (1982), *The Religion of Protestants*, Oxford (esp. ch. 5, 'Popular and Unpopular Religion')

R. Colls (1977), *The Collier's Rant*, London

J. Contreras (1982), *El sancto oficio de la inquisición en Galicia 1560–1700*, Madrid

B. Cousin (1983), *Le miracle et le quotidien: Les ex-voto provençaux, images d'une société*, Aix-en-Provence

Culturas populares: diferencias, divergencias, conflictos (1986), Madrid

H. Cunningham (1980), *Leisure in the Industrial Revolution*, London
P. Curry (1989), *Prophecy and Power: Astrology in Early Modern England*, Cambridge
T.C. Curtis and W. Speck (1976), 'The Societies for the Reformation of Manners', *Literature and History* 3, 45–64

R. Darnton (1984), *The Great Cat Massacre*, New York
C.S.L. Davies (1985), 'Popular Religion and the Pilgrimage of Grace', in Fletcher and Stevenson, ch.2
N.Z. Davis (1982), 'From Popular Religion to Religious Cultures', in Ozment 321–36
N.Z. Davis (1992), 'Toward Mixtures and Margins', *American Historical Review* 97, 1409–16
J.-P. Dedieu (1979), 'Christianization in New Castille: Catechism, Communion, Mass and Confirmation in the Toledo Archbishopric, 1540–1650', English trans in *Culture and Control in Counter-Reformation in Spain*, ed. A.J. Cruz and M.E. Perry, Minneapolis, ch.1
J.-P. Dedieu (1987), 'The Inquisition and Popular Culture in New Castille', in Haliczer, ch.7
J. Deetz (1977), *In Small Things Forgotten*, New York
R. Dekker (1982), *Holland in beroering*, Baarn
R. Dekker (1987), 'Women in Revolt', *Theory and Society* 16, 337–62
R. Dekker and L. van de Pol (1981), *The Tradition of Female Transvestism in Early Modern Europe*, English trans London 1989
J. Delumeau (1992), *La religion de ma mère: les femmes et la transmission de la foi*, Paris
T. van Deursen (1978–80), *Plain Lives in a Golden Age*, English trans Cambridge 1991
T. van Deursen (1986), 'Volkskultuur in wisselwerking met de elitecultuur in de vroegmoderne tijd', in *Religieuse Volkscultuur*, ed. G. Rooijakkers and T. van der Zee, Nijmegen, 54–70
J. Devlin (1987), *The Superstitious Mind*, New Haven and London
M. Dinges (1987), 'Materiellen Kultur und Alltag – die Unterschichten in Bordeaux im 16./17.Jht', *Francia* 15 (1987), 257–78
G. Duboscq (1979, ed.), *La religion populaire*, Paris
R. van Dülmen (1983, ed.), *Kultur der einfachen Leute*, Munich
R. van Dülmen (1992, ed), *Dynamik der Tradition*, Frankfurt
R. van Dülmen and N. Schindler (1984, eds), *Volkskultur: zur Wiederentdeckung des vergessenen Alltags*, Frankfurt
R. van Dülmen (1985), *Theatre of Horror: Crime and Punishment in Early Modern Germany*, English trans Cambridge 1990
E. Duffy (1986), 'The Godly and the Multitude in Stuart England', *The 17th Century* 1, 31–55

E. Duffy (1992), *The Stripping of the Altars: Traditional Religion in England 1400–1580*, New Haven

A. Dutu (1985), 'Popular Literature, Print and Common Culture', *Cahiers roumains d'études littéraires* 2, 4–17

F. Egmond (1987), 'The Noble and the Ignoble Bandit', *Ethnologia Europaea* 17, 139–56

J. Fabian (1978), 'Popular Culture in Africa', *Africa* 48, 315–34

C.A. Ferguson (1959), 'Diglossia', reprinted in *Language and Social Context*, ed. P.P. Giglioli, Harmondsworth 1972, ch.11

J. Fiske (1989), *Understanding Popular Culture*, London

A. Fletcher and J. Stevenson (1985, eds), *Order and Disorder in Early Modern England*, Cambridge

M.R. Forster (1992), *The Counter-Reformation in the Villages: Religion and Reform in the Bishopric of Speyer, 1560–1720*, Ithaca

W. Frijhoff (1978), 'Prophétie et société dans les Provinces-Unies', in M.-S. Dupont-Bouchat et al, *Prophètes et sorcières dans les Pays-Bas*, Paris, 263–362

W. Frijhoff (1979), 'Official and Popular Religion', in Vrijhoff and Waardenburg, ch.3

W. Frijhoff (1986), 'Vraagtekens bij het vroegmoderne kerstenings-offensief', in *Religieuze Volkskultuur*, ed. G. Rooiakkers and T. van der Zee, Nijmegen, 71–98

W. Frijhoff (1990), 'The Meaning of the Marvelous: on Religious Experience in the Early Seventeenth-Century Netherlands', in *Experiences and Explanations*, ed. L. Laeyendecker et al, Ljouwert, 79–101

M.-H. Froeschlé-Chopard (1980), *La religion populaire en Provence*, Paris

J. Frykman and O. Löfgren (1979), *Culture Builders: a Historical Anthropology of Middle-Class Life*, revised English trans New Brunswick 1987

V. Gammon (1981), 'Babylonian Performances: the Rise and Suppression of Popular Church Music, 1660–1870', in Yeo and Yeo 62–88

R. García Carcel (1980), *Herejia y sociedad en el siglo xvi: la inquisición en Valencia, 1530–1609*, Barcelona

B. Garnot (1990), *Le peuple au siècle des Lumières*, Paris

C. Garrett (1985), 'Spirit Possession, Oral Tradition and the Camisard Revolt', in Bertrand, 43–61

D. Garrioch (1987), 'Verbal Insults in 18th-century Paris', in *The Social History of Language*, ed. P. Burke and R. Porter, Cambridge, ch.5

R. Gawthrop and G. Strauss (1984), 'Protestantism and Literacy in Early Modern Germany', *P&P* 104, 31–55

Ernest Gellner (1987, unpub), 'High and Low Culture in Islam and Europe'

D. Gentilcore (1992), *From Bishop to Witch: the System of the Sacred in Early Modern Terra d'Otranto*, Manchester

B. Geremek (1978, ed.), *Kultura elitarna a kultura masowa w Polce poznego sredniowiecza*, Warsaw

C. Ginzburg (1979, ed.) 'Religione delle classi popolari', *Quaderni Storici* 41

C. Ginzburg (1978), 'The Dovecote has opened its Eyes', English trans. in Henningsen and Tedeschi (1986), 190–8

C. Ginzburg (1989), *Ecstasies*, English trans London 1990

C. Gluck (1978), 'The People in History: Recent Trends in Japanese Historiography', *Journal of Asian Studies* 38, 25–50

W. Godzich and N. Spadaccini (1986, eds), *Literature among Discourses: the Spanish Golden Age*, Minnesota

J. Goring (1983), *Godly Exercises or the Devil's Dance? Puritanism and Popular Culture in Pre-Civil War England*, London

P.F. Grendler (1982), 'What Zuanne read in School', *Sixteenth Century Journal* 13, 41–53

K. von Greyerz (1984, ed), *Religion and Society in Early Modern Europe*, London

A. Griessinger (1981), *Das symbolische Kapital der Ehre*, Frankfurt

J. Gripsrud (1989), 'High Culture Revisited', *Cultural Studies* 3, 194–207

R. Guha (1982–8, ed.), *Subaltern Studies*, 6 vols, Delhi

R. Guha (1983), *Elementary Aspects of Peasant Insurgency*, Delhi

V. Guidetti (1988), *Le missioni popolari dei Gesuiti in Italia*, Milan

A.J. Gurevich (1981), *Medieval Popular Culture*, English trans. Cambridge 1987

A.J. Gurevitch (1983), 'Popular and Scholarly Medieval Traditions', *Journal of Medieval History* 9, 71–90

R. Habermas (1991), *Wallfahrt und Aufruhr. Zum Wunderglauben im Bayern der frühen Neuzeit*, Frankfurt

S. Haliczer (1987, ed.), *Inquisition and Society in Early Modern Europe*, London and Sydney

S. Hall (1981), 'Notes on Deconstructing the Popular', in R. Samuel, ed., *People's History and Socialist Theory*, London, 227–40

T. Harris (1987), *Popular Politics in Restoration London*, Cambridge

T. Harris (1989), 'The Problem of Popular Political Culture in Seventeenth-century London', *History of European Ideas* 10, 43–58

T. Harris (forthcoming), 'Problematizing Popular Culture', in *Popular*

Culture in England c1500–1850

D. Hebdige (1979), *Subculture: the Meaning of Style*

J. Held (1983), 'Goyas Reflexion der Volkskultur in Spanien', in *Kultur zwischen Bürgertum und Volk*, ed. J. Held, Berlin, 149–62

G. Henningsen (1990), 'The Ladies from Outside', in Ankarloo and Henningsen, 191–215

G. Henningsen and J. Tedeschi (1986, eds), *The Inquisition in Early Modern Europe*, Dekalb

John Henry (1991), 'Doctors and Healers: Popular Culture and the Medical profession', in Pumfrey, 191–221

E.J. Hobsbawm and J.W. Scott (1980), 'Political Shoemakers', *P&P* 89, 86–114

E.J. Hobsbawm and T. Ranger (1983, eds), *The Invention of Tradition*, Cambridge

H. Hoerger (1984), 'Organisational Forms of Popular Piety in Rural Old Bavaria', in Greyerz, 212–22

C. Holmes (1984), 'Popular Culture? Witches, Magistrates and Divines in Early Modern England', in Kaplan, ch.5

C. Holmes (1985), 'Drainers and Fenmen: the Problem of Popular Political Consciousness in the 17th Century', in Fletcher and Stevenson, ch.6

E. Horowitz (1989), 'The Eve of the Circumcision', *Journal of Social History* 23, 45–69

E. Horowitz (1992), 'Toward a Social History of Jewish Popular Religion', *Journal of Religious History* 17, 138–51

R. Houston (1982), 'The Literacy Myth: Illiteracy in Scotland, 1630–1760', *P&P* 96, 81–102

R.P.-C. Hsia (1988, ed), *The German people and the Reformation*, Ithaca

R.P.-C. Hsia (1989), *Social Discipline in the Reformation: Central Europe 1550–1750*, London

R. Ileto (1979), *Pasyon and Revolution*, Manila

M. Ingram (1985), 'The Reform of Popular Culture?' in Reay, ch.4

M. Ingram (1985), 'Ridings, Rough Music and Mocking Rhymes in Early Modern England', in Reay, ch.5

R.M. Isherwood (1981), 'Entertainment in the Parisian Fairs in the Eighteenth Century', *Journal of Modern History* 53, 24–48

R.M. Isherwood (1986), *Farce and Fantasy: Popular Entertainment in Eighteenth-Century Paris*, Oxford

D. Johnson, A.J. Nathan and E.S. Rawski (1985, eds), *Popular Culture in Late Imperial China*, Berkeley

G. Jordan and N. Rogers (1989), 'Admirals as Heroes', *Journal of British Studies* 28

H. Kamen (1993), *The Phoenix and the Flame: Catalonia and the Counter-Reformation*, New Haven and London

S. Kaplan (1984, ed.), *Understanding Popular Culture*, Berlin

W. Kaschuba (1988), *Volkskultur zwischen feudalen und bürgerlichen Gesellschaft*, Frankfurt

R.D.G. Kelley (1992), 'Notes on Deconstructing the Folk', *American Historical Review* 97, 1400–08

S. Kinser (1983), 'Les combats de Carnaval et de Carême', *Annales E.S.C.* 38, 65–98

S. Kinser (1986), 'Presentation and Representation: Carnival at Nuremberg, 1450–1550', *Representations* 13, 1–41

J. Kittelson (1985), 'Visitations and Popular Religious Culture: Further Reports from Strasbourg', in *Pietas and Societas*, ed. K.C. Sessions and P.N. Bebb, Kirksville, 89–101

G. Klaniczay (1990), *The Uses of Supernatural Power*, Cambridge

C. Klapisch (1980), 'The Medieval Italian Mattinata', *Journal of Family History*, 2–24

C. Klapisch (1984), 'Le chiavi fiorentine di Barbablu', *Quaderni Storici* 57, 765–92

Jürgen Kuczynski (1980–1), *Geschichte des Alltags des Deutsche Volkes, 1600–1810*, 2 vols, Berlin

N. Kumar (1988), *The Artisans of Banaras*, Princeton

D. Kunzle (1978), 'World Upside Down', in *The Reversible World*, ed. B. Babcock, Ithaca

T. Laqueur (1989), 'Crowds, Carnival and the State in English Executions, 1604–1868', in *The First Modern Society*, ed. A.L. Beier et al, Cambridge, 305–55

F. Laroque (1988), *Shakespeare's Festive World*, English trans Cambridge 1991

T.J. Jackson Lears (1985), 'The Concept of Cultural Hegemony: Problems and Possibilities', *American Historical Review* 90, 567–93

F. Lebrun (1976), 'Le "Traité des Superstitions" de J.-B. Thiers', *Annales de Bretagne* 83, 443–65

J. Le Goff and J.-C. Schmitt (1981, eds), *Le Charivari*, Paris

E. Le Roy Ladurie (1979), *Carnival*, English trans London 1980

G. Levi (1985), *Inheriting Power*, English trans Chicago 1988

L.W. Levine (1992), 'The Folklore of Industrial Society', *American Historical Review* 97, 1369–99

D.S. Likhacev and A.M. Pancenko (1976), *Smechovej mir drevnej Rusi*, Moscow

João Luis Lisboa (1989), 'Popular Knowledge in the 18th Century Almanacs', *History of European Ideas* 11, 509–13

O. Löfgren (1987), 'Deconstructing Swedishness', *Anthropology at Home*, ed. A. Jackson, London, 74–93

J. Lotman (1984), 'The Poetics of Everyday Behaviour in Russian Eighteenth-Century Culture', in *The Semiotics of Russian Culture*, ed. J. Lotman and B.A. Uspenskii, Ann Arbor, 231–56

G. Lottes (1984), 'Popular Culture and the Early Modern State in Germany', in Kaplan, 173–9

A. Lottin (1979), 'Contre-réforme et religion populaire: un mariage difficile mais réussi aux 16e et 17e siècles en Flandre et en Hainaut', in Dubuscq, 53–63

H.-J. Lüsebrink (1979), 'Mandrin', *Revue de l'histoire moderne* 26, 345–64

Keith P. Luria (1991), *Territories of Grace: Cultural Change in the Seventeenth-Century Diocese of Grenoble*, Berkeley

N. McKendrick et al (1982), *The Birth of a Consumer Society*, London

R. Mandrou (1977), 'Cultures populaires et savantes', in Beauroy, 17–38

D. Marchesini (1992), *Il bisogno di scrivere: usi della scrittura nell'Italia moderna*, Rome and Bari

J. Marco (1977), *Literatura popular en España en los siglos xviii y xix*, Madrid

L.S. Marcus (1986), *The Politics of Mirth: Jonson, Herrick, Milton, Marvell and the Defense of Old Holiday Pastimes*, Chicago

J. Martin (1987), 'Popular Culture and the Shaping of Popular Heresy in Renaissance Venice', in Haliczer, ch.6

R. Da Matta (1978), *Carnaval, Malandros e Heróis*, Rio

H. Medick (1983), 'Plebeian Culture in the Transition to Capitalism', in *Culture, Ideology and Politics*, ed. R. Samuel etc, London, 84–108

H. Medick (1984), 'Village Spinning Bees, Sexual Culture and Free Time in Early Modern Germany', in *Interest and Emotion*, ed D. Sabean and H. Medick, Cambridge, 317–39

L. de Mello e Souza (1987), *O Diabo e a Terra da Santa Cruz*, São Paulo

Ruth-E. Mohrmann (1993), 'Everyday Culture in Early Modern Times', *New Literary History* 24, 75–86

M. Molho (1976), *Cervantes: raíces folkloricos*, Madrid

P.N. Moogk (1979), 'Thieving Buggers and Stupid Sluts: Insults and Popular Culture in New France', *William and Mary Quarterly* 36, 523–47

R. Muchembled (1978), *Popular Culture and Elite Culture in France*, English trans Baton Rouge 1985

R. Muchembled (1989), *La violence au village*, Turnhout

C. Mukerji (1983), *From Graven Images: Patterns of Modern Materialism*

C. Mukerji and M. Schudson (1991, eds), *Rethinking Popular Culture*, Berkeley

M. Mullett (1987), *Popular Culture and Popular Protest in Late Medieval and Early Modern Europe*

M. Mullett (1989), 'Popular Culture and the Counter-Reformation', *History of European Ideas* 11, 493–9

S.T. Nalle (1987), 'Popular Culture in Cuenca on the Eve of the Catholic Reformation', in Haliczer, ch.4

S.T. Nalle (1992), 'A Saint for All Seasons: the Cult of San Julián', in *Culture and Control in Counter-Reformation Spain*, ed. A.J. Cruz and M.E. Perry, Minneapolis, ch.2

O. Niccoli (1987), *Prophecy and People in Renaissance Italy*, English trans Princeton 1990

H. van Nierop (1991), 'A Beggars' Banquet', *European History Quarterly* 21, 419–43

S. Nigro (1983), *Le brache di san Griffone: novellistica e predicazione tra '400 e '500*, Bari

J. Obelkevich (1979, ed.), *Religion and the People*, Chapel Hill

J. Obelkevich, L. Roper and R. Samuel (1986, eds), *Disciplines of Faith*, London

L.S. O'Connell (1980), 'The Elizabethan Bourgeois Hero-Tale', in *After the Reformation*, ed. B. Malament, Manchester, 267–87

R. O'Hanlon and D. Washbrook (1991), 'Approaches to the Study of Colonialism and Culture in India', *History Workshop Journal* 32, 110–27

M. O'Neil (1984), '*Sacerdote ovvero strione*: Ecclesiastical and Superstitious Remedies in 16th-Century Italy', in Kaplan ch.4

M. O'Neil (1987), 'Magical Healing, Love Magic and the Inquisition in Late Sixteenth-Century Modena', in Haliczer ch.5

R. Ortiz (1978), *A morte branca do feiticeiro negro*, Petrópolis

G.N. Parker (1980), 'An Educational Revolution? The Growth of Literacy and Schooling in Early Modern Europe', *Tijdschrift voor Geschiedenis* 93, 210–20

G.N. Parker (1992), 'Success and Failure during the First Century of the Reformation', *Past and Present* 136, 43–82

R. Paulson (1979), *Popular and Polite Art in the Age of Hogarth and Fielding*, Notre Dame

H. Payne (1979), 'Elite v Popular Mentality in the Eighteenth Century', *Studies in Eighteenth-Century Culture* 8, 5–32

J. Pereira Pereira (1988), 'La religiosidad y sociabilidad popular como aspectos del conflicto social', in *Equipo Madrid, Carlos III, Madrid y la Ilustración*, Madrid, 223–54

M.I. Pereira de Queiroz (1992), *O carnaval brasileiro*, S. Paulo

E.M. Peters (1987), 'Religion and Culture, Popular and Unpopular,

1500–1800', *Journal of Modern History* 59, 317–30

R. Porter (1985), 'The Patient's View', *Theory and Society* 14, 175–98

Stephen Pumfrey, Paolo Rossi and Maurice Slawinski (1991, eds), *Science, Culture and Popular Belief in Renaissance Europe*, Manchester.

E.S. Rawski (1979), *Education and Popular Literacy in Ch'ing China*, Ann Arbor

B. Reay (1985, ed.), *Popular Culture in Seventeenth-Century England*, London

B. Reay (1985), 'Popular Culture in Early Modern England', in Reay, ch.1

B. Reay (1985), 'Popular Religion', in Reay, ch.3

A. Redondo (1987), 'La religion populaire espagnole au 16e siècle', in *Culturas populares*, 329–69

J. Revel (1984), 'Forms of Expertise: Intellectuals and "Popular" Culture in France (1650–1800)', in Kaplan, ch.10

J. Revel (1986), 'La culture populaire: sur les usages et les abus d'un outil historiographique', in *Culturas populares*, 223–40

Brian Rigby (1991), *Popular Culture in Modern France: a Study of Cultural Discourse*, London

M.-J. del Río (1988), 'Represión y control de fiestas y diversiones en el Madrid de Carlos III', in *Equipo Madrid, Carlos III, Madrid y la Ilustración*, Madrid, 299–330

D. Roche (1981), *The People of Paris*, English trans Leamington Spa 1987

D. Roche (1985), 'Les idées sociales, politiques et religieuses d'un artisan parisien au 18e siècle', in Bertrand, 63–72

P. Rogers (1985), *Literature and Popular Culture in Eighteenth-Century England*

D. Rollison (1981), 'Property, Ideology and Popular Culture in a Gloucestershire Village', *P&P*, 93, 70–97

H. Roodenburg (1983), 'De autobiografie van Isabella de Moerloose', *Tijdschrift voor Geschiedenis* 90, 311–42

H. Roodenburg (1990), *Onder censuur: De kerkelijke tucht in de gereformeerde gemeente van Amsterdam, 1578–1700*, The Hague

L. Roper (1989), *The Holy Household: Women and Morals in Reformation Augsburg*, Oxford

P.L. Rossi (1991), 'Society, Culture and the Dissemination of Learning', in Pumfrey, 143–75

W. Rowe and V. Schelling (1991), *Memory and Modernity: Popular Culture in Latin America*, London

H.-C. Rublack (1992), 'Success and Failure of the Reformation: Popular

"Apologies" from the 17th and 18th Centuries', in *Germania Illustrata*, ed. A. Fix and S. Karant-Nunn, Kirksville, 141–65

G. Ruggiero (1993), *Binding Passions: Tales of Magic, Marriage and Power at the End of the Renaissance*, New York

D. Sabean (1984), *Power in the Blood*, Cambridge

R. Samuel (1981, ed.), *People's History and Socialist Theory*, London

R. Sandgruber (1982), *Die Anfänge der Konsumgesellschaft*, Vienna

J. Scarisbrick (1984), *The Reformation and the English People*, London

M. Scharfe (1984), 'The Distances between the Lower Classes and Official Religion: Examples from 18thc Württemberg', in Greyerz, 157–74

R. Schenda (1985), 'Orale und literarische Kommunikationsformen', in Brückner et al, 447–64

W. Schieder (ed, 1986), *Volksreligiosität in der modernen Sozialgeschichte*, Göttingen.

N. Schindler (1984), 'Spuren in die Geschichte der "anderen" Zivilisation', in van Dülmen and Schindler, 13–77

N. Schindler (1992), *Widerspenstige Leute*, Frankfurt

A.J. Schutte (1980), 'Printing, Piety and the People in Italy', *Archiv für Reformationsgeschichte* 71, 5–19

J. Scott (1987), *Weapons of the Weak: Everyday Forms of Peasant Resistance*, New Haven

T. Scott (1991), 'The Common People in the German Reformation', *Historical Journal* 34, 183–92

R.W. Scribner (1981), *For the Sake of Simple Folk*, Cambridge

R.W. Scribner (1987), *Popular Culture and Popular Movements in Reformation Germany*, London

R.W. Scribner (1989a), 'Is a History of Popular Culture Possible?', *History of European Ideas* 10, 175–92

R.W. Scribner (1989b), 'Popular Piety and Modes of Visual Perception in Late-Medieval and Reformation Germany', *Journal of Religious History* 15, 448–69

R.W. Scribner (1990), 'The Impact of the Reformation on Daily Life', in *Mensch und Objekt im Mittelalter*, 315–43

R.W. Scribner (1993, ed.), *Popular Religion in Germany*, Manchester

P. Seleski (forthcoming), 'Women, Work and Cultural Change in Eighteenth and Early Nineteenth-Century London', in Harris

J. Sharpe (1985), 'The People and the Law', in Reay, ch.7

M. Shiach (1989), *Discourse on Popular Culture*, Cambridge

D.H. Shively (1991), 'Popular Culture', *Cambridge History of Japan* 4, ed. J.W. Hall, Cambridge, 706–69

G. Sider (1980), 'The Ties that Bind', *Social History* 5, 1–39

L. Silver (1986), 'The State of Research in Northern European Art of the Renaissance Era', *Art Bulletin* 68, 518–35

J. Simpson (1991), 'The Local Legend: a Product of Popular Culture', *Rural History* 2, 25–30

M. Southwold (1982), 'True Buddhism and Village Buddhism in Sri Lanka', in J. Davis (ed) *Religious Organisation and Religious Experience*, New York, 137–52

M. Spufford (1981), *Small Books and Pleasant Histories*, London

P. Stallybrass and A. White (1986), *The Politics and Poetics of Transgression*, London

J. Stevenson (1985), 'The Moral Economy of the English Crowd: Myth and Reality', in Fletcher and Stevenson, ch.8

L.C. Stevenson (1986), *Praise and Paradox: Merchants and Craftsmen in Elizabethan Popular Literature*, Cambridge

R. Storch (1982, ed.), *Popular Culture and Custom in Nineteenth-Century England*, London

G. Strauss (1991), 'The Dilemma of Popular History', *P&P* 132, 130–49

I. Taddei (1991), *Fête, jeunesse et pouvoirs: l'Abbaye des Nobles Enfants de Lausanne*, Lausanne

J. Tazbir (1980), 'Hexenprozesse in Polen', *Archiv für Reformationsgeschichte* 71, 280–307

K.V. Thomas (1977), 'The Place of Laughter in Tudor and Stuart England', *Times Literary Supplement* 21 Jan 1977

K.V. Thomas (1986), 'The Meaning of Literacy in Early Modern England' in *The Written Word*, ed. G. Baumann, Oxford, 97–131

E.P. Thomspon (1991), *Customs in Common*, new ed. Harmondsworth 1993

A. Torre (1986), 'Village Ceremonial Life and Politics in 18th-century Piedmont', in Obelkevich, Roper and Samuel, ch.13

A. Torre (1992), 'Politics Cloaked in Worship: State, Church and Local Power in Piedmont 1570–1770', in *P&P* 134, 42–92

J.M. Ultee (1976), 'The Suppression of Fêtes', *Catholic Historical Review* 62

D. Underdown (1985), *Revel, Riot and Rebellion*, Oxford

C. Velay-Vallantin (1992), *L'histoire des contes*, Paris

M. Vovelle (1981, ed), *Les intermédiaires culturels*, Paris

M. Vovelle (1982), *Idéologies et mentalités* (part 3, 'la populaire en question')

P.F. Vrijhof and J. Waardenburg, (1979, eds), *Official and Popular Religion*, The Hague.

J. Walter (1980), 'Grain Riots and Popular Attitudes to the Law:

Maldon and the Crisis of 1629', in Brewer and Styles, ch.2

J. Walter (1985), 'A Rising of the People? The Oxfordshire Rising of 1596', *P&P* 107

A. Walthall (1986), *Social Protest and Popular Culture in Eighteenth-Century Japan*, Tucson

T. Watt (1991), *Cheap Print and Popular Piety 1550–1640*, Cambridge

C. Webster (1982), 'Paracelus and Demons: Science as a Synthesis of Popular Belief', in Zambelli, 3–20

R. Weimann (1978), *Shakespeare and the Popular Tradition in the Theater*, English trans., Baltimore

G. Wiegelmann (1980, ed.), *Geschichte der Alltagskultur*

M.E. Wiesner (1988), 'Women's Response to the Reformation', in *Hsia*, 148–71

K. Wilson (1988), 'Admiral Vernon', *P&P* 121, 74–109

S. Wilson (1989), 'Popular Culture: What do you mean?', *History of European Ideas* 11, 515–19

K. Wrightson (1980), 'Two Concepts of Order', in Brewer and Styles, ch.1

K. Wrightson (1981), 'Alehouses, Order and Reformation in Rural England, 1590–1660', in Yeo and Yeo, 1–22

H. Wunder (1979), 'The Mentality of Rebellious Peasants', in *The German Peasant War*, ed. R.W. Scribner and G. Benecke, London, ch.12

N. Wurzbach (1981), *Die englische Strassenballade*, Munich

E. Yeo and S. Yeo (1981, eds), *Popular Culture and Class Conflict*, Brighton

P. Zambelli (1982, ed.), *Scienze, credenze occulte, livelli di cultura*, Florence

G. Zarri (1990), *Le sante vive*, Turin

Index

fandango (Spanish), dance for
couples, 118
farandoulo (Provençal), dance in
line, 117
farsantes (Spanish), players, 97
Fauriel, Claude (1772–1844),
French scholar, 5, 20, 288, 290
Faust, 171f, 313n42
Feijoó, Benito (1676–1764),
Spanish Benedictine, 242,
322n73
Fernández de Moratín, Nicolas
(1737–80), Spanish critic, 242,
322n74
Fiorillo, Silvio (d.c1632),
Neapolitan actor, 114, 306n50
Flavel, John (c1630–91), English
divine, 45, 134
Fletcher, Andrew (1655–1716),
Scottish politician, 72
Folz, Hans (c1450–1513), poet of
Nuremberg, 103
Fontenelle, Bernard de
(1657–1757), French writer, 274
forlana, lively dance from Friuli,
116f
Fortis, Alberto (1741–1803),
Italian antiquary, 7, 10, 142,
178, 287, 291
Foster, George, contemporary
American anthropologist, 87,
336
Fox, George (d.1661), Quaker, 39
Francis, St, 101, 155
Franck, Sebastian (1499–1542),
German heretic, 27, 281f,
328n74
François de Sales, St (1567–1622),
bishop of Geneva, 221
Frazer, Sir James (1854–1941),
British anthropologist, 191, 209f
Frederick, the emperor, 153, 170
Frederick the Great, King of
Prussia, 151, 170, 172
Friese, Friedrich, 17th-century
German antiquary, 282, 328n74
Fullone, Pietro, 17th-century
Sicilian poet, 105

Gaal, Georg von (1783–1855),
Hungarian folklorist, 6, 291n10
Gaismair, Michael (c1491–1532),
Austrian peasant leader, 175,
314n54
gangarilla (Spanish), troupe of
actors, 98
García, Carlos, 16th-century
Spanish writer, 47, 69, 298n53
Garrett, Almeida (1799–1854),
Portuguese writer, 17
gavotte (French), dance from
Dauphiné, 116
Gay, John (1685–1732), English
writer, 61, 300n83
Geijer, Erik Gustaf (1783–1847),
Swedish poet and historian, 5, 7,
10, 17, 288, 290
Geiler von Kaisersberg, Johan
(1445–1510), German preacher,
216, 319n25
Geneviève of Brabant, popular
heroine, 164
Gengenbach, Pamphilus
(c1480–c1525), Swiss
playwright, 156, 228
Gent, Thomas (1693–1778),
English printer, 40, 297n41
George, St, 85, 149, 172f, 177, 194,
209, 216, 313n46
George II, King of England, 154
George III, King of England, 154
Gerhardt, Paul (1604–76), German
hymn writer, 226
Gerhoh von Reichersberg
(1093–1169), German
Augustinian, 217
Gerson, Jean (1363–1429), French
cleric, 217
Giberti, Gian Matteo (1495–1543),
bishop of Verona, 211, 220
giravoli (Italian), cunning men,
107
Glinka, Mikhail (1804–57),
Russian composer, 7
Gluckman, Max, contemporary
British anthropologist, 201f
Goethe, Johan Wolfgang von